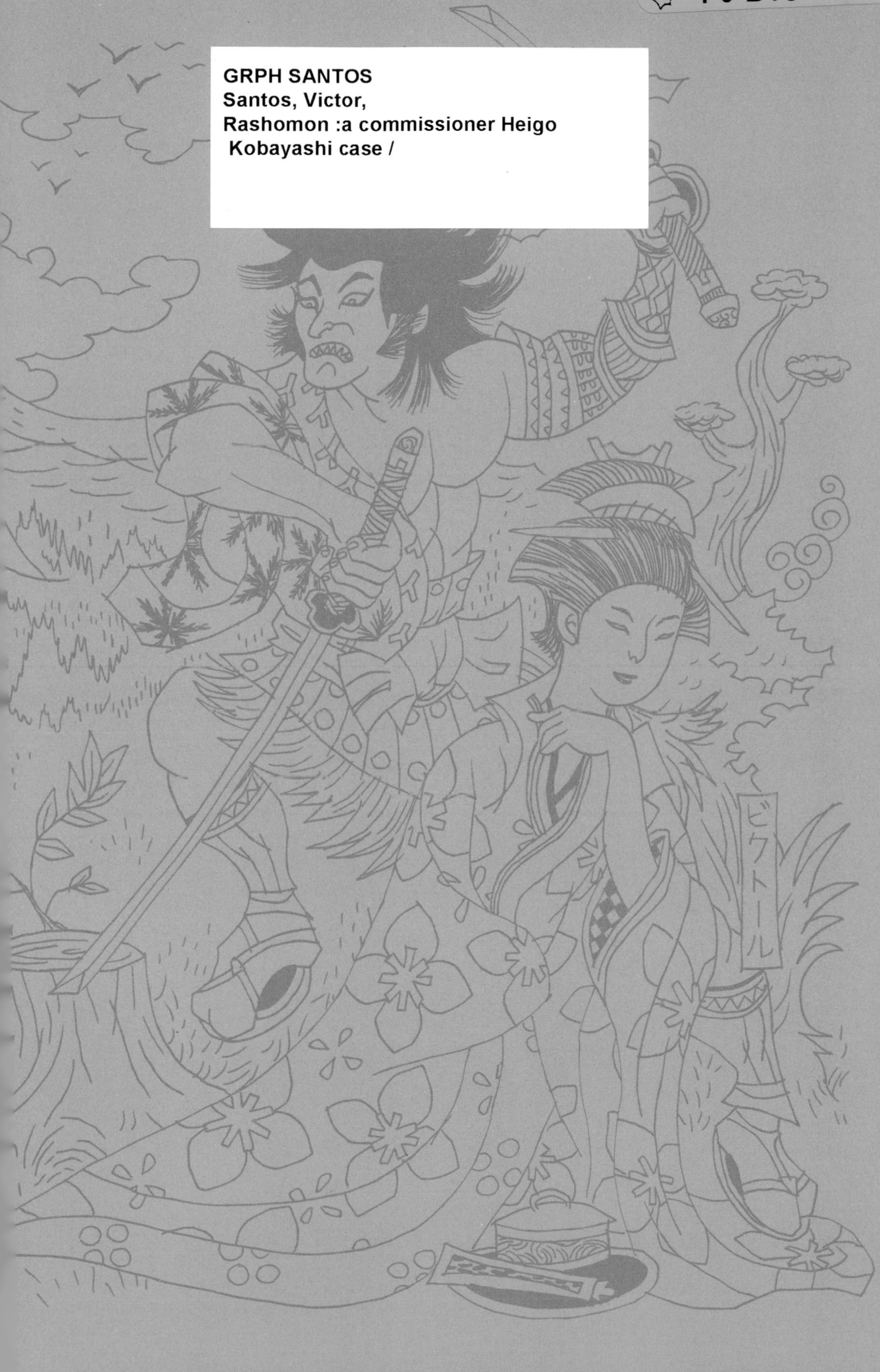
ビクトール

RASHOMON

A COMMISSIONER
HEIGO
KOBAYASHI
CASE

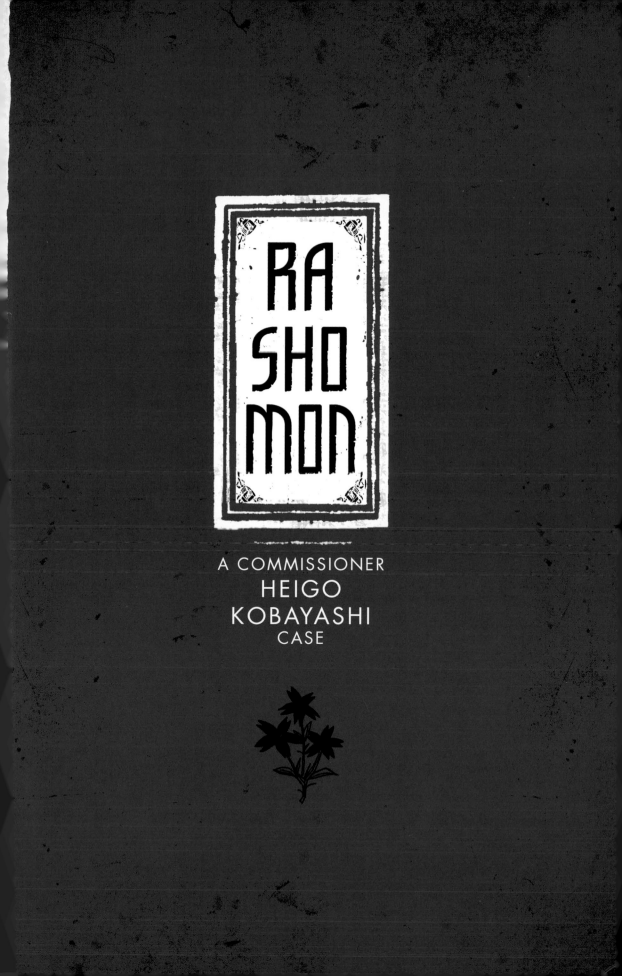

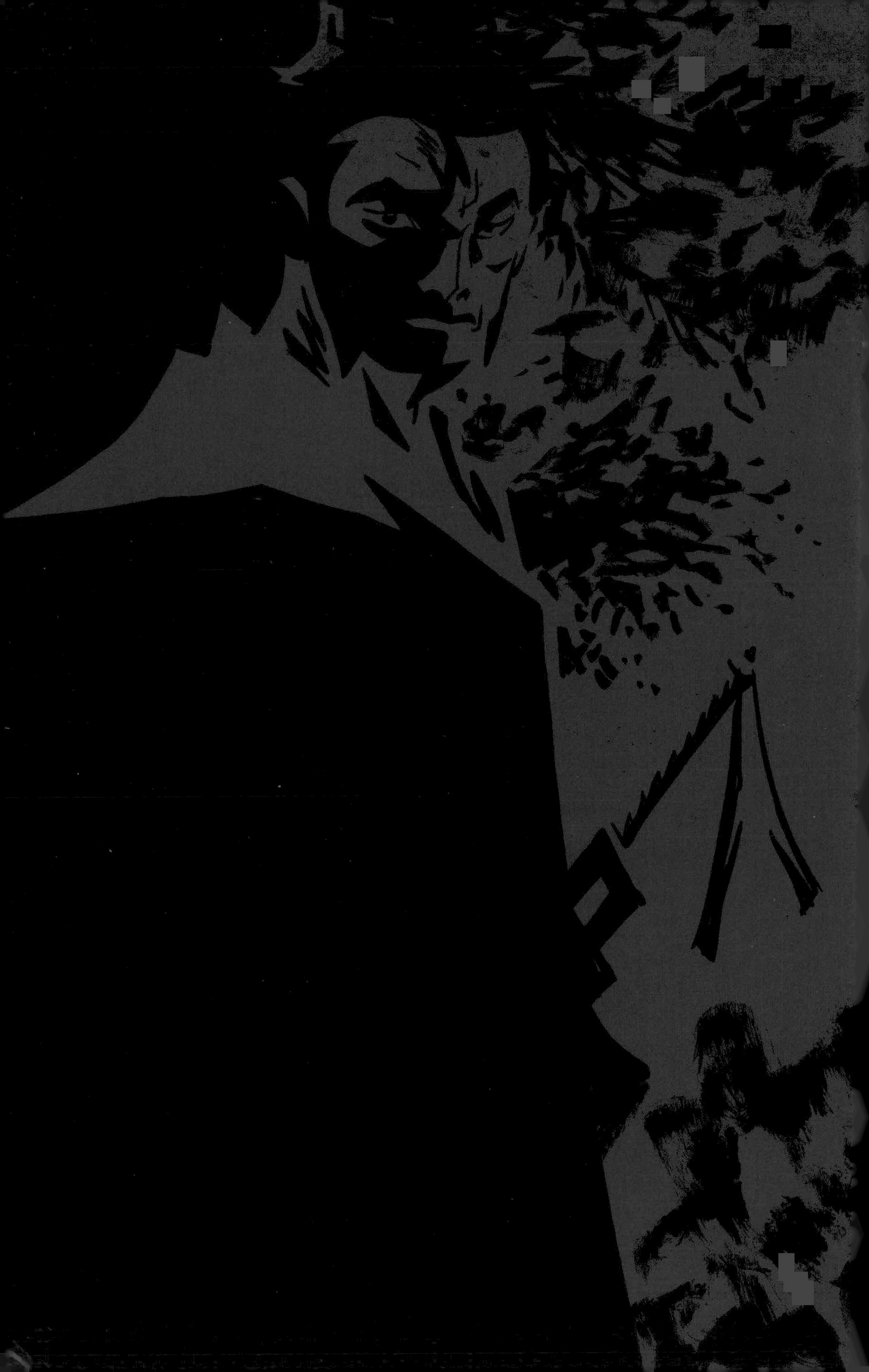

RASHOMON

A COMMISSIONER
HEIGO
KOBAYASHI
CASE

STORY AND ART BY
Victor Santos

LETTERS BY
Ryane Hill
& John J. Hill

TRANSLATIONS BY
Katie LaBarbera

DARK HORSE BOOKS

PRESIDENT & PUBLISHER
MIKE RICHARDSON

COLLECTION EDITOR
SPENCER CUSHING

COLLECTION ASSISTANT EDITOR
KEVIN BURKHALTER

DESIGNER
ETHAN KIMBERLING

DIGITAL ART TECHNICIAN
CHRISTINA MCKENZIE

Published by Dark Horse Books
A division of Dark Horse Comics, Inc.
10956 SE Main Street
Milwaukie, OR 97222

First edition: October 2017
ISBN 978-1-50670-317-6

10 9 8 7 6 5 4 3 2 1
Printed in China

International Licensing: (503) 905-2377

Comic Shop Locator Service: (888) 266-4226

This volume collects *Rashomon* Volumes 1 and 2 originally published in Spain by Norma Editorial.

Library of Congress Cataloging-in-Publication Data

Names: Santos, Victor, 1977- author, illustrator. | Hill, John J. (Letterer), letterer. | LaBarbera, Katie, translator.
Title: Rashomon : a commissioner Heigo Kobayashi case / story and art by Victor Santos ; letters by John J. Hill ; translations by Katie LaBarbera.
Description: First edition. | Milwaukie, OR : Dark Horse Books, 2017. | "This volume collects Rashomon Volumes 1 and 2 originally published in Spain by Norma Editorial."
Identifiers: LCCN 2017023746 | ISBN 9781506703176 (hardback)
Subjects: LCSH: Graphic novels. | BISAC: COMICS & GRAPHIC NOVELS / Crime & Mystery. | COMICS & GRAPHIC NOVELS / Literary. | COMICS & GRAPHIC NOVELS / General.
Classification: LCC PN6777.S29 R3713 2017 | DDC 741.5/946--dc23
LC record available at https://lccn.loc.gov/2017023746

TABLE OF CONTENTS

RASHOMON

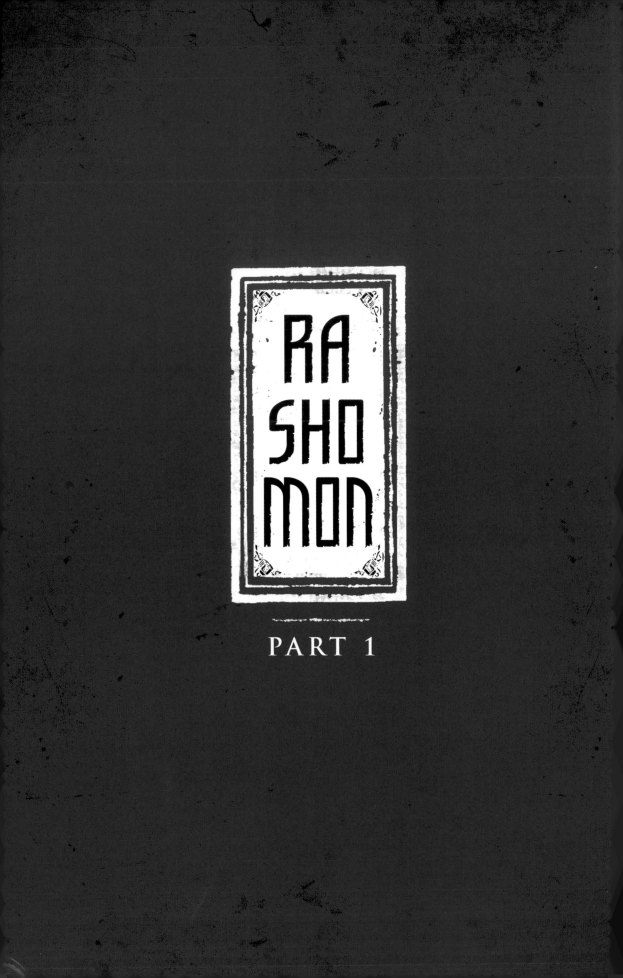

PART 1

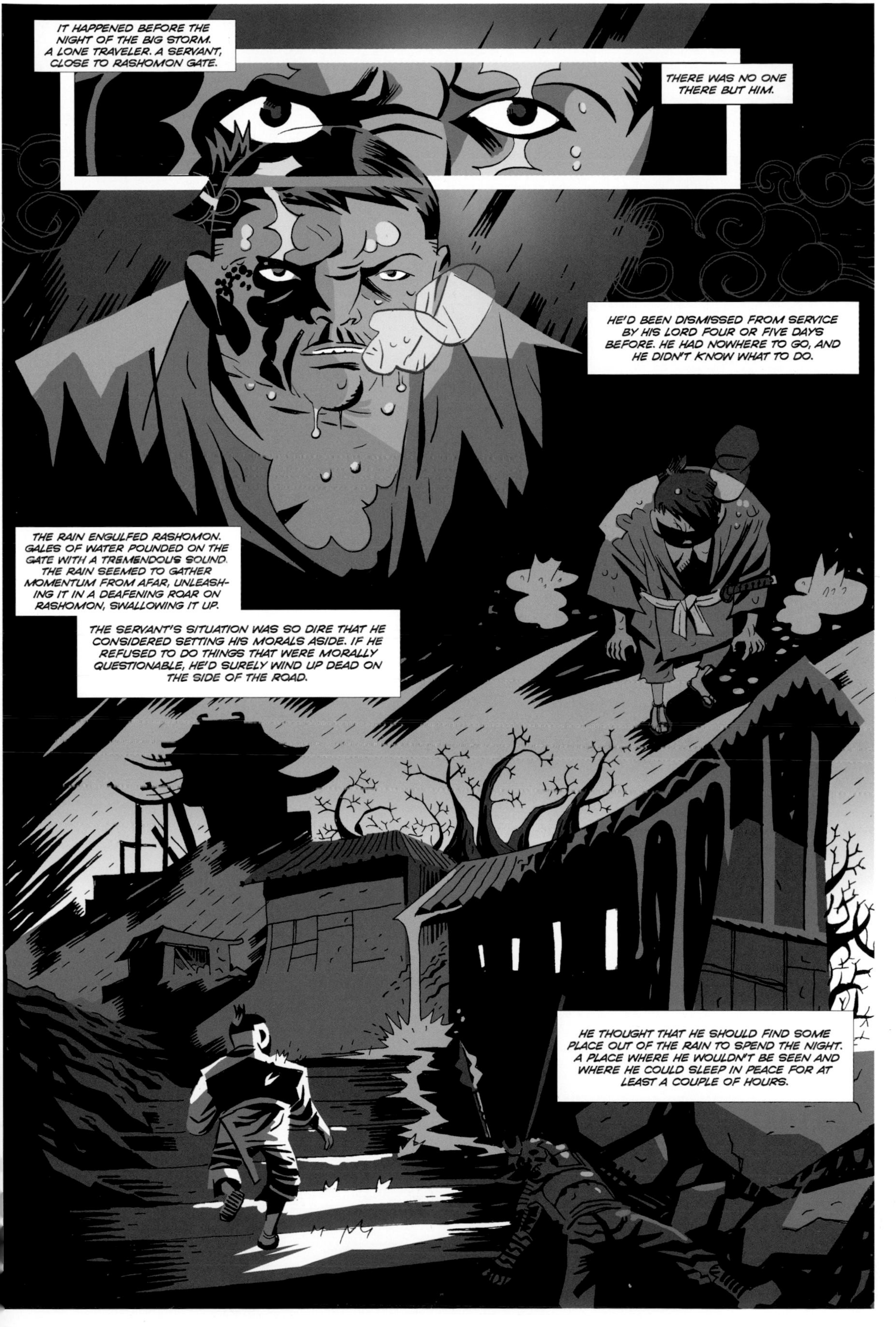
IT HAPPENED BEFORE THE NIGHT OF THE BIG STORM. A LONE TRAVELER. A SERVANT, CLOSE TO RASHOMON GATE.
THERE WAS NO ONE THERE BUT HIM.
HE'D BEEN DISMISSED FROM SERVICE BY HIS LORD FOUR OR FIVE DAYS BEFORE. HE HAD NOWHERE TO GO, AND HE DIDN'T KNOW WHAT TO DO.
THE RAIN ENGULFED RASHOMON. GALES OF WATER POUNDED ON THE GATE WITH A TREMENDOUS SOUND. THE RAIN SEEMED TO GATHER MOMENTUM FROM AFAR, UNLEASHING IT IN A DEAFENING ROAR ON RASHOMON, SWALLOWING IT UP.
THE SERVANT'S SITUATION WAS SO DIRE THAT HE CONSIDERED SETTING HIS MORALS ASIDE. IF HE REFUSED TO DO THINGS THAT WERE MORALLY QUESTIONABLE, HE'D SURELY WIND UP DEAD ON THE SIDE OF THE ROAD.
HE THOUGHT THAT HE SHOULD FIND SOME PLACE OUT OF THE RAIN TO SPEND THE NIGHT. A PLACE WHERE HE WOULDN'T BE SEEN AND WHERE HE COULD SLEEP IN PEACE FOR AT LEAST A COUPLE OF HOURS.

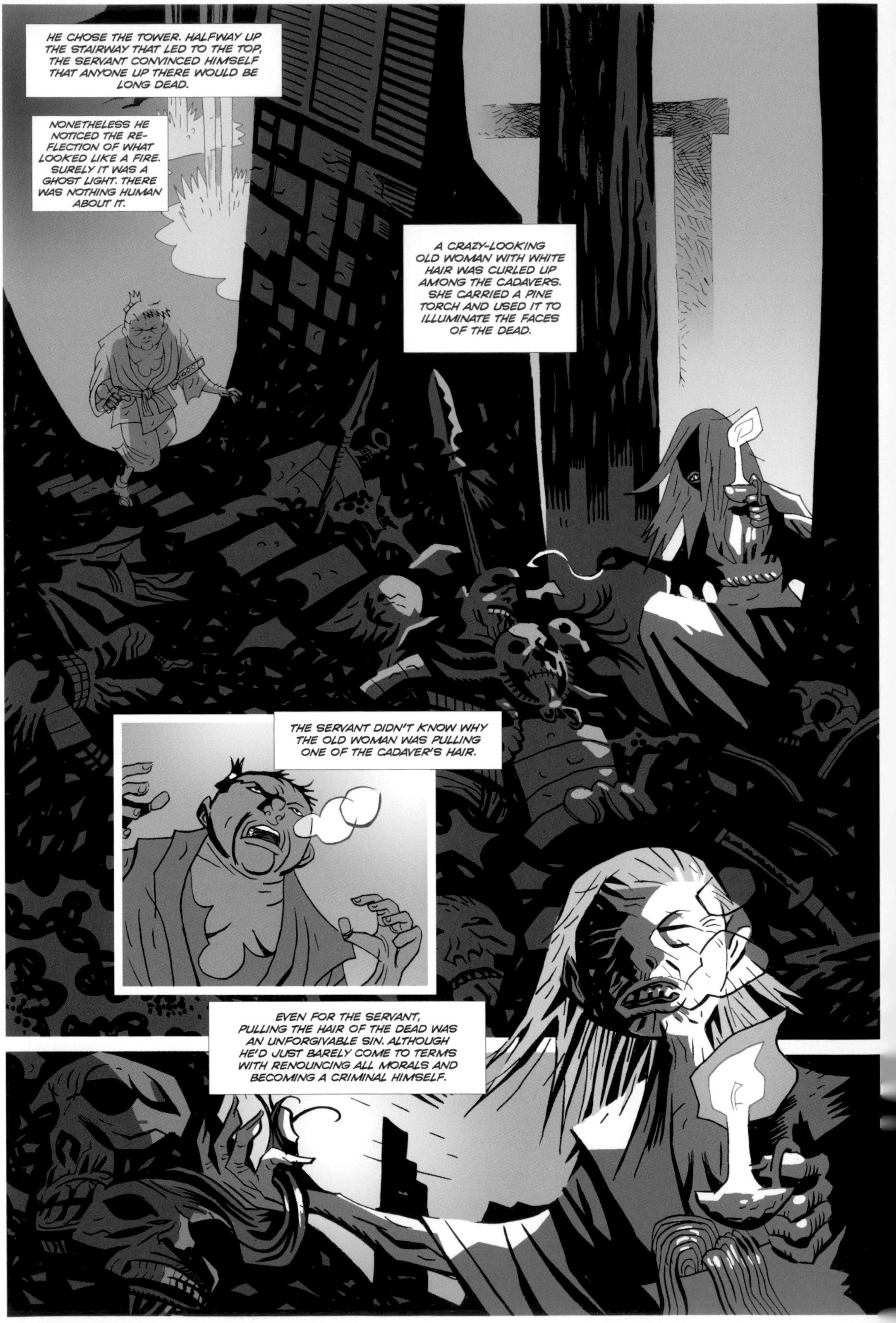
HE CHOSE THE TOWER. HALFWAY UP THE STAIRWAY THAT LED TO THE TOP, THE SERVANT CONVINCED HIMSELF THAT ANYONE UP THERE WOULD BE LONG DEAD.
NONETHELESS HE NOTICED THE RE-FLECTION OF WHAT LOOKED LIKE A FIRE. SURELY IT WAS A GHOST LIGHT. THERE WAS NOTHING HUMAN ABOUT IT.
A CRAZY-LOOKING OLD WOMAN WITH WHITE HAIR WAS CURLED UP AMONG THE CADAVERS. SHE CARRIED A PINE TORCH AND USED IT TO ILLUMINATE THE FACES OF THE DEAD.
THE SERVANT DIDN'T KNOW WHY THE OLD WOMAN WAS PULLING ONE OF THE CADAVER'S HAIR.
EVEN FOR THE SERVANT, PULLING THE HAIR OF THE DEAD WAS AN UNFORGIVABLE SIN. ALTHOUGH HE'D JUST BARELY COME TO TERMS WITH RENOUNCING ALL MORALS AND BECOMING A CRIMINAL HIMSELF.

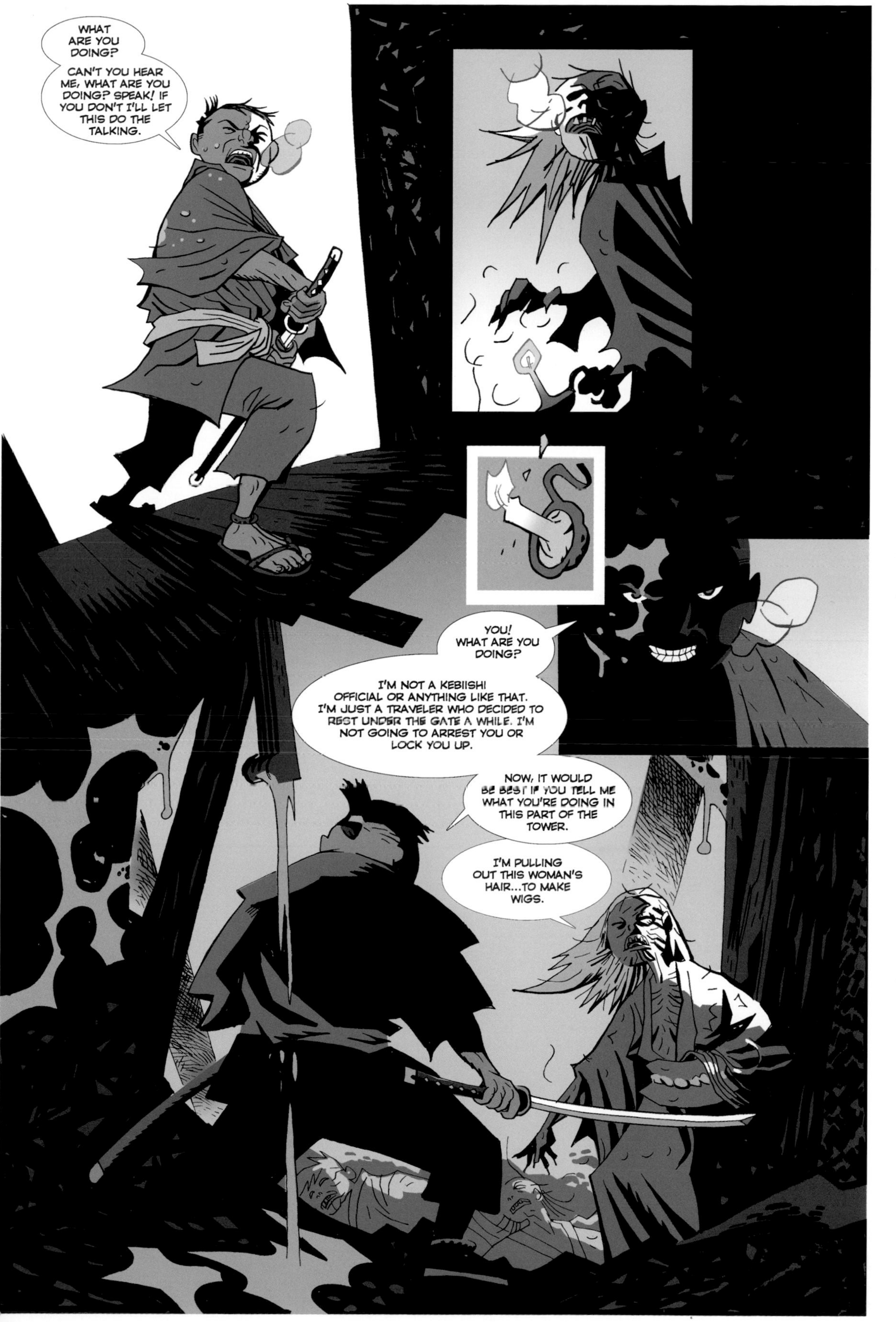
WHAT ARE YOU DOING?
CAN'T YOU HEAR ME, WHAT ARE YOU DOING? SPEAK! IF YOU DON'T I'LL LET THIS DO THE TALKING.
YOU! WHAT ARE YOU DOING?
I'M NOT A KEBIISHI OFFICIAL OR ANYTHING LIKE THAT. I'M JUST A TRAVELER WHO DECIDED TO REST UNDER THE GATE A WHILE. I'M NOT GOING TO ARREST YOU OR LOCK YOU UP.
NOW, IT WOULD BE BEST IF YOU TELL ME WHAT YOU'RE DOING IN THIS PART OF THE TOWER.
I'M PULLING OUT THIS WOMAN'S HAIR...TO MAKE WIGS.

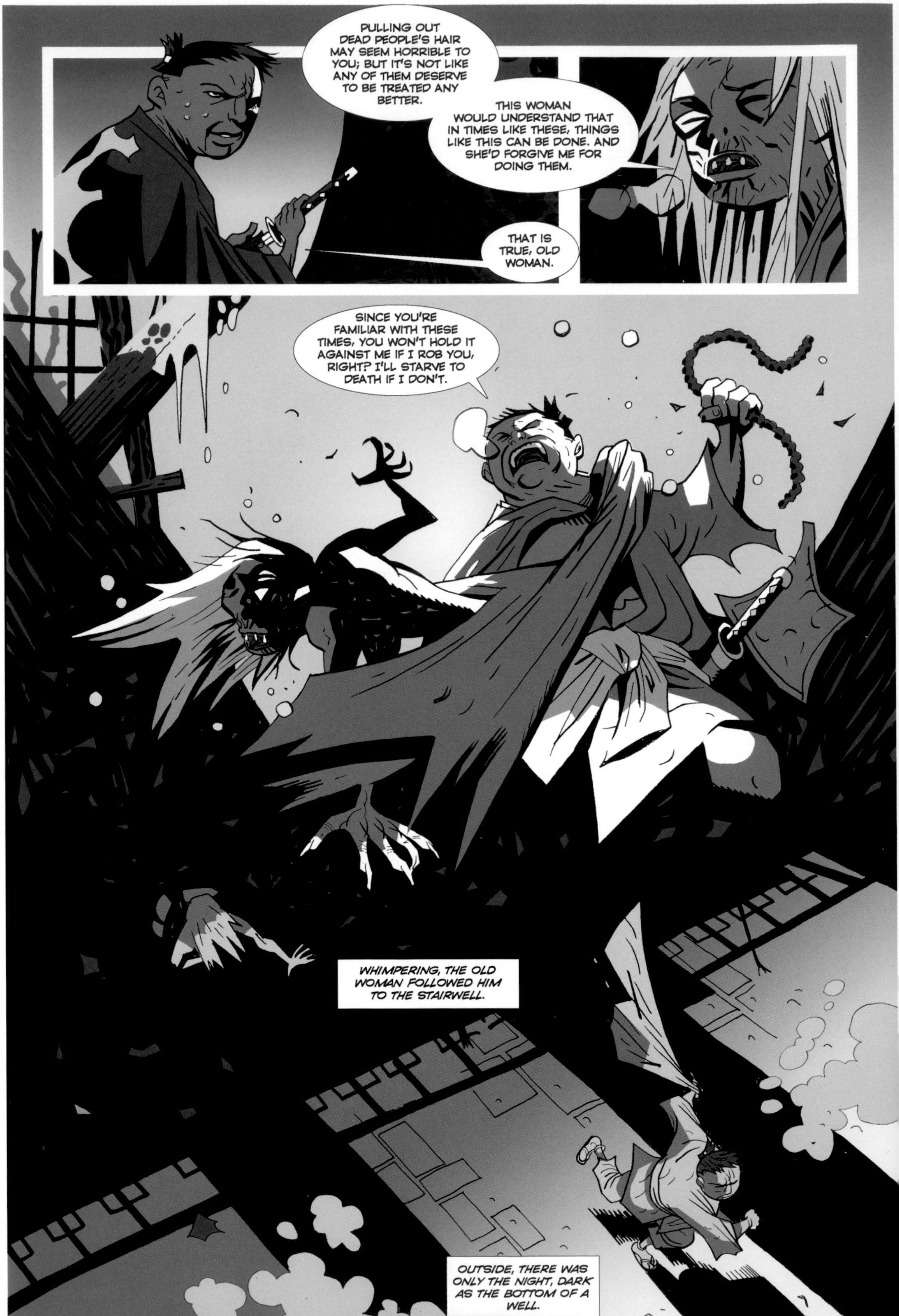
PULLING OUT DEAD PEOPLE'S HAIR MAY SEEM HORRIBLE TO YOU; BUT IT'S NOT LIKE ANY OF THEM DESERVE TO BE TREATED ANY BETTER.
THIS WOMAN WOULD UNDERSTAND THAT IN TIMES LIKE THESE, THINGS LIKE THIS CAN BE DONE. AND SHE'D FORGIVE ME FOR DOING THEM.
THAT IS TRUE, OLD WOMAN.
SINCE YOU'RE FAMILIAR WITH THESE TIMES, YOU WON'T HOLD IT AGAINST ME IF I ROB YOU, RIGHT? I'LL STARVE TO DEATH IF I DON'T.
WHIMPERING, THE OLD WOMAN FOLLOWED HIM TO THE STAIRWELL.
OUTSIDE, THERE WAS ONLY THE NIGHT, DARK AS THE BOTTOM OF A WELL.

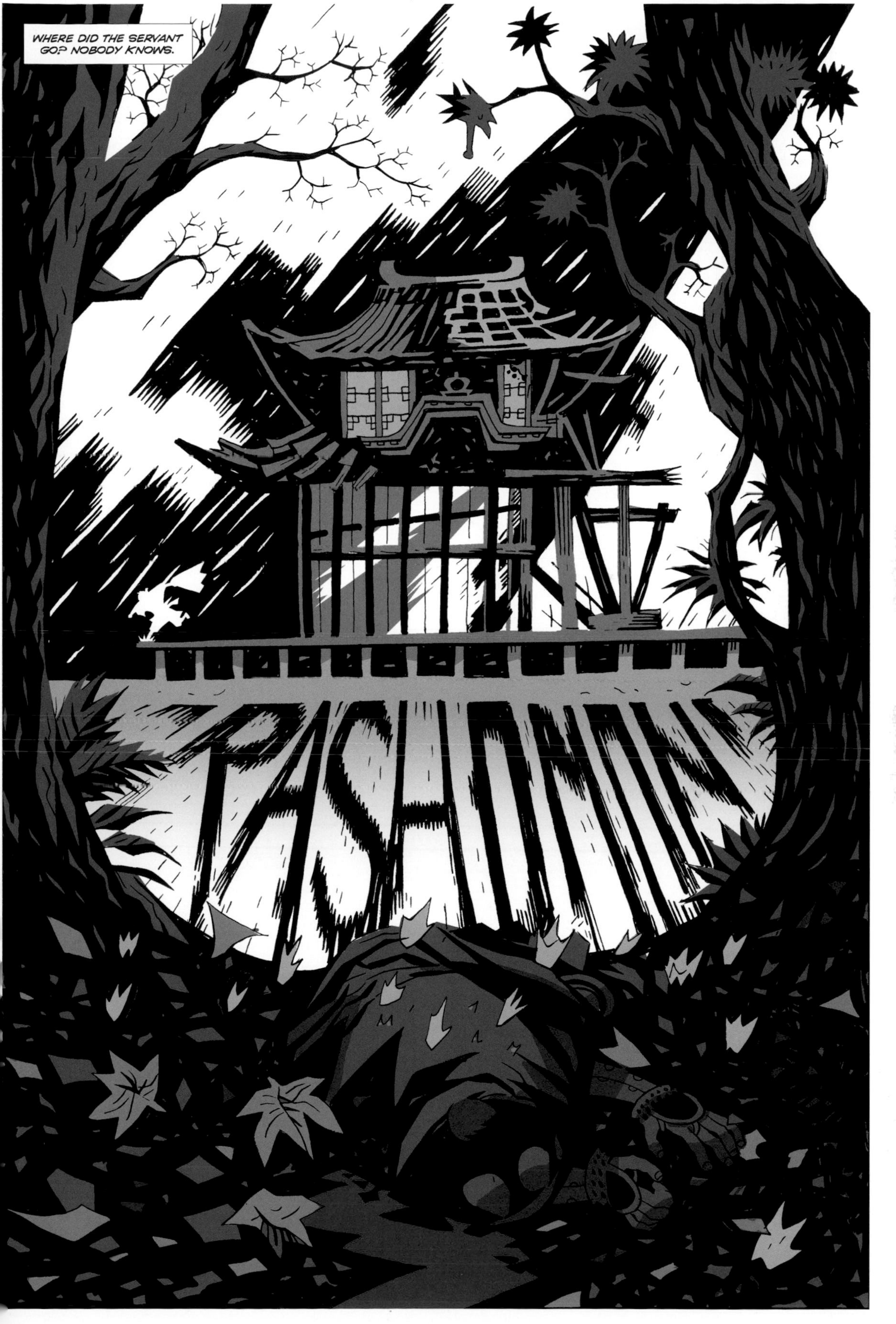
WHERE DID THE SERVANT GO? NOBODY KNOWS.

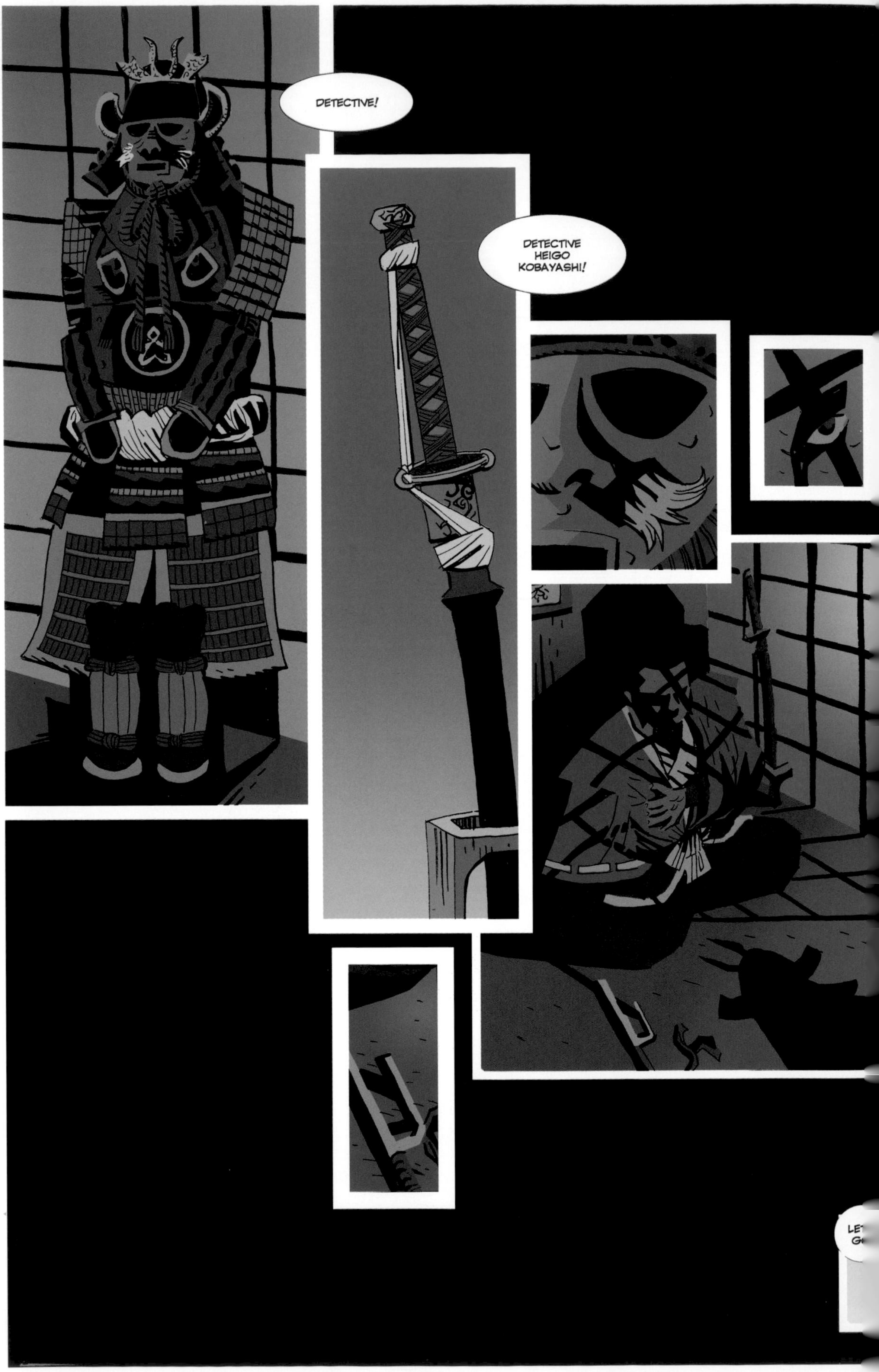
DETECTIVE!
DETECTIVE HEIGO KOBAYASHI!

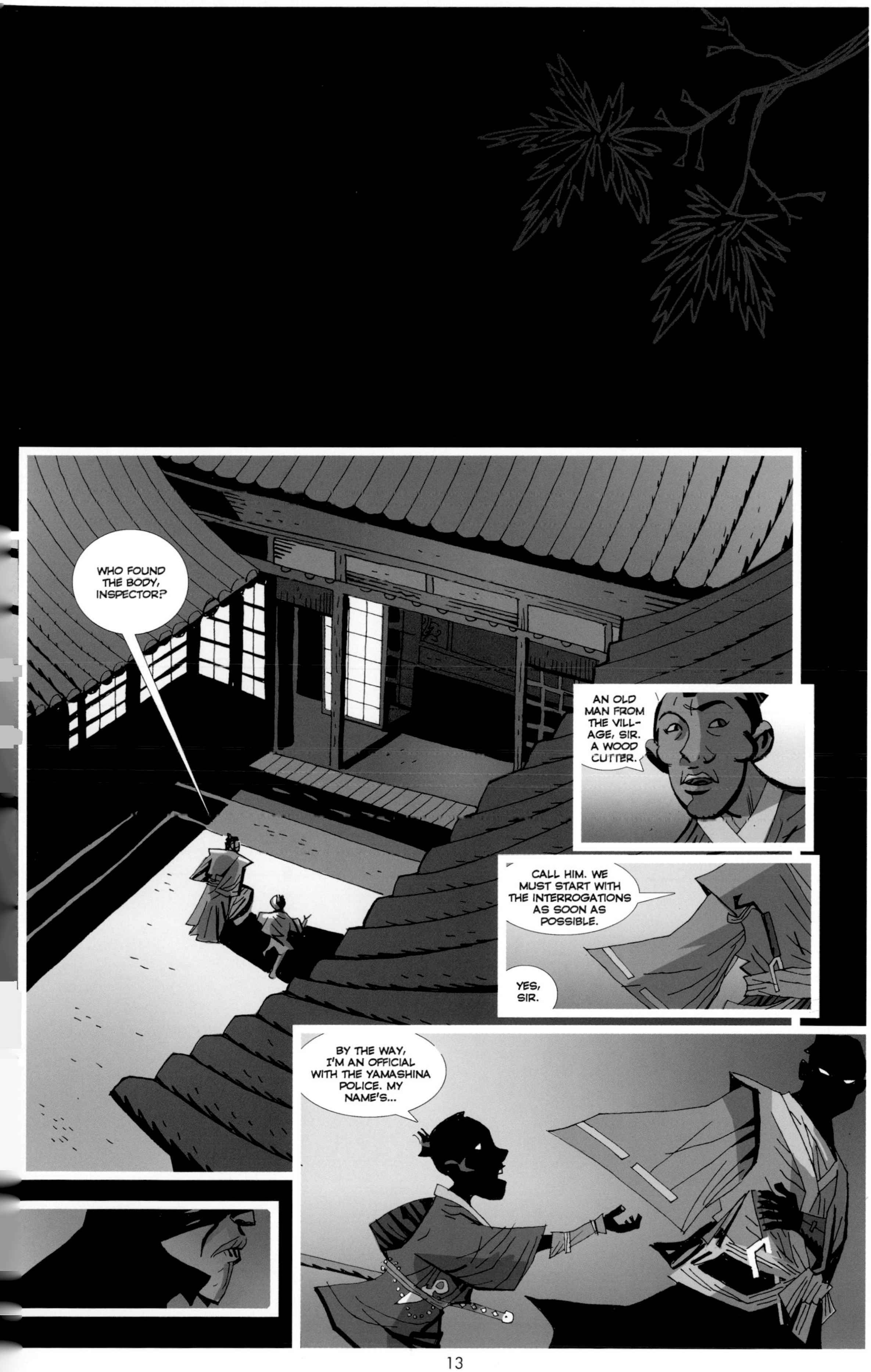
WHO FOUND THE BODY, INSPECTOR?
AN OLD MAN FROM THE VILL-AGE, SIR. A WOOD CUTTER.
CALL HIM. WE MUST START WITH THE INTERROGATIONS AS SOON AS POSSIBLE.
YES, SIR.
BY THE WAY, I'M AN OFFICIAL WITH THE YAMASHINA POLICE. MY NAME'S...

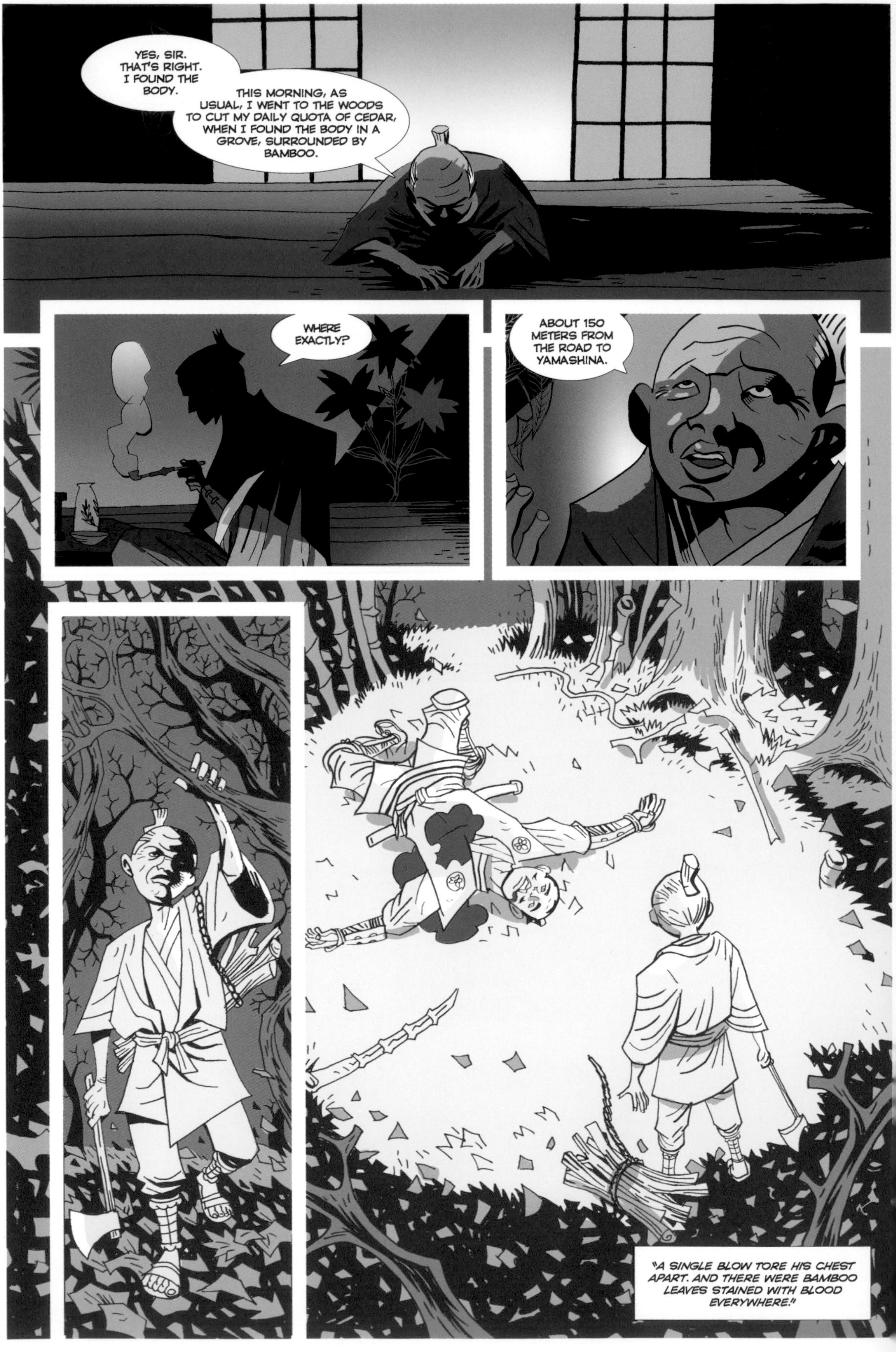
YES, SIR. THAT'S RIGHT. I FOUND THE BODY.
THIS MORNING, AS USUAL, I WENT TO THE WOODS TO CUT MY DAILY QUOTA OF CEDAR, WHEN I FOUND THE BODY IN A GROVE, SURROUNDED BY BAMBOO.
WHERE EXACTLY?
ABOUT 150 METERS FROM THE ROAD TO YAMASHINA.
"A SINGLE BLOW TORE HIS CHEST APART. AND THERE WERE BAMBOO LEAVES STAINED WITH BLOOD EVERYWHERE."

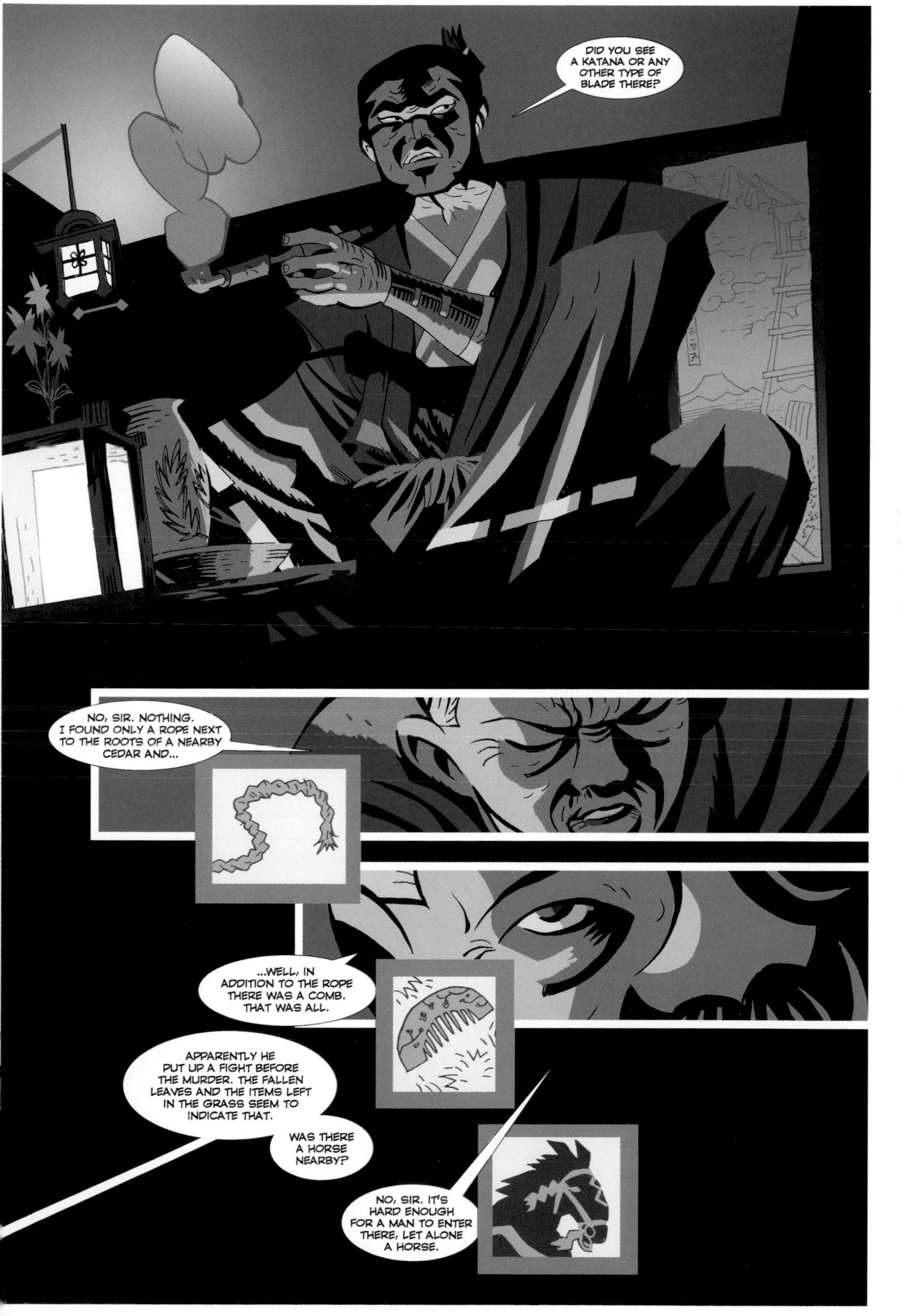
DID YOU SEE A KATANA OR ANY OTHER TYPE OF BLADE THERE?
NO, SIR. NOTHING. I FOUND ONLY A ROPE NEXT TO THE ROOTS OF A NEARBY CEDAR AND...
...WELL, IN ADDITION TO THE ROPE THERE WAS A COMB. THAT WAS ALL.
APPARENTLY HE PUT UP A FIGHT BEFORE THE MURDER. THE FALLEN LEAVES AND THE ITEMS LEFT IN THE GRASS SEEM TO INDICATE THAT.
WAS THERE A HORSE NEARBY?
NO, SIR. IT'S HARD ENOUGH FOR A MAN TO ENTER THERE, LET ALONE A HORSE.

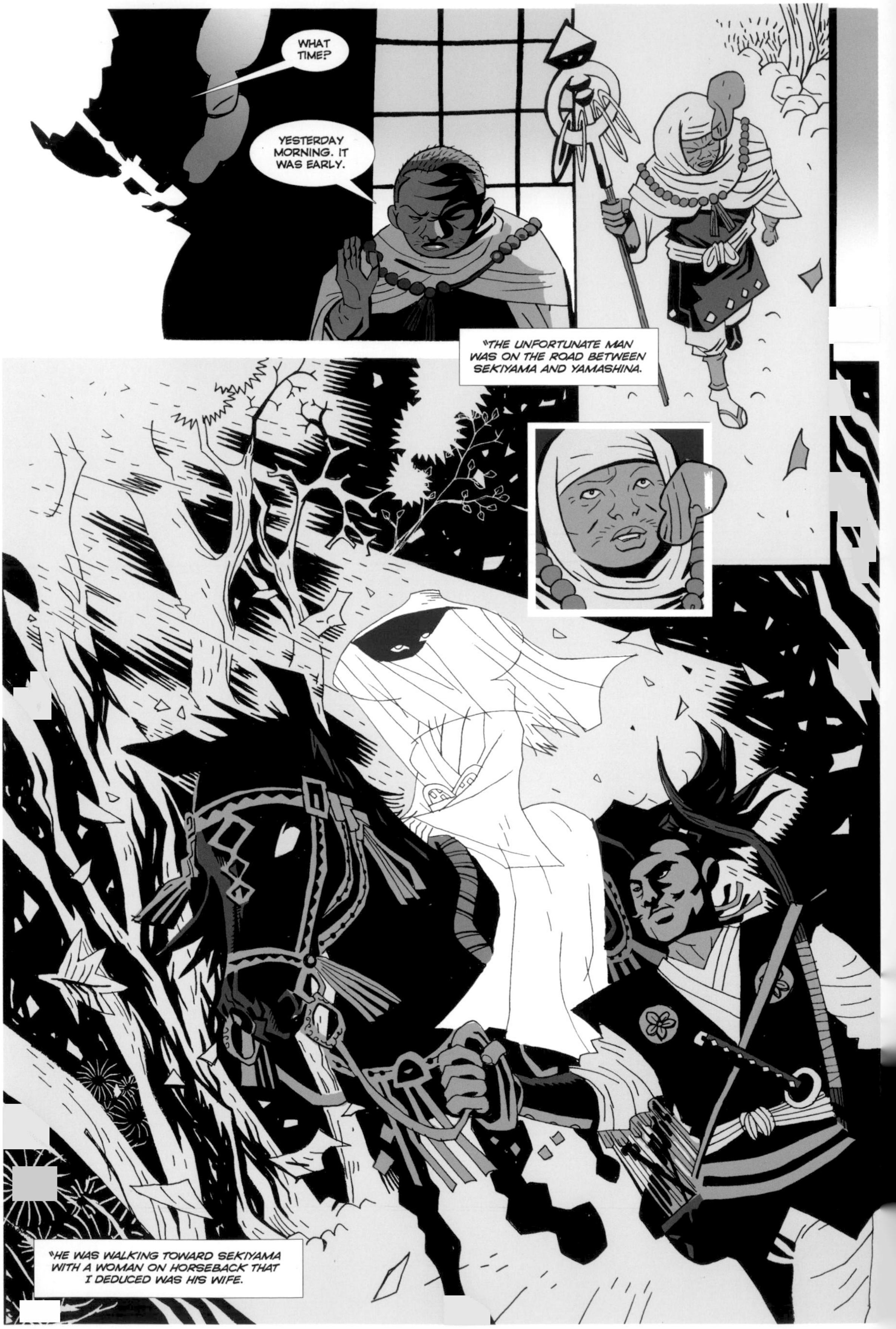
WHAT TIME?
YESTERDAY MORNING. IT WAS EARLY.
"THE UNFORTUNATE MAN WAS ON THE ROAD BETWEEN SEKIYAMA AND YAMASHINA.
"HE WAS WALKING TOWARD SEKIYAMA WITH A WOMAN ON HORSEBACK THAT I DEDUCED WAS HIS WIFE.

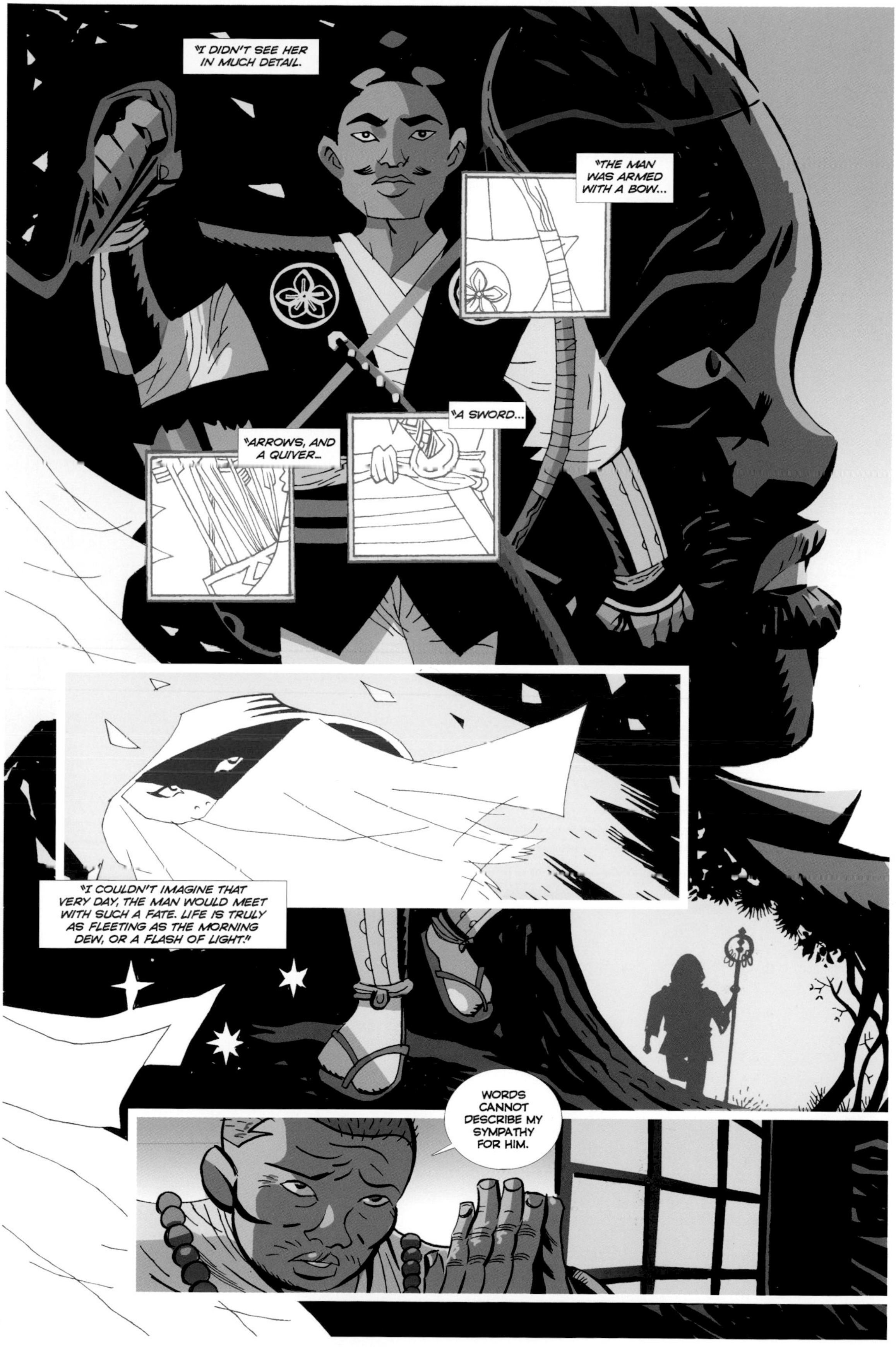
"I DIDN'T SEE HER IN MUCH DETAIL.
"THE MAN WAS ARMED WITH A BOW...
"A SWORD...
"ARROWS, AND A QUIVER...
"I COULDN'T IMAGINE THAT VERY DAY, THE MAN WOULD MEET WITH SUCH A FATE. LIFE IS TRULY AS FLEETING AS THE MORNING DEW, OR A FLASH OF LIGHT."
WORDS CANNOT DESCRIBE MY SYMPATHY FOR HIM.

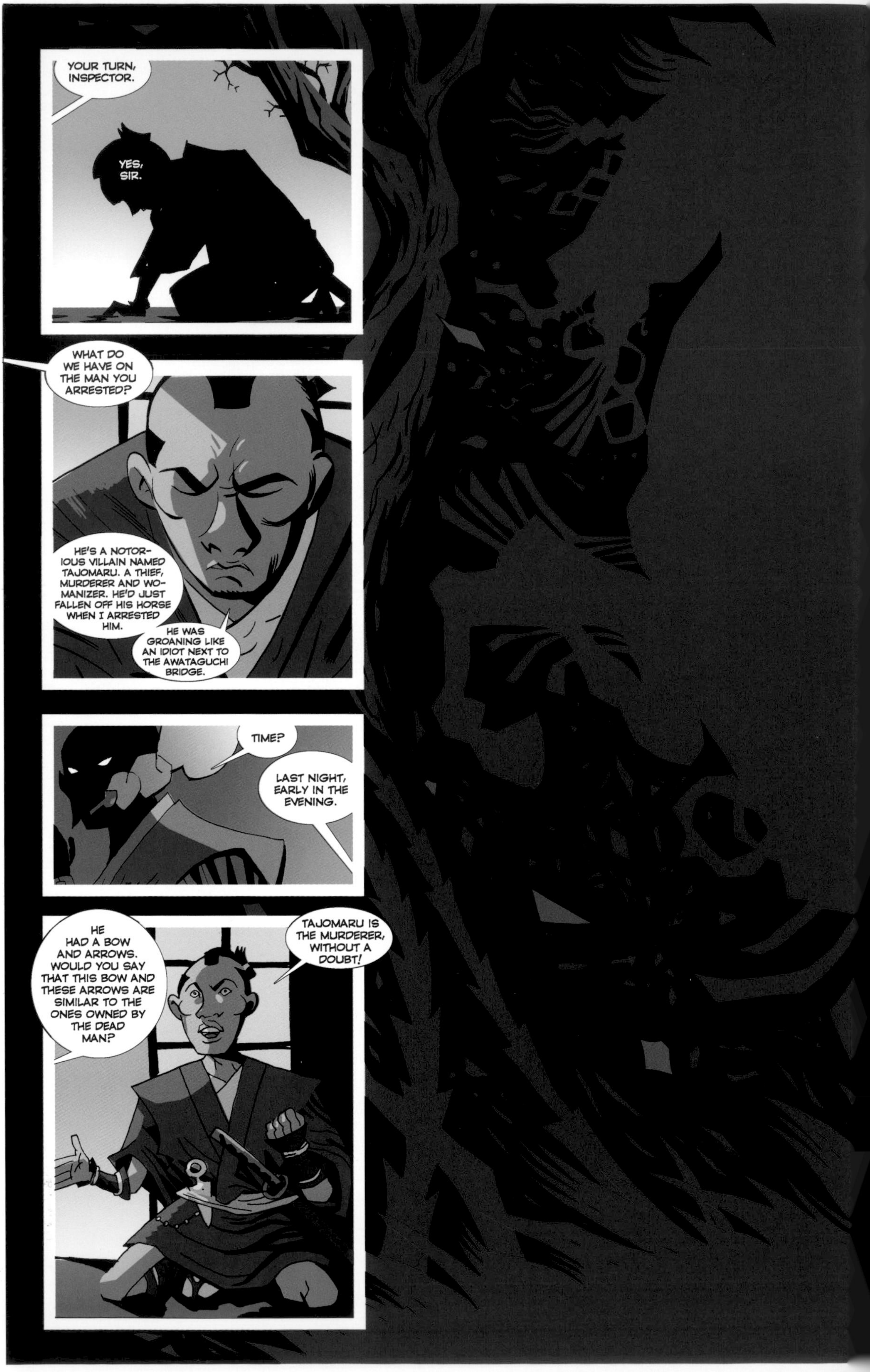
YOUR TURN, INSPECTOR.
YES, SIR.
WHAT DO WE HAVE ON THE MAN YOU ARRESTED?
HE'S A NOTORIOUS VILLAIN NAMED TAJOMARU. A THIEF, MURDERER AND WOMANIZER. HE'D JUST FALLEN OFF HIS HORSE WHEN I ARRESTED HIM.
HE WAS GROANING LIKE AN IDIOT NEXT TO THE AWATAGUCHI BRIDGE.
TIME?
LAST NIGHT, EARLY IN THE EVENING.
HE HAD A BOW AND ARROWS. WOULD YOU SAY THAT THIS BOW AND THESE ARROWS ARE SIMILAR TO THE ONES OWNED BY THE DEAD MAN?
TAJOMARU IS THE MURDERER, WITHOUT A DOUBT!

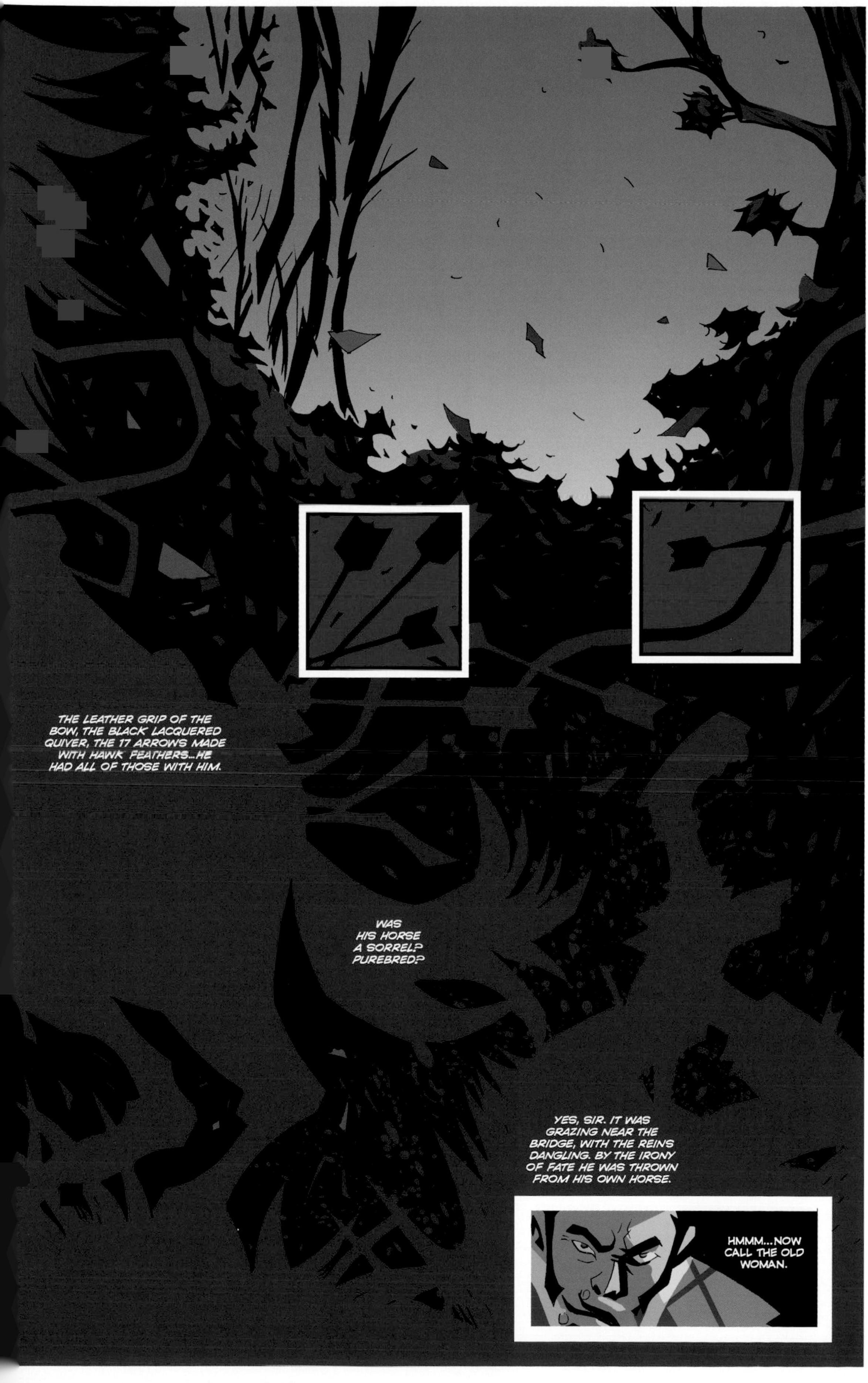
THE LEATHER GRIP OF THE BOW, THE BLACK LACQUERED QUIVER, THE 17 ARROWS MADE WITH HAWK FEATHERS...HE HAD ALL OF THOSE WITH HIM.
WAS HIS HORSE A SORREL? PUREBRED?
YES, SIR. IT WAS GRAZING NEAR THE BRIDGE, WITH THE REINS DANGLING. BY THE IRONY OF FATE HE WAS THROWN FROM HIS OWN HORSE.
HMMM...NOW CALL THE OLD WOMAN.

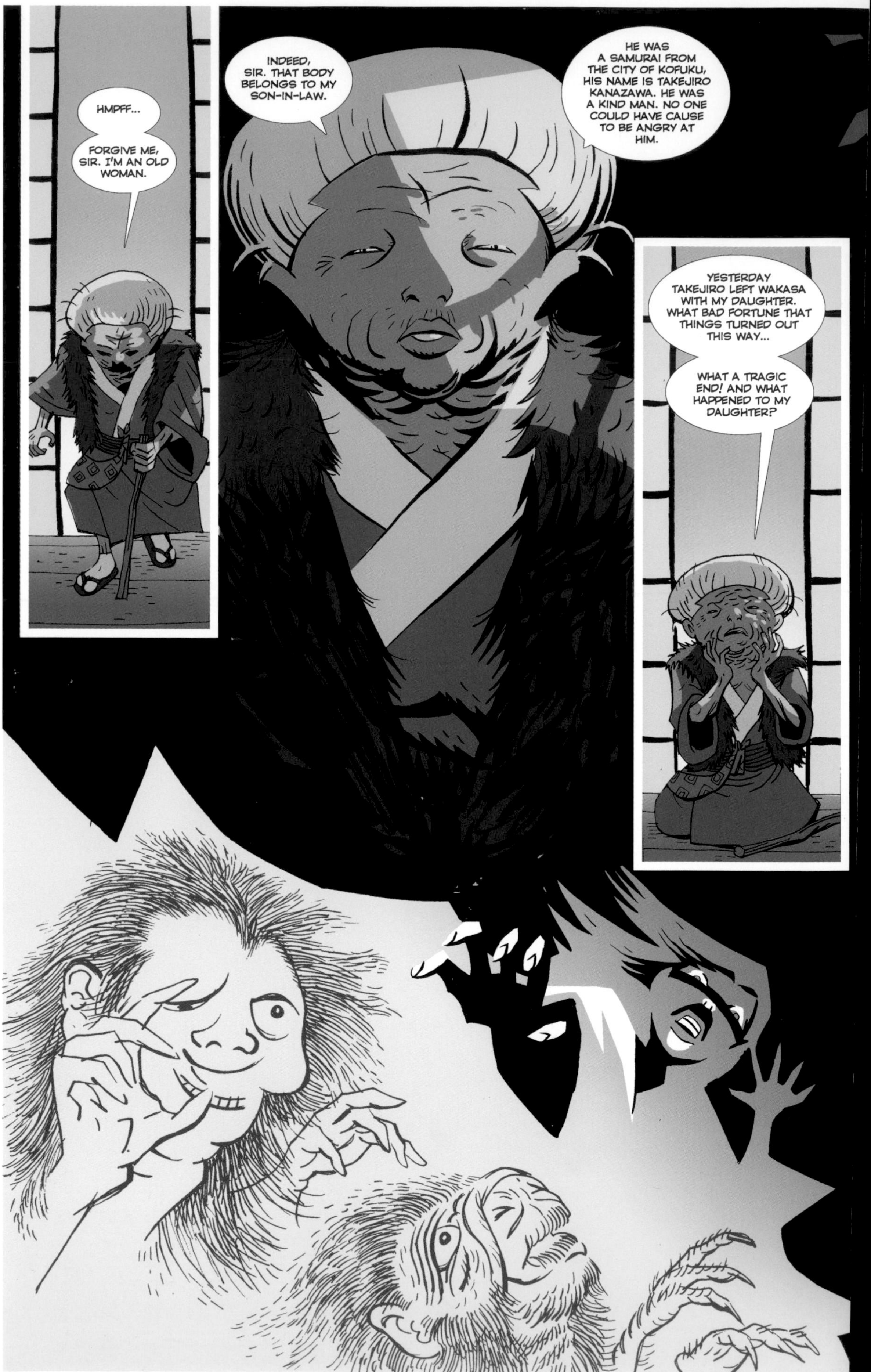
HMPFF...
FORGIVE ME, SIR. I'M AN OLD WOMAN.
INDEED, SIR. THAT BODY BELONGS TO MY SON-IN-LAW.
HE WAS A SAMURAI FROM THE CITY OF KOFUKU, HIS NAME IS TAKEJIRO KANAZAWA. HE WAS A KIND MAN. NO ONE COULD HAVE CAUSE TO BE ANGRY AT HIM.
YESTERDAY TAKEJIRO LEFT WAKASA WITH MY DAUGHTER. WHAT BAD FORTUNE THAT THINGS TURNED OUT THIS WAY...
WHAT A TRAGIC END! AND WHAT HAPPENED TO MY DAUGHTER?

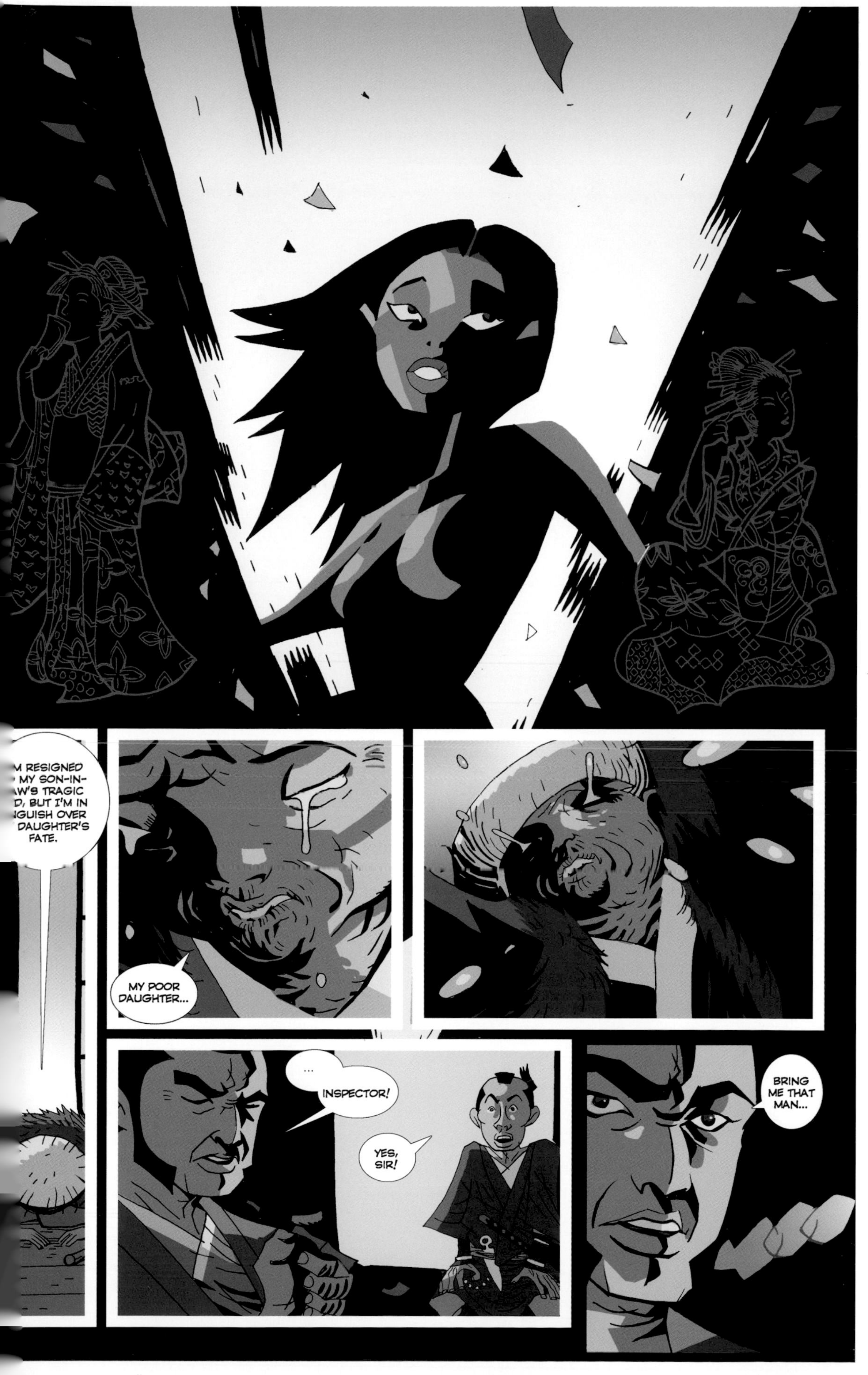

M RESIGNED MY SON-IN-AW'S TRAGIC D, BUT I'M IN NGUISH OVER DAUGHTER'S FATE.
MY POOR DAUGHTER...
...
INSPECTOR!
YES, SIR!
BRING ME THAT MAN...

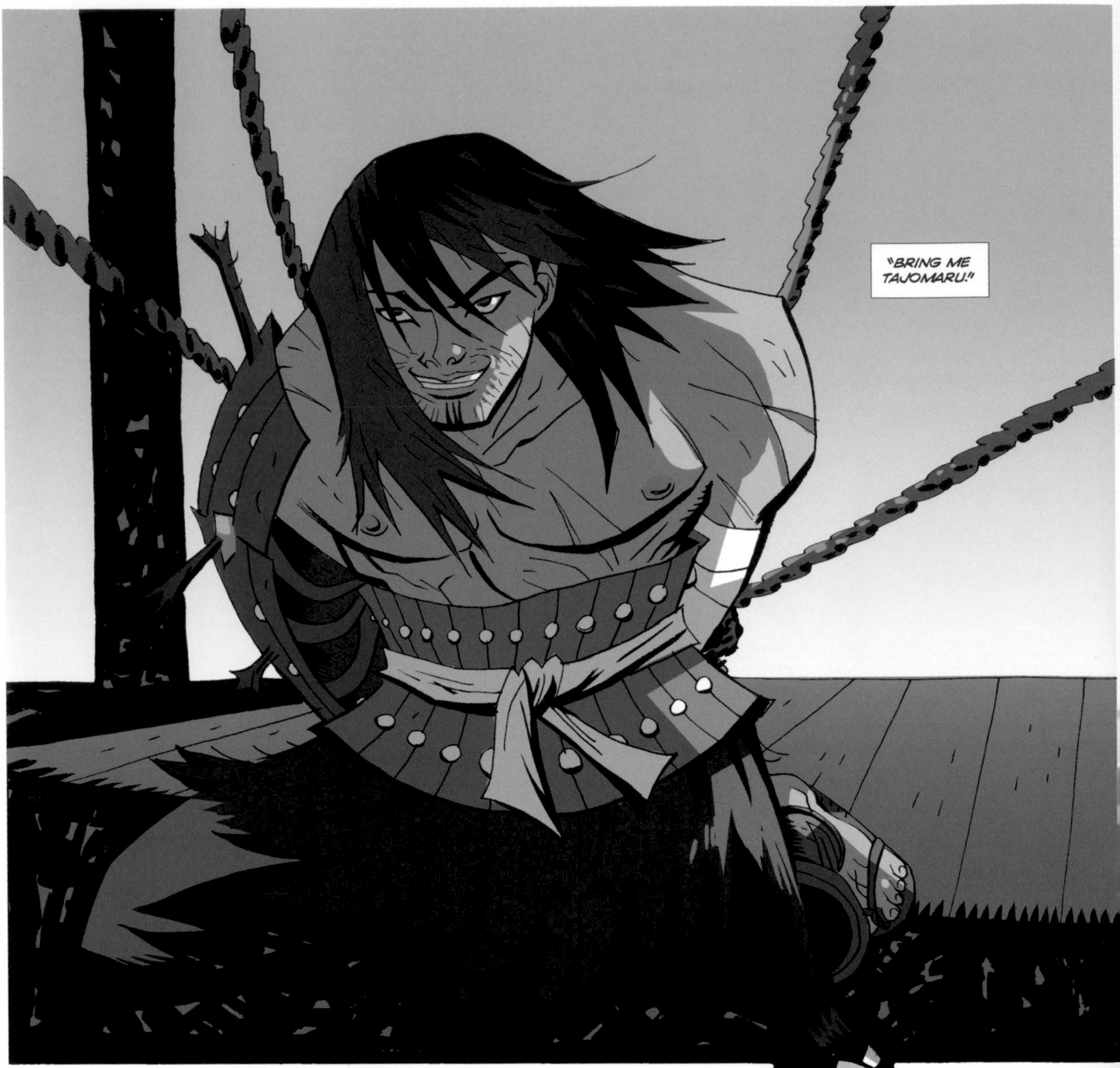
"BRING ME TAJOMARU."
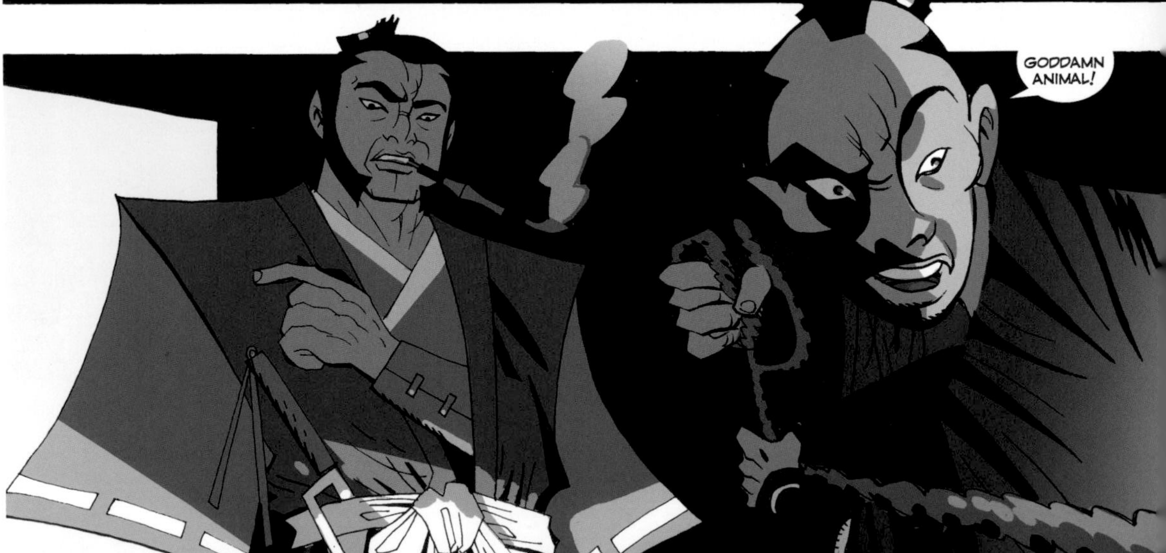
GODDAMN ANIMAL!

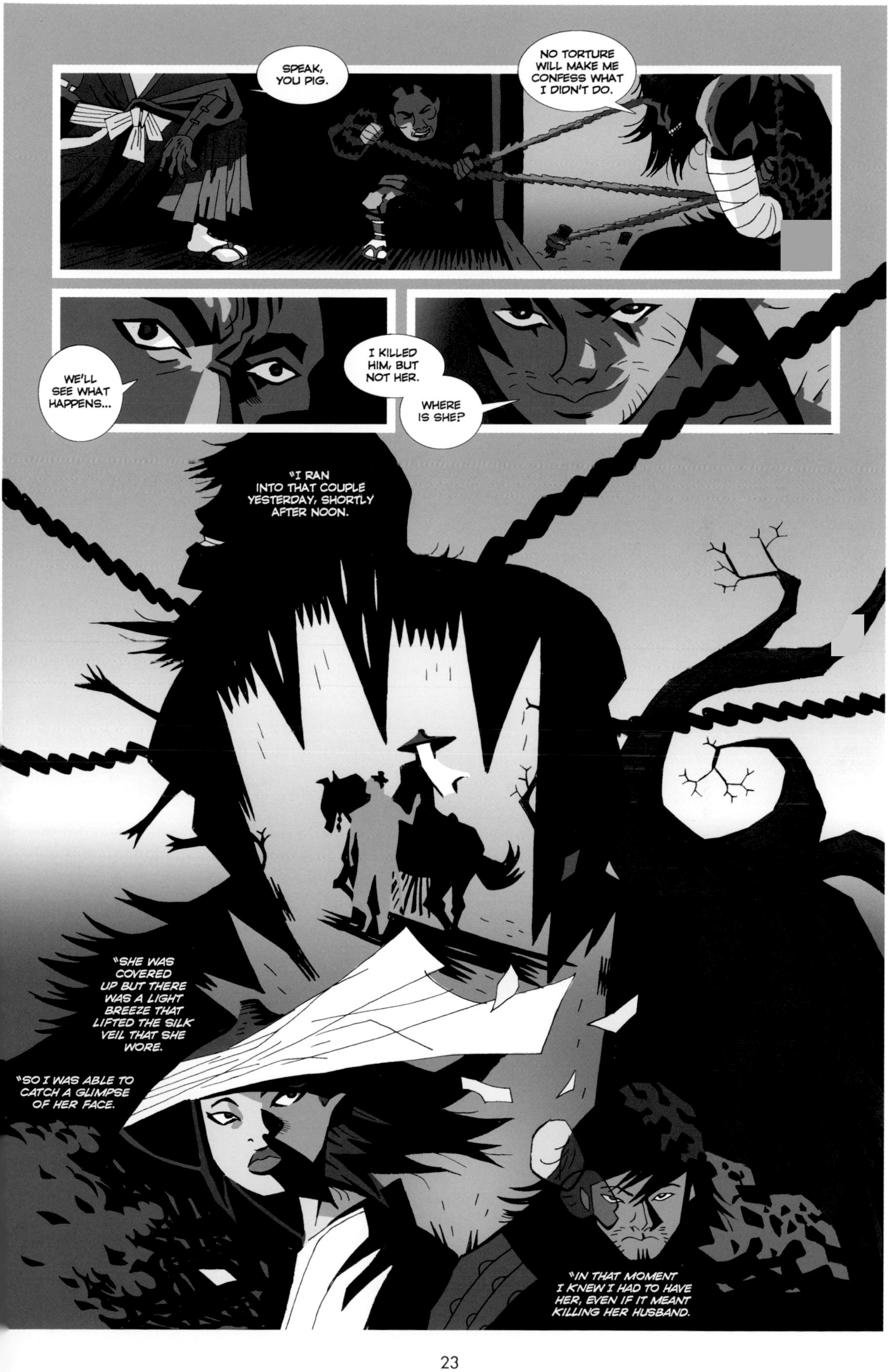
SPEAK, YOU PIG.
NO TORTURE WILL MAKE ME CONFESS WHAT I DIDN'T DO.
WE'LL SEE WHAT HAPPENS...
I KILLED HIM, BUT NOT HER.
WHERE IS SHE?
"I RAN INTO THAT COUPLE YESTERDAY, SHORTLY AFTER NOON.
"SHE WAS COVERED UP BUT THERE WAS A LIGHT BREEZE THAT LIFTED THE SILK VEIL THAT SHE WORE.
"SO I WAS ABLE TO CATCH A GLIMPSE OF HER FACE.
"IN THAT MOMENT I KNEW I HAD TO HAVE HER, EVEN IF IT MEANT KILLING HER HUSBAND.

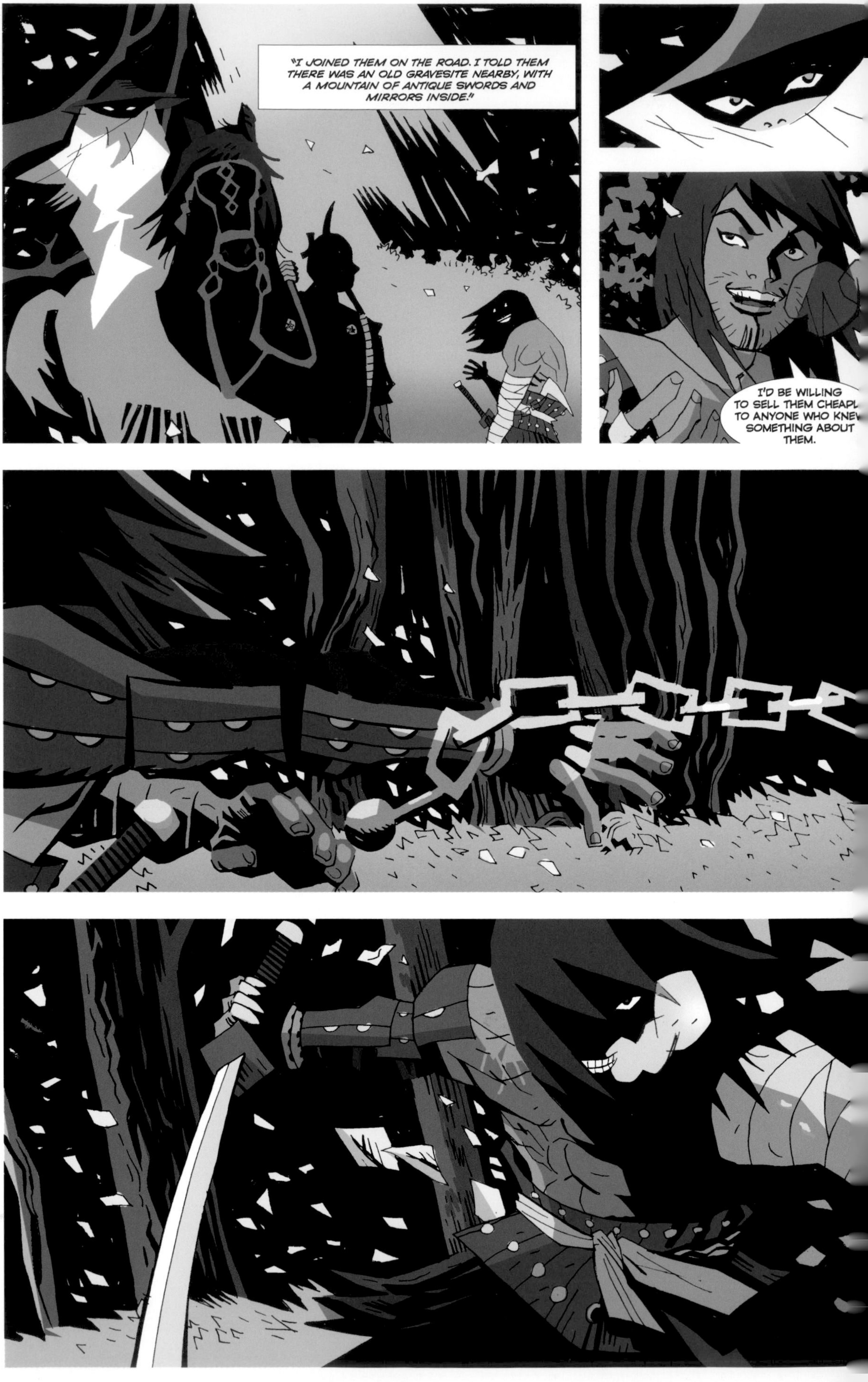
"I JOINED THEM ON THE ROAD. I TOLD THEM THERE WAS AN OLD GRAVESITE NEARBY, WITH A MOUNTAIN OF ANTIQUE SWORDS AND MIRRORS INSIDE."
I'D BE WILLING TO SELL THEM CHEAPL TO ANYONE WHO KNEV SOMETHING ABOUT THEM.

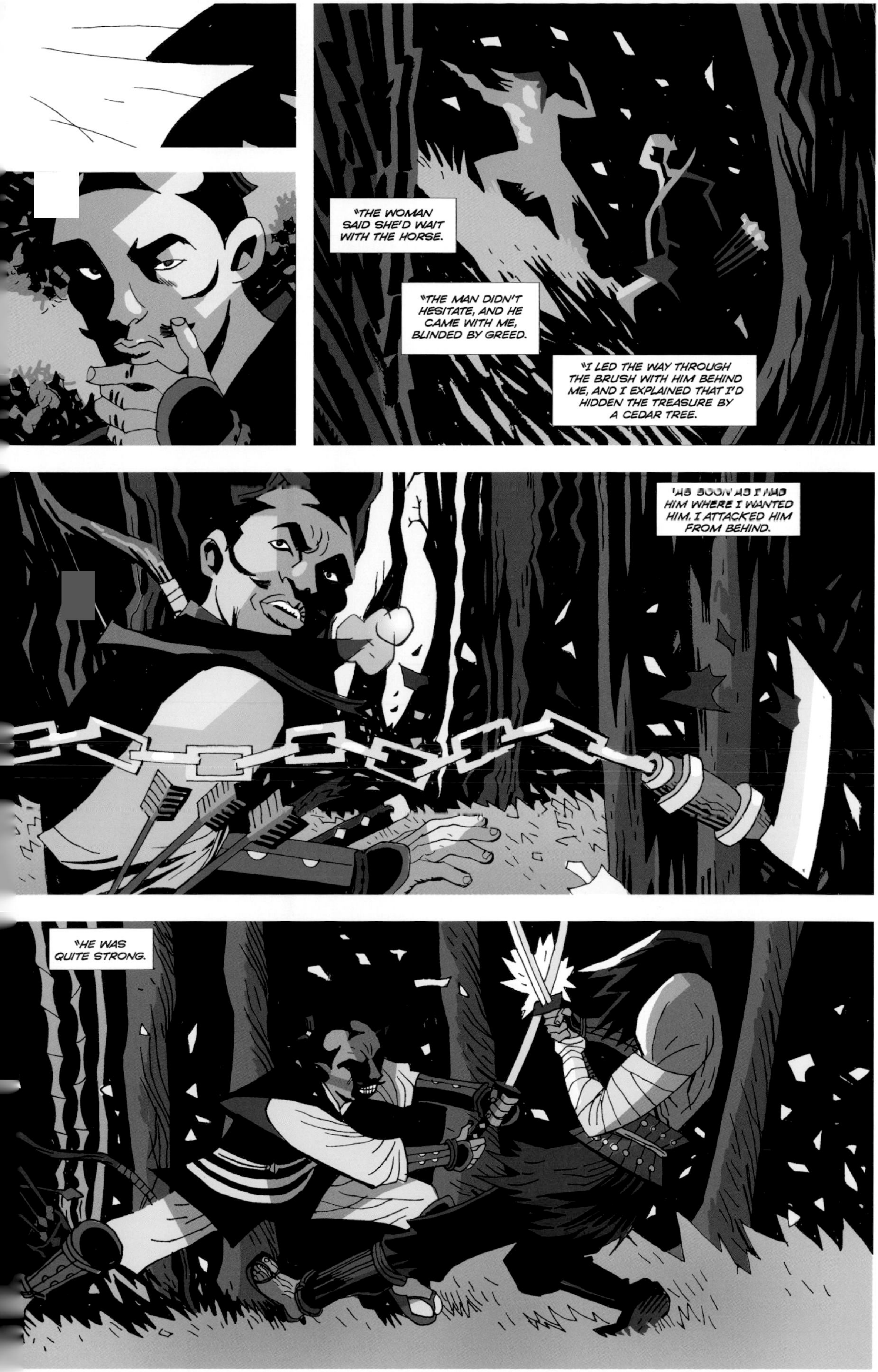
"THE WOMAN SAID SHE'D WAIT WITH THE HORSE.
"THE MAN DIDN'T HESITATE, AND HE CAME WITH ME, BLINDED BY GREED.
"I LED THE WAY THROUGH THE BRUSH WITH HIM BEHIND ME, AND I EXPLAINED THAT I'D HIDDEN THE TREASURE BY A CEDAR TREE.
"AS SOON AS I HAD HIM WHERE I WANTED HIM, I ATTACKED HIM FROM BEHIND.
"HE WAS QUITE STRONG.

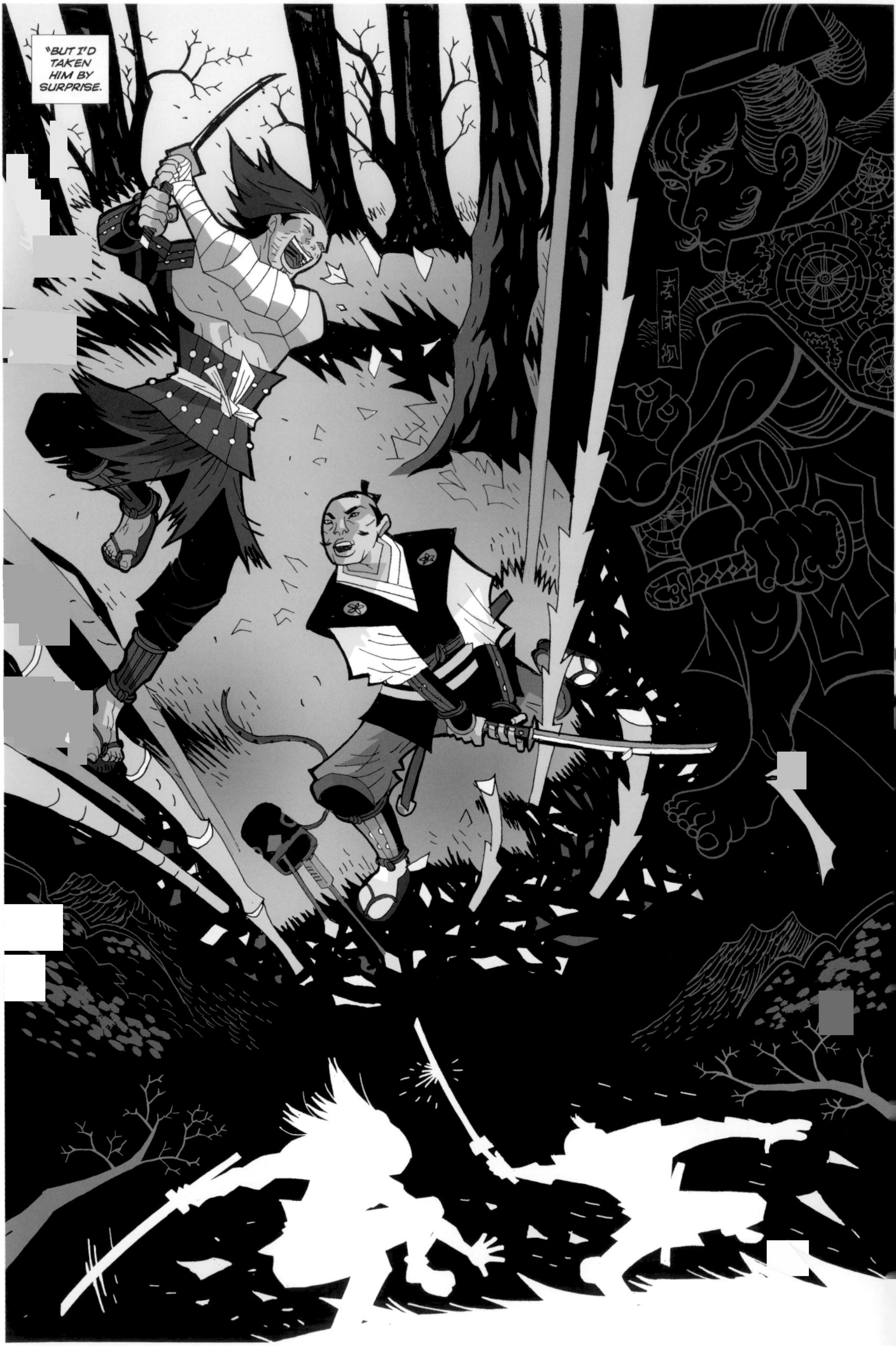
"BUT I'D TAKEN HIM BY SURPRISE.

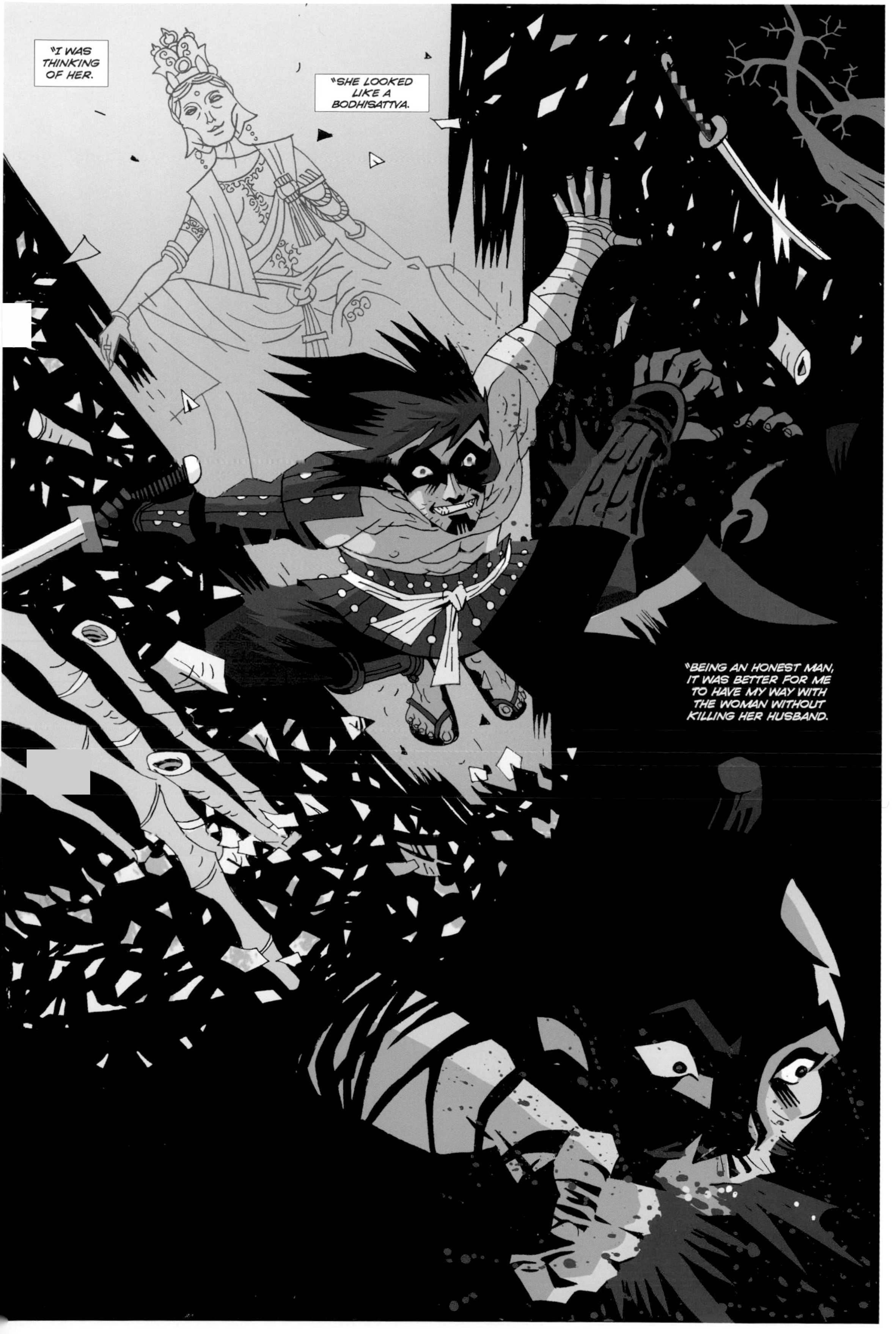
"I WAS THINKING OF HER.
"SHE LOOKED LIKE A BODHISATTVA.
"BEING AN HONEST MAN, IT WAS BETTER FOR ME TO HAVE MY WAY WITH THE WOMAN WITHOUT KILLING HER HUSBAND.

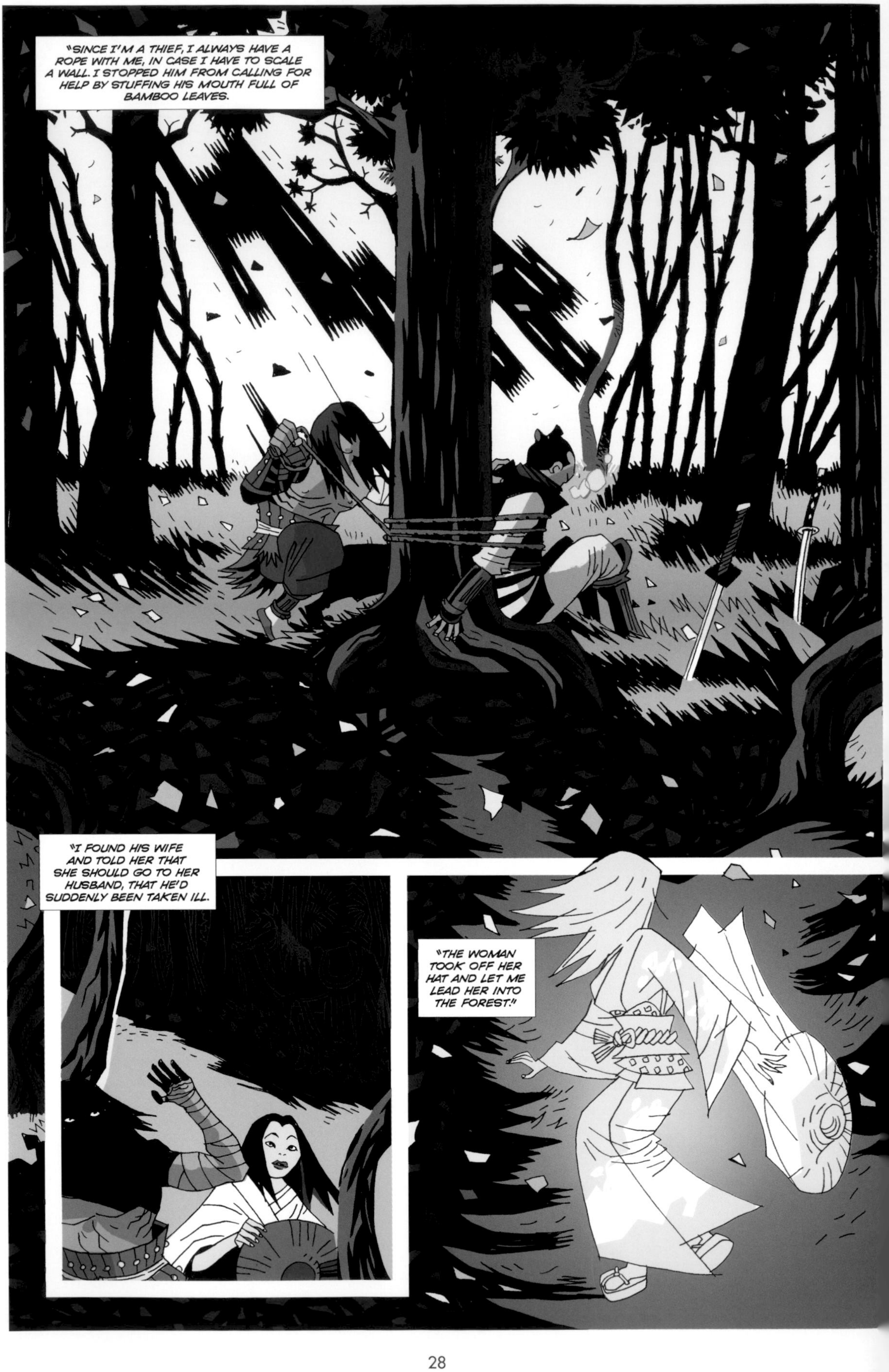
"SINCE I'M A THIEF, I ALWAYS HAVE A ROPE WITH ME, IN CASE I HAVE TO SCALE A WALL. I STOPPED HIM FROM CALLING FOR HELP BY STUFFING HIS MOUTH FULL OF BAMBOO LEAVES.
"I FOUND HIS WIFE AND TOLD HER THAT SHE SHOULD GO TO HER HUSBAND, THAT HE'D SUDDENLY BEEN TAKEN ILL.
"THE WOMAN TOOK OFF HER HAT AND LET ME LEAD HER INTO THE FOREST."

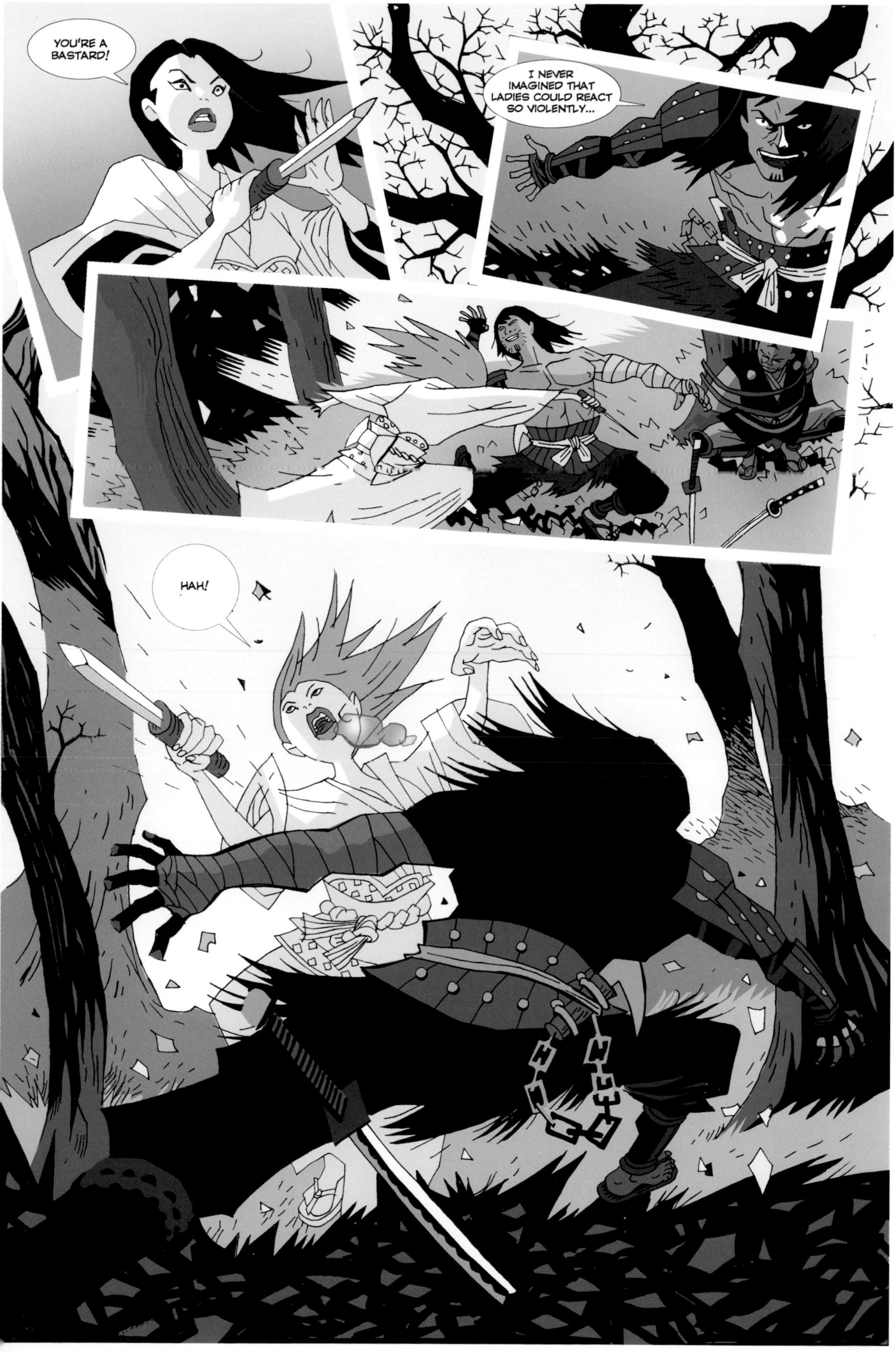
YOU'RE A BASTARD!
I NEVER IMAGINED THAT LADIES COULD REACT SO VIOLENTLY...
HAH!

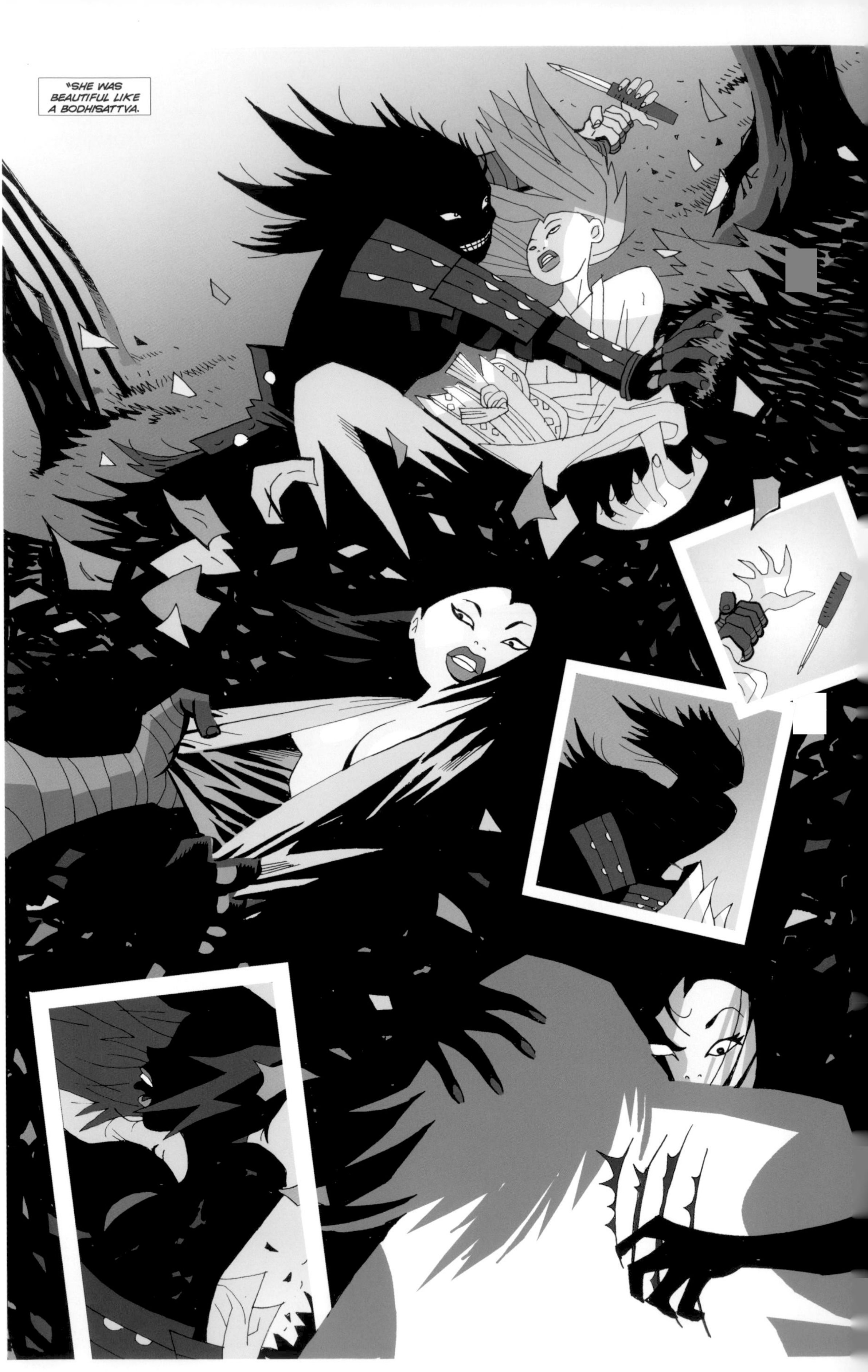
"SHE WAS BEAUTIFUL LIKE A BODHISATTVA.

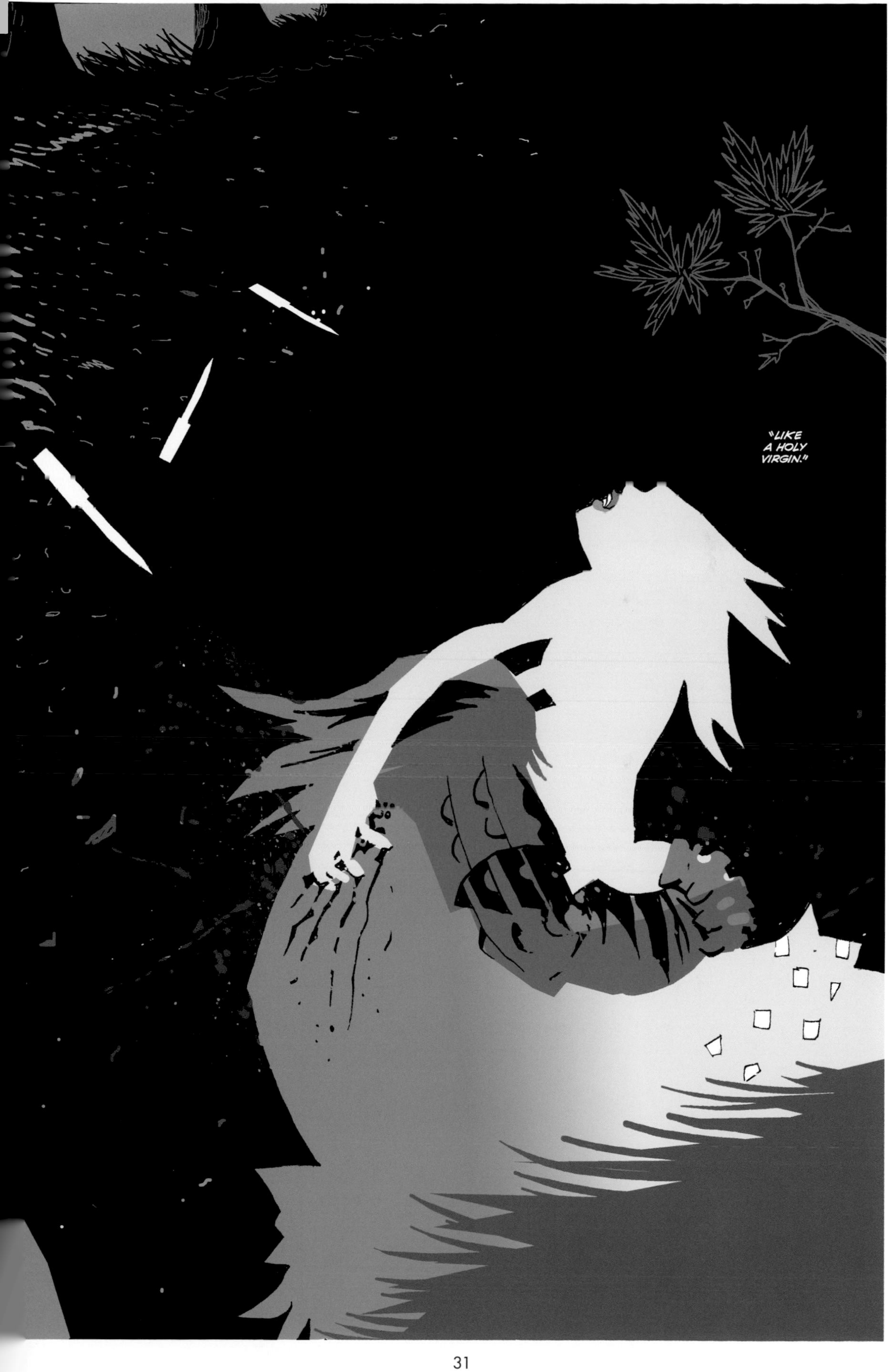
"LIKE A HOLY VIRGIN."

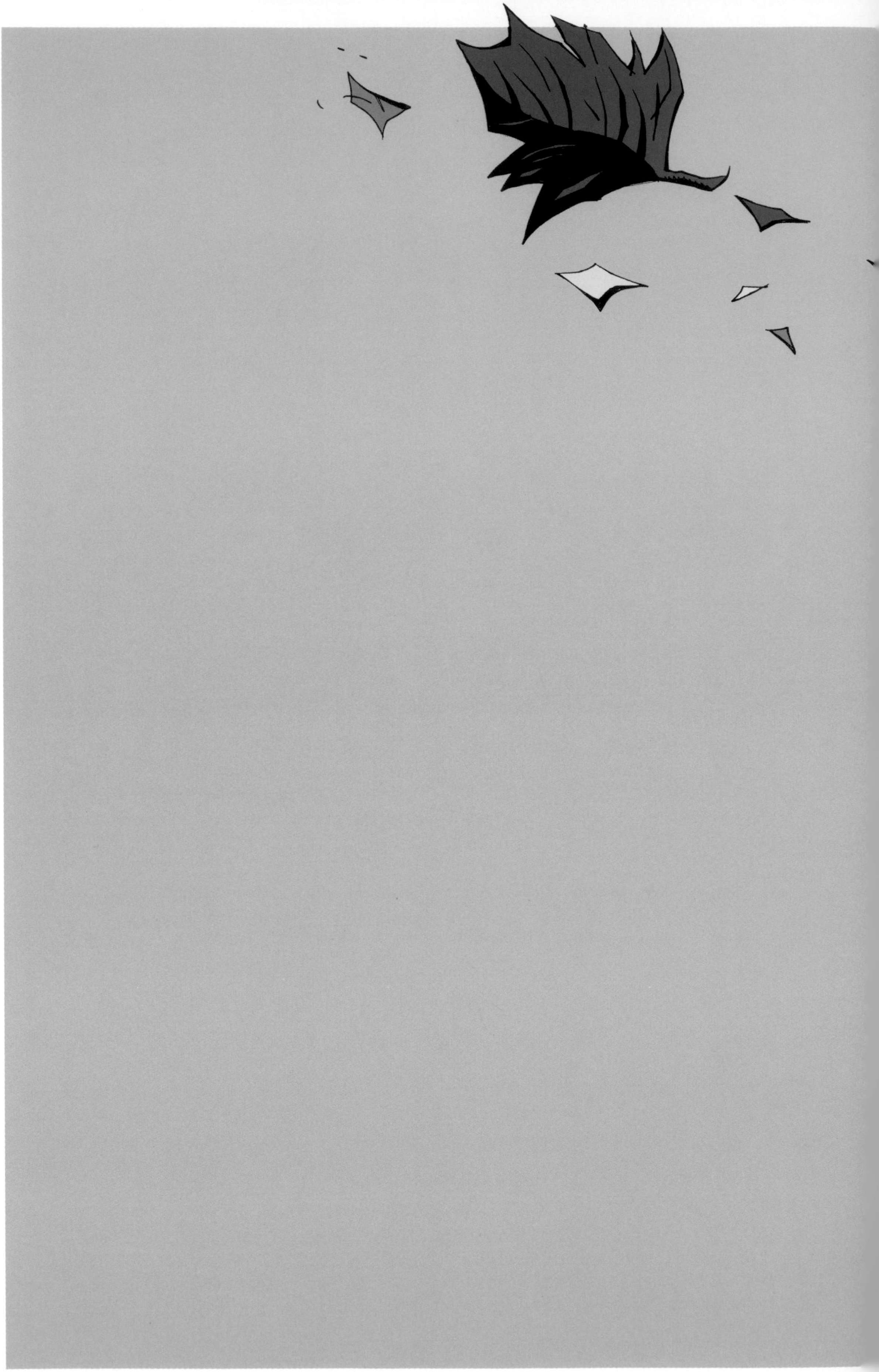

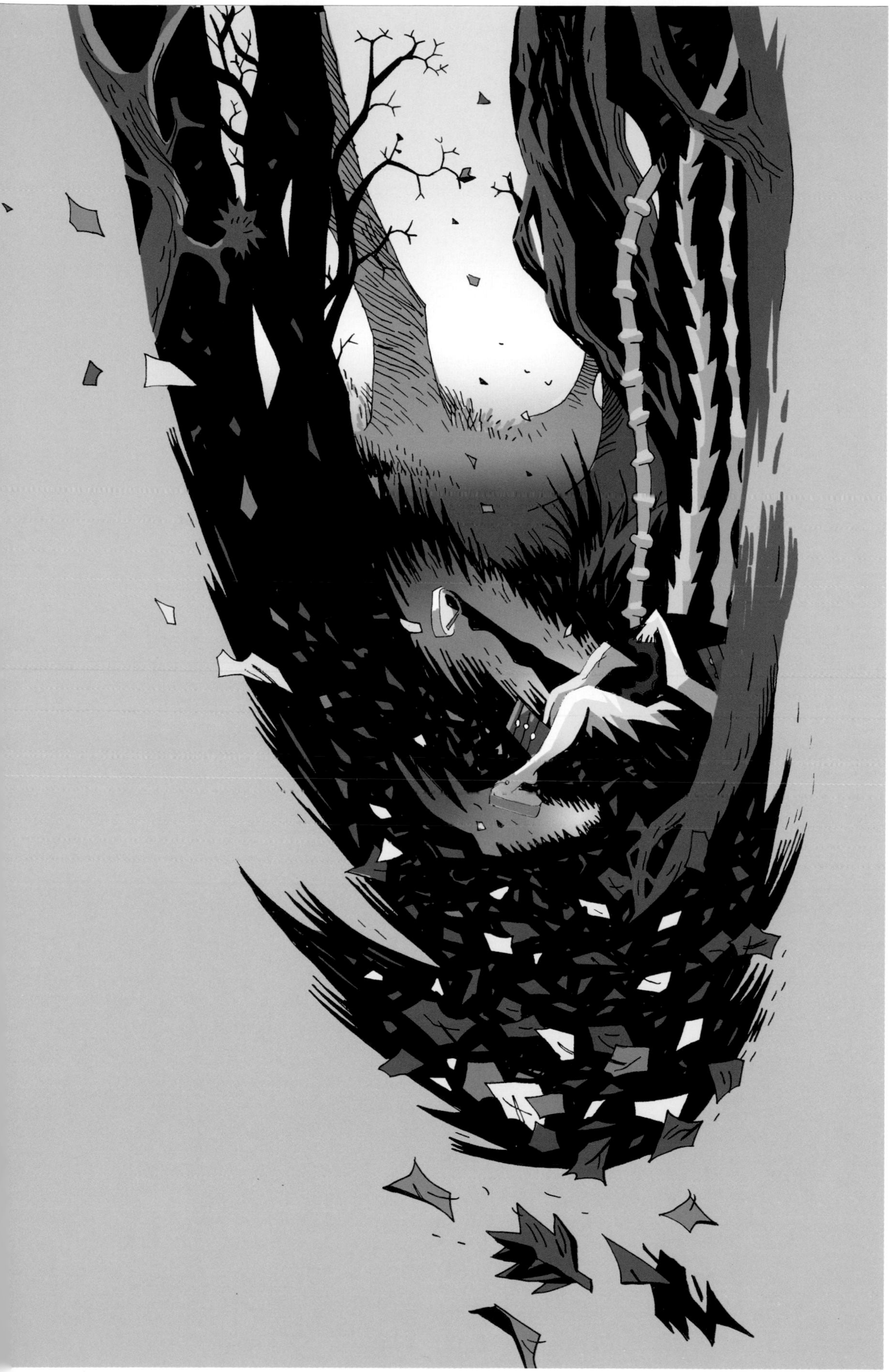

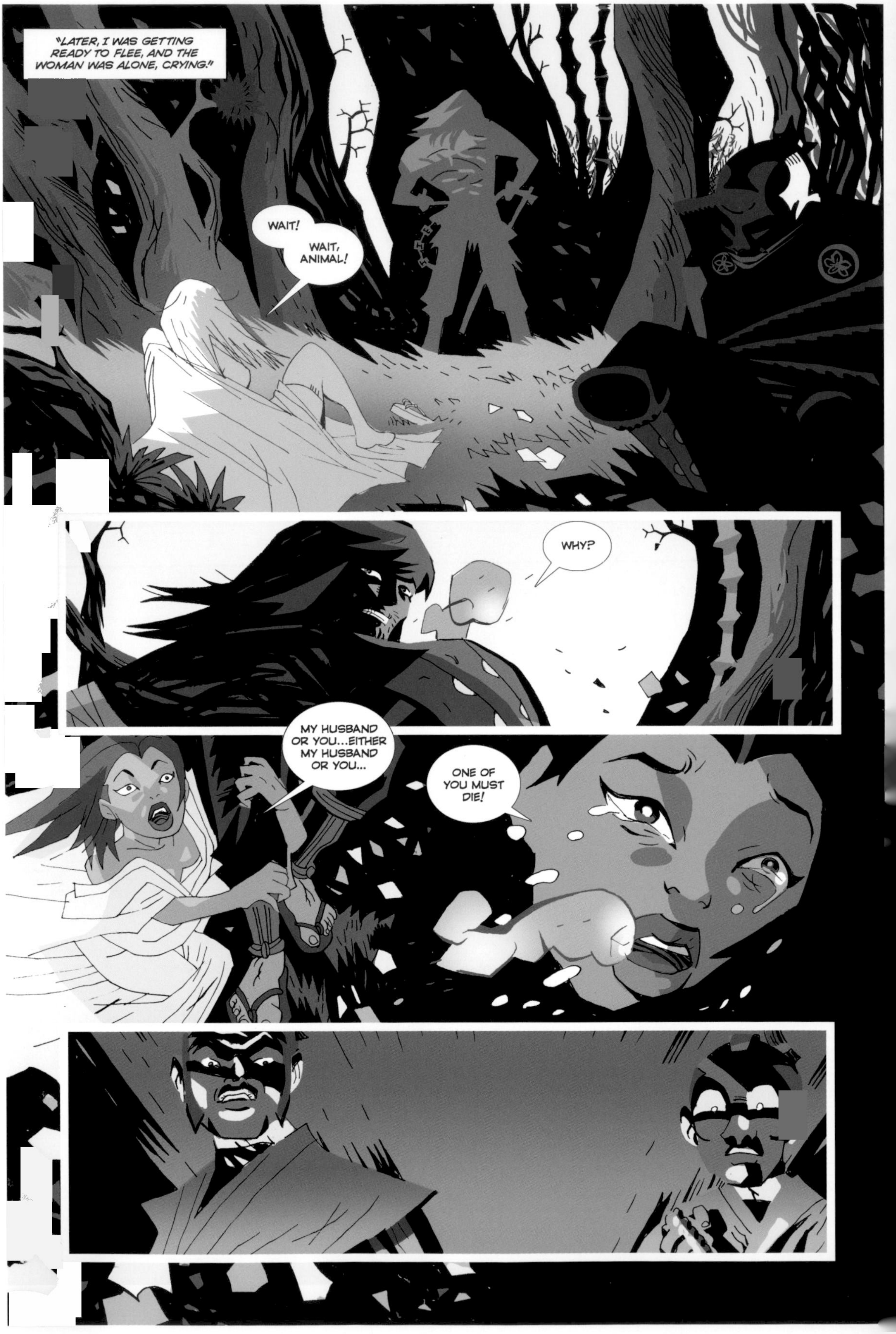
"LATER, I WAS GETTING READY TO FLEE, AND THE WOMAN WAS ALONE, CRYING."
WAIT!
WAIT, ANIMAL!
WHY?
MY HUSBAND OR YOU...EITHER MY HUSBAND OR YOU...
ONE OF YOU MUST DIE!

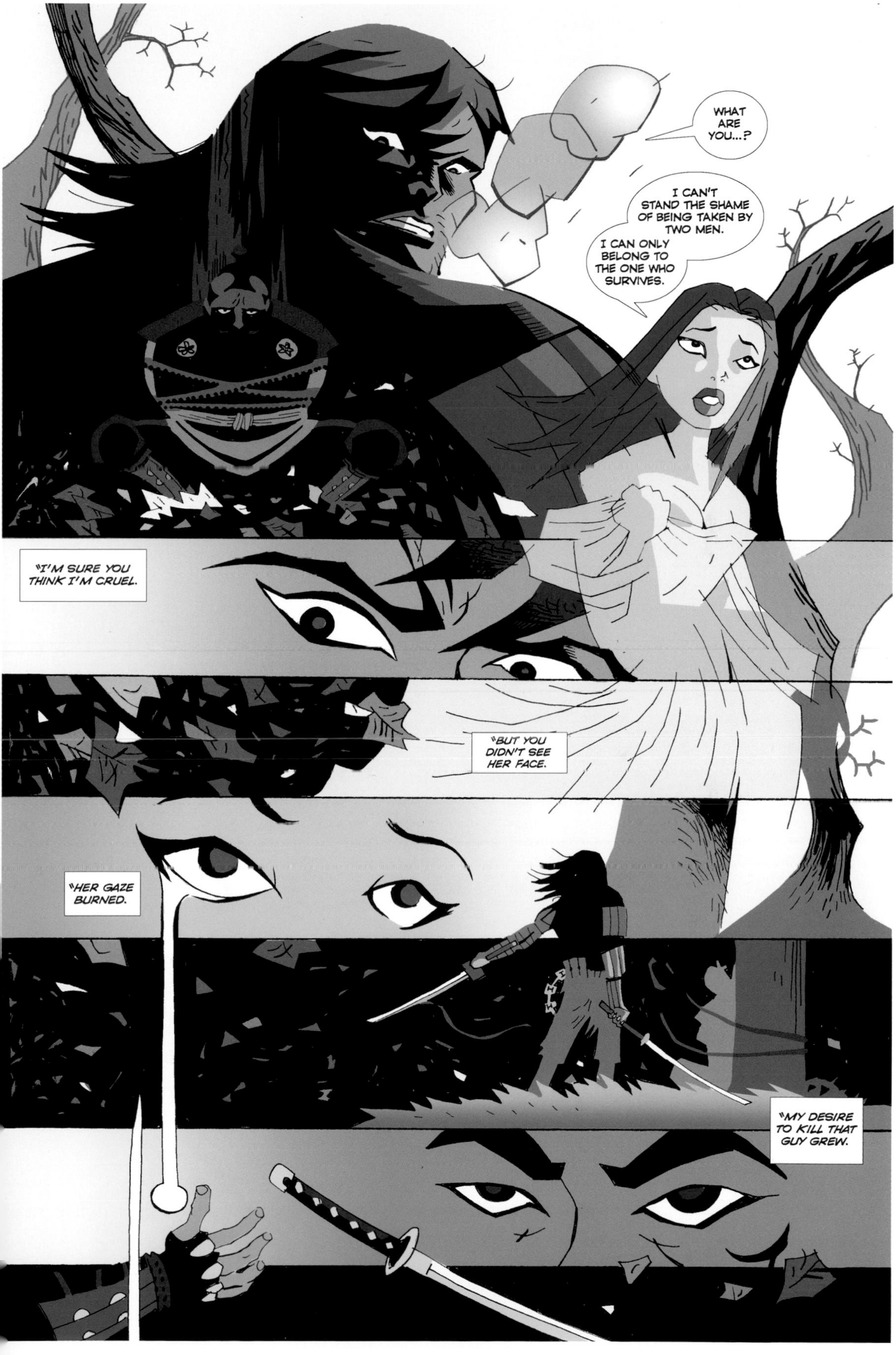
WHAT ARE YOU...?
I CAN'T STAND THE SHAME OF BEING TAKEN BY TWO MEN.
I CAN ONLY BELONG TO THE ONE WHO SURVIVES.
"I'M SURE YOU THINK I'M CRUEL.
"BUT YOU DIDN'T SEE HER FACE.
"HER GAZE BURNED.
"MY DESIRE TO KILL THAT GUY GREW.

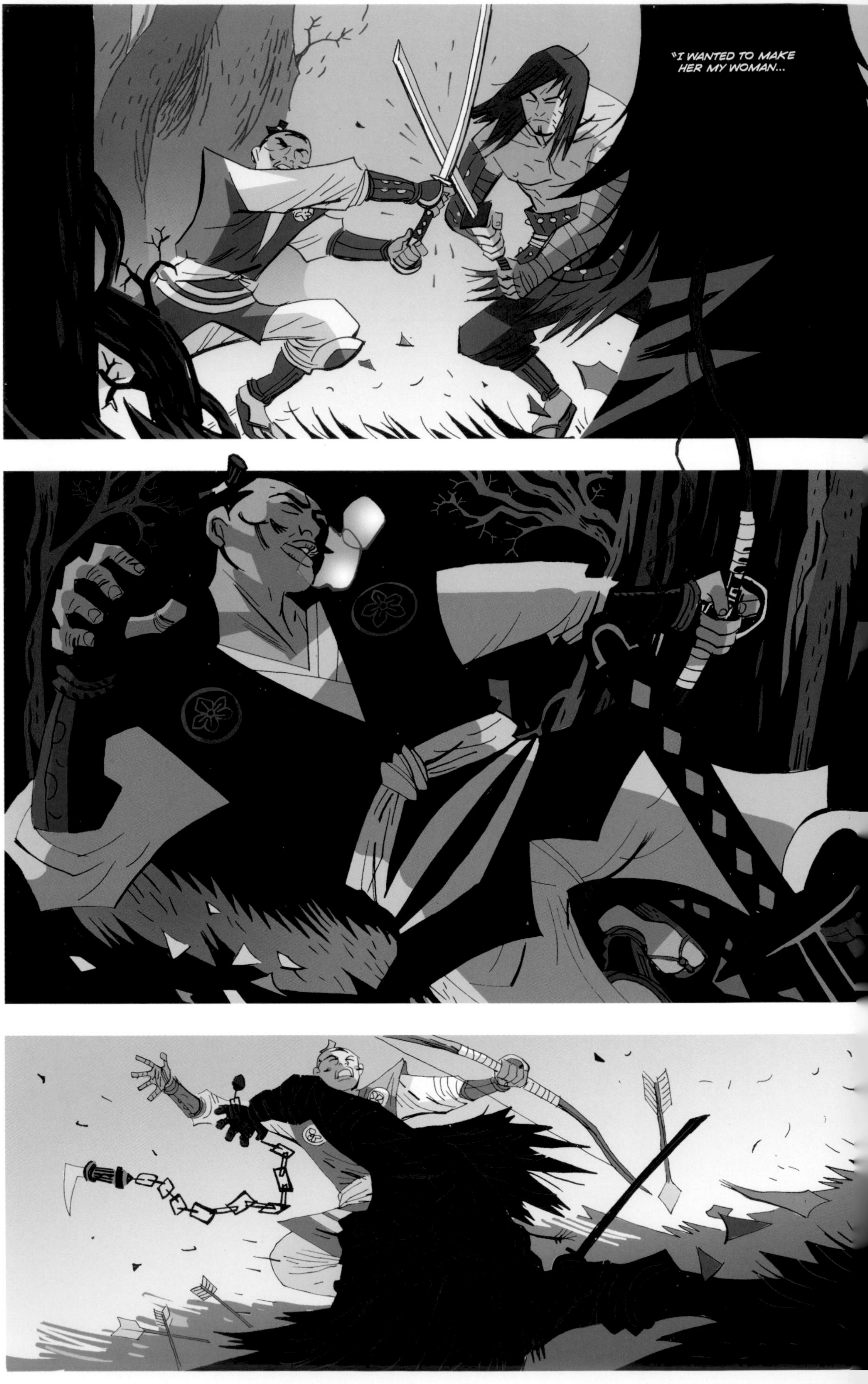
"I WANTED TO MAKE HER MY WOMAN...

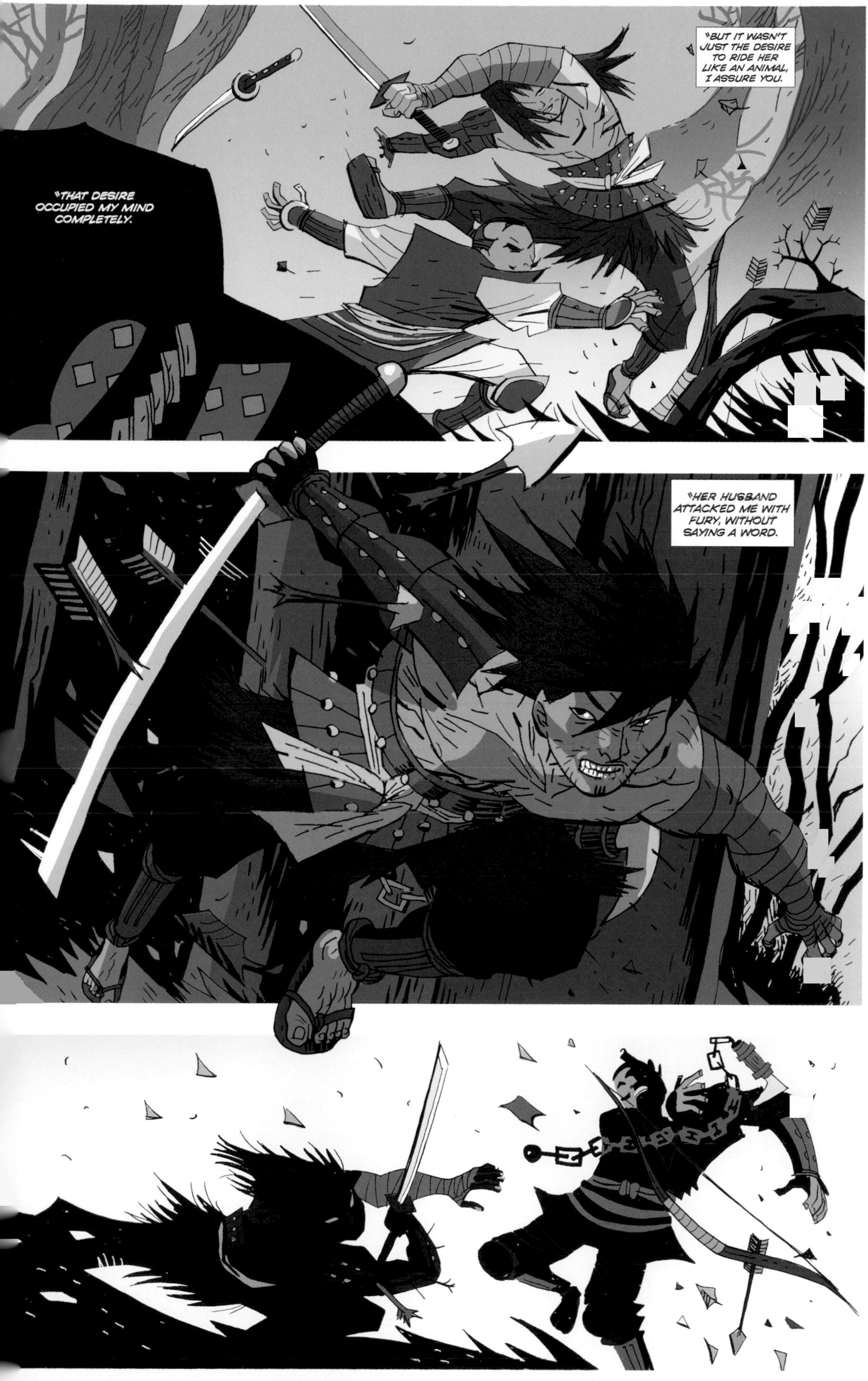
"THAT DESIRE OCCUPIED MY MIND COMPLETELY.
"BUT IT WASN'T JUST THE DESIRE TO RIDE HER LIKE AN ANIMAL, I ASSURE YOU.
"HER HUSBAND ATTACKED ME WITH FURY, WITHOUT SAYING A WORD.

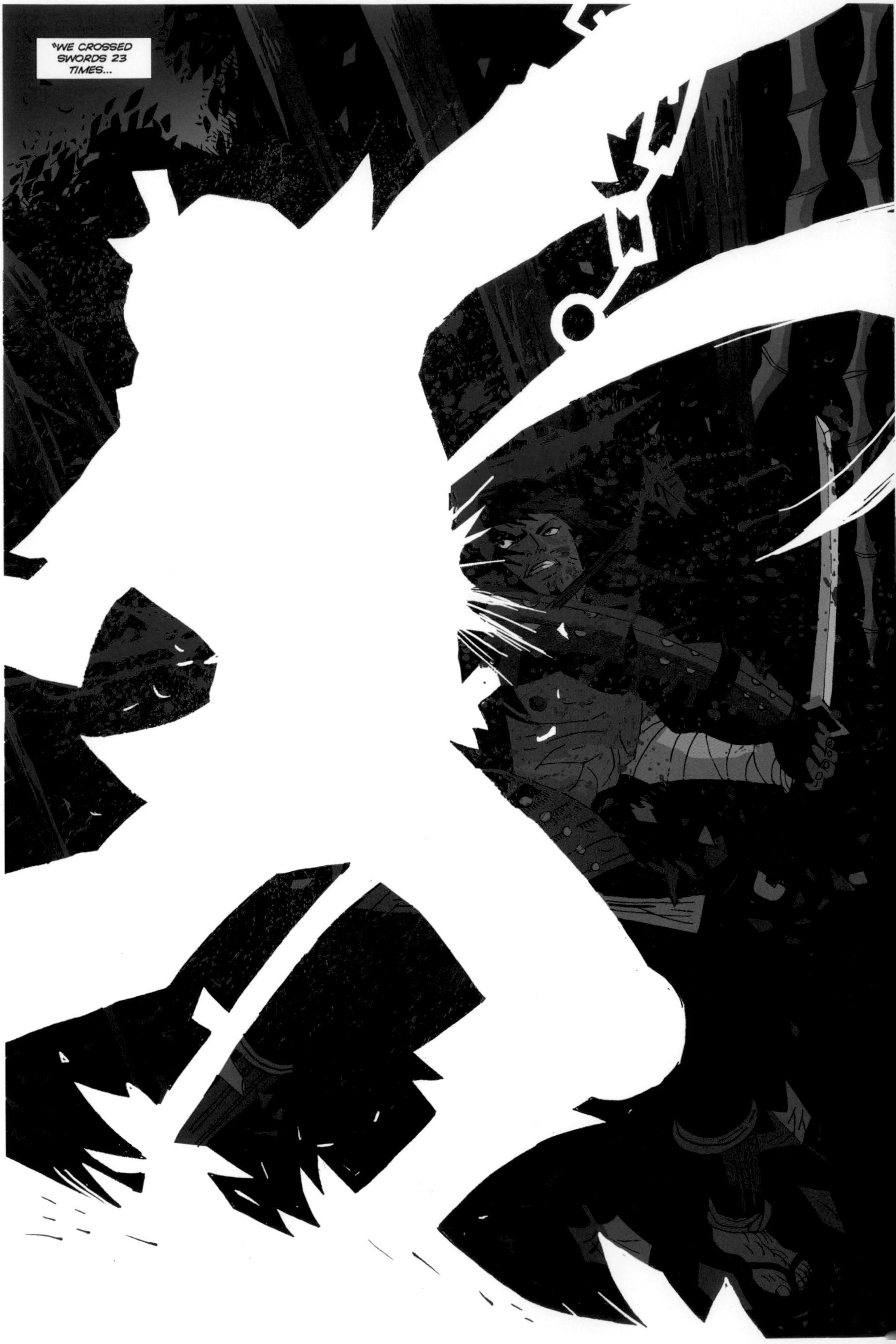
"WE CROSSED SWORDS 23 TIMES...

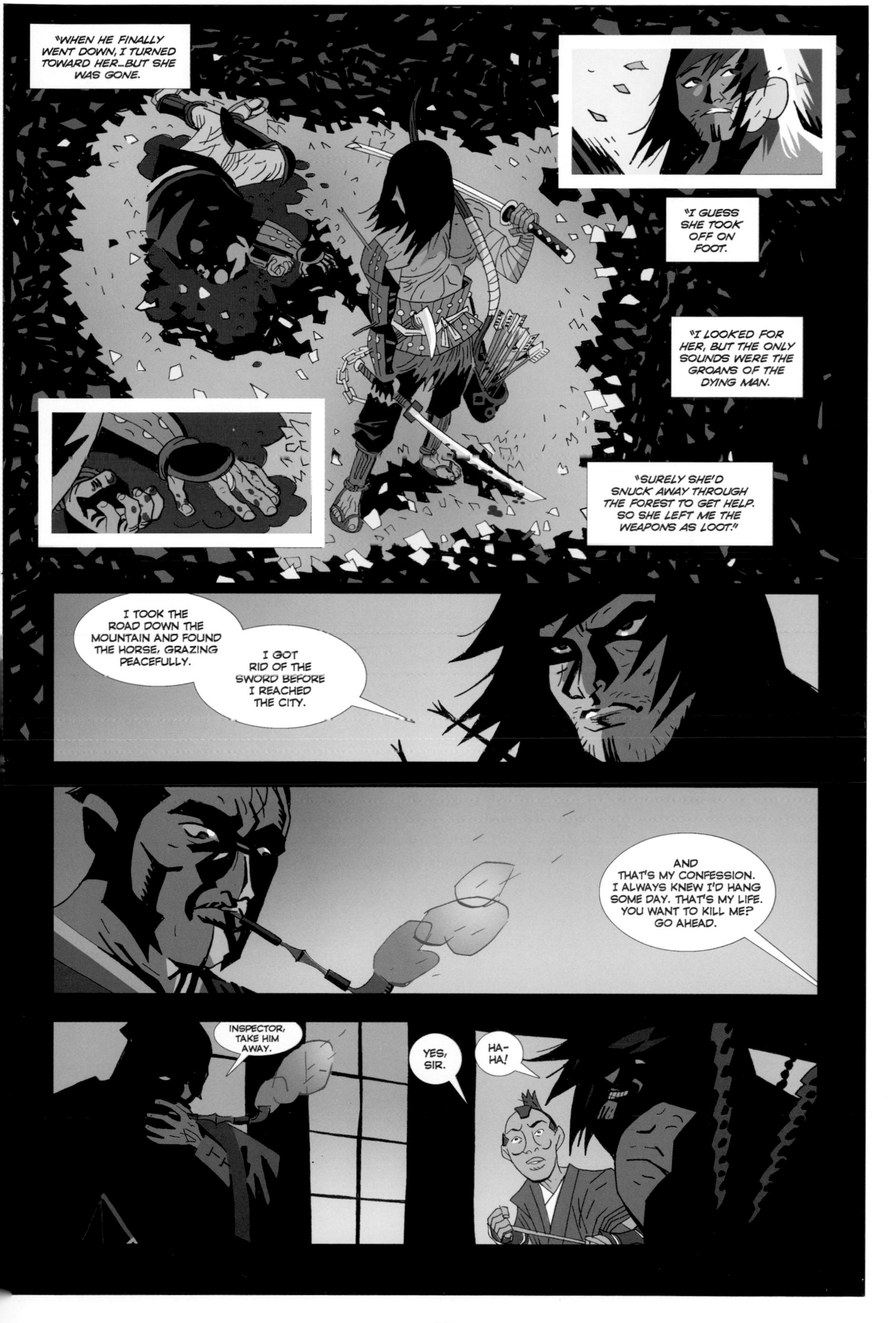
"WHEN HE FINALLY WENT DOWN, I TURNED TOWARD HER...BUT SHE WAS GONE.
"I GUESS SHE TOOK OFF ON FOOT.
"I LOOKED FOR HER, BUT THE ONLY SOUNDS WERE THE GROANS OF THE DYING MAN.
"SURELY SHE'D SNUCK AWAY THROUGH THE FOREST TO GET HELP. SO SHE LEFT ME THE WEAPONS AS LOOT."
I TOOK THE ROAD DOWN THE MOUNTAIN AND FOUND THE HORSE, GRAZING PEACEFULLY.
I GOT RID OF THE SWORD BEFORE I REACHED THE CITY.
AND THAT'S MY CONFESSION. I ALWAYS KNEW I'D HANG SOME DAY. THAT'S MY LIFE. YOU WANT TO KILL ME? GO AHEAD.
INSPECTOR, TAKE HIM AWAY.
YES, SIR.
HA-HA!

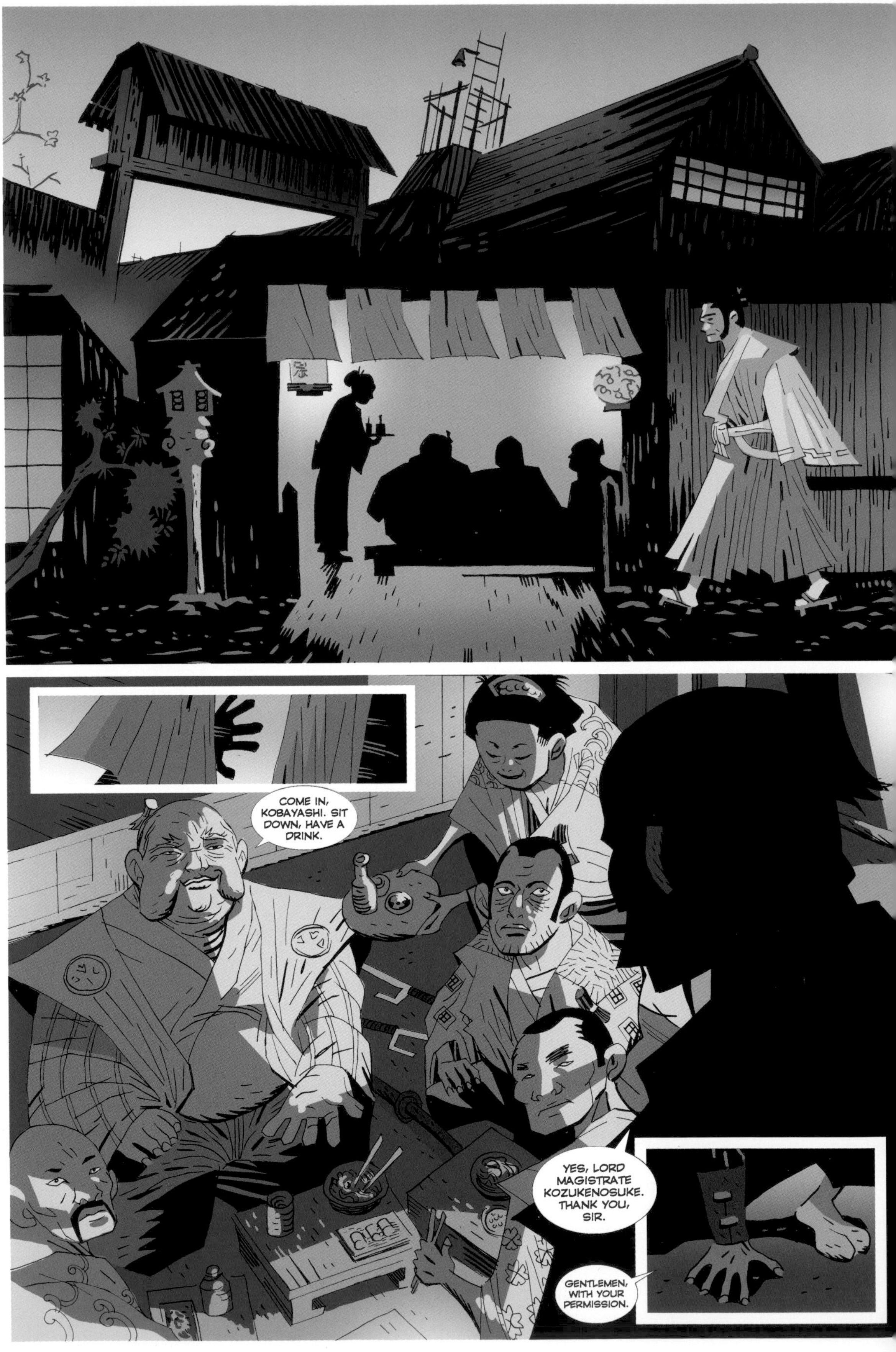
COME IN, KOBAYASHI. SIT DOWN, HAVE A DRINK.
YES, LORD MAGISTRATE KOZUKENOSUKE. THANK YOU, SIR.
GENTLEMEN, WITH YOUR PERMISSION.

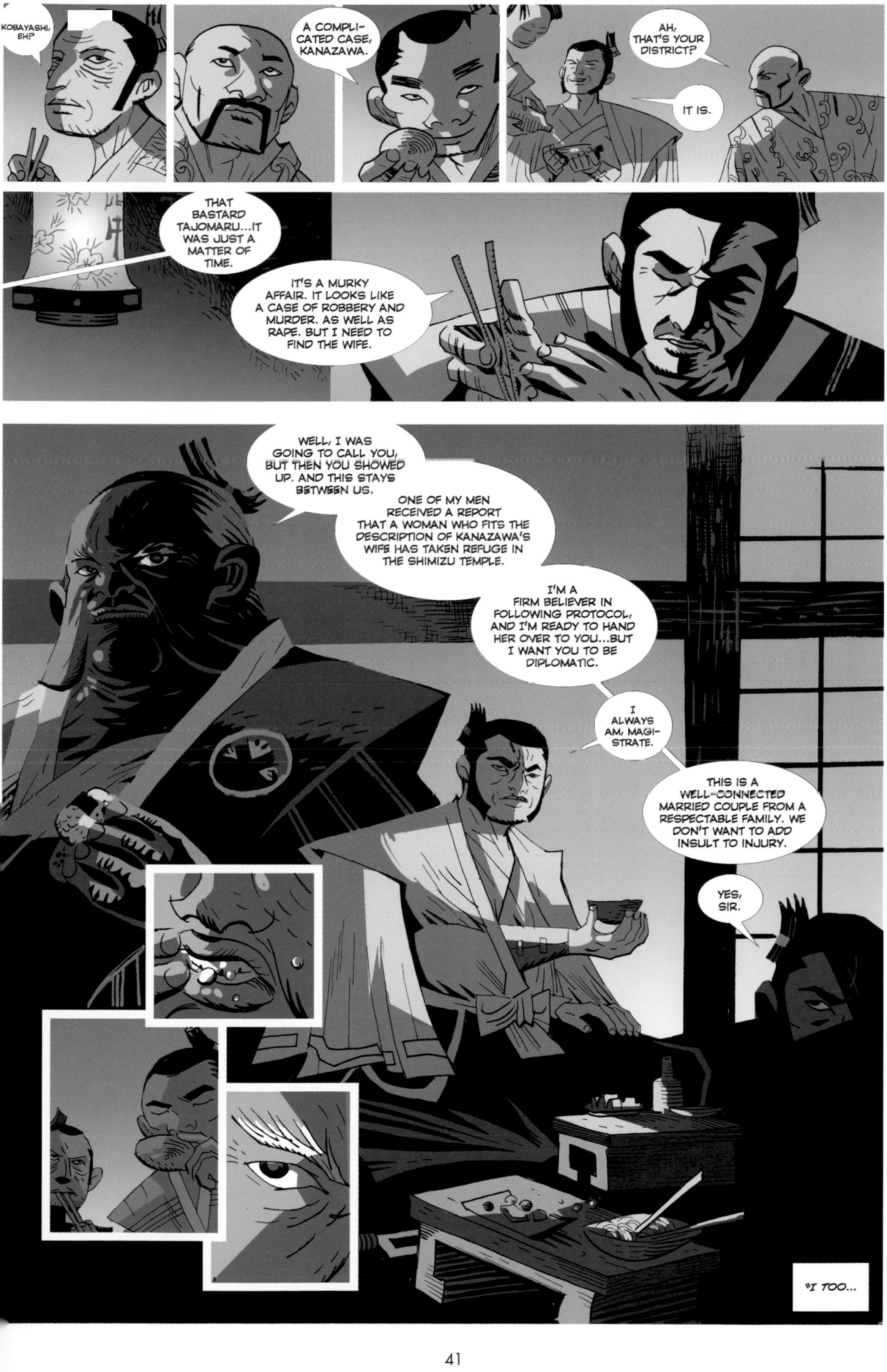
KOBAYASHI, EH?
A COMPLI-CATED CASE, KANAZAWA.
AH, THAT'S YOUR DISTRICT?
IT IS.
THAT BASTARD TAJOMARU...IT WAS JUST A MATTER OF TIME.
IT'S A MURKY AFFAIR. IT LOOKS LIKE A CASE OF ROBBERY AND MURDER. AS WELL AS RAPE. BUT I NEED TO FIND THE WIFE.
WELL, I WAS GOING TO CALL YOU, BUT THEN YOU SHOWED UP. AND THIS STAYS BETWEEN US.
ONE OF MY MEN RECEIVED A REPORT THAT A WOMAN WHO FITS THE DESCRIPTION OF KANAZAWA'S WIFE HAS TAKEN REFUGE IN THE SHIMIZU TEMPLE.
I'M A FIRM BELIEVER IN FOLLOWING PROTOCOL, AND I'M READY TO HAND HER OVER TO YOU...BUT I WANT YOU TO BE DIPLOMATIC.
I ALWAYS AM, MAGI-STRATE.
THIS IS A WELL-CONNECTED MARRIED COUPLE FROM A RESPECTABLE FAMILY. WE DON'T WANT TO ADD INSULT TO INJURY.
YES, SIR.
"I TOO...

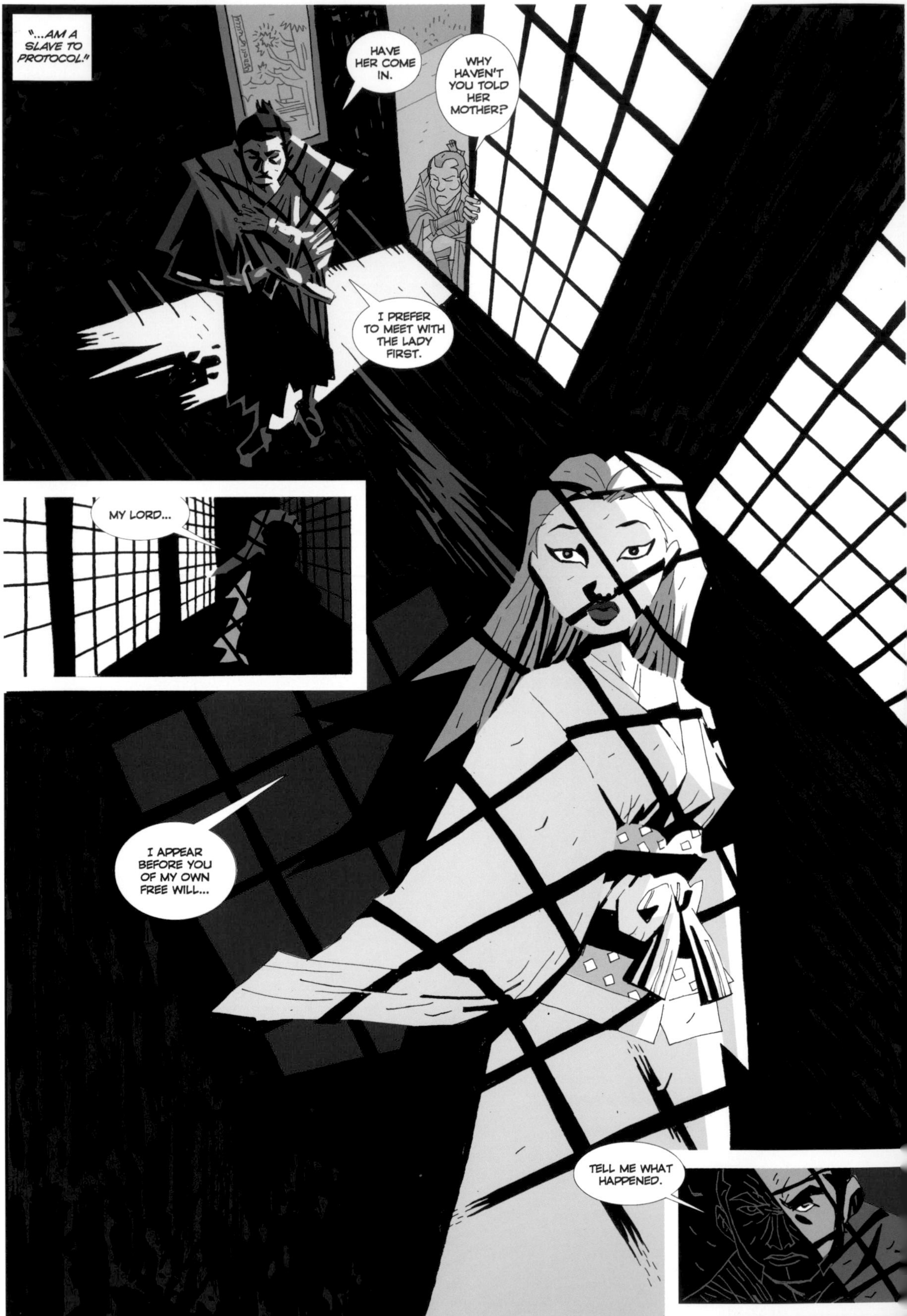
"...AM A SLAVE TO PROTOCOL."
HAVE HER COME IN.
WHY HAVEN'T YOU TOLD HER MOTHER?
I PREFER TO MEET WITH THE LADY FIRST.
MY LORD...
I APPEAR BEFORE YOU OF MY OWN FREE WILL...
TELL ME WHAT HAPPENED.

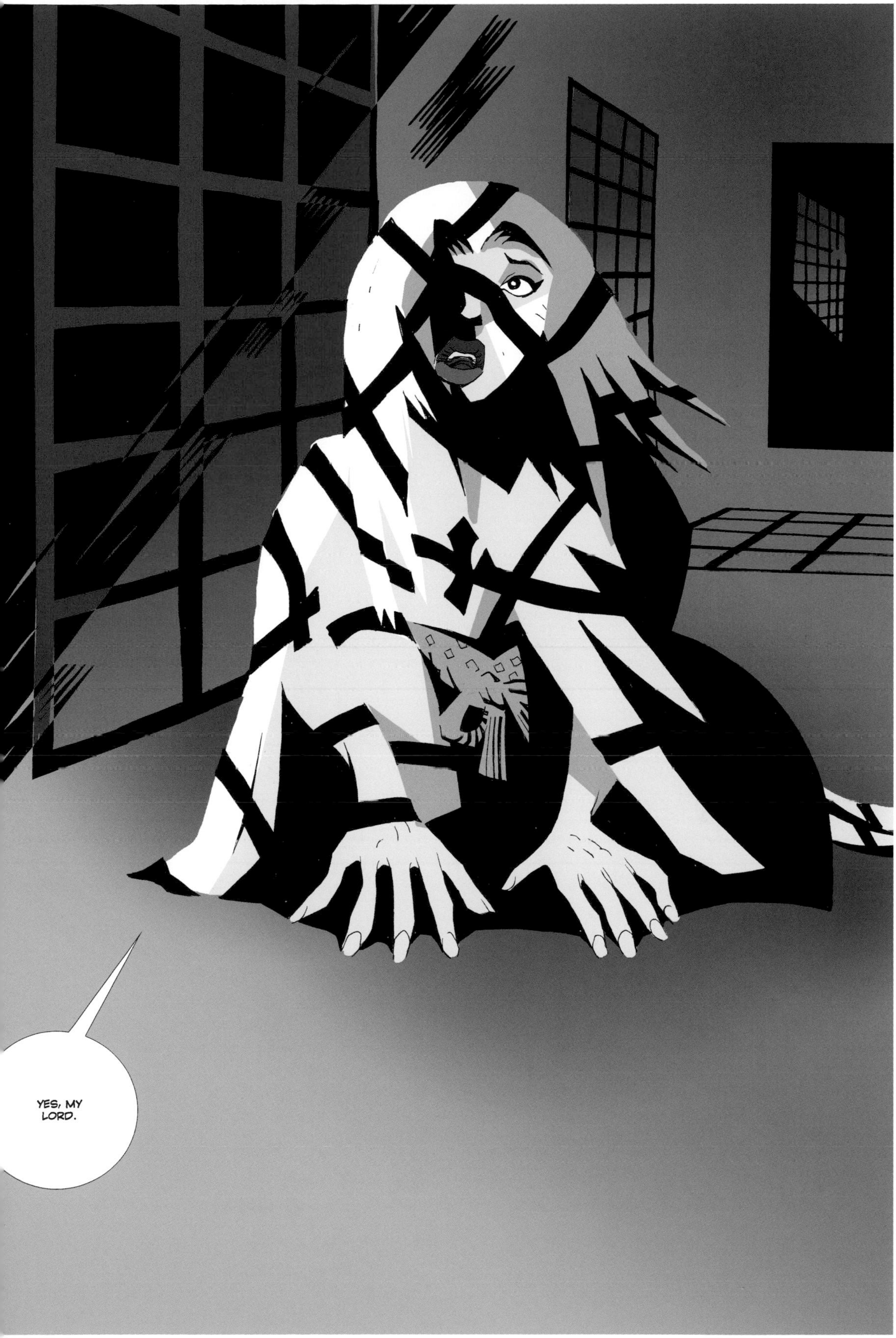
YES, MY LORD.

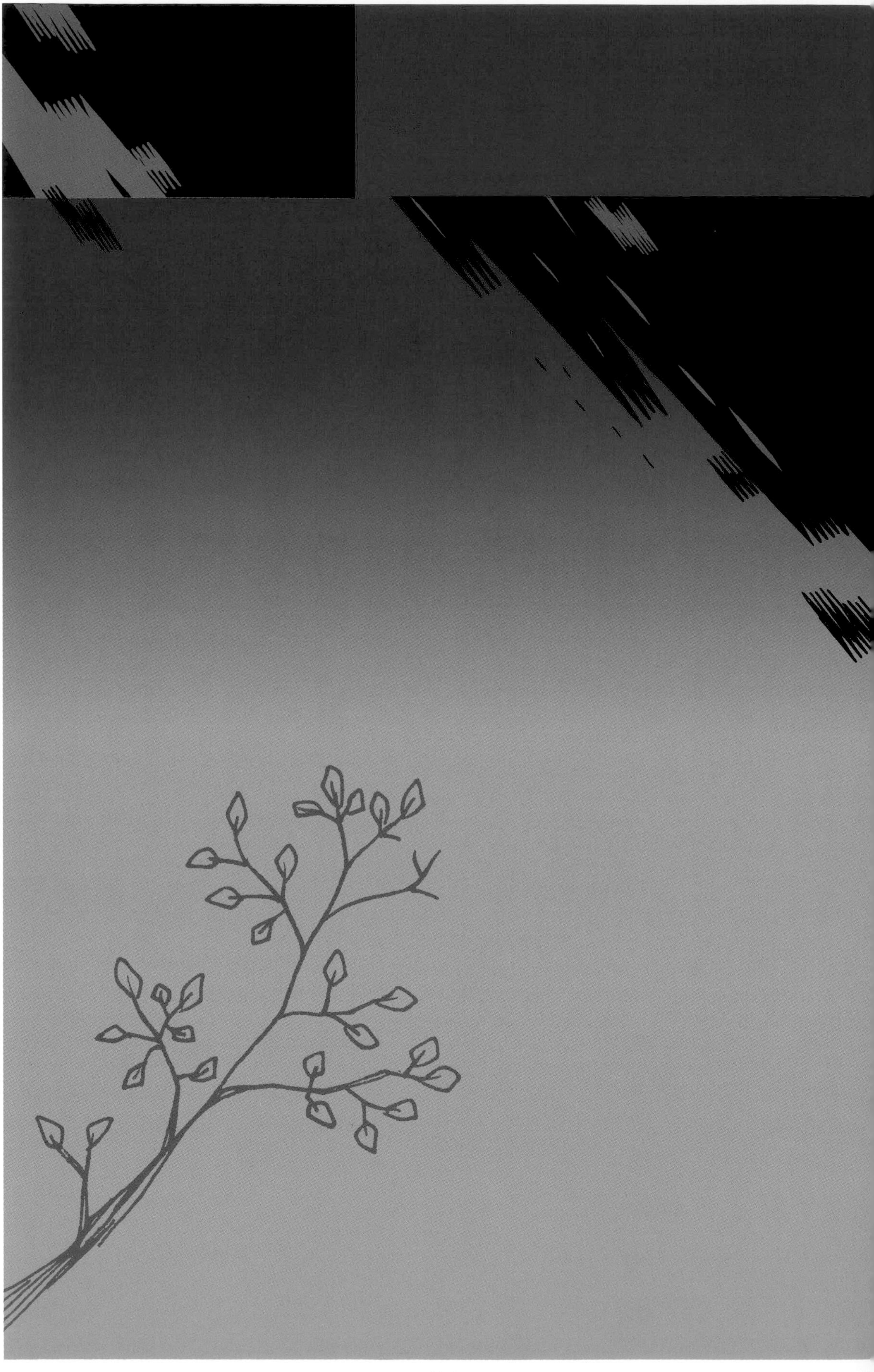

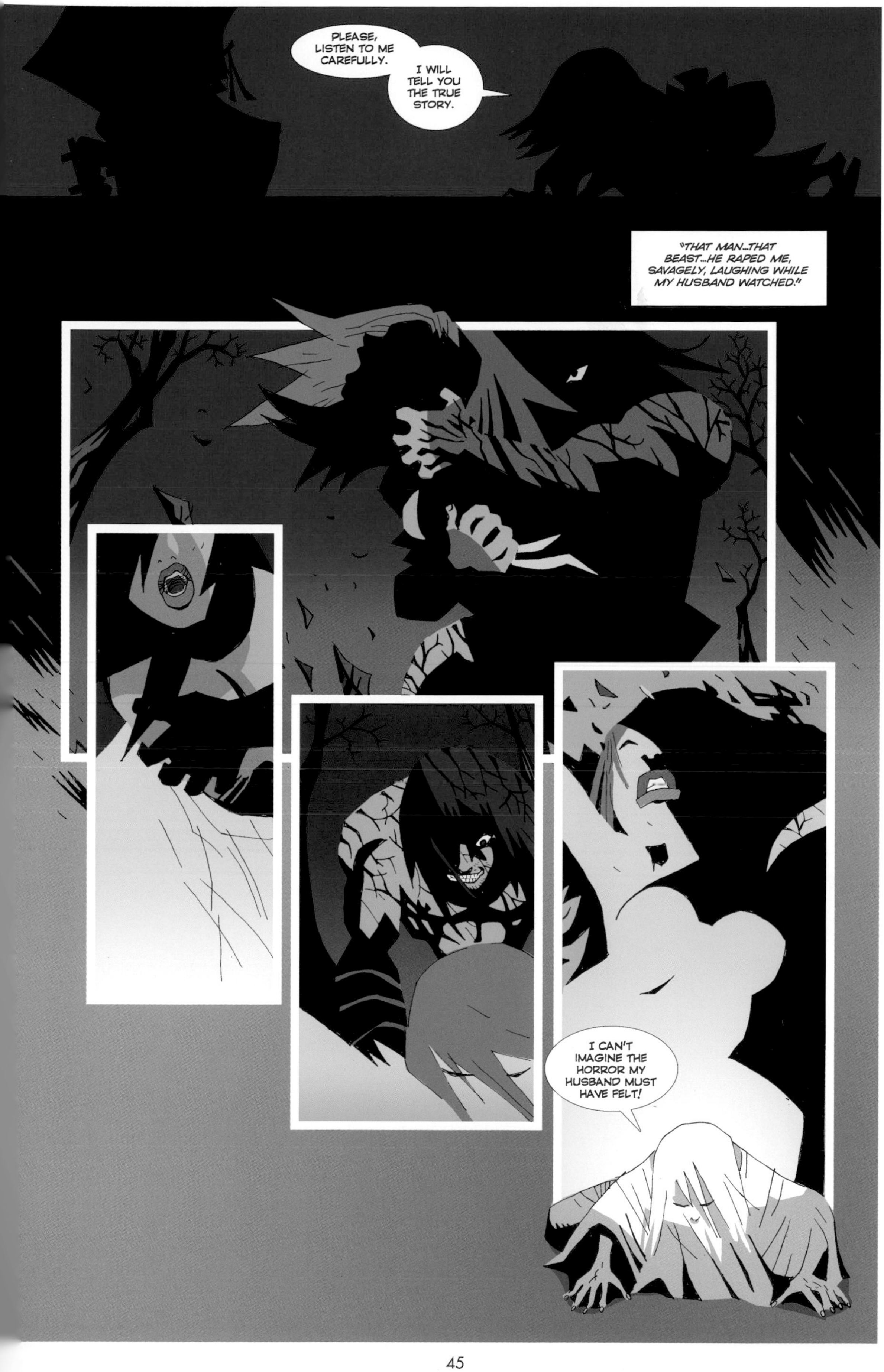
PLEASE, LISTEN TO ME CAREFULLY.
I WILL TELL YOU THE TRUE STORY.
"THAT MAN...THAT BEAST...HE RAPED ME, SAVAGELY, LAUGHING WHILE MY HUSBAND WATCHED."
I CAN'T IMAGINE THE HORROR MY HUSBAND MUST HAVE FELT!

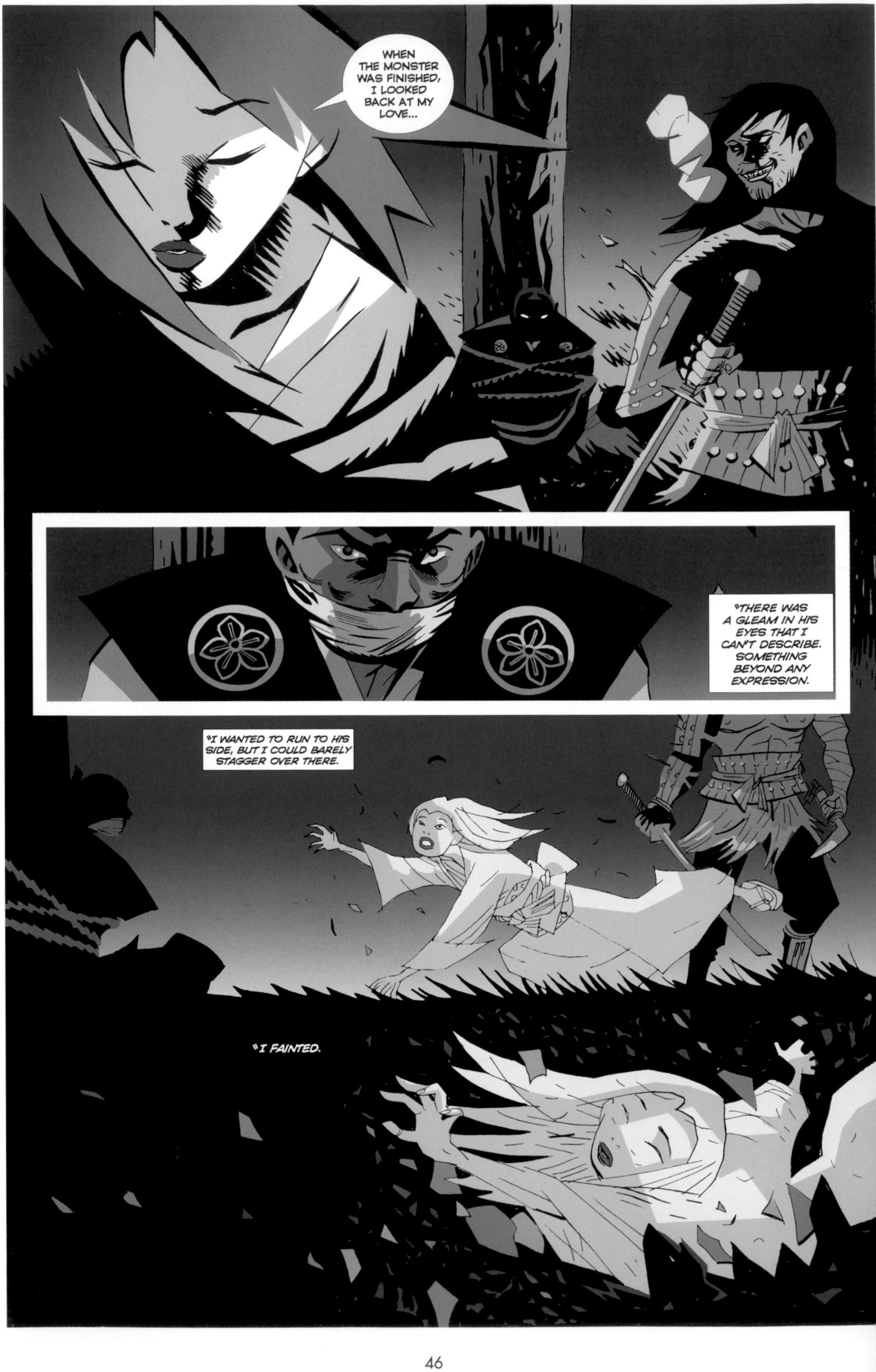
WHEN THE MONSTER WAS FINISHED, I LOOKED BACK AT MY LOVE...
"THERE WAS A GLEAM IN HIS EYES THAT I CAN'T DESCRIBE. SOMETHING BEYOND ANY EXPRESSION.
"I WANTED TO RUN TO HIS SIDE, BUT I COULD BARELY STAGGER OVER THERE.
"I FAINTED.

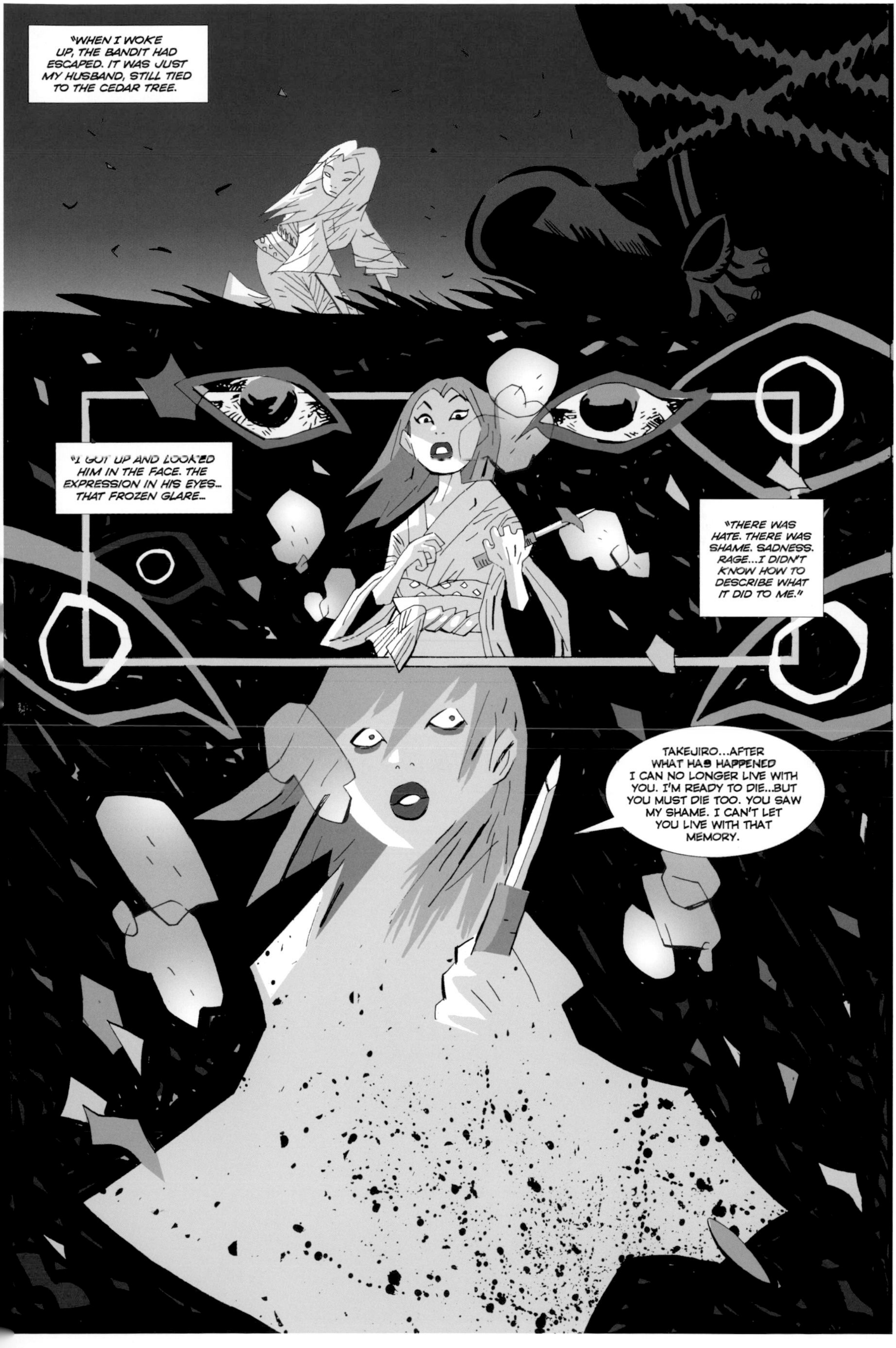
"WHEN I WOKE UP, THE BANDIT HAD ESCAPED. IT WAS JUST MY HUSBAND, STILL TIED TO THE CEDAR TREE.
"I GOT UP AND LOOKED HIM IN THE FACE. THE EXPRESSION IN HIS EYES... THAT FROZEN GLARE...
"THERE WAS HATE. THERE WAS SHAME. SADNESS. RAGE...I DIDN'T KNOW HOW TO DESCRIBE WHAT IT DID TO ME."
TAKEJIRO...AFTER WHAT HAS HAPPENED I CAN NO LONGER LIVE WITH YOU. I'M READY TO DIE...BUT YOU MUST DIE TOO. YOU SAW MY SHAME. I CAN'T LET YOU LIVE WITH THAT MEMORY.

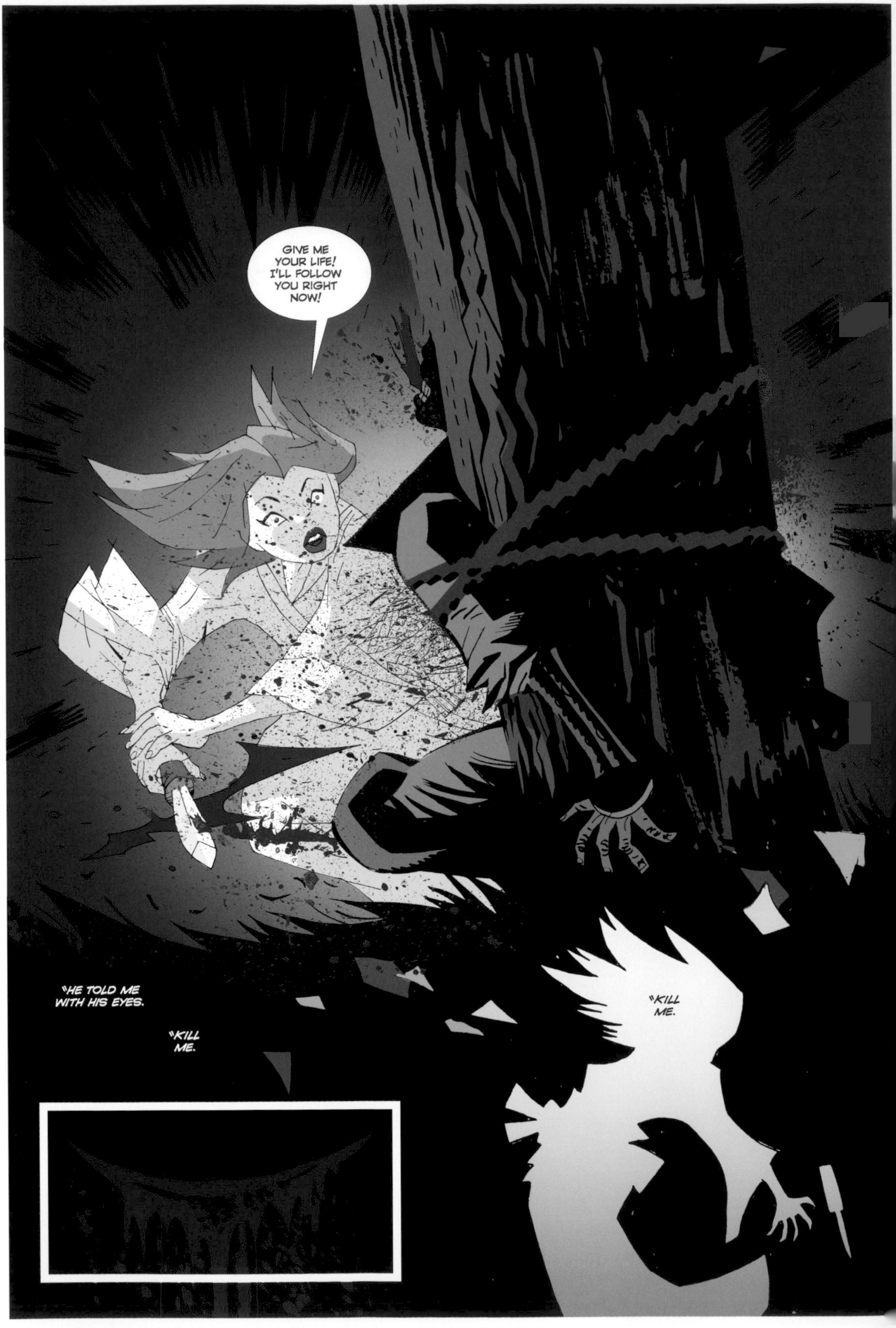
GIVE ME YOUR LIFE! I'LL FOLLOW YOU RIGHT NOW!
"HE TOLD ME WITH HIS EYES.
"KILL ME.
"KILL ME.

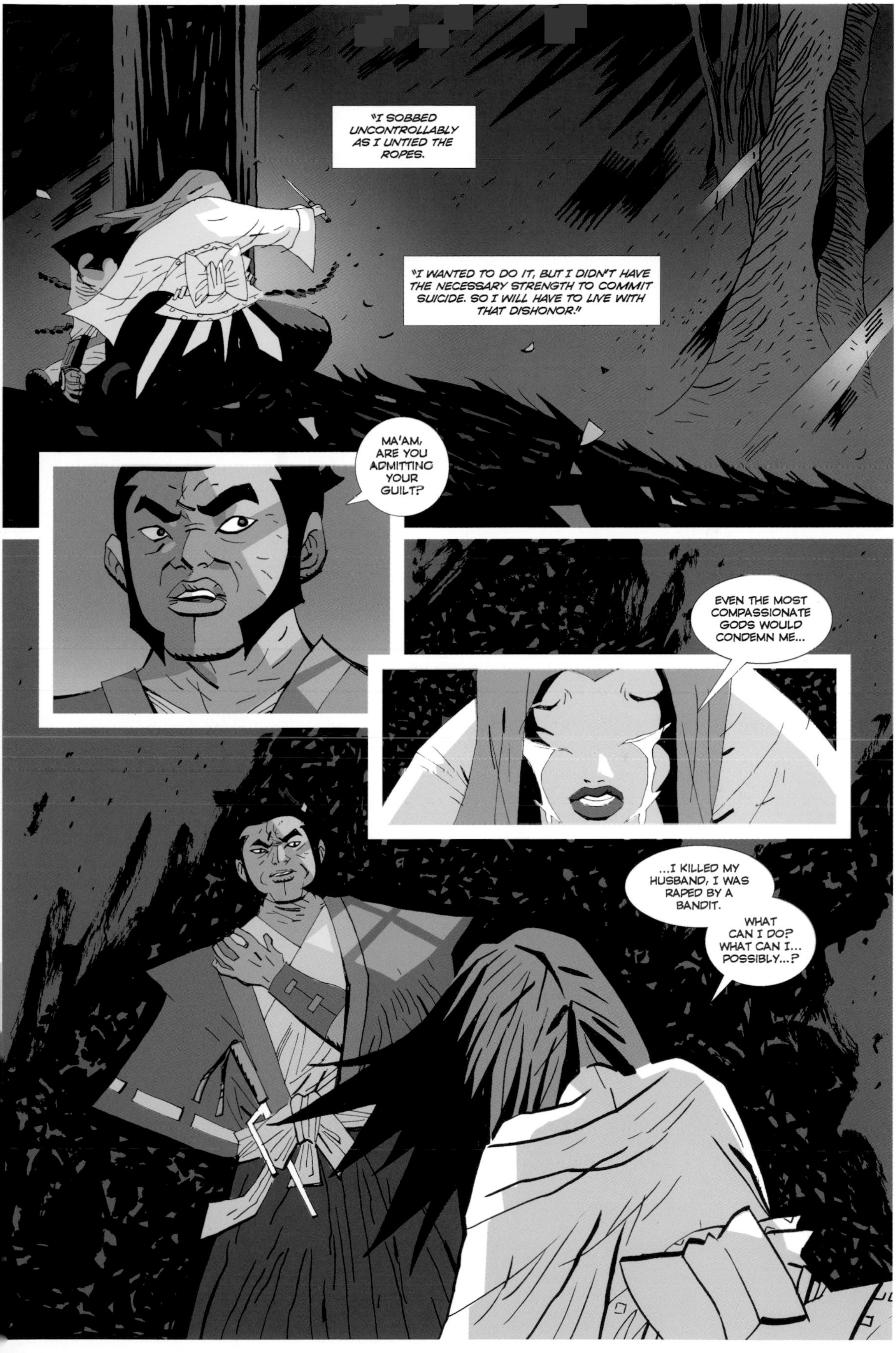
"I SOBBED UNCONTROLLABLY AS I UNTIED THE ROPES.
"I WANTED TO DO IT, BUT I DIDN'T HAVE THE NECESSARY STRENGTH TO COMMIT SUICIDE. SO I WILL HAVE TO LIVE WITH THAT DISHONOR."
MA'AM, ARE YOU ADMITTING YOUR GUILT?
EVEN THE MOST COMPASSIONATE GODS WOULD CONDEMN ME...
...I KILLED MY HUSBAND, I WAS RAPED BY A BANDIT.
WHAT CAN I DO? WHAT CAN I... POSSIBLY...?

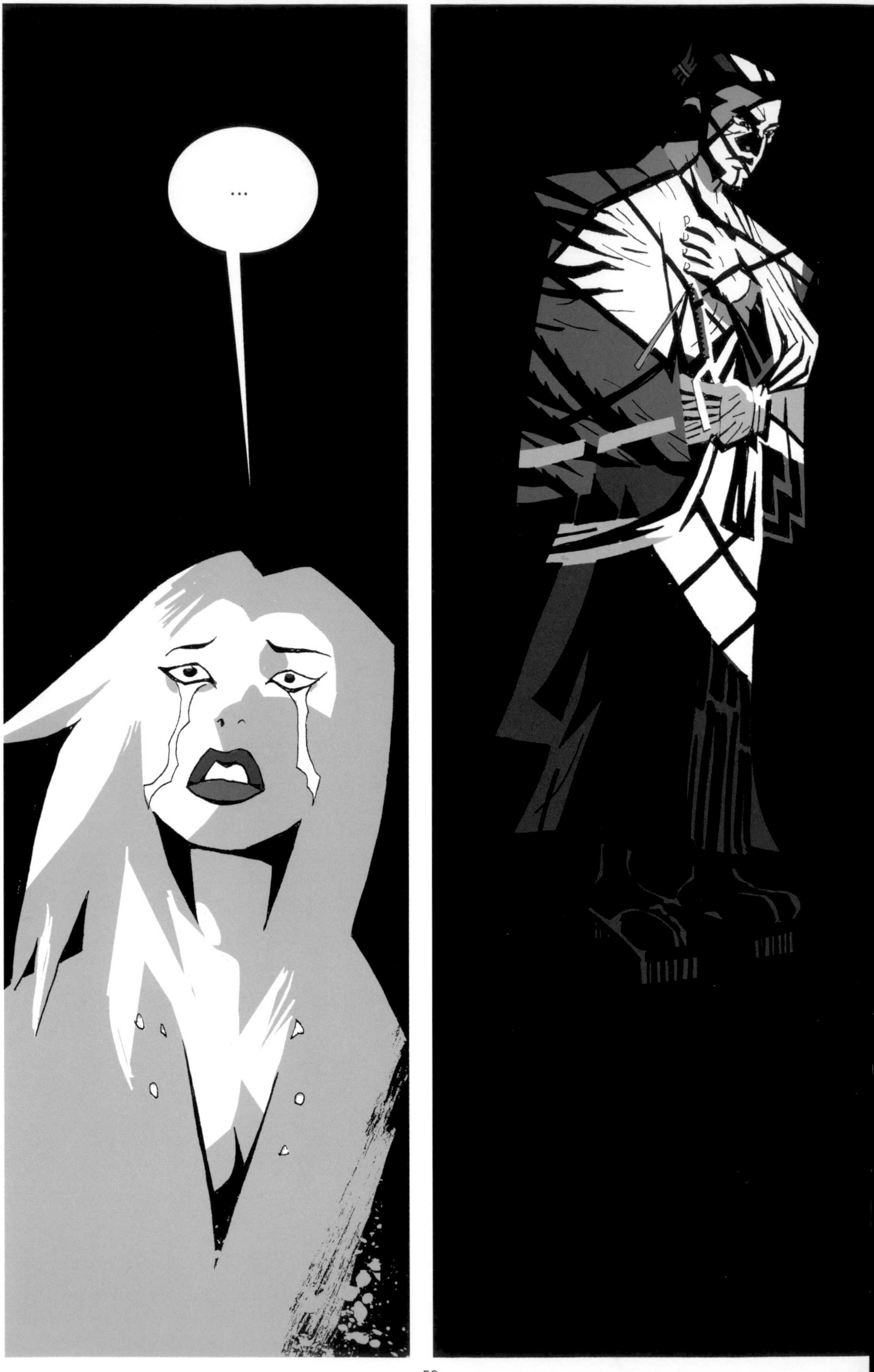
...

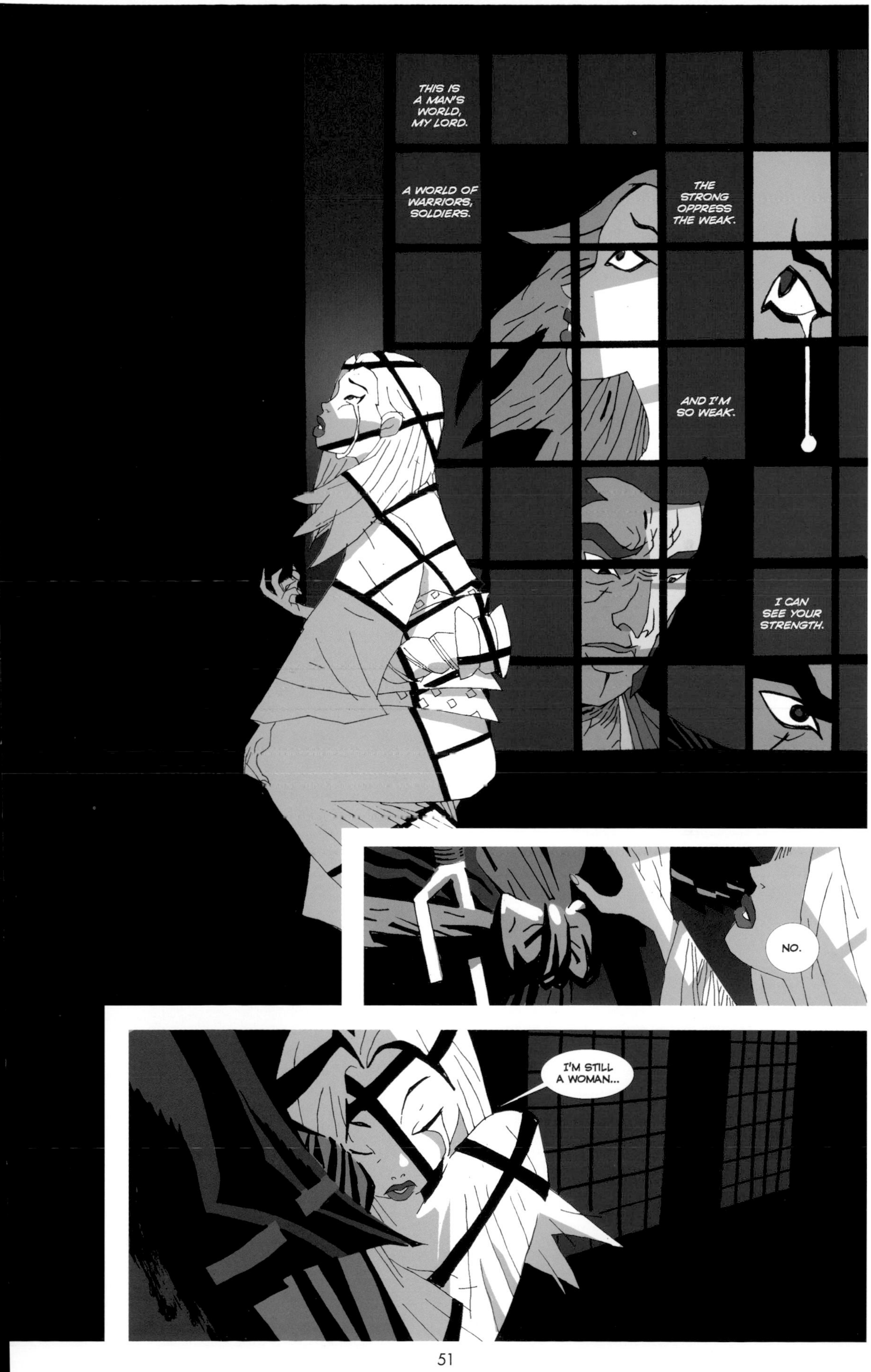
THIS IS A MAN'S WORLD, MY LORD.
A WORLD OF WARRIORS, SOLDIERS.
THE STRONG OPPRESS THE WEAK.
AND I'M SO WEAK.
I CAN SEE YOUR STRENGTH.
NO.
I'M STILL A WOMAN...

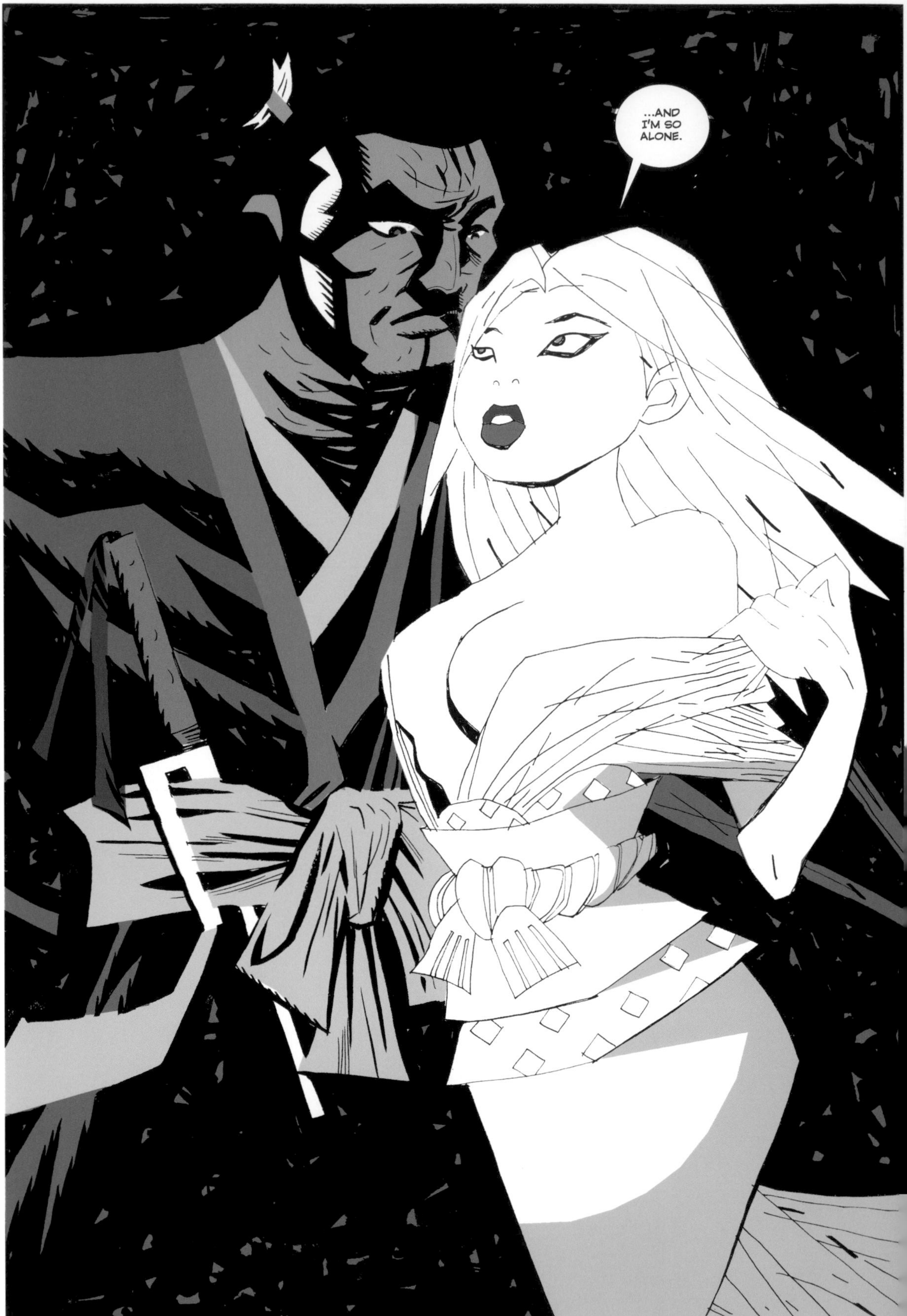
...AND I'M SO ALONE.

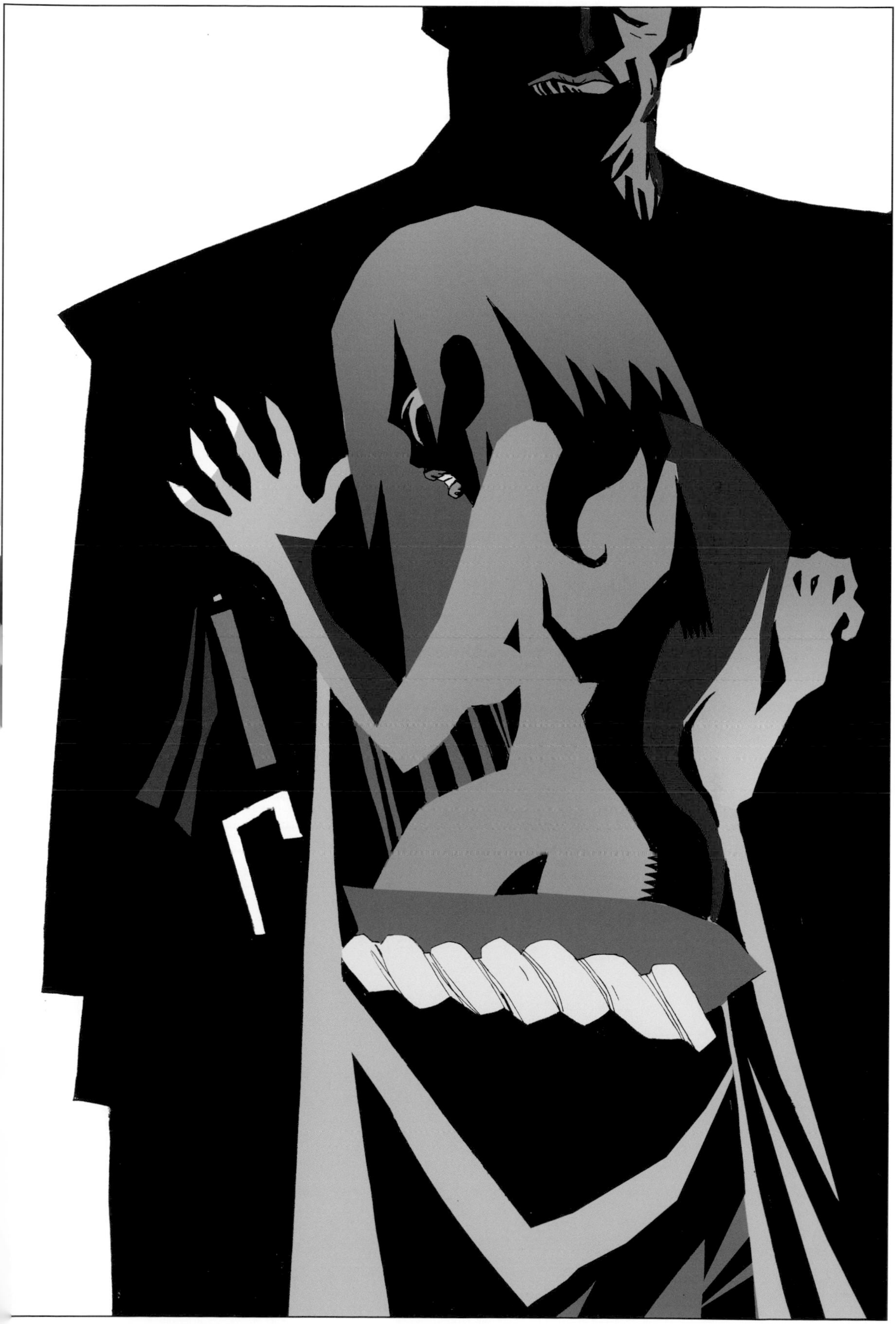

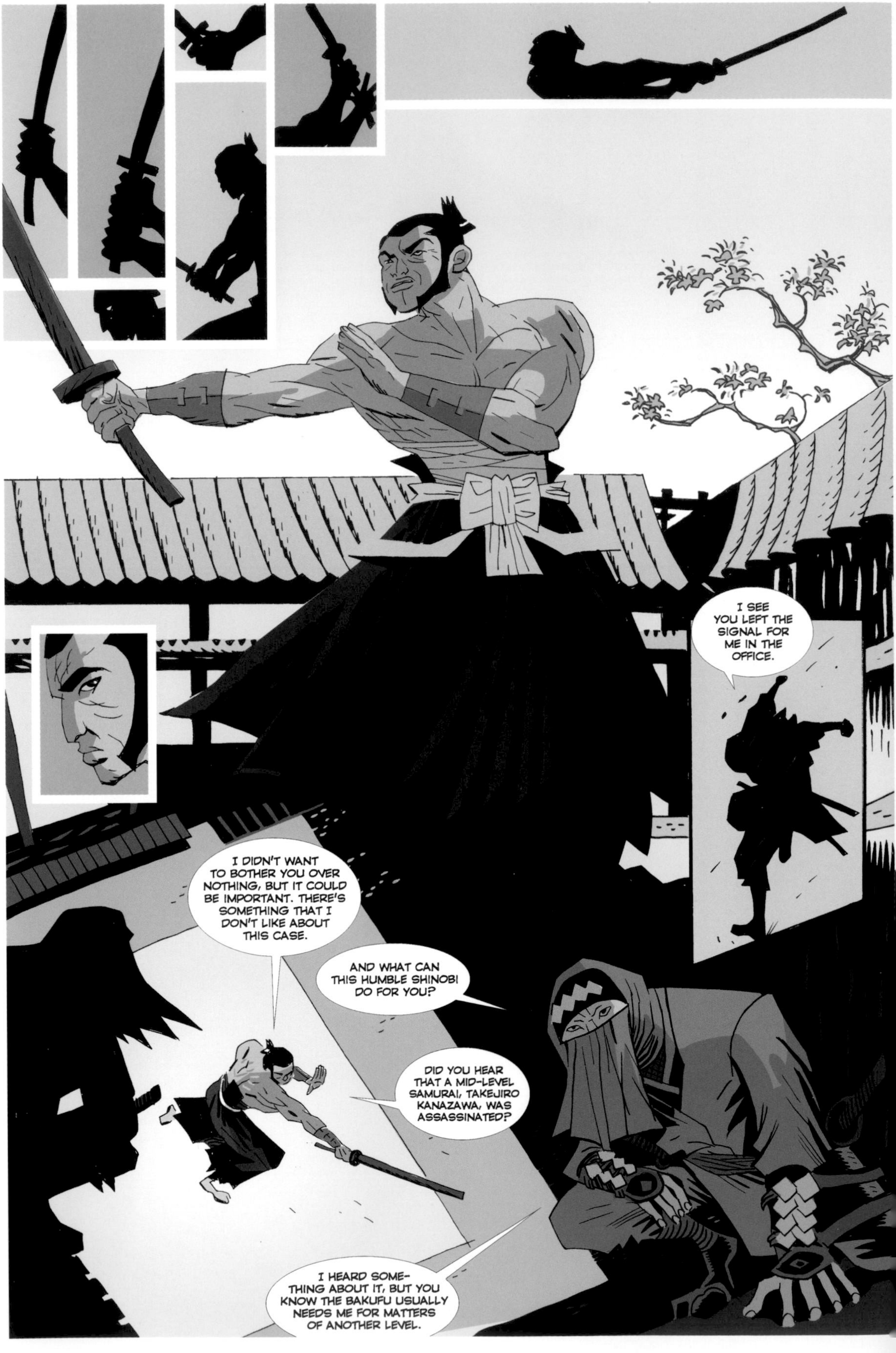
I SEE YOU LEFT THE SIGNAL FOR ME IN THE OFFICE.
I DIDN'T WANT TO BOTHER YOU OVER NOTHING, BUT IT COULD BE IMPORTANT. THERE'S SOMETHING THAT I DON'T LIKE ABOUT THIS CASE.
AND WHAT CAN THIS HUMBLE SHINOBI DO FOR YOU?
DID YOU HEAR THAT A MID-LEVEL SAMURAI, TAKEJIRO KANAZAWA, WAS ASSASSINATED?
I HEARD SOME-THING ABOUT IT, BUT YOU KNOW THE BAKUFU USUALLY NEEDS ME FOR MATTERS OF ANOTHER LEVEL.

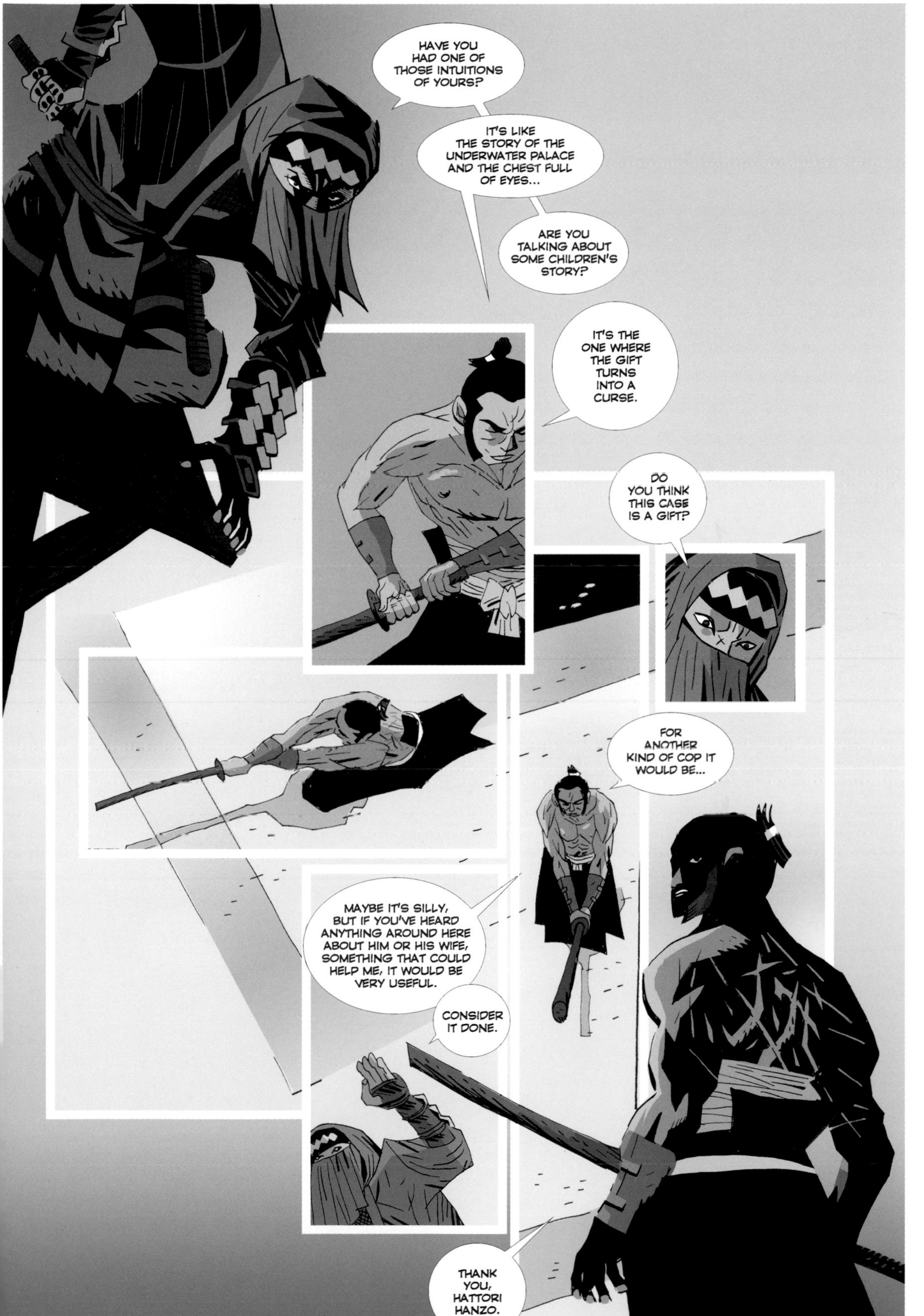
HAVE YOU HAD ONE OF THOSE INTUITIONS OF YOURS?
IT'S LIKE THE STORY OF THE UNDERWATER PALACE AND THE CHEST FULL OF EYES...
ARE YOU TALKING ABOUT SOME CHILDREN'S STORY?
IT'S THE ONE WHERE THE GIFT TURNS INTO A CURSE.
DO YOU THINK THIS CASE IS A GIFT?
FOR ANOTHER KIND OF COP IT WOULD BE...
MAYBE IT'S SILLY, BUT IF YOU'VE HEARD ANYTHING AROUND HERE ABOUT HIM OR HIS WIFE, SOMETHING THAT COULD HELP ME, IT WOULD BE VERY USEFUL.
CONSIDER IT DONE.
THANK YOU, HATTORI HANZO.

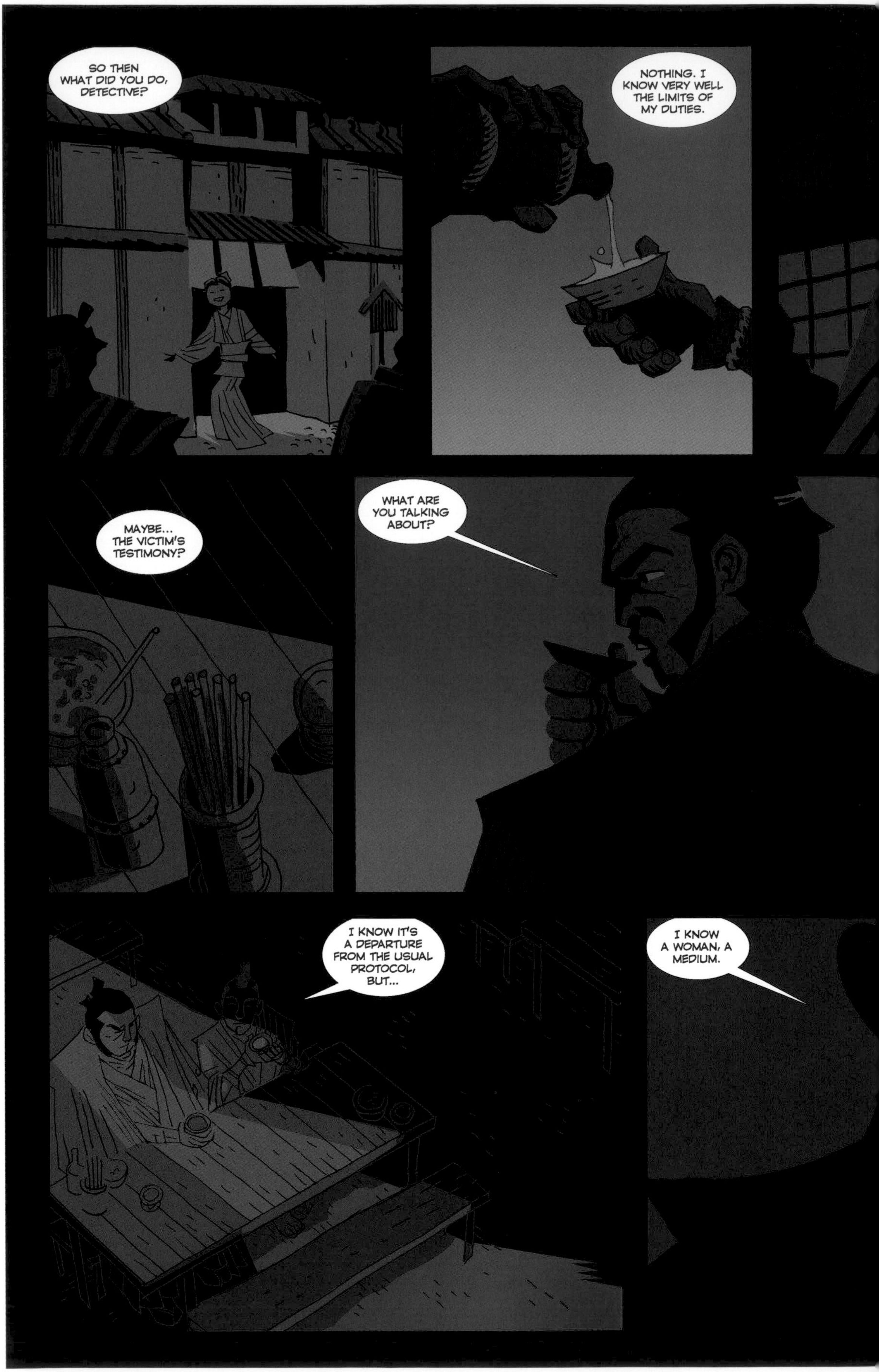
SO THEN WHAT DID YOU DO, DETECTIVE?
NOTHING. I KNOW VERY WELL THE LIMITS OF MY DUTIES.
MAYBE... THE VICTIM'S TESTIMONY?
WHAT ARE YOU TALKING ABOUT?
I KNOW IT'S A DEPARTURE FROM THE USUAL PROTOCOL, BUT...
I KNOW A WOMAN, A MEDIUM.

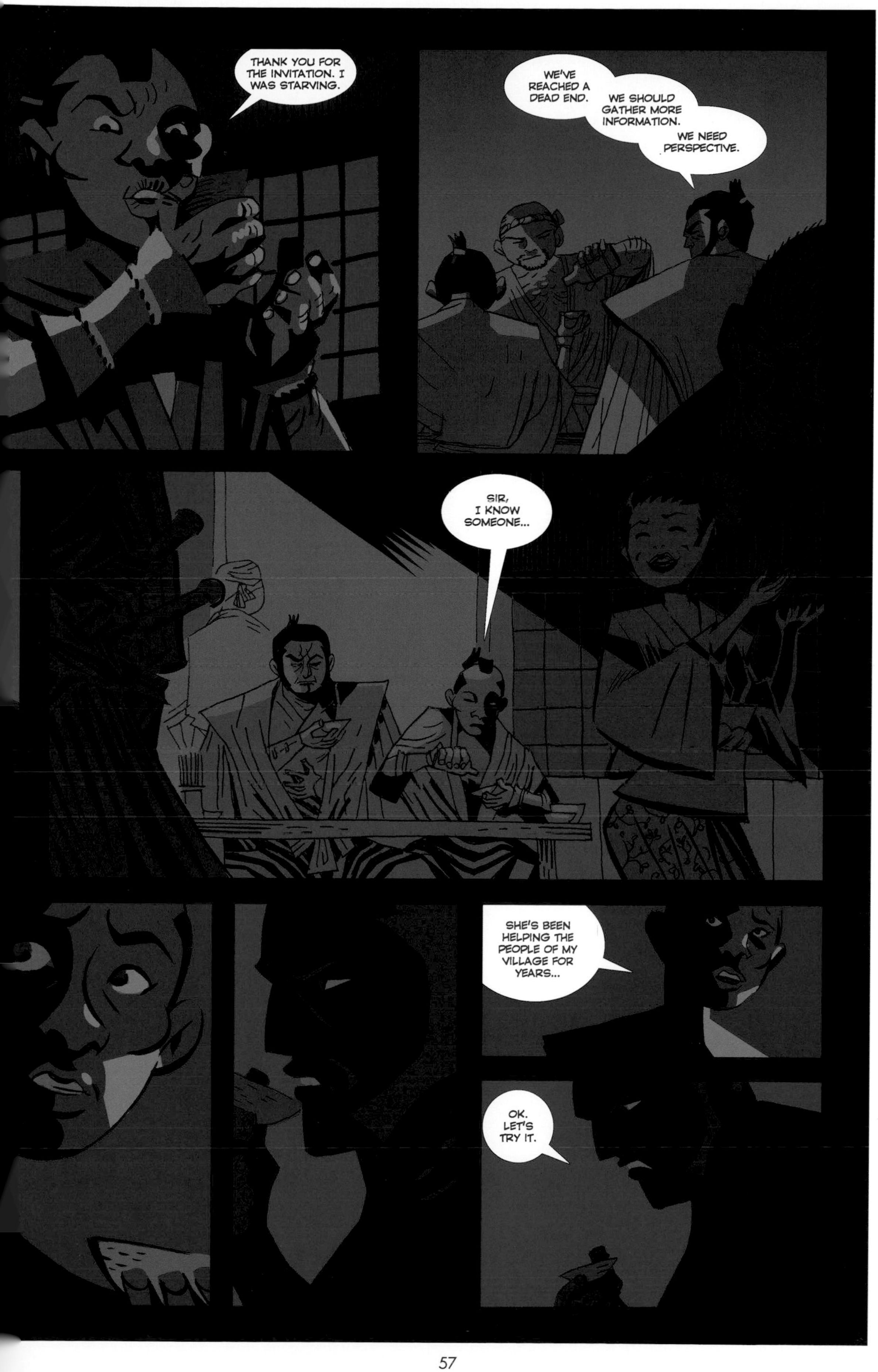
THANK YOU FOR THE INVITATION. I WAS STARVING.
WE'VE REACHED A DEAD END.
WE SHOULD GATHER MORE INFORMATION.
WE NEED PERSPECTIVE.
SIR, I KNOW SOMEONE...
SHE'S BEEN HELPING THE PEOPLE OF MY VILLAGE FOR YEARS...
OK. LET'S TRY IT.

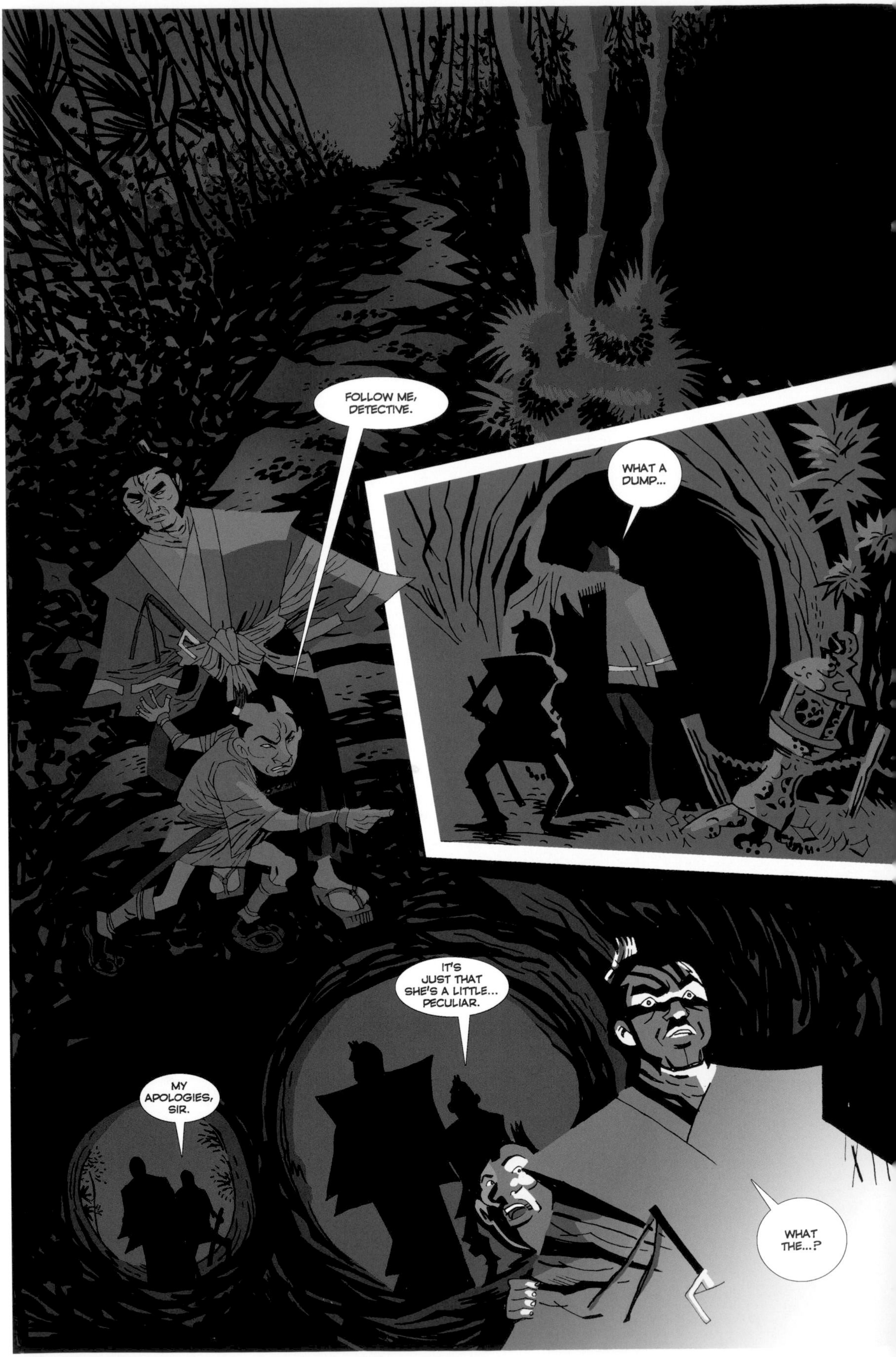
FOLLOW ME, DETECTIVE.
WHAT A DUMP...
MY APOLOGIES, SIR.
IT'S JUST THAT SHE'S A LITTLE... PECULIAR.
WHAT THE...?

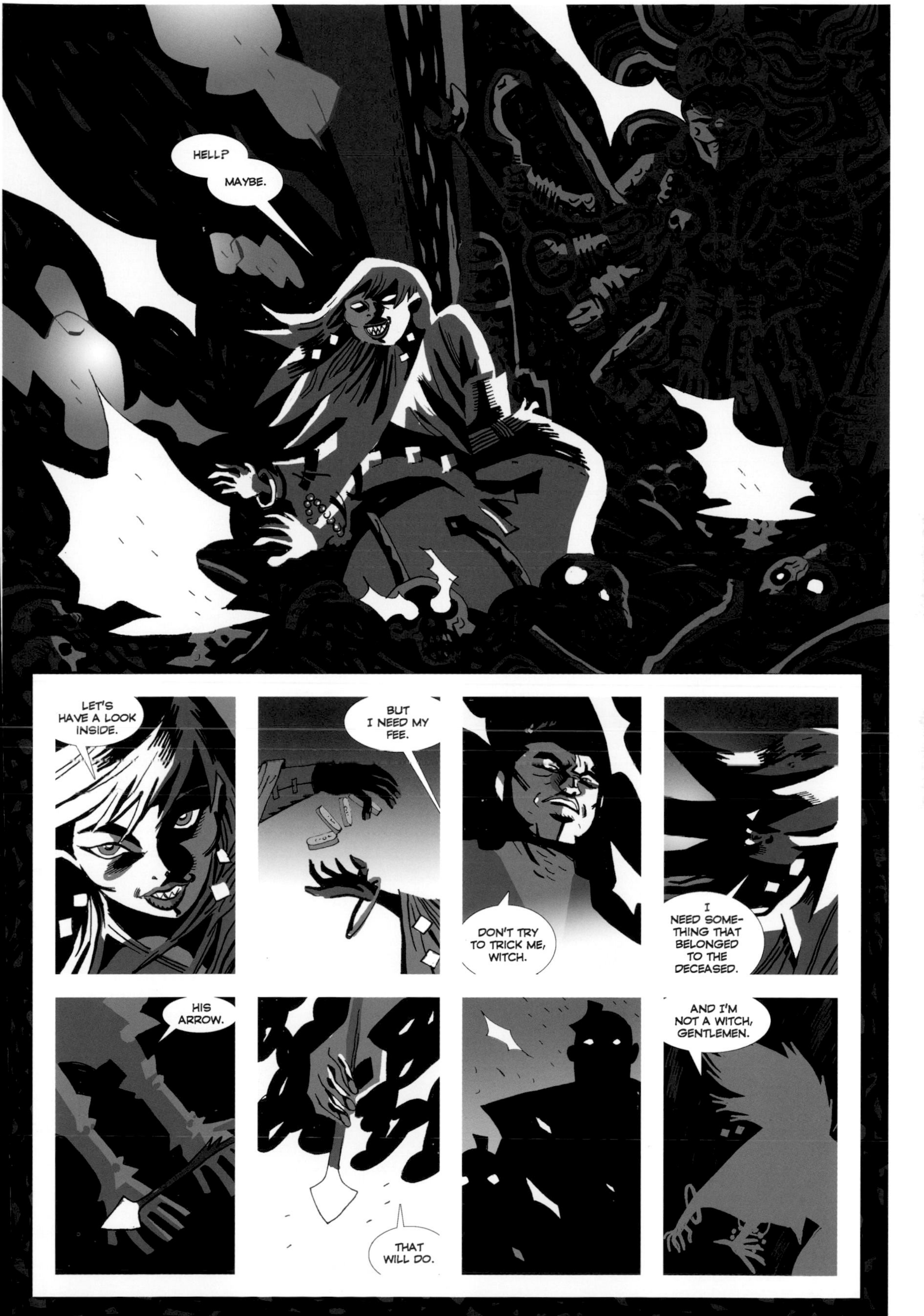
HELL?
MAYBE.
LET'S HAVE A LOOK INSIDE.
BUT I NEED MY FEE.
DON'T TRY TO TRICK ME, WITCH.
I NEED SOME-THING THAT BELONGED TO THE DECEASED.
HIS ARROW.
THAT WILL DO.
AND I'M NOT A WITCH, GENTLEMEN.

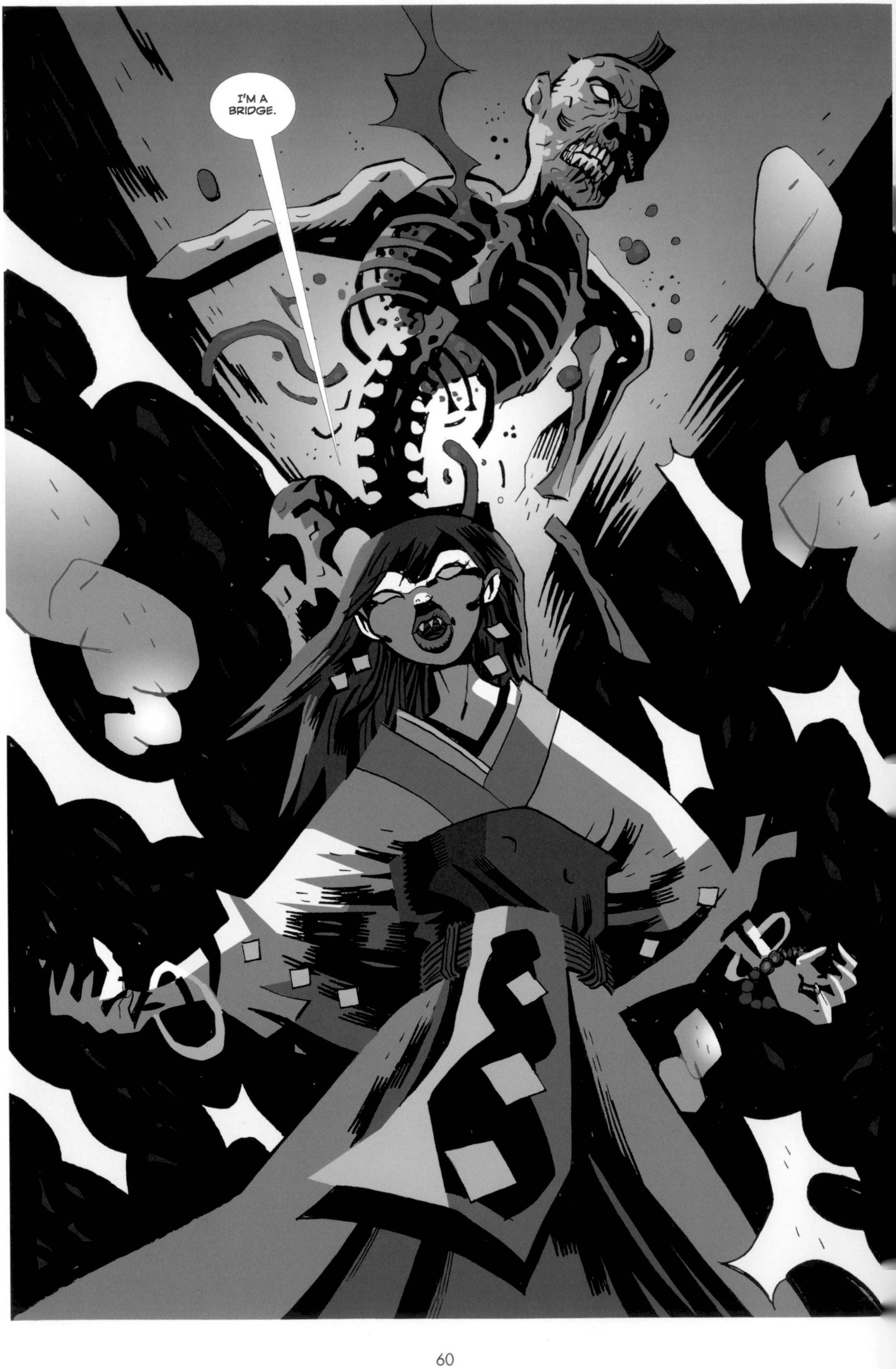
I'M A BRIDGE.

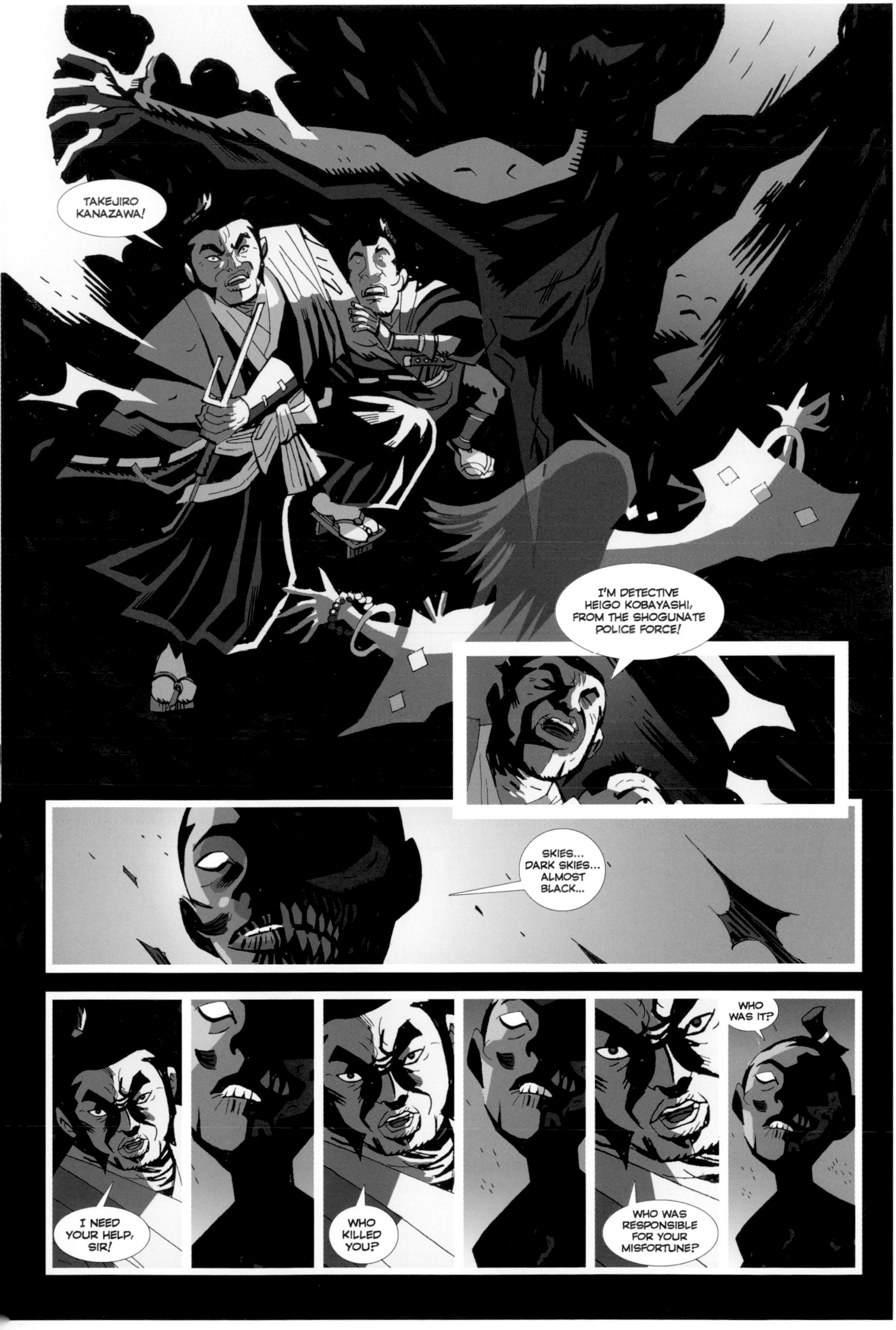
TAKEJIRO KANAZAWA!
I'M DETECTIVE HEIGO KOBAYASHI, FROM THE SHOGUNATE POLICE FORCE!
SKIES... DARK SKIES... ALMOST BLACK...
I NEED YOUR HELP, SIR!
WHO KILLED YOU?
WHO WAS RESPONSIBLE FOR YOUR MISFORTUNE?
WHO WAS IT?

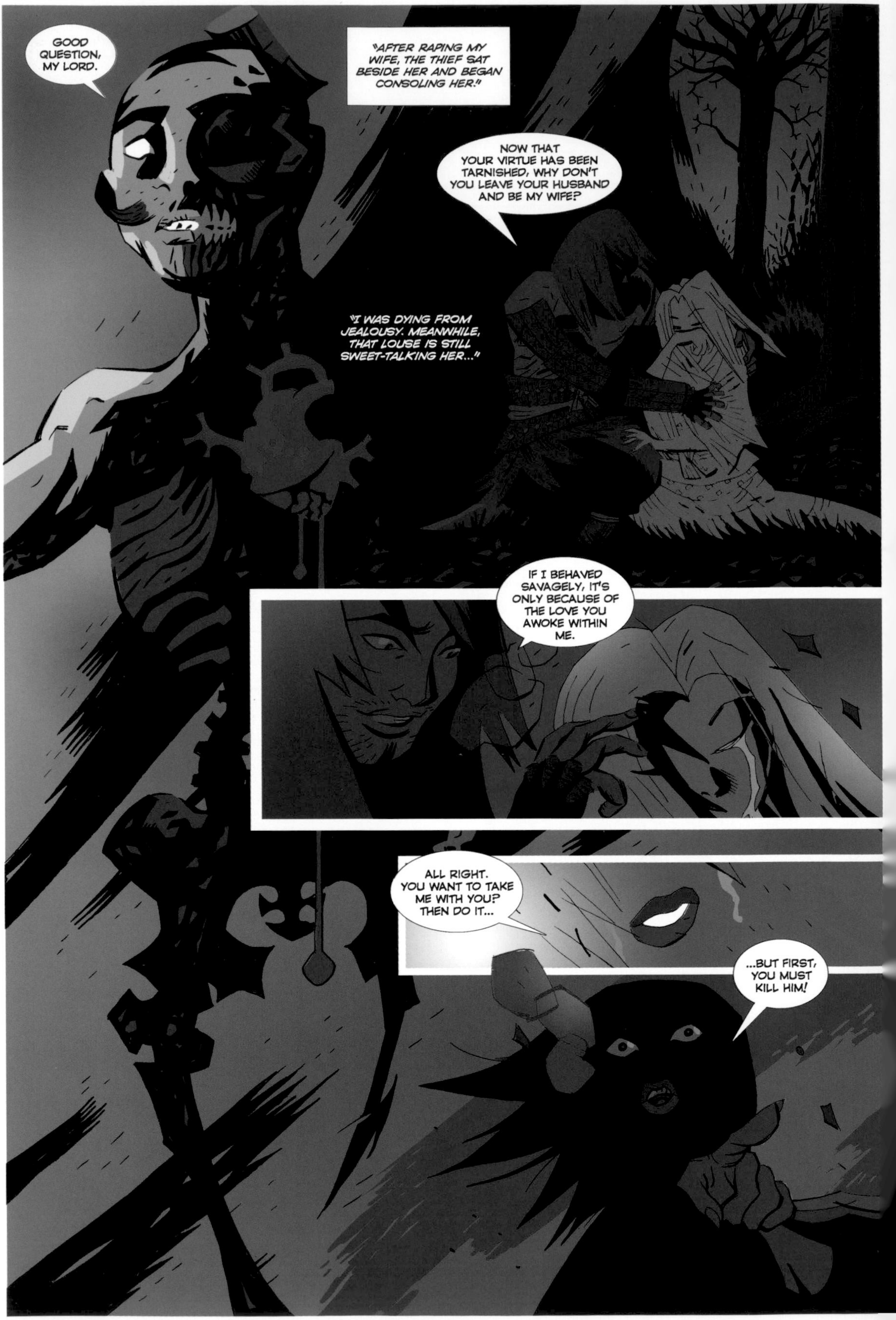
GOOD QUESTION, MY LORD.
"AFTER RAPING MY WIFE, THE THIEF SAT BESIDE HER AND BEGAN CONSOLING HER."
NOW THAT YOUR VIRTUE HAS BEEN TARNISHED, WHY DON'T YOU LEAVE YOUR HUSBAND AND BE MY WIFE?
"I WAS DYING FROM JEALOUSY. MEANWHILE, THAT LOUSE IS STILL SWEET-TALKING HER..."
IF I BEHAVED SAVAGELY, IT'S ONLY BECAUSE OF THE LOVE YOU AWOKE WITHIN ME.
ALL RIGHT. YOU WANT TO TAKE ME WITH YOU? THEN DO IT...
...BUT FIRST, YOU MUST KILL HIM!

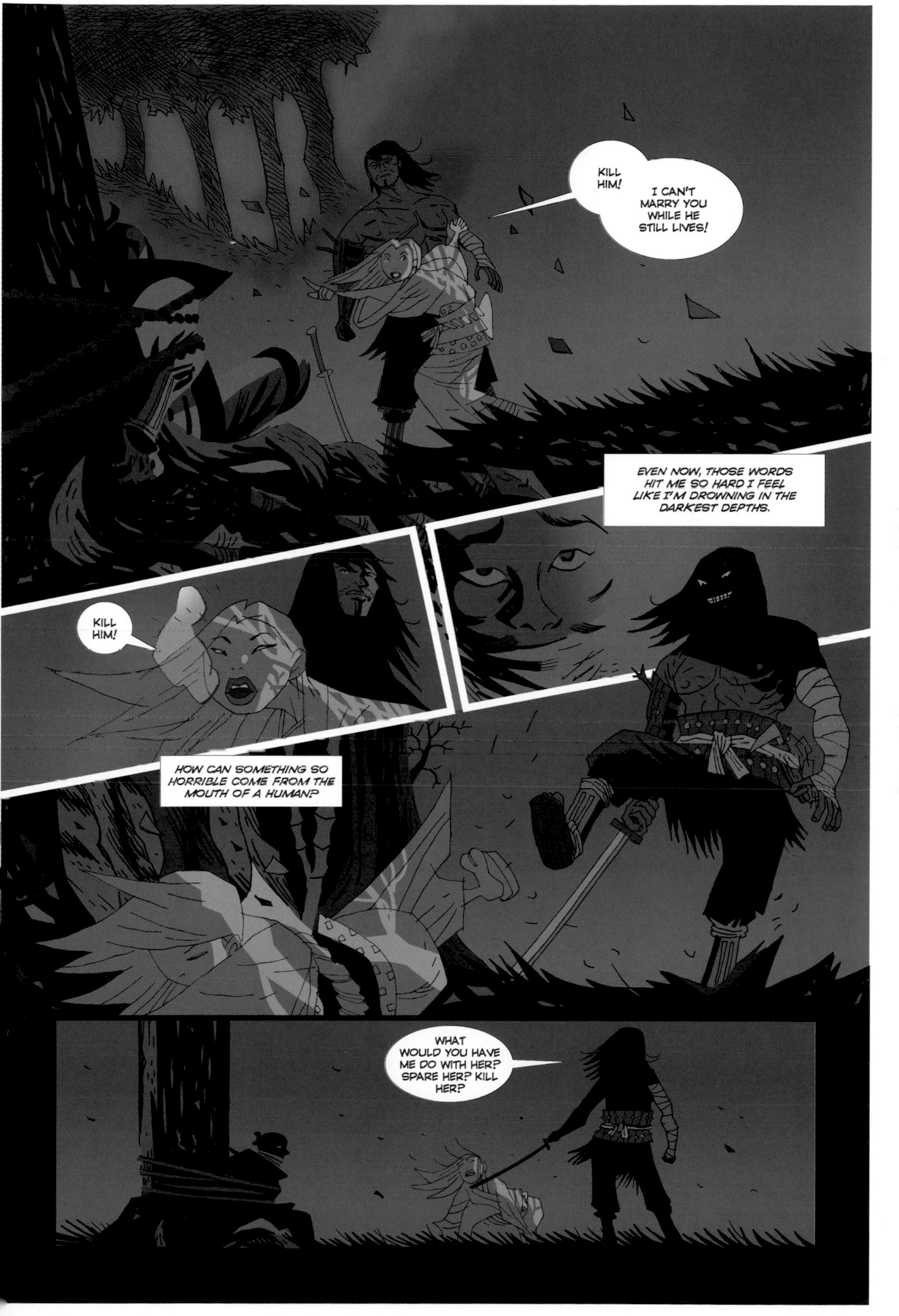
KILL HIM!
I CAN'T MARRY YOU WHILE HE STILL LIVES!
EVEN NOW, THOSE WORDS HIT ME SO HARD I FEEL LIKE I'M DROWNING IN THE DARKEST DEPTHS.
KILL HIM!
HOW CAN SOMETHING SO HORRIBLE COME FROM THE MOUTH OF A HUMAN?
WHAT WOULD YOU HAVE ME DO WITH HER? SPARE HER? KILL HER?

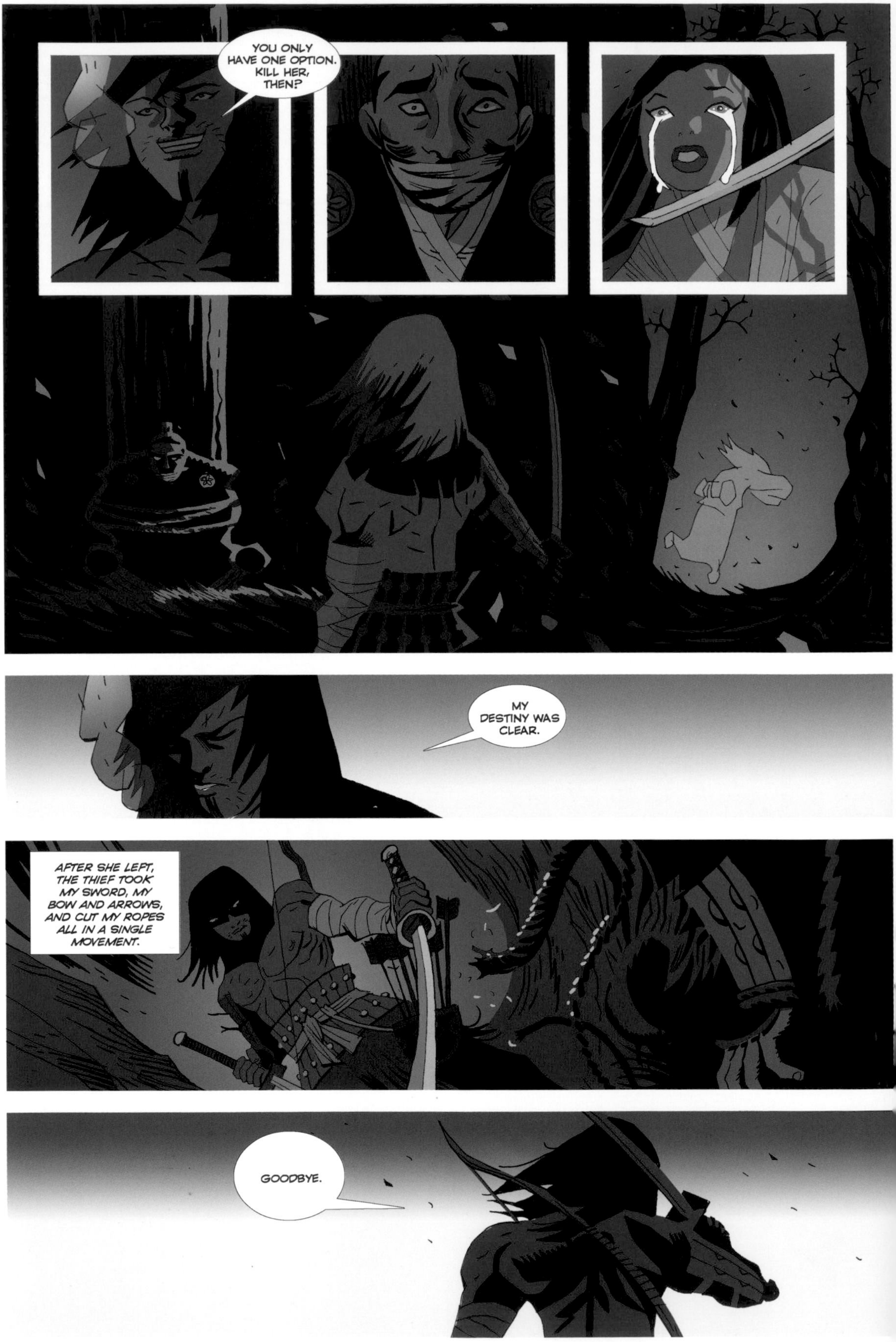
YOU ONLY HAVE ONE OPTION. KILL HER, THEN?
MY DESTINY WAS CLEAR.
AFTER SHE LEFT, THE THIEF TOOK MY SWORD, MY BOW AND ARROWS, AND CUT MY ROPES ALL IN A SINGLE MOVEMENT.
GOODBYE.

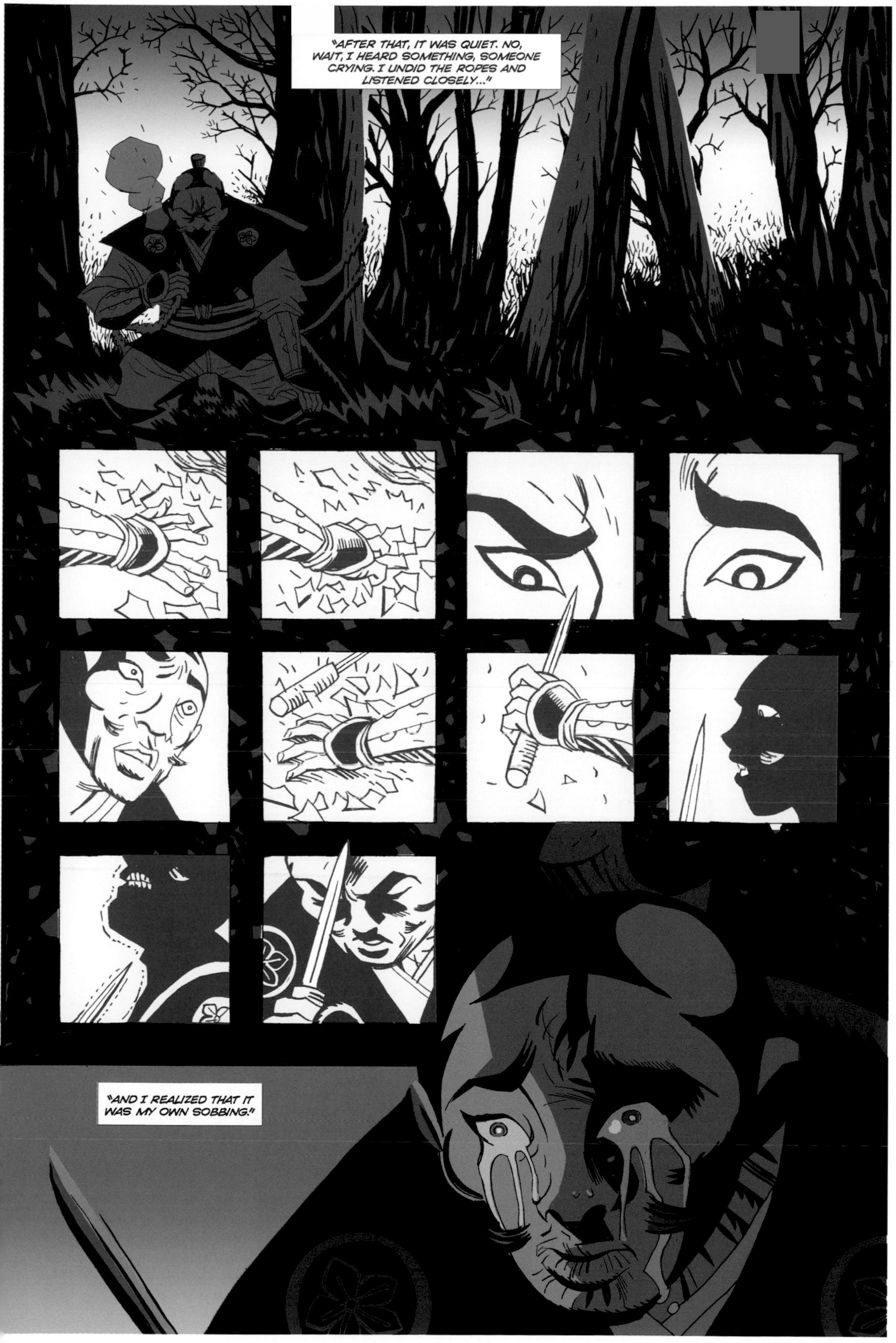
"AFTER THAT, IT WAS QUIET. NO, WAIT, I HEARD SOMETHING, SOMEONE CRYING. I UNDID THE ROPES AND LISTENED CLOSELY..."
"AND I REALIZED THAT IT WAS MY OWN SOBBING."

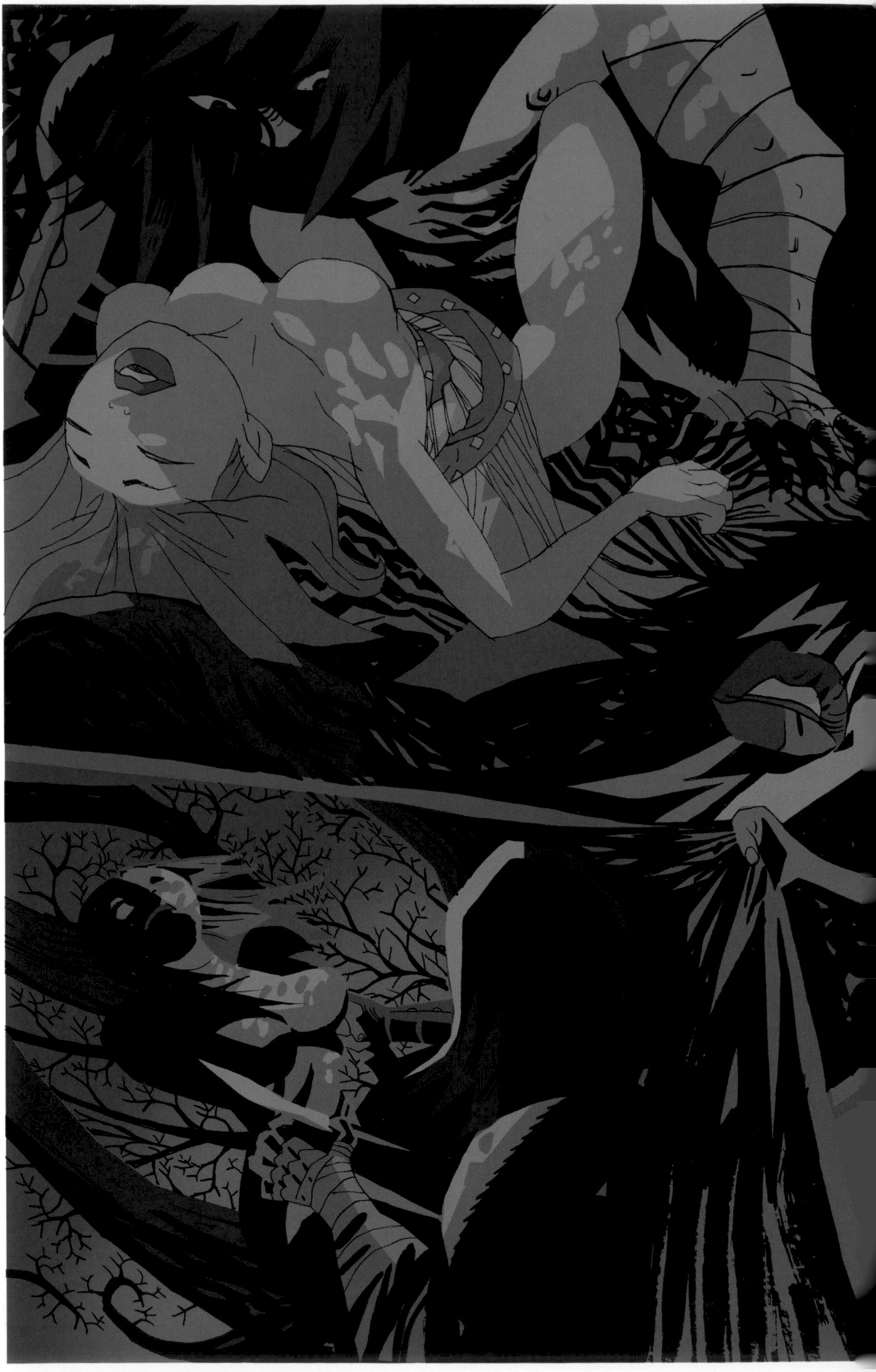

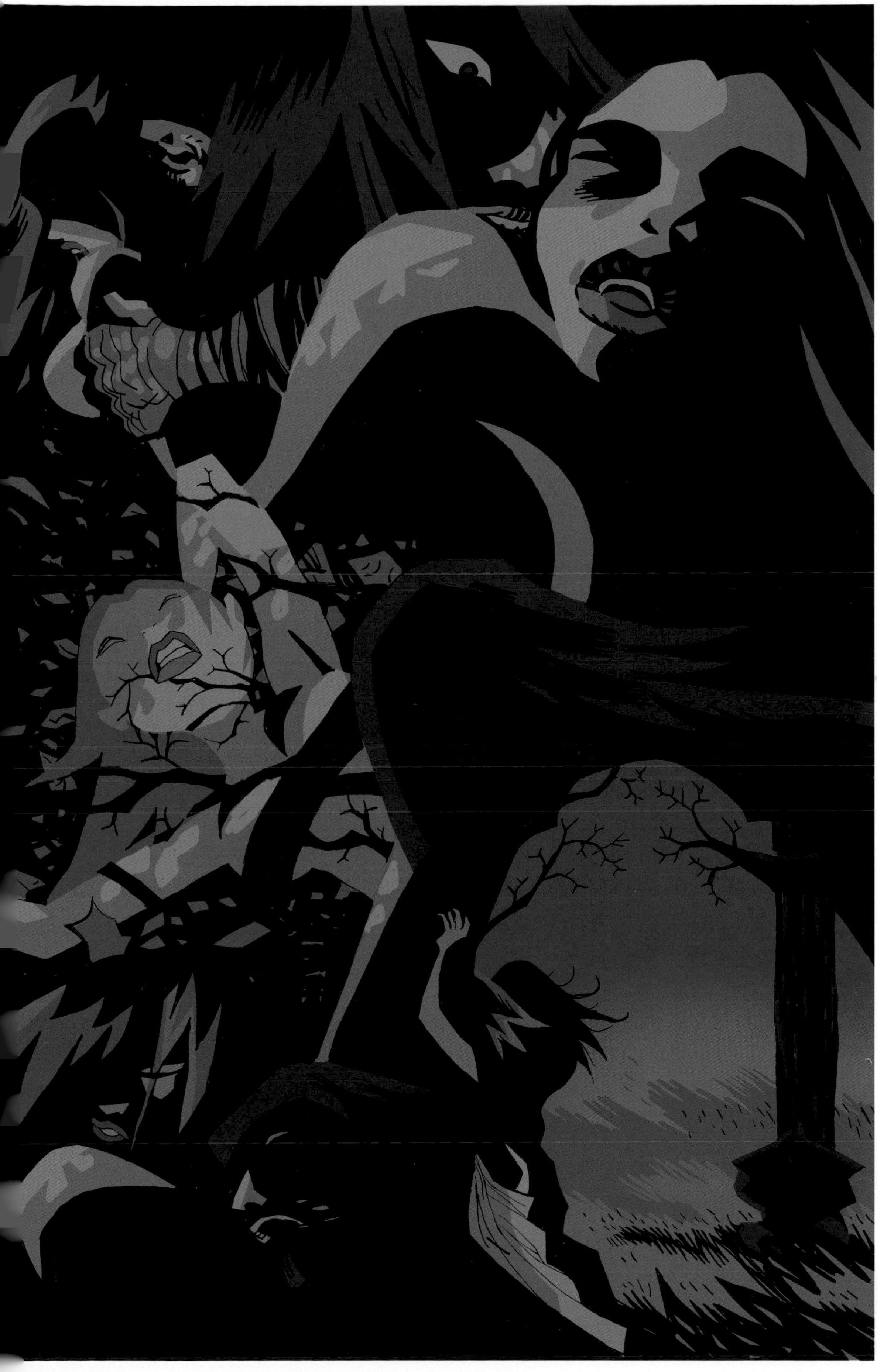

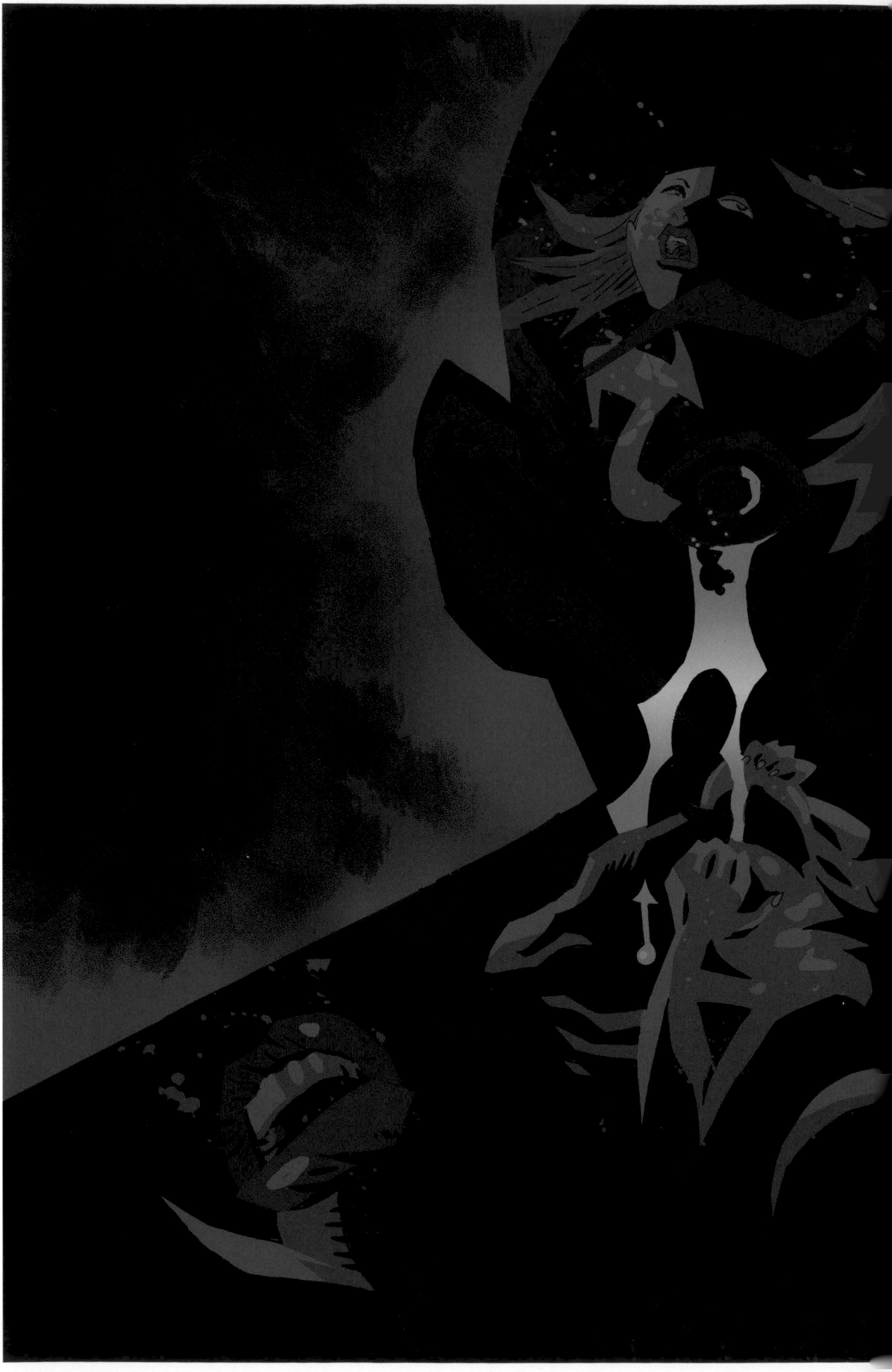

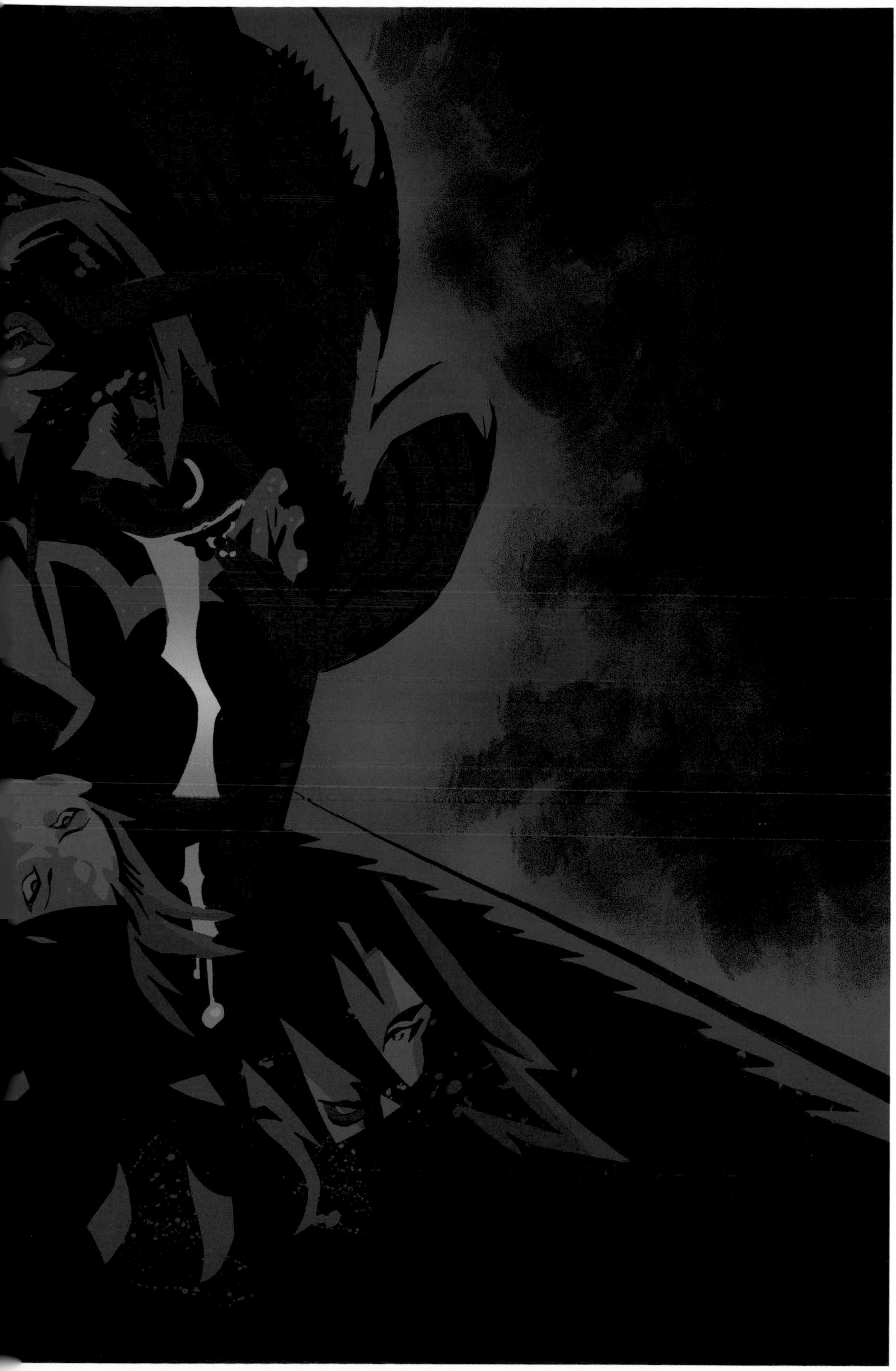

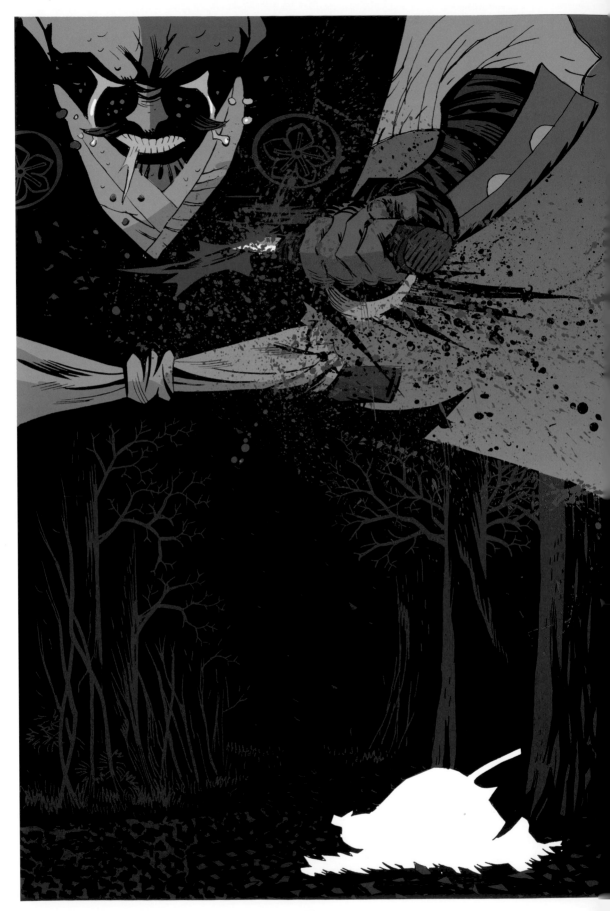

"I DIDN'T FEEL ANY PAIN.

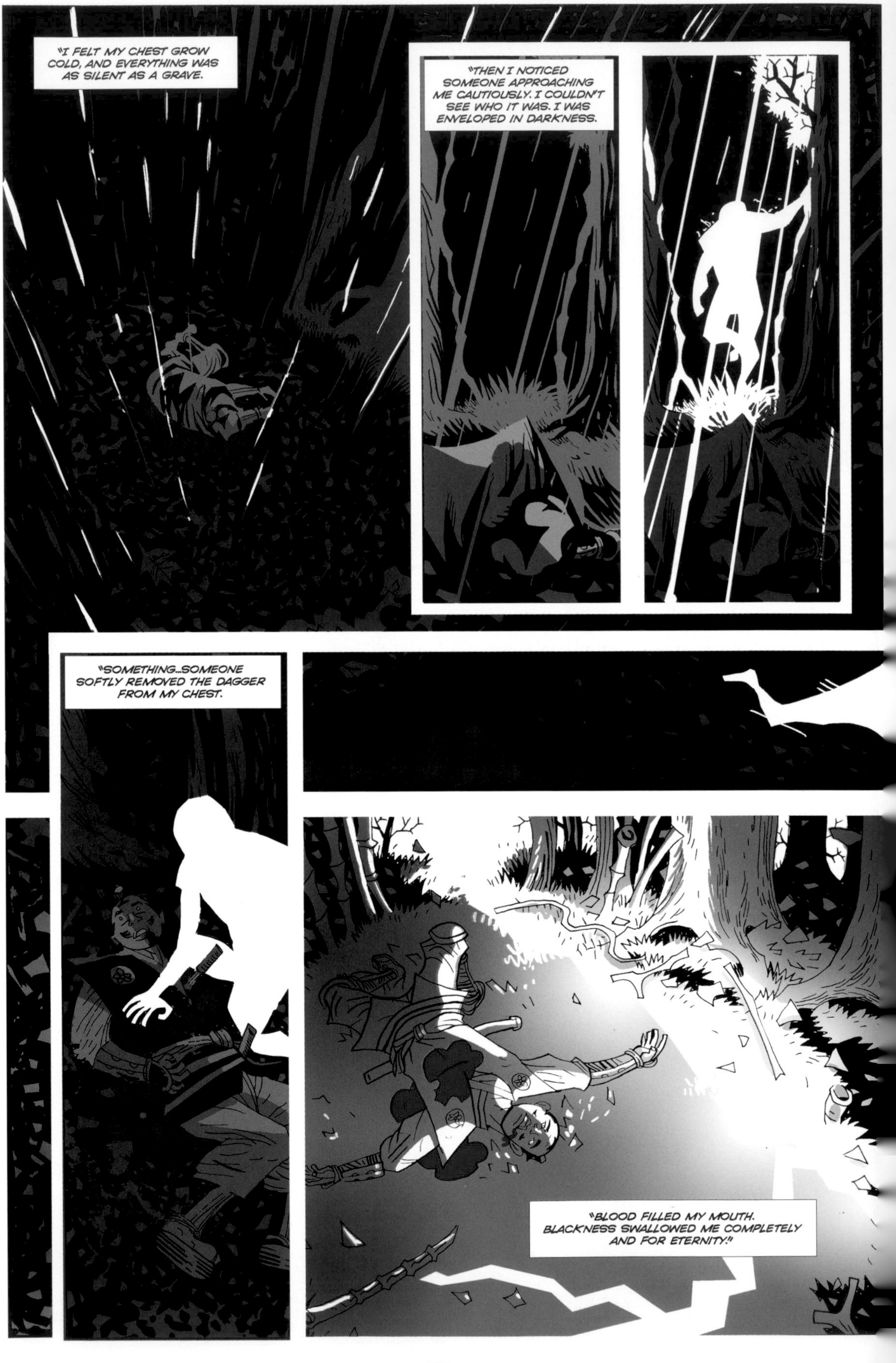
"I FELT MY CHEST GROW COLD, AND EVERYTHING WAS AS SILENT AS A GRAVE.
"THEN I NOTICED SOMEONE APPROACHING ME CAUTIOUSLY. I COULDN'T SEE WHO IT WAS. I WAS ENVELOPED IN DARKNESS.
"SOMETHING...SOMEONE SOFTLY REMOVED THE DAGGER FROM MY CHEST.
"BLOOD FILLED MY MOUTH. BLACKNESS SWALLOWED ME COMPLETELY AND FOR ETERNITY."

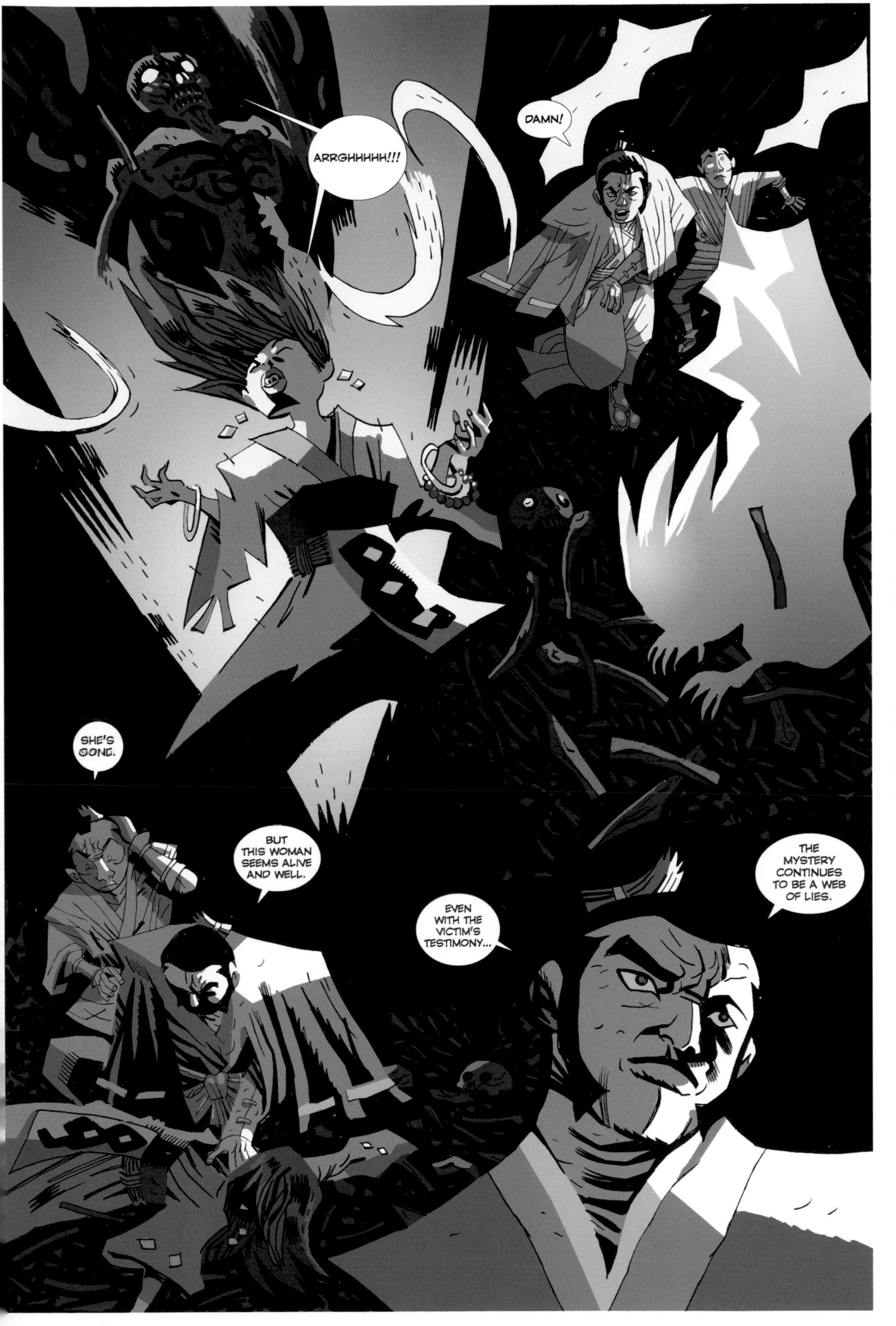
ARRGHHHHH!!!
DAMN!
SHE'S GONE.
BUT THIS WOMAN SEEMS ALIVE AND WELL.
EVEN WITH THE VICTIM'S TESTIMONY...
THE MYSTERY CONTINUES TO BE A WEB OF LIES.

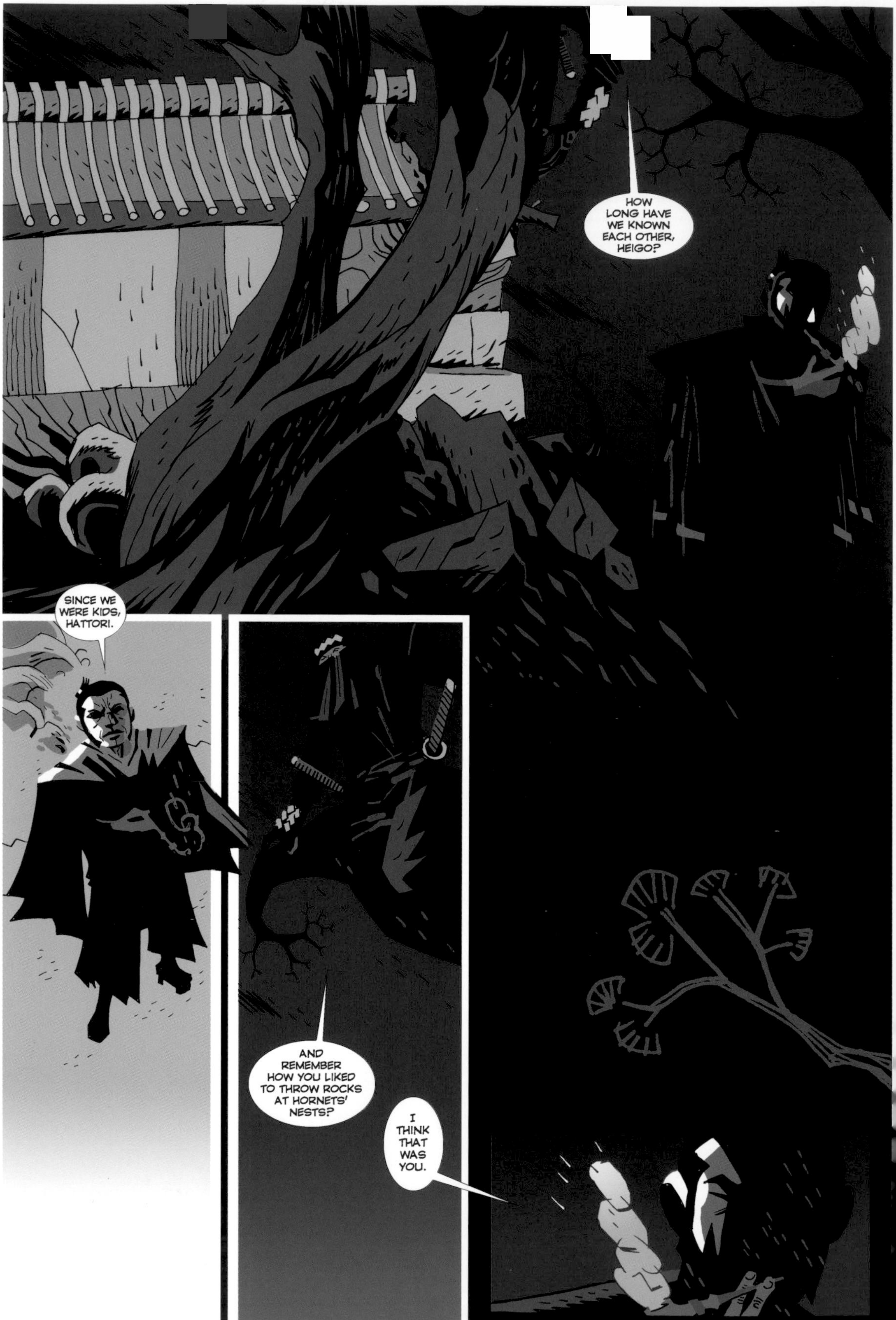
HOW LONG HAVE WE KNOWN EACH OTHER, HEIGO?
SINCE WE WERE KIDS, HATTORI.
AND REMEMBER HOW YOU LIKED TO THROW ROCKS AT HORNETS' NESTS?
I THINK THAT WAS YOU.

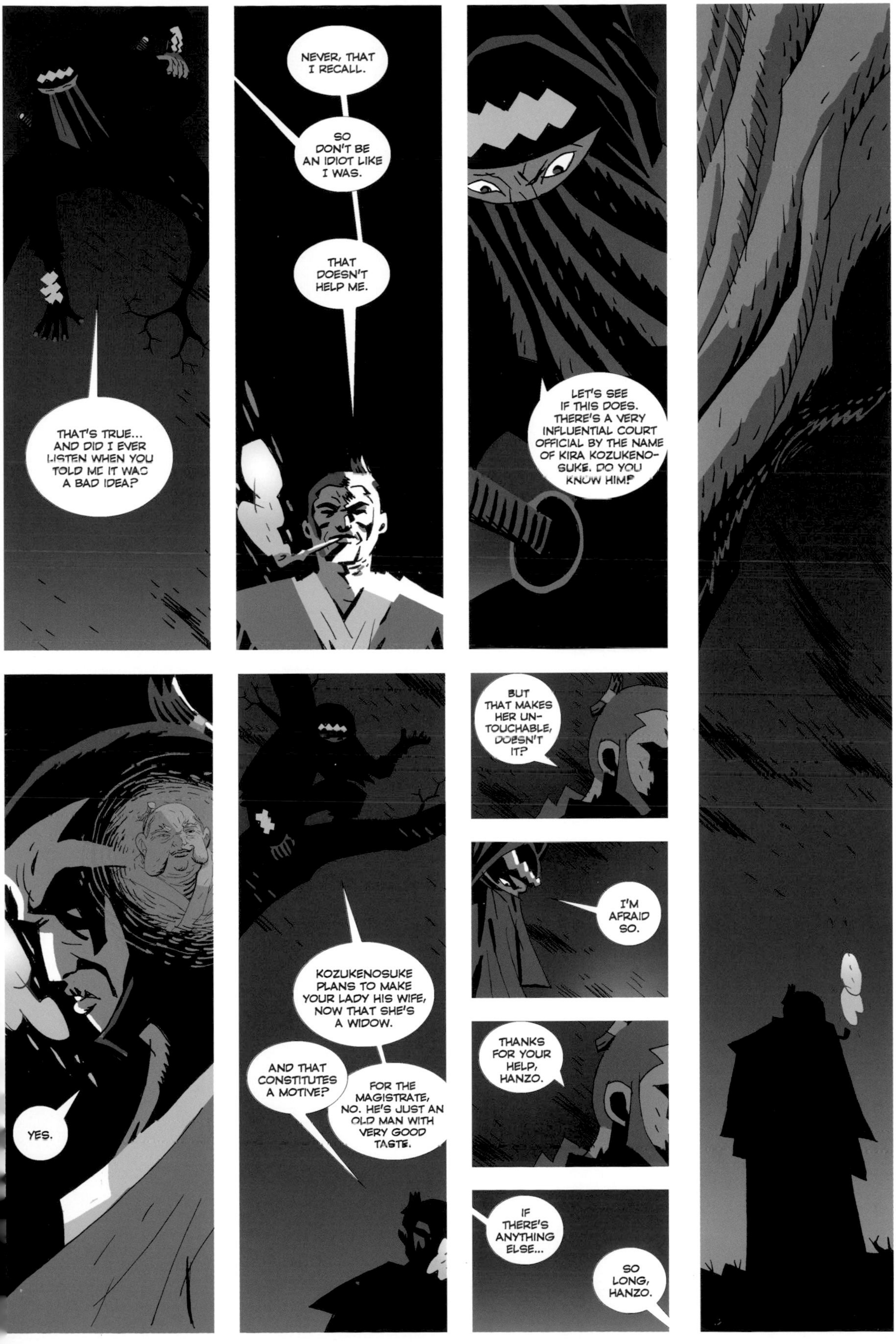
THAT'S TRUE... AND DID I EVER LISTEN WHEN YOU TOLD ME IT WAS A BAD IDEA?
NEVER, THAT I RECALL.
SO DON'T BE AN IDIOT LIKE I WAS.
THAT DOESN'T HELP ME.
LET'S SEE IF THIS DOES. THERE'S A VERY INFLUENTIAL COURT OFFICIAL BY THE NAME OF KIRA KOZUKENO-SUKE. DO YOU KNOW HIM?
YES.
KOZUKENOSUKE PLANS TO MAKE YOUR LADY HIS WIFE, NOW THAT SHE'S A WIDOW.
AND THAT CONSTITUTES A MOTIVE?
FOR THE MAGISTRATE, NO. HE'S JUST AN OLD MAN WITH VERY GOOD TASTE.
BUT THAT MAKES HER UN-TOUCHABLE, DOESN'T IT?
I'M AFRAID SO.
THANKS FOR YOUR HELP, HANZO.
IF THERE'S ANYTHING ELSE...
SO LONG, HANZO.

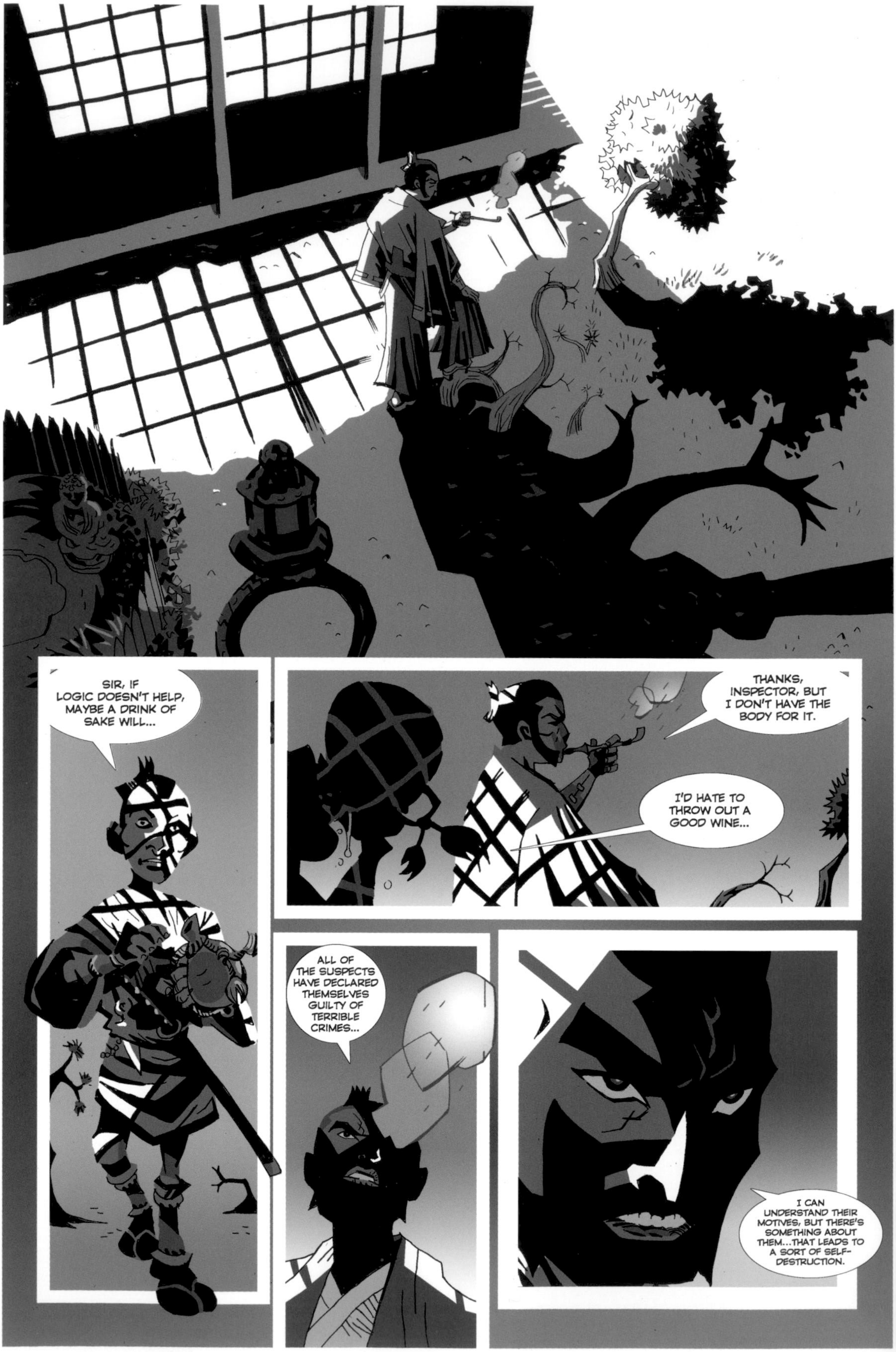
SIR, IF LOGIC DOESN'T HELP, MAYBE A DRINK OF SAKE WILL...
THANKS, INSPECTOR, BUT I DON'T HAVE THE BODY FOR IT.
I'D HATE TO THROW OUT A GOOD WINE...
ALL OF THE SUSPECTS HAVE DECLARED THEMSELVES GUILTY OF TERRIBLE CRIMES...
I CAN UNDERSTAND THEIR MOTIVES, BUT THERE'S SOMETHING ABOUT THEM...THAT LEADS TO A SORT OF SELF-DESTRUCTION.

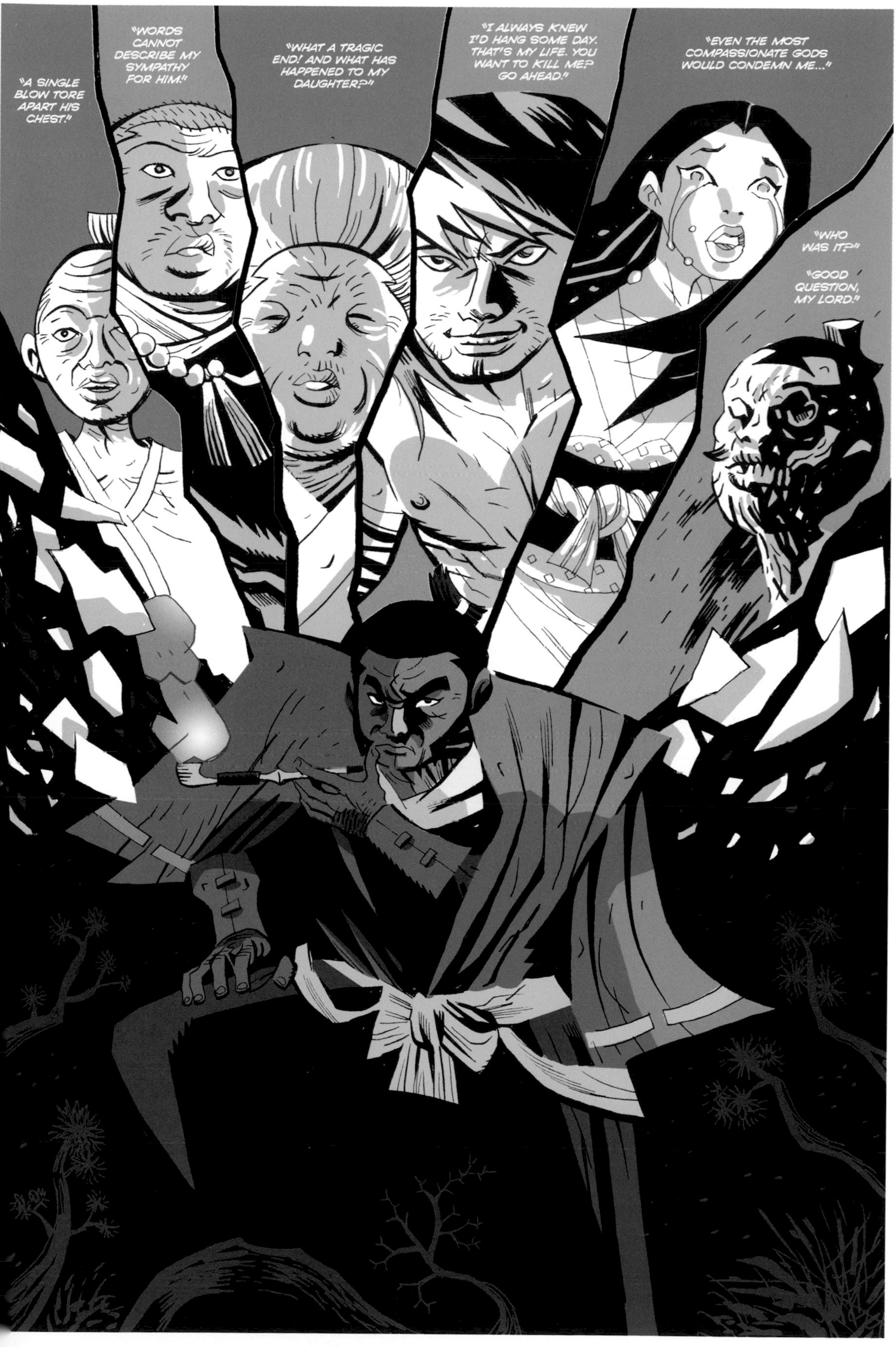
"A SINGLE BLOW TORE APART HIS CHEST."
"WORDS CANNOT DESCRIBE MY SYMPATHY FOR HIM."
"WHAT A TRAGIC END! AND WHAT HAS HAPPENED TO MY DAUGHTER?"
"I ALWAYS KNEW I'D HANG SOME DAY. THAT'S MY LIFE. YOU WANT TO KILL ME? GO AHEAD."
"EVEN THE MOST COMPASSIONATE GODS WOULD CONDEMN ME..."
"WHO WAS IT?"
"GOOD QUESTION, MY LORD."

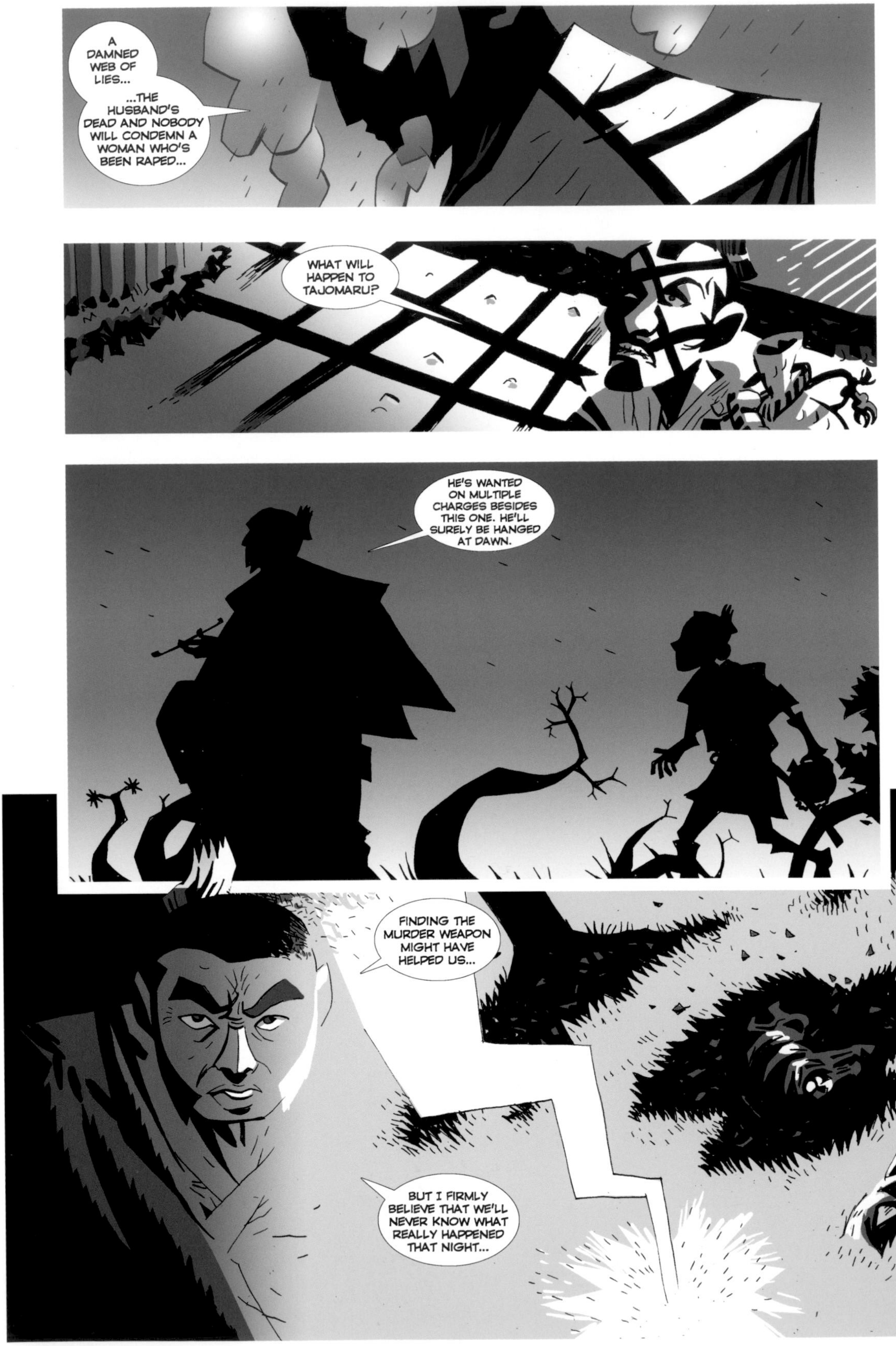
A DAMNED WEB OF LIES...
...THE HUSBAND'S DEAD AND NOBODY WILL CONDEMN A WOMAN WHO'S BEEN RAPED...
WHAT WILL HAPPEN TO TAJOMARU?
HE'S WANTED ON MULTIPLE CHARGES BESIDES THIS ONE. HE'LL SURELY BE HANGED AT DAWN.
FINDING THE MURDER WEAPON MIGHT HAVE HELPED US...
BUT I FIRMLY BELIEVE THAT WE'LL NEVER KNOW WHAT REALLY HAPPENED THAT NIGHT...

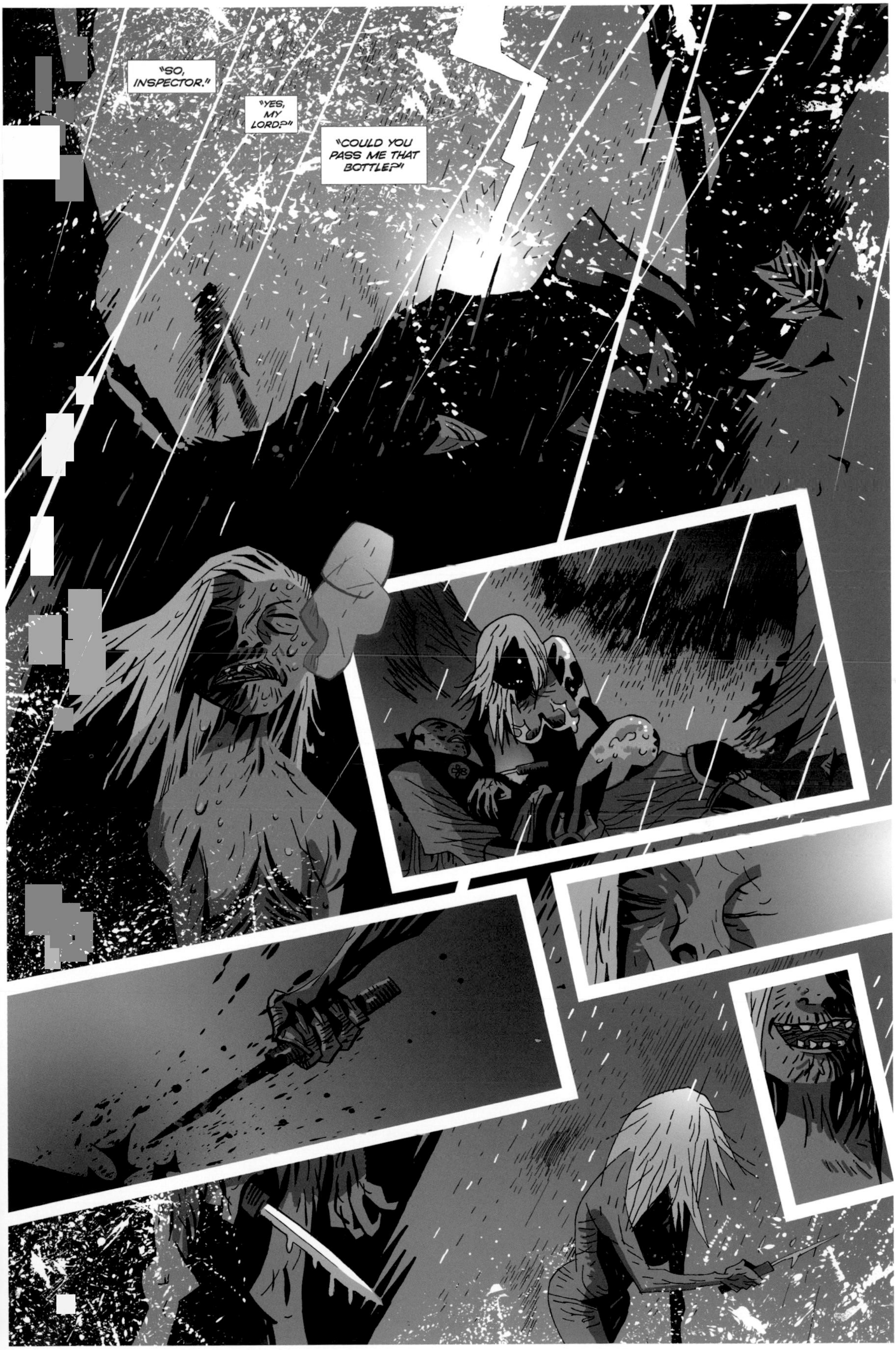
"SO, INSPECTOR."
"YES, MY LORD?"
"COULD YOU PASS ME THAT BOTTLE?"

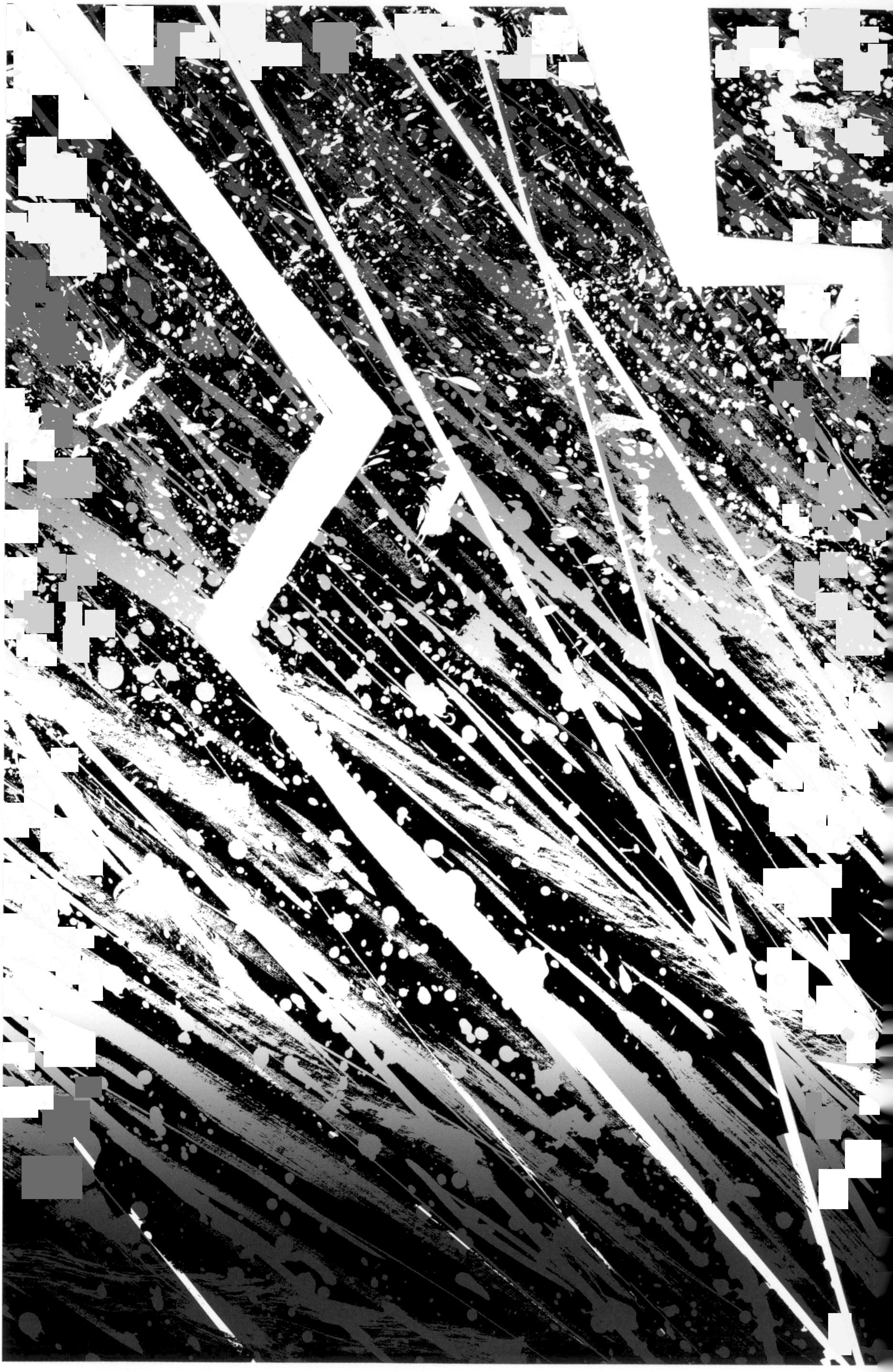

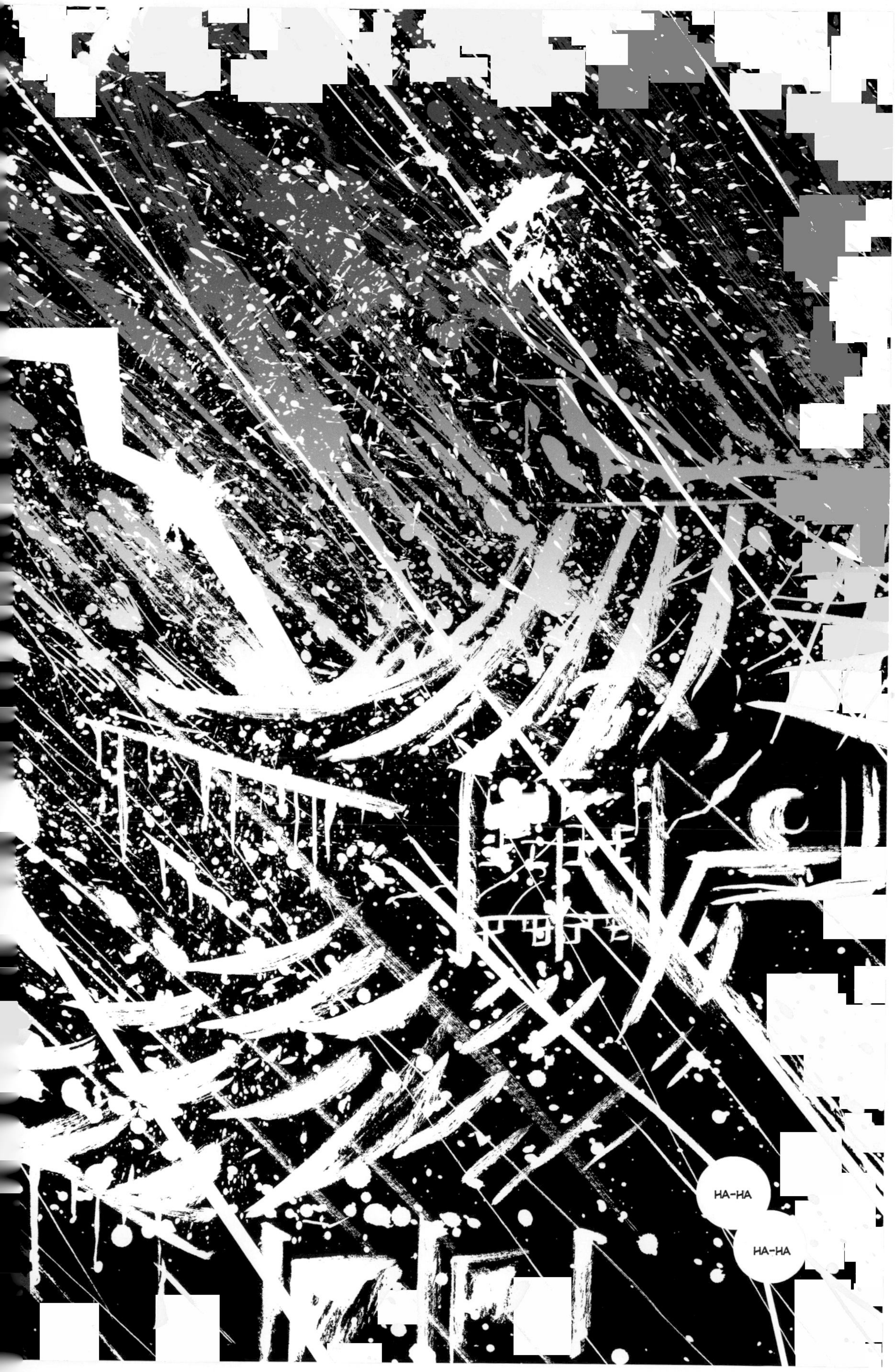
HA-HA
HA-HA

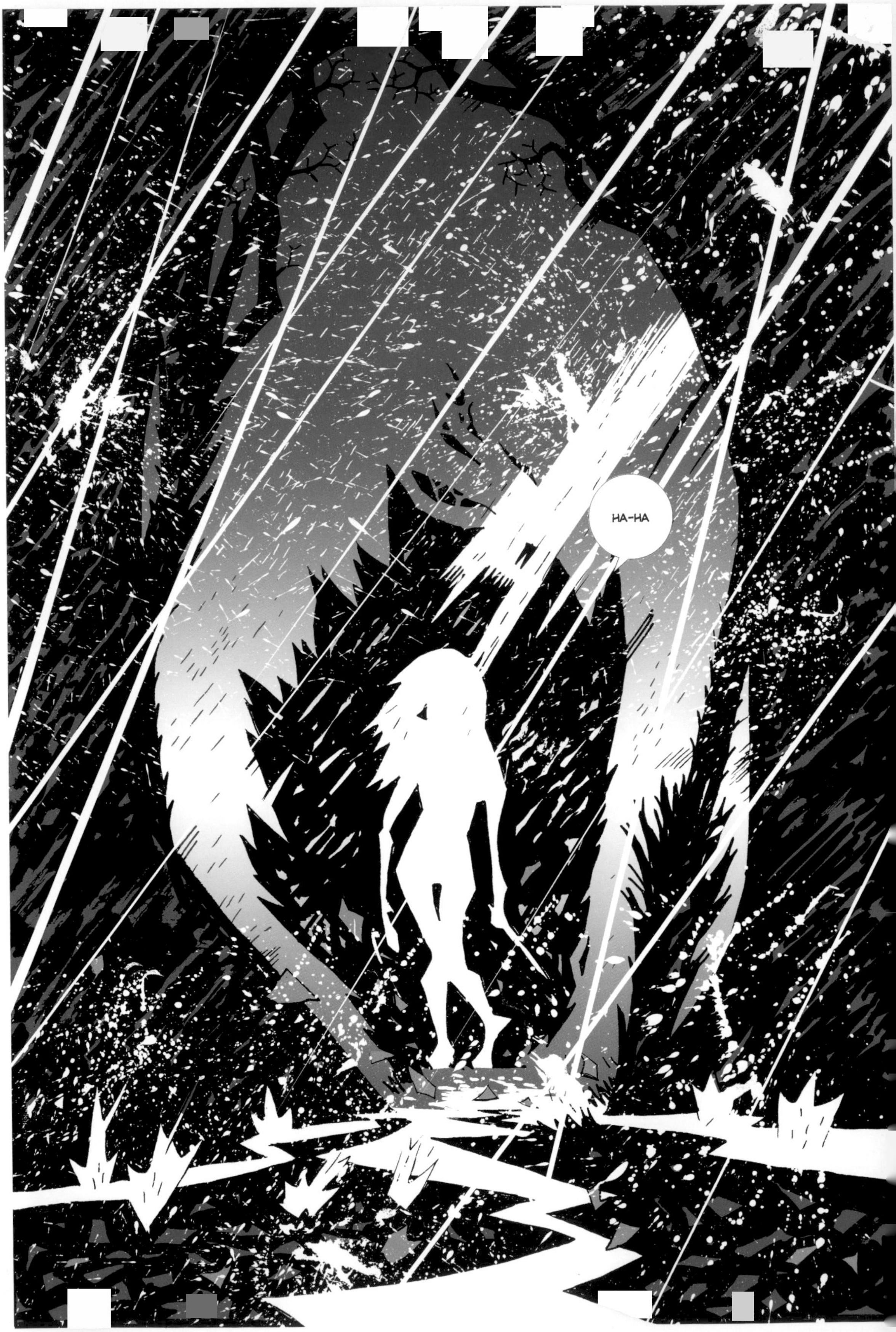
HA-HA

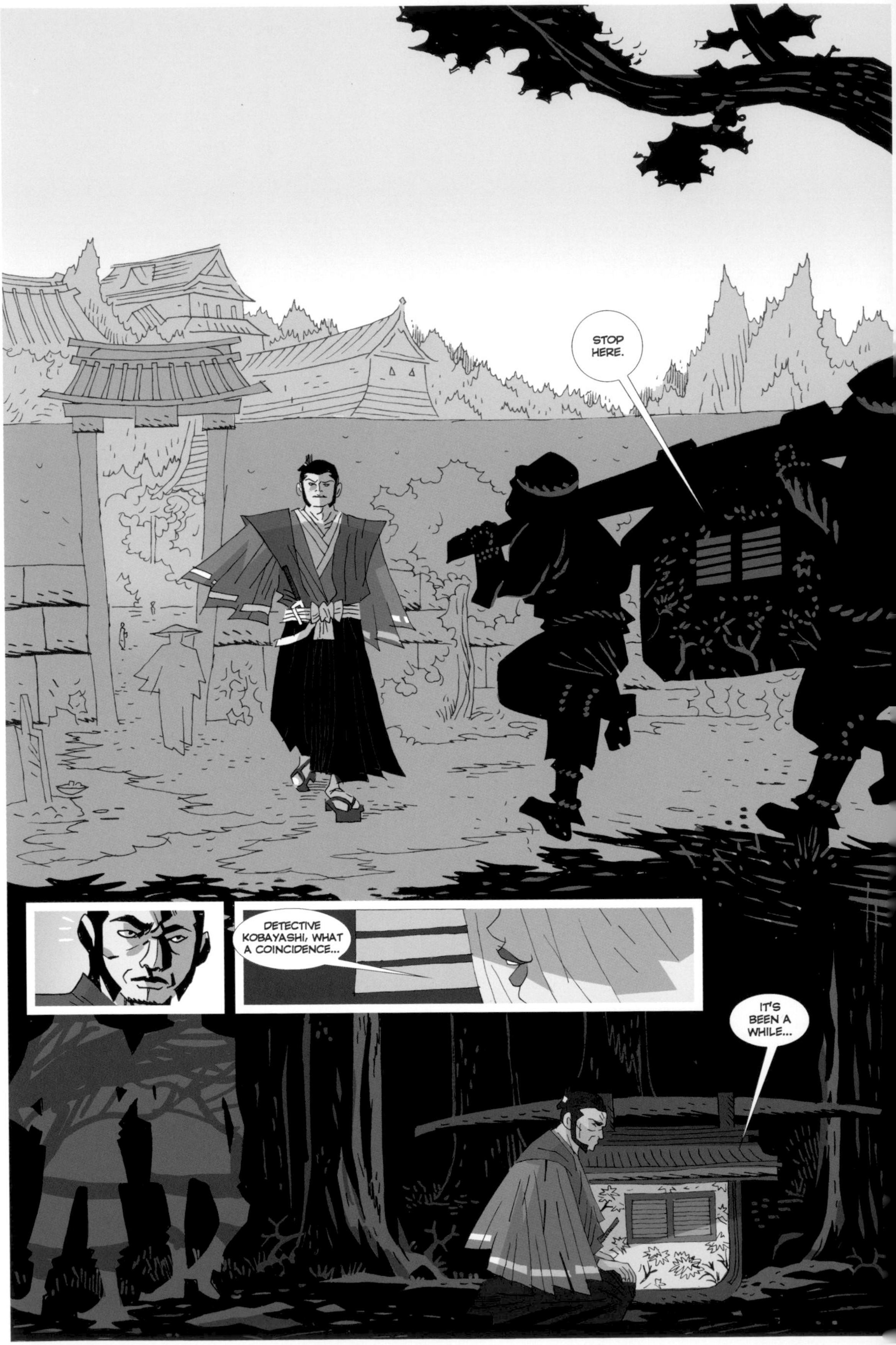
STOP HERE.
DETECTIVE KOBAYASHI, WHAT A COINCIDENCE...
IT'S BEEN A WHILE...

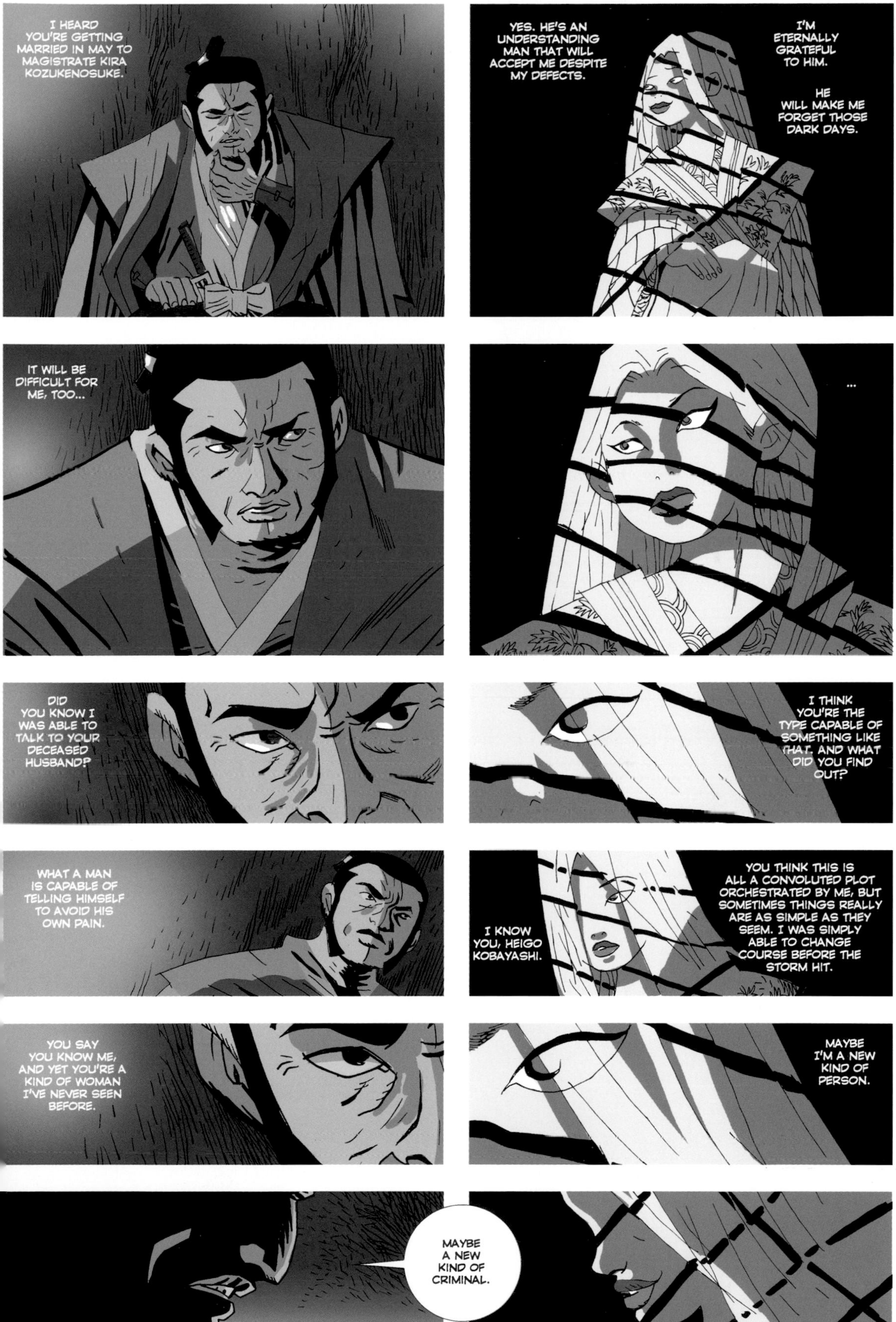
I HEARD YOU'RE GETTING MARRIED IN MAY TO MAGISTRATE KIRA KOZUKENOSUKE.
YES. HE'S AN UNDERSTANDING MAN THAT WILL ACCEPT ME DESPITE MY DEFECTS.
I'M ETERNALLY GRATEFUL TO HIM.
HE WILL MAKE ME FORGET THOSE DARK DAYS.
IT WILL BE DIFFICULT FOR ME, TOO...
...
DID YOU KNOW I WAS ABLE TO TALK TO YOUR DECEASED HUSBAND?
I THINK YOU'RE THE TYPE CAPABLE OF SOMETHING LIKE THAT. AND WHAT DID YOU FIND OUT?
WHAT A MAN IS CAPABLE OF TELLING HIMSELF TO AVOID HIS OWN PAIN.
I KNOW YOU, HEIGO KOBAYASHI.
YOU THINK THIS IS ALL A CONVOLUTED PLOT ORCHESTRATED BY ME, BUT SOMETIMES THINGS REALLY ARE AS SIMPLE AS THEY SEEM. I WAS SIMPLY ABLE TO CHANGE COURSE BEFORE THE STORM HIT.
YOU SAY YOU KNOW ME, AND YET YOU'RE A KIND OF WOMAN I'VE NEVER SEEN BEFORE.
MAYBE I'M A NEW KIND OF PERSON.
MAYBE A NEW KIND OF CRIMINAL.

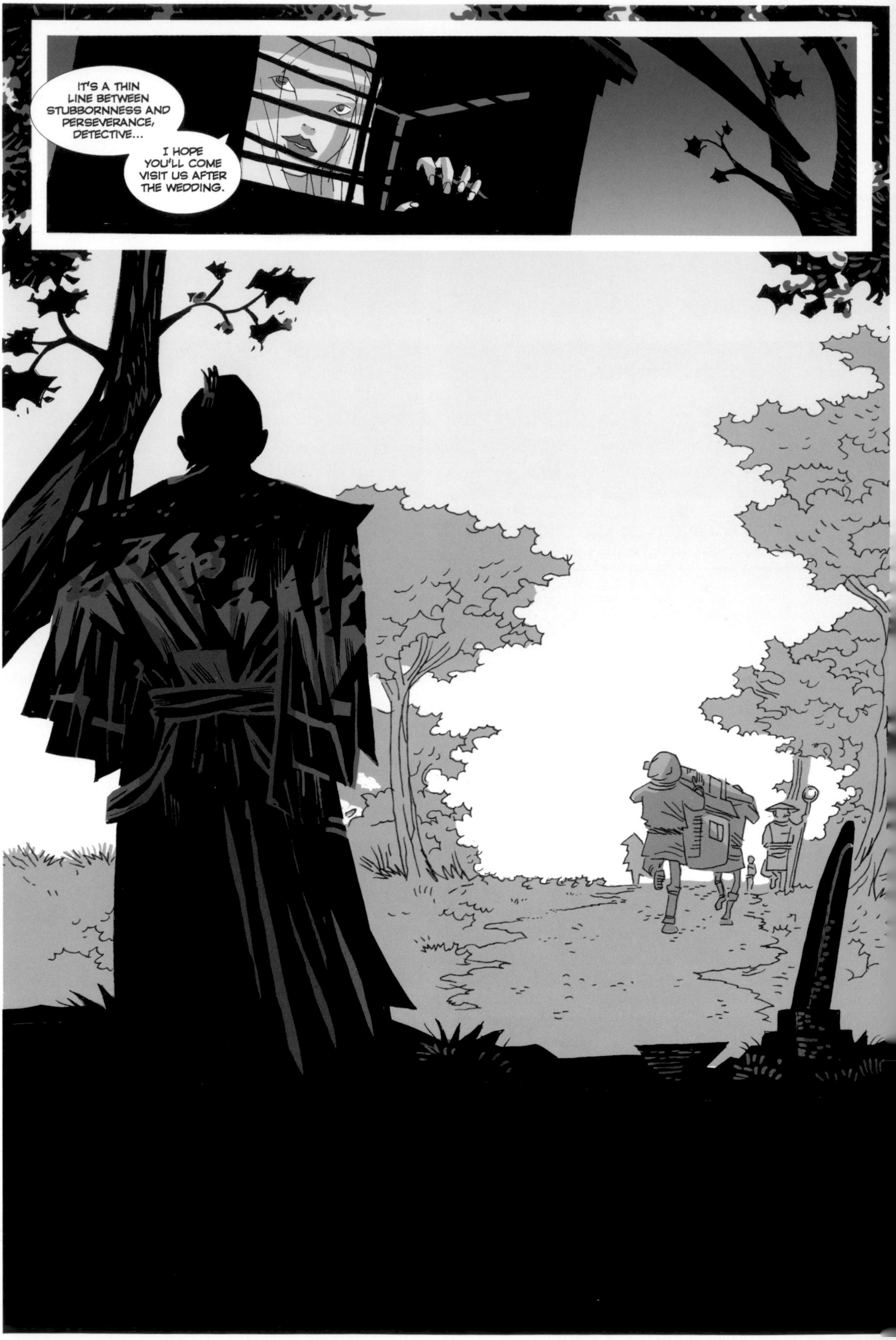
IT'S A THIN LINE BETWEEN STUBBORNNESS AND PERSEVERANCE, DETECTIVE...
I HOPE YOU'LL COME VISIT US AFTER THE WEDDING.

RA SHO MON

PART 2

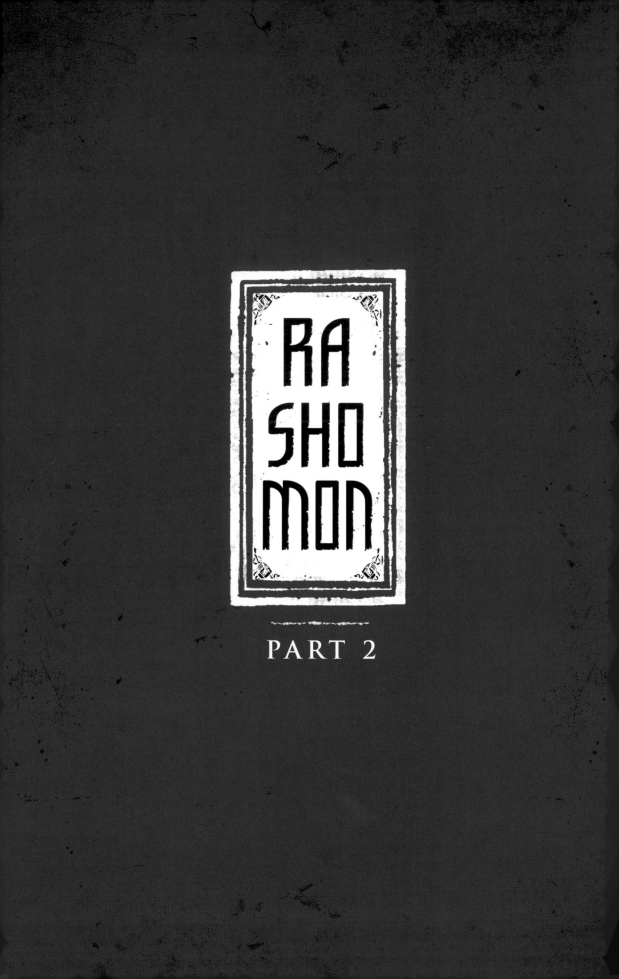

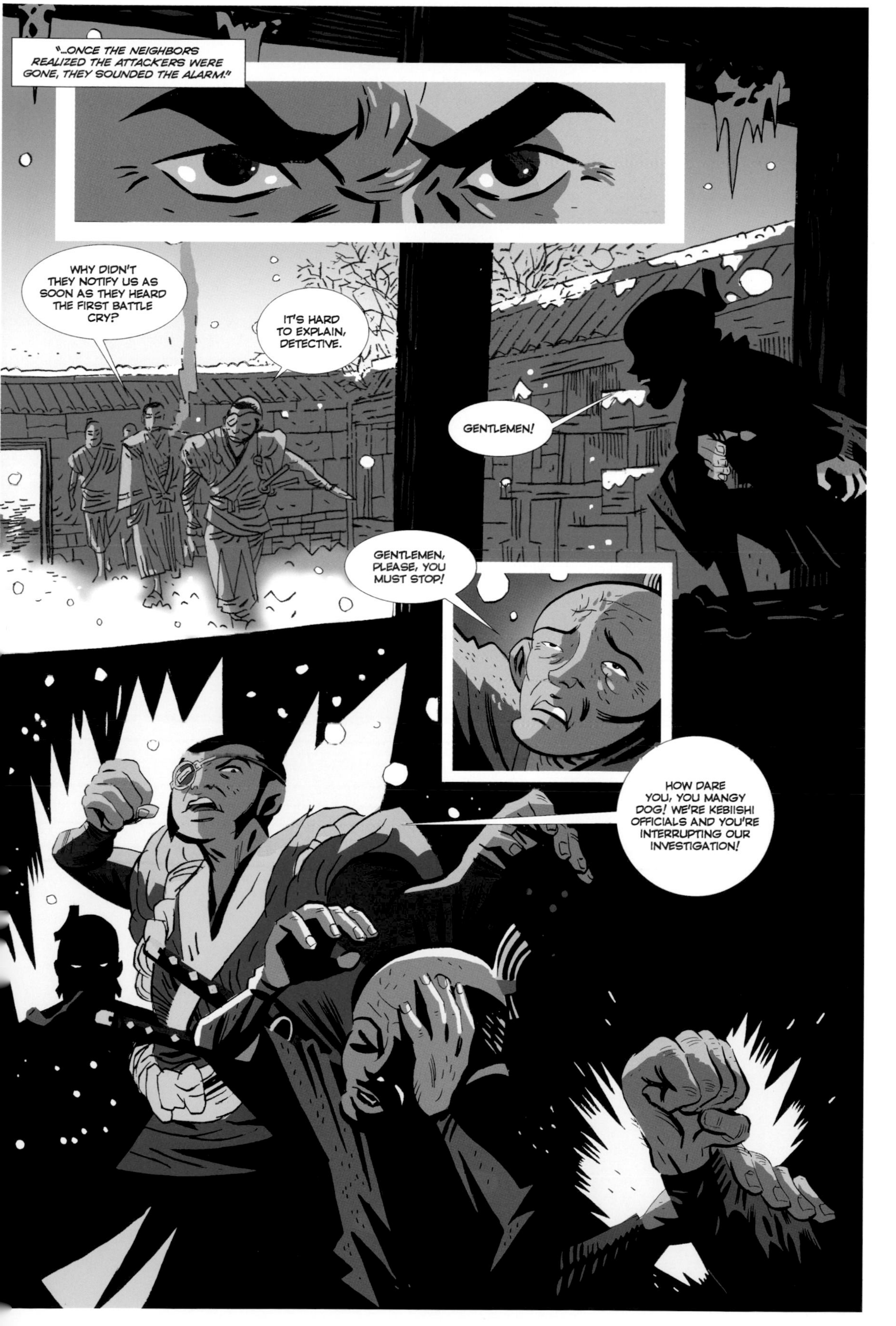
"...ONCE THE NEIGHBORS REALIZED THE ATTACKERS WERE GONE, THEY SOUNDED THE ALARM."
WHY DIDN'T THEY NOTIFY US AS SOON AS THEY HEARD THE FIRST BATTLE CRY?
IT'S HARD TO EXPLAIN, DETECTIVE.
GENTLEMEN!
GENTLEMEN, PLEASE, YOU MUST STOP!
HOW DARE YOU, YOU MANGY DOG! WE'RE KEBIISHI OFFICIALS AND YOU'RE INTERRUPTING OUR INVESTIGATION!

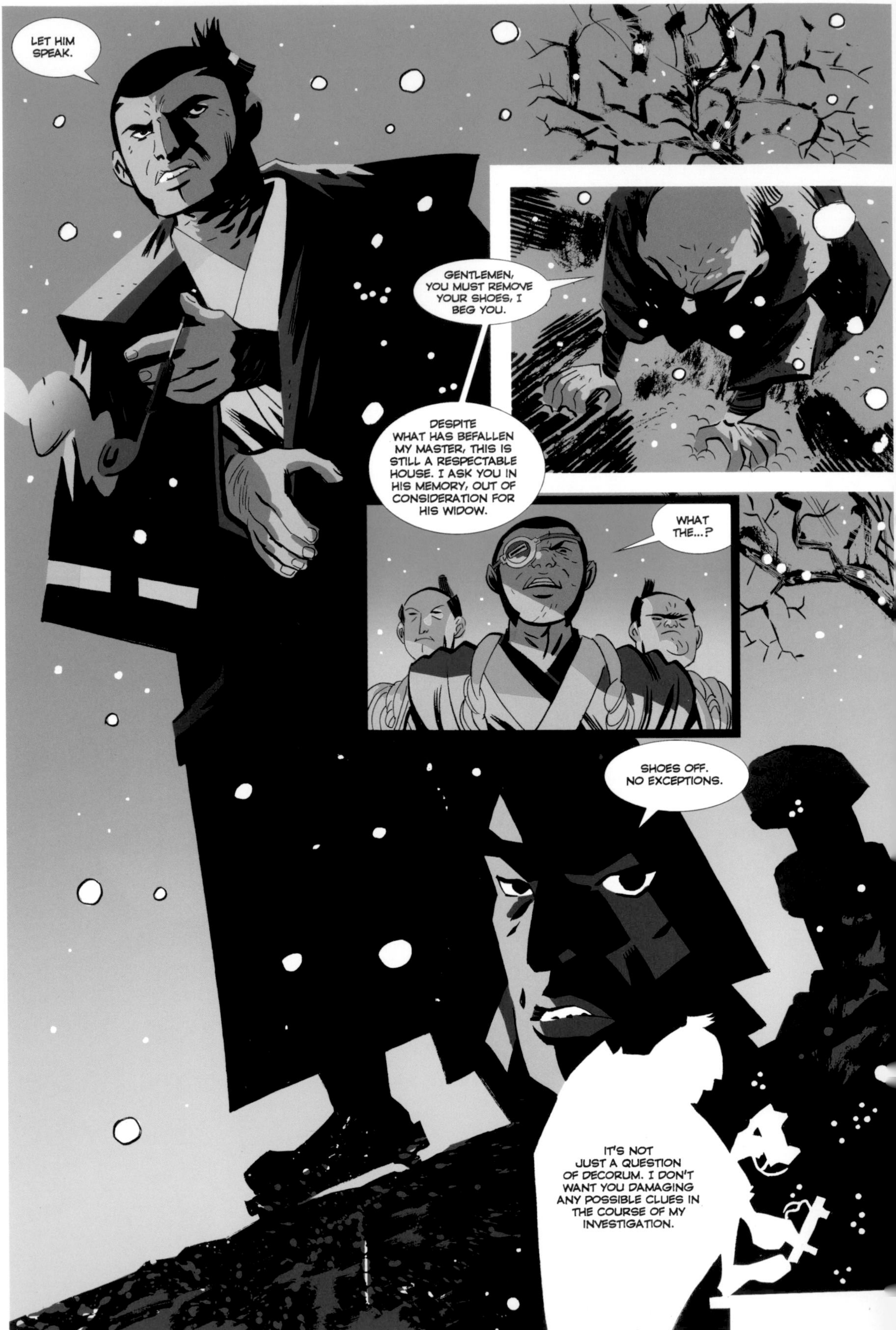
LET HIM SPEAK.
GENTLEMEN, YOU MUST REMOVE YOUR SHOES, I BEG YOU.
DESPITE WHAT HAS BEFALLEN MY MASTER, THIS IS STILL A RESPECTABLE HOUSE. I ASK YOU IN HIS MEMORY, OUT OF CONSIDERATION FOR HIS WIDOW.
WHAT THE...?
SHOES OFF. NO EXCEPTIONS.
IT'S NOT JUST A QUESTION OF DECORUM. I DON'T WANT YOU DAMAGING ANY POSSIBLE CLUES IN THE COURSE OF MY INVESTIGATION.

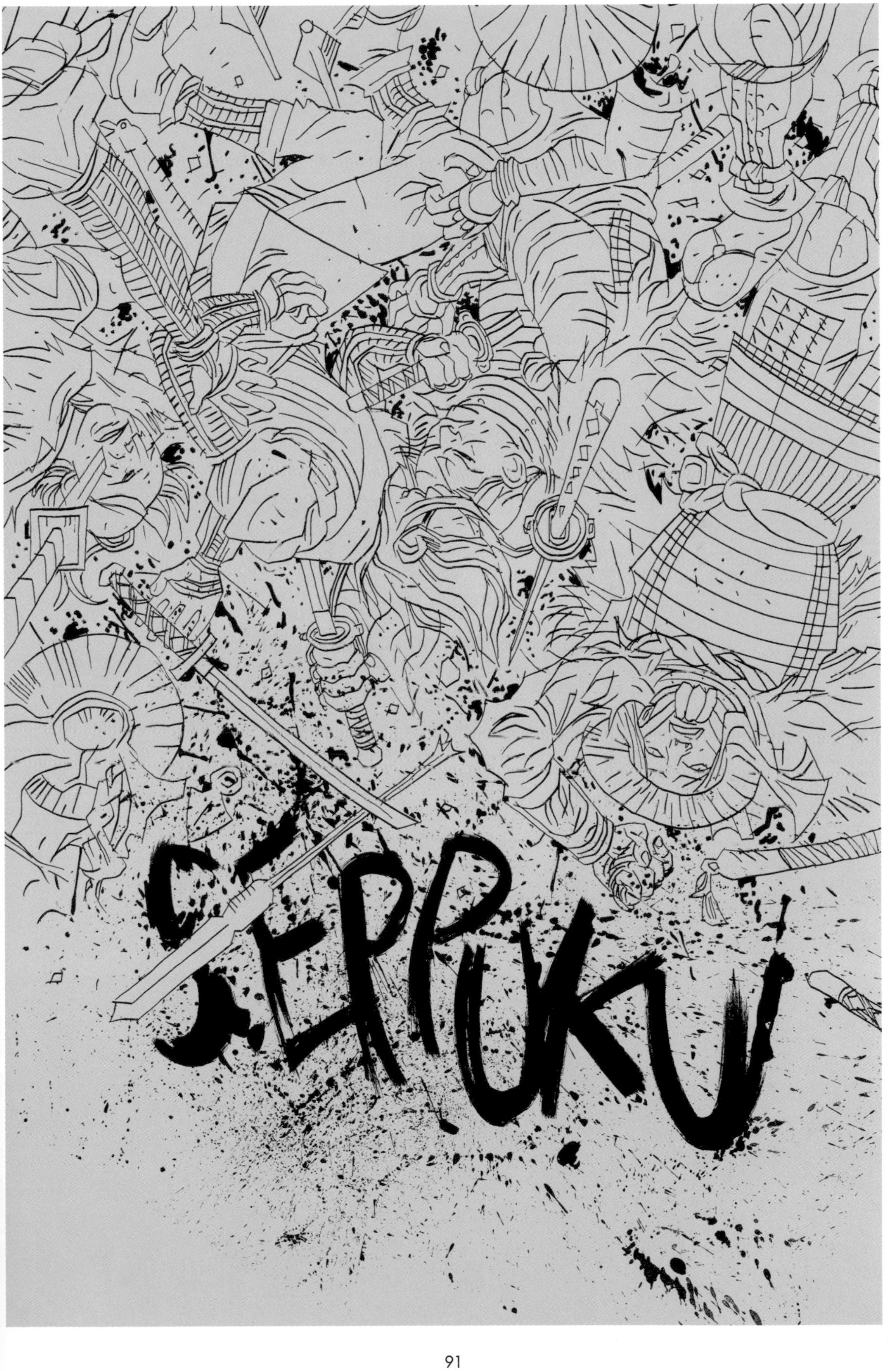
SEPPUKU

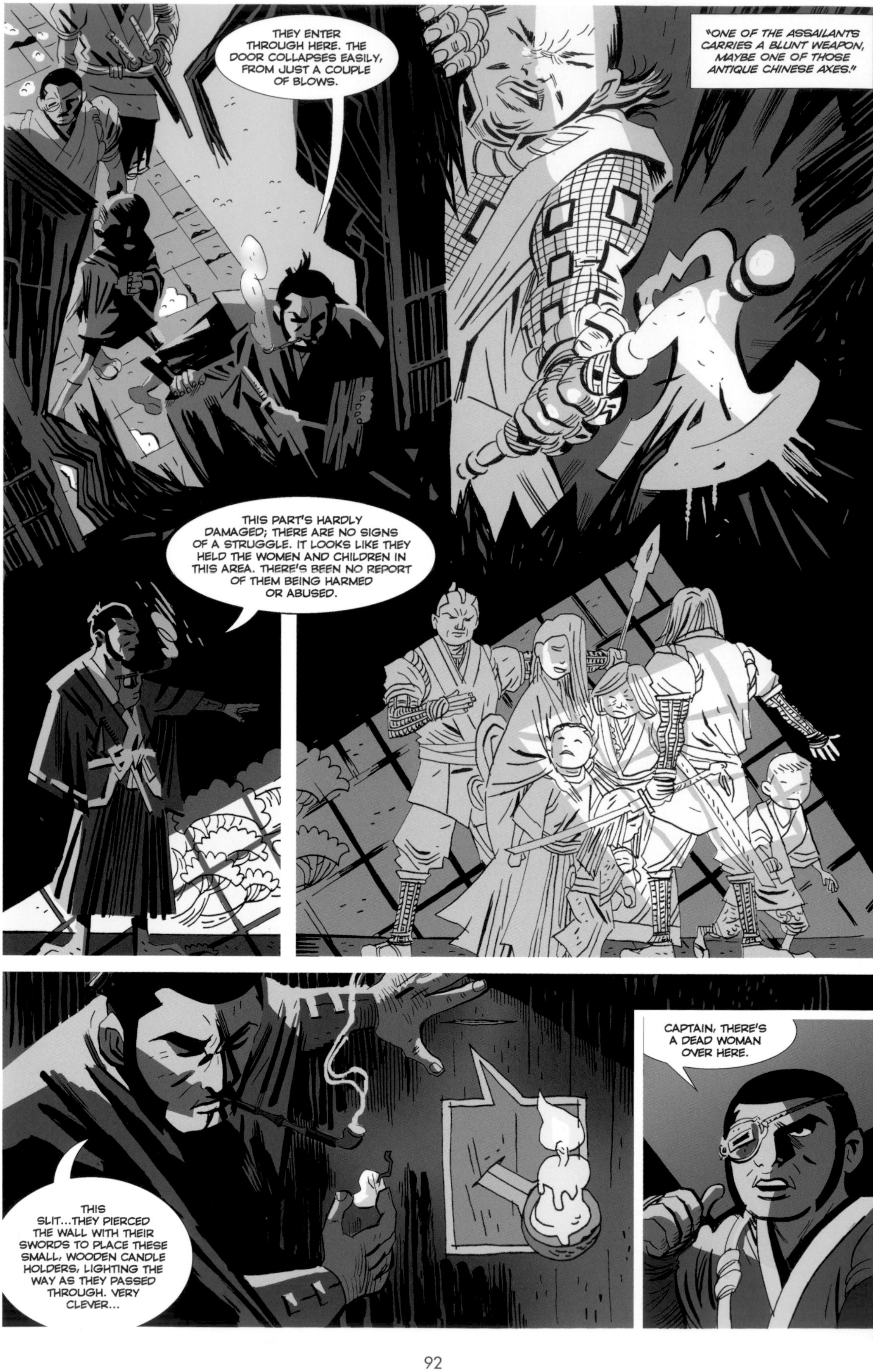
THEY ENTER THROUGH HERE. THE DOOR COLLAPSES EASILY, FROM JUST A COUPLE OF BLOWS.
"ONE OF THE ASSAILANTS CARRIES A BLUNT WEAPON, MAYBE ONE OF THOSE ANTIQUE CHINESE AXES."
THIS PART'S HARDLY DAMAGED; THERE ARE NO SIGNS OF A STRUGGLE. IT LOOKS LIKE THEY HELD THE WOMEN AND CHILDREN IN THIS AREA. THERE'S BEEN NO REPORT OF THEM BEING HARMED OR ABUSED.
THIS SLIT...THEY PIERCED THE WALL WITH THEIR SWORDS TO PLACE THESE SMALL, WOODEN CANDLE HOLDERS, LIGHTING THE WAY AS THEY PASSED THROUGH. VERY CLEVER...
CAPTAIN, THERE'S A DEAD WOMAN OVER HERE.

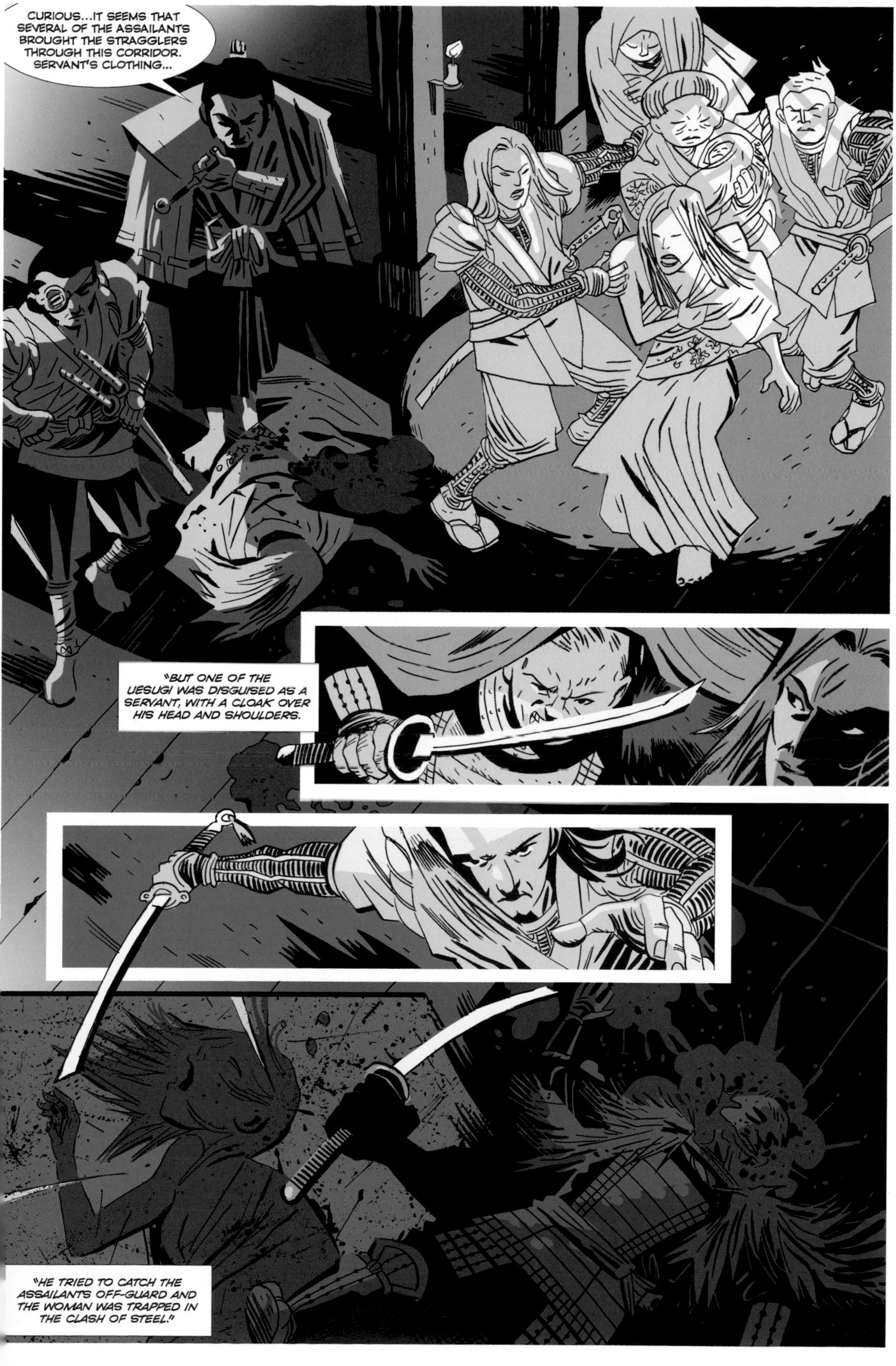
CURIOUS...IT SEEMS THAT SEVERAL OF THE ASSAILANTS BROUGHT THE STRAGGLERS THROUGH THIS CORRIDOR. SERVANT'S CLOTHING...
"BUT ONE OF THE UESUGI WAS DISGUISED AS A SERVANT, WITH A CLOAK OVER HIS HEAD AND SHOULDERS.
"HE TRIED TO CATCH THE ASSAILANTS OFF-GUARD AND THE WOMAN WAS TRAPPED IN THE CLASH OF STEEL."

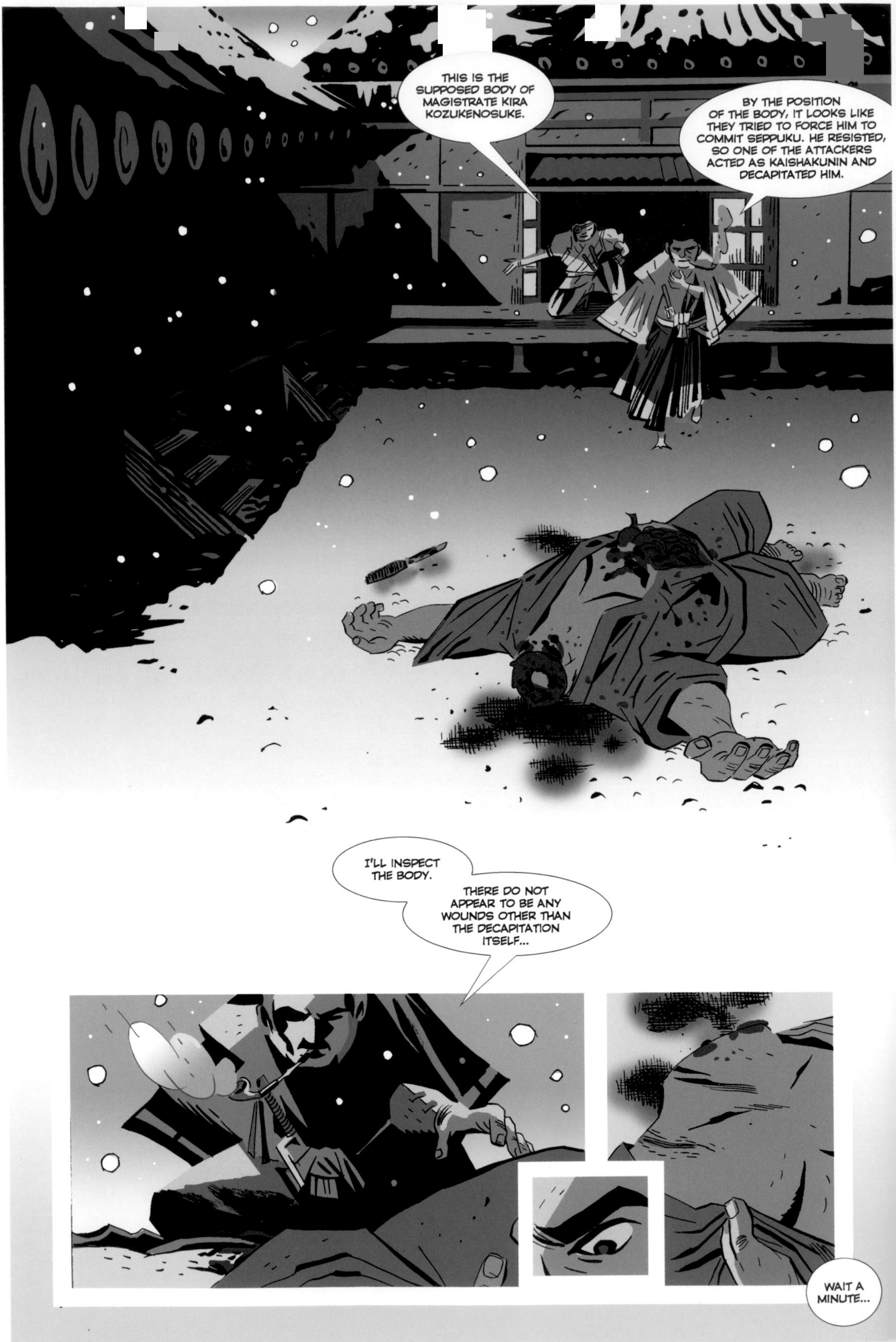
THIS IS THE SUPPOSED BODY OF MAGISTRATE KIRA KOZUKENOSUKE.
BY THE POSITION OF THE BODY, IT LOOKS LIKE THEY TRIED TO FORCE HIM TO COMMIT SEPPUKU. HE RESISTED, SO ONE OF THE ATTACKERS ACTED AS KAISHAKUNIN AND DECAPITATED HIM.
I'LL INSPECT THE BODY.
THERE DO NOT APPEAR TO BE ANY WOUNDS OTHER THAN THE DECAPITATION ITSELF...
WAIT A MINUTE...

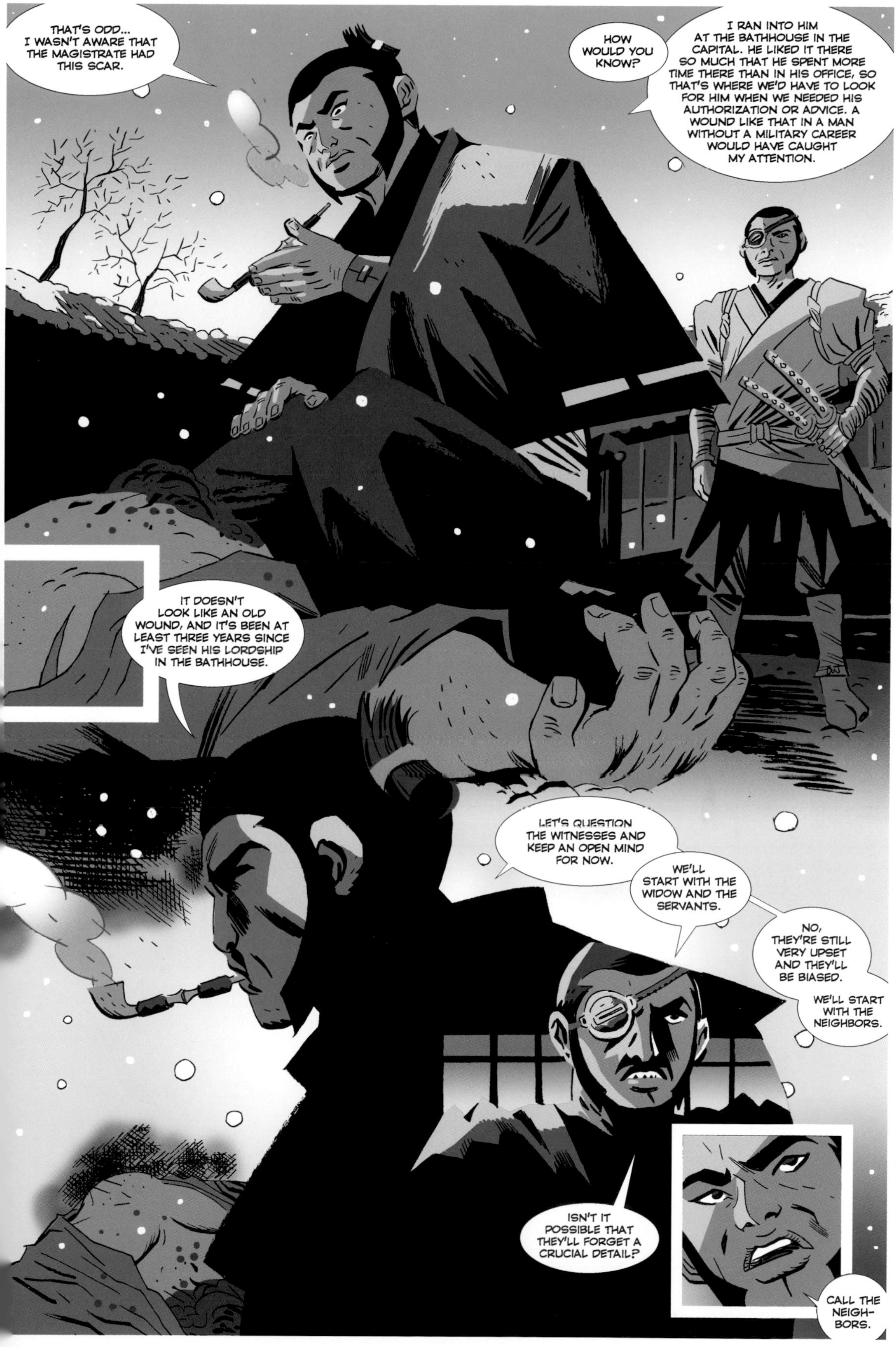
THAT'S ODD... I WASN'T AWARE THAT THE MAGISTRATE HAD THIS SCAR.
HOW WOULD YOU KNOW?
I RAN INTO HIM AT THE BATHHOUSE IN THE CAPITAL. HE LIKED IT THERE SO MUCH THAT HE SPENT MORE TIME THERE THAN IN HIS OFFICE, SO THAT'S WHERE WE'D HAVE TO LOOK FOR HIM WHEN WE NEEDED HIS AUTHORIZATION OR ADVICE. A WOUND LIKE THAT IN A MAN WITHOUT A MILITARY CAREER WOULD HAVE CAUGHT MY ATTENTION.
IT DOESN'T LOOK LIKE AN OLD WOUND, AND IT'S BEEN AT LEAST THREE YEARS SINCE I'VE SEEN HIS LORDSHIP IN THE BATHHOUSE.
LET'S QUESTION THE WITNESSES AND KEEP AN OPEN MIND FOR NOW.
WE'LL START WITH THE WIDOW AND THE SERVANTS.
NO, THEY'RE STILL VERY UPSET AND THEY'LL BE BIASED.
WE'LL START WITH THE NEIGHBORS.
ISN'T IT POSSIBLE THAT THEY'LL FORGET A CRUCIAL DETAIL?
CALL THE NEIGH-BORS.

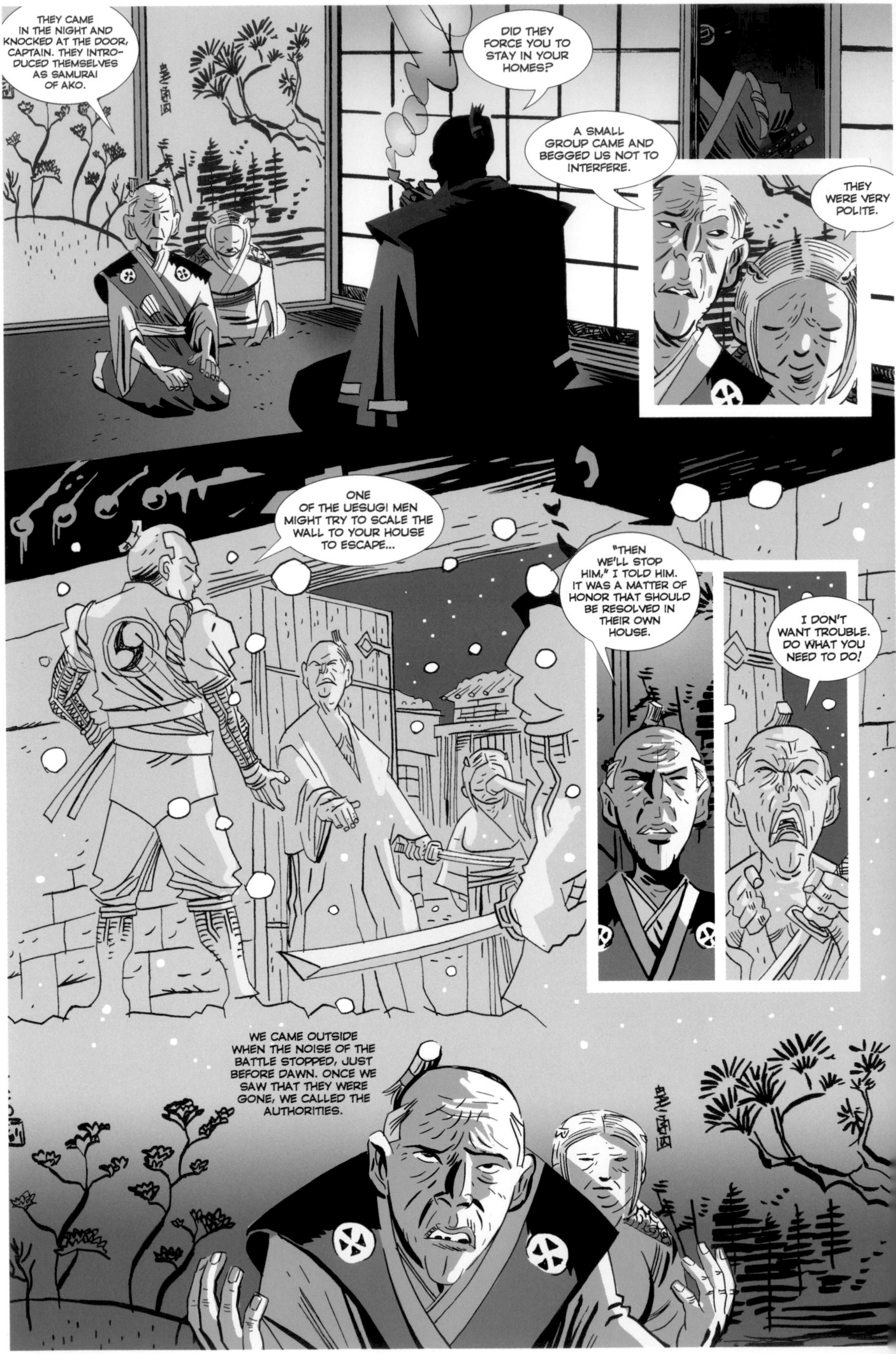
THEY CAME IN THE NIGHT AND KNOCKED AT THE DOOR, CAPTAIN. THEY INTRO-DUCED THEMSELVES AS SAMURAI OF AKO.
DID THEY FORCE YOU TO STAY IN YOUR HOMES?
A SMALL GROUP CAME AND BEGGED US NOT TO INTERFERE.
THEY WERE VERY POLITE.
ONE OF THE UESUGI MEN MIGHT TRY TO SCALE THE WALL TO YOUR HOUSE TO ESCAPE...
"THEN WE'LL STOP HIM," I TOLD HIM. IT WAS A MATTER OF HONOR THAT SHOULD BE RESOLVED IN THEIR OWN HOUSE.
I DON'T WANT TROUBLE. DO WHAT YOU NEED TO DO!
WE CAME OUTSIDE WHEN THE NOISE OF THE BATTLE STOPPED, JUST BEFORE DAWN. ONCE WE SAW THAT THEY WERE GONE, WE CALLED THE AUTHORITIES.

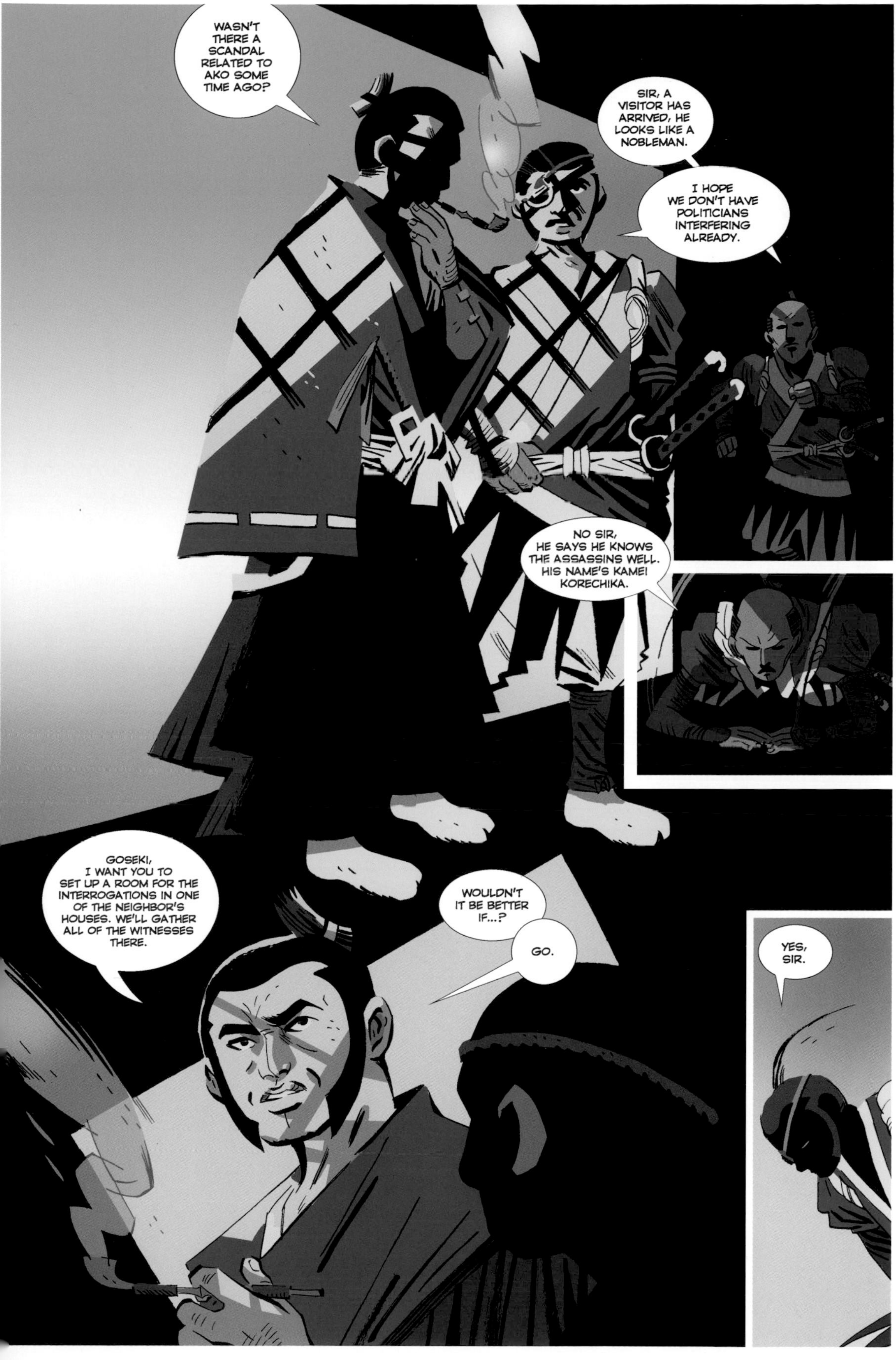
WASN'T THERE A SCANDAL RELATED TO AKO SOME TIME AGO?
SIR, A VISITOR HAS ARRIVED, HE LOOKS LIKE A NOBLEMAN.
I HOPE WE DON'T HAVE POLITICIANS INTERFERING ALREADY.
NO SIR, HE SAYS HE KNOWS THE ASSASSINS WELL. HIS NAME'S KAMEI KORECHIKA.
GOSEKI, I WANT YOU TO SET UP A ROOM FOR THE INTERROGATIONS IN ONE OF THE NEIGHBOR'S HOUSES. WE'LL GATHER ALL OF THE WITNESSES THERE.
WOULDN'T IT BE BETTER IF...?
GO.
YES, SIR.

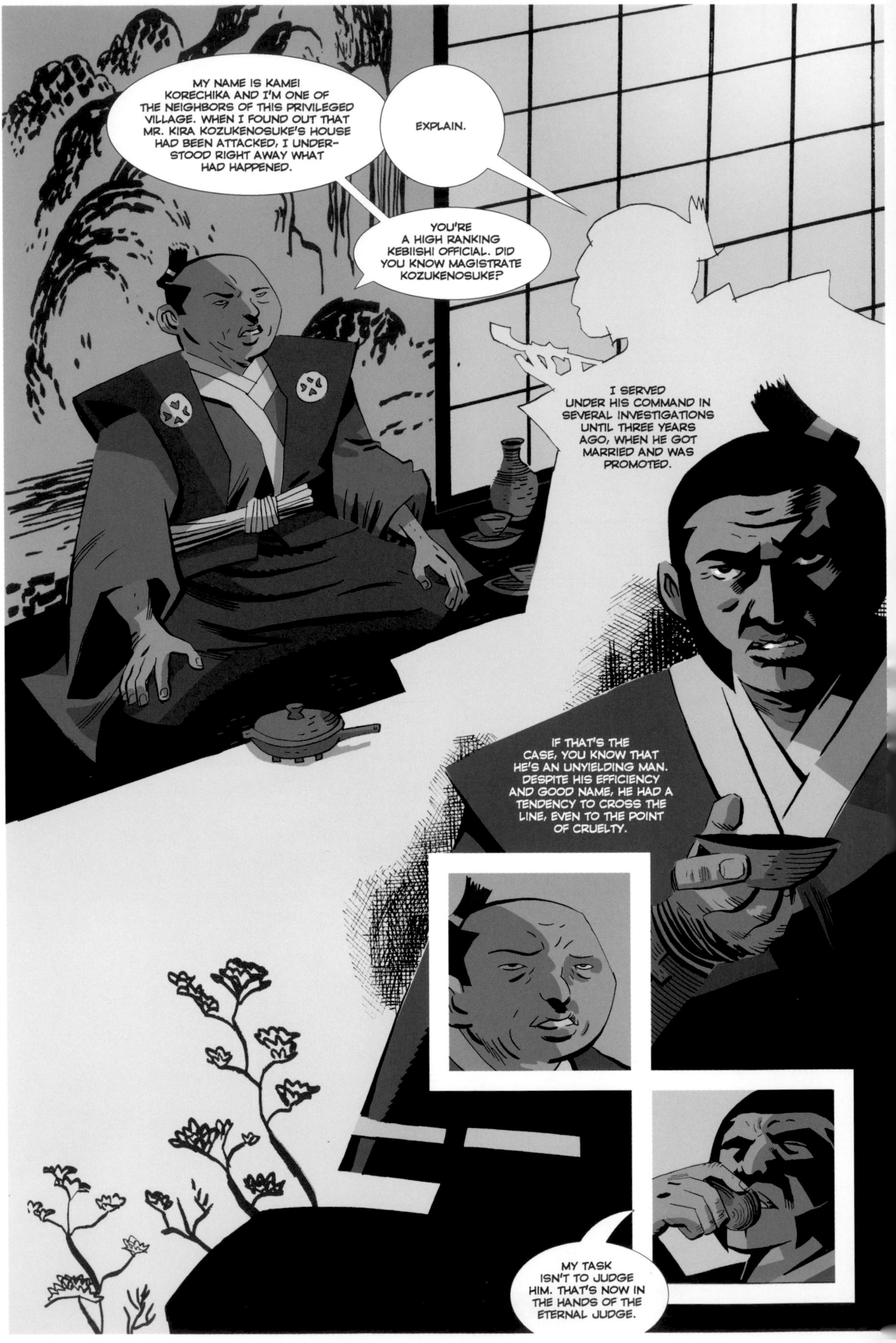
MY NAME IS KAMEI KORECHIKA AND I'M ONE OF THE NEIGHBORS OF THIS PRIVILEGED VILLAGE. WHEN I FOUND OUT THAT MR. KIRA KOZUKENOSUKE'S HOUSE HAD BEEN ATTACKED, I UNDERSTOOD RIGHT AWAY WHAT HAD HAPPENED.
EXPLAIN.
YOU'RE A HIGH RANKING KEBIISHI OFFICIAL. DID YOU KNOW MAGISTRATE KOZUKENOSUKE?
I SERVED UNDER HIS COMMAND IN SEVERAL INVESTIGATIONS UNTIL THREE YEARS AGO, WHEN HE GOT MARRIED AND WAS PROMOTED.
IF THAT'S THE CASE, YOU KNOW THAT HE'S AN UNYIELDING MAN. DESPITE HIS EFFICIENCY AND GOOD NAME, HE HAD A TENDENCY TO CROSS THE LINE, EVEN TO THE POINT OF CRUELTY.
MY TASK ISN'T TO JUDGE HIM. THAT'S NOW IN THE HANDS OF THE ETERNAL JUDGE.

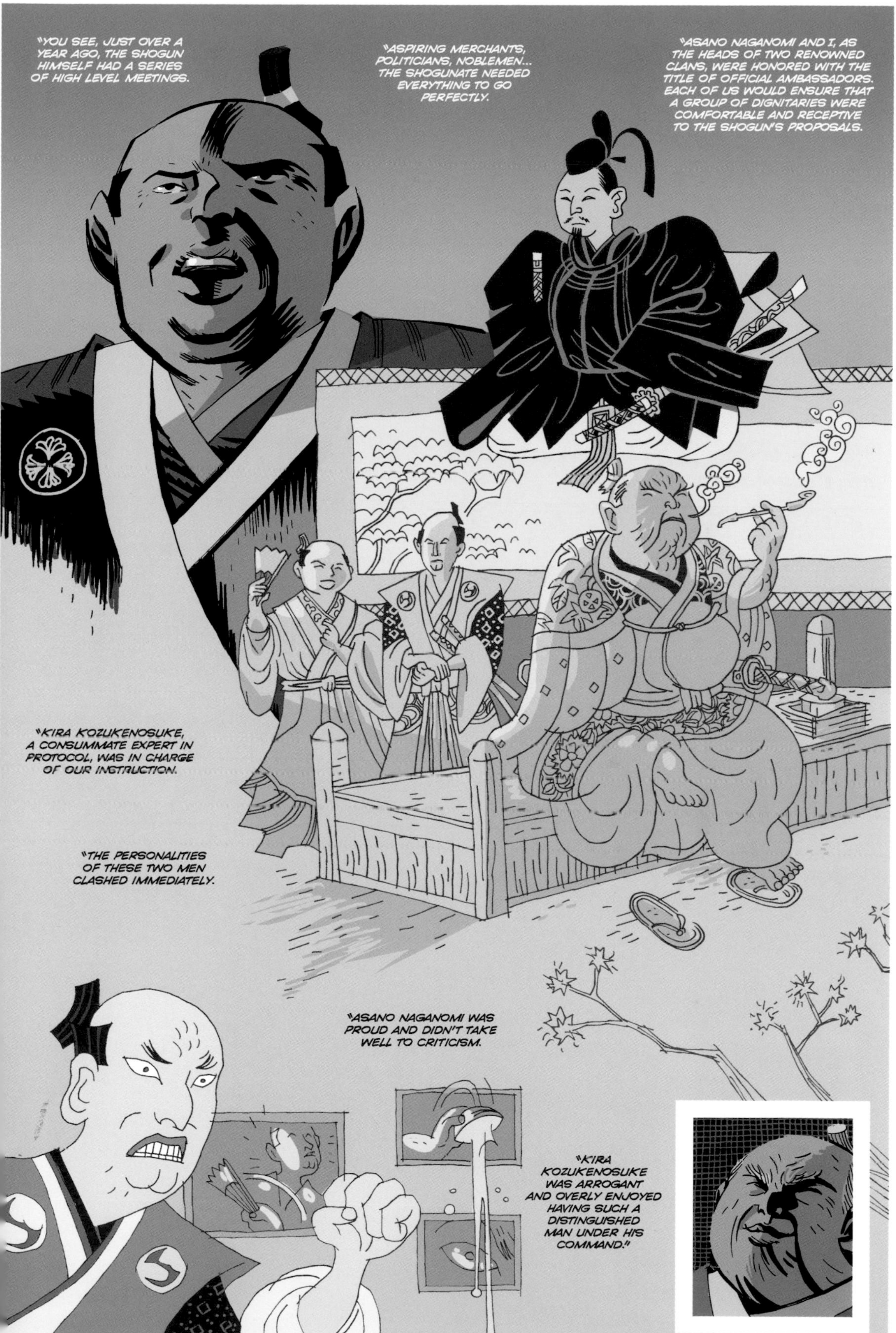
"YOU SEE, JUST OVER A YEAR AGO, THE SHOGUN HIMSELF HAD A SERIES OF HIGH LEVEL MEETINGS.
"ASPIRING MERCHANTS, POLITICIANS, NOBLEMEN... THE SHOGUNATE NEEDED EVERYTHING TO GO PERFECTLY.
"ASANO NAGANOMI AND I, AS THE HEADS OF TWO RENOWNED CLANS, WERE HONORED WITH THE TITLE OF OFFICIAL AMBASSADORS. EACH OF US WOULD ENSURE THAT A GROUP OF DIGNITARIES WERE COMFORTABLE AND RECEPTIVE TO THE SHOGUN'S PROPOSALS.
"KIRA KOZUKENOSUKE, A CONSUMMATE EXPERT IN PROTOCOL, WAS IN CHARGE OF OUR INSTRUCTION.
"THE PERSONALITIES OF THESE TWO MEN CLASHED IMMEDIATELY.
"ASANO NAGANOMI WAS PROUD AND DIDN'T TAKE WELL TO CRITICISM.
"KIRA KOZUKENOSUKE WAS ARROGANT AND OVERLY ENJOYED HAVING SUCH A DISTINGUISHED MAN UNDER HIS COMMAND."

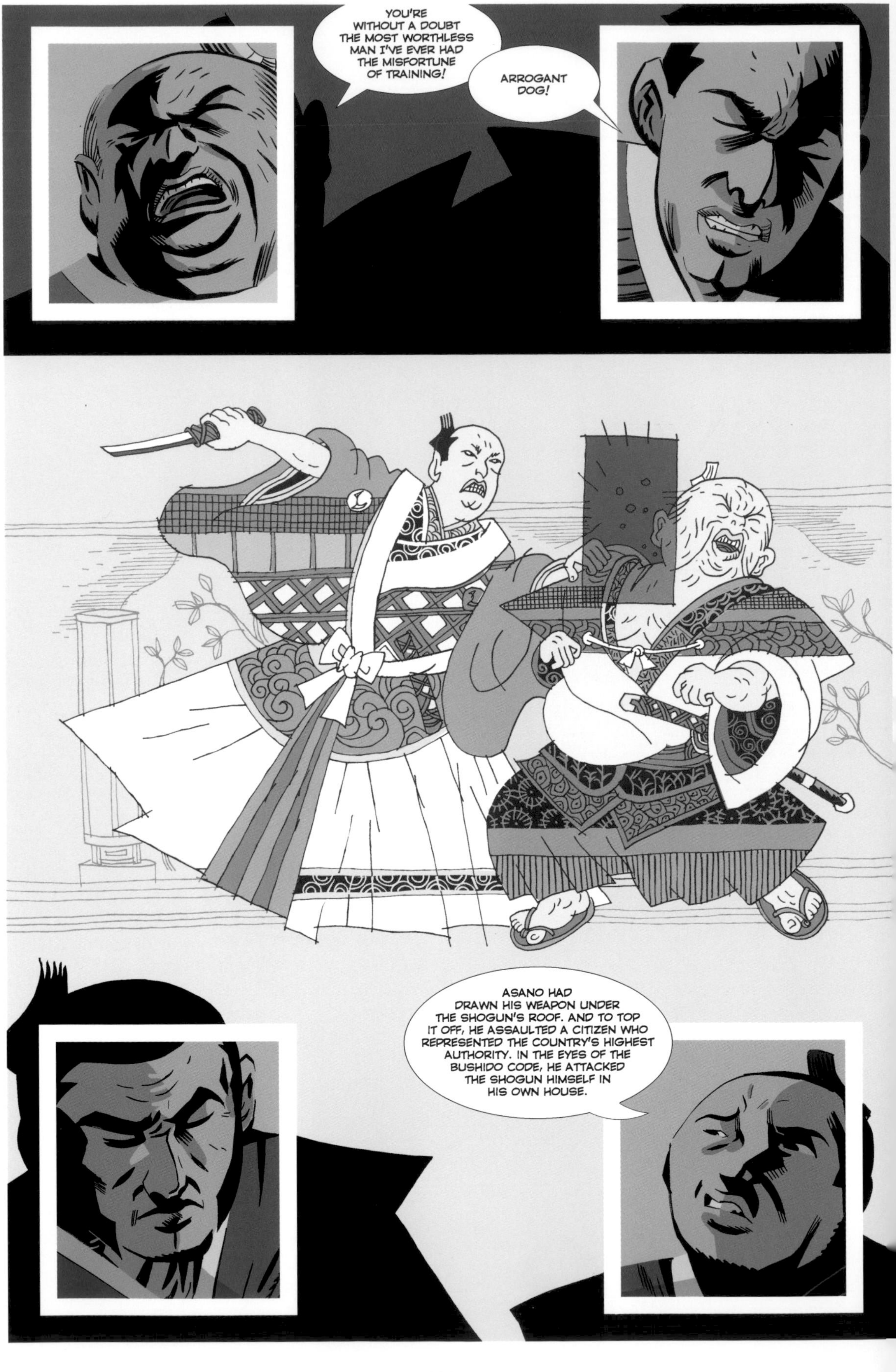
YOU'RE WITHOUT A DOUBT THE MOST WORTHLESS MAN I'VE EVER HAD THE MISFORTUNE OF TRAINING!
ARROGANT DOG!
ASANO HAD DRAWN HIS WEAPON UNDER THE SHOGUN'S ROOF. AND TO TOP IT OFF, HE ASSAULTED A CITIZEN WHO REPRESENTED THE COUNTRY'S HIGHEST AUTHORITY. IN THE EYES OF THE BUSHIDO CODE, HE ATTACKED THE SHOGUN HIMSELF IN HIS OWN HOUSE.

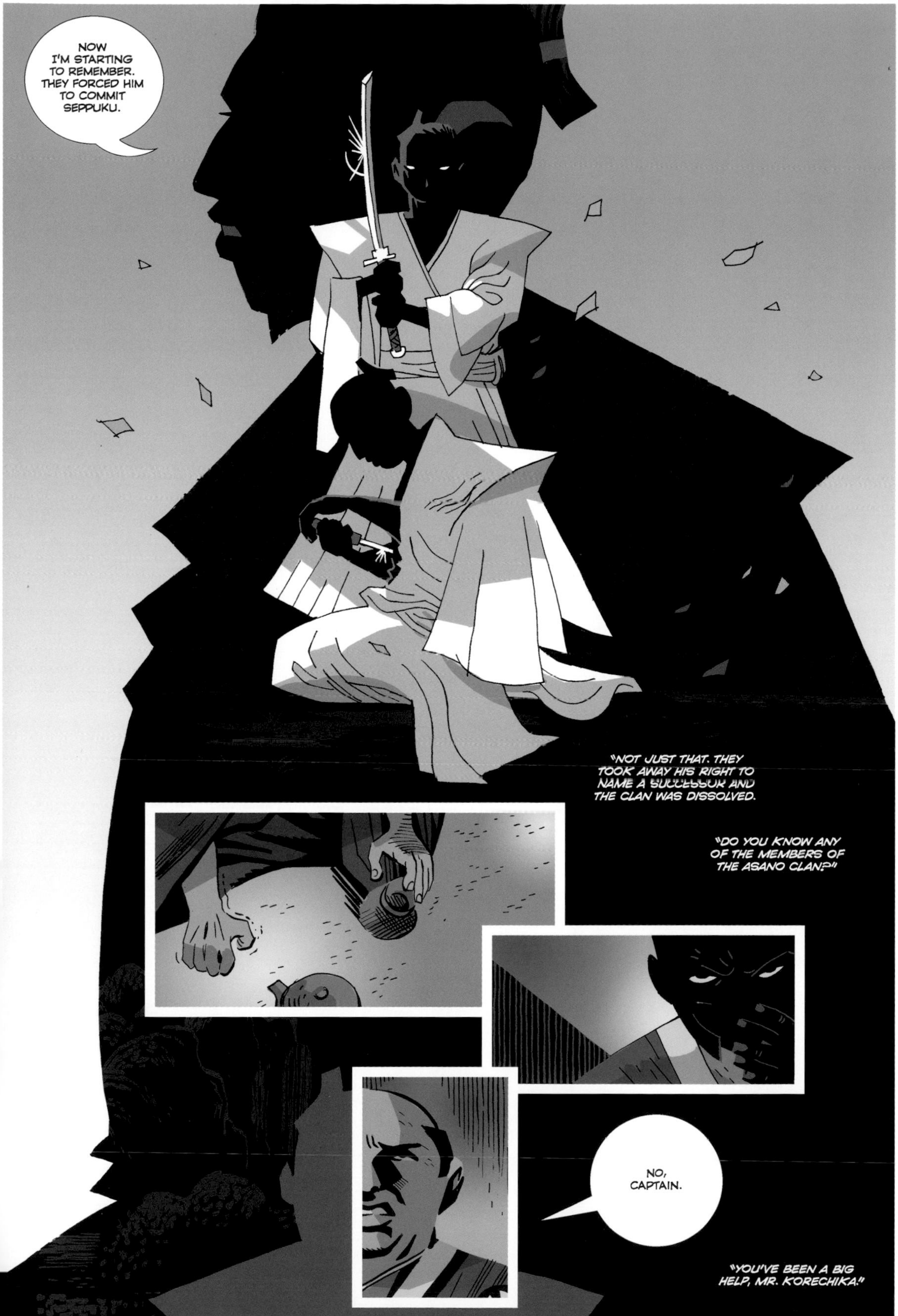
NOW I'M STARTING TO REMEMBER. THEY FORCED HIM TO COMMIT SEPPUKU.
"NOT JUST THAT. THEY TOOK AWAY HIS RIGHT TO NAME A SUCCESSOR AND THE CLAN WAS DISSOLVED.
"DO YOU KNOW ANY OF THE MEMBERS OF THE ASANO CLAN?"
NO, CAPTAIN.
"YOU'VE BEEN A BIG HELP, MR. KORECHIKA."

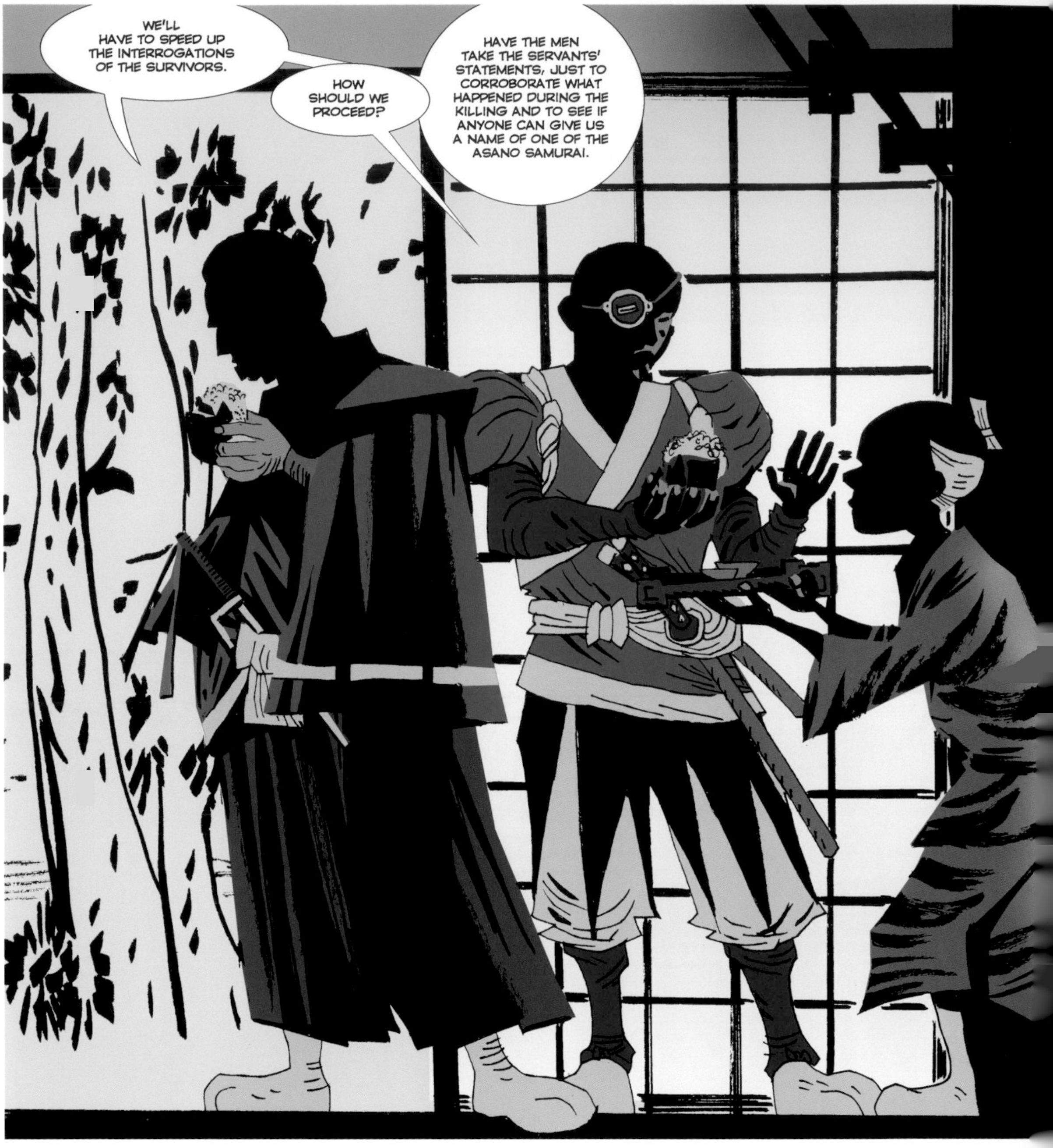
WE'LL HAVE TO SPEED UP THE INTERROGATIONS OF THE SURVIVORS.
HOW SHOULD WE PROCEED?
HAVE THE MEN TAKE THE SERVANTS' STATEMENTS, JUST TO CORROBORATE WHAT HAPPENED DURING THE KILLING AND TO SEE IF ANYONE CAN GIVE US A NAME OF ONE OF THE ASANO SAMURAI.

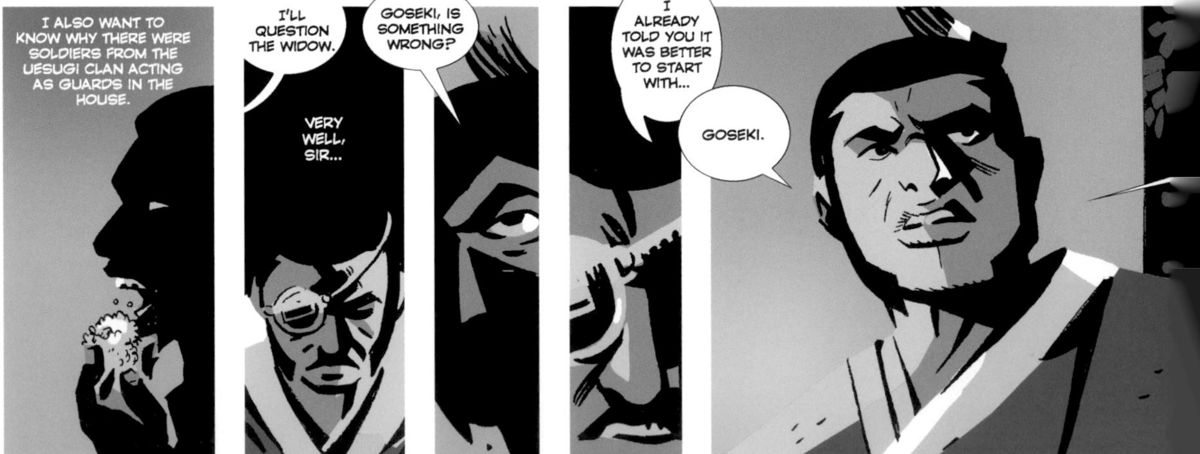
I ALSO WANT TO KNOW WHY THERE WERE SOLDIERS FROM THE UESUGI CLAN ACTING AS GUARDS IN THE HOUSE.
I'LL QUESTION THE WIDOW.
VERY WELL, SIR...
GOSEKI, IS SOMETHING WRONG?
I ALREADY TOLD YOU IT WAS BETTER TO START WITH...
GOSEKI.

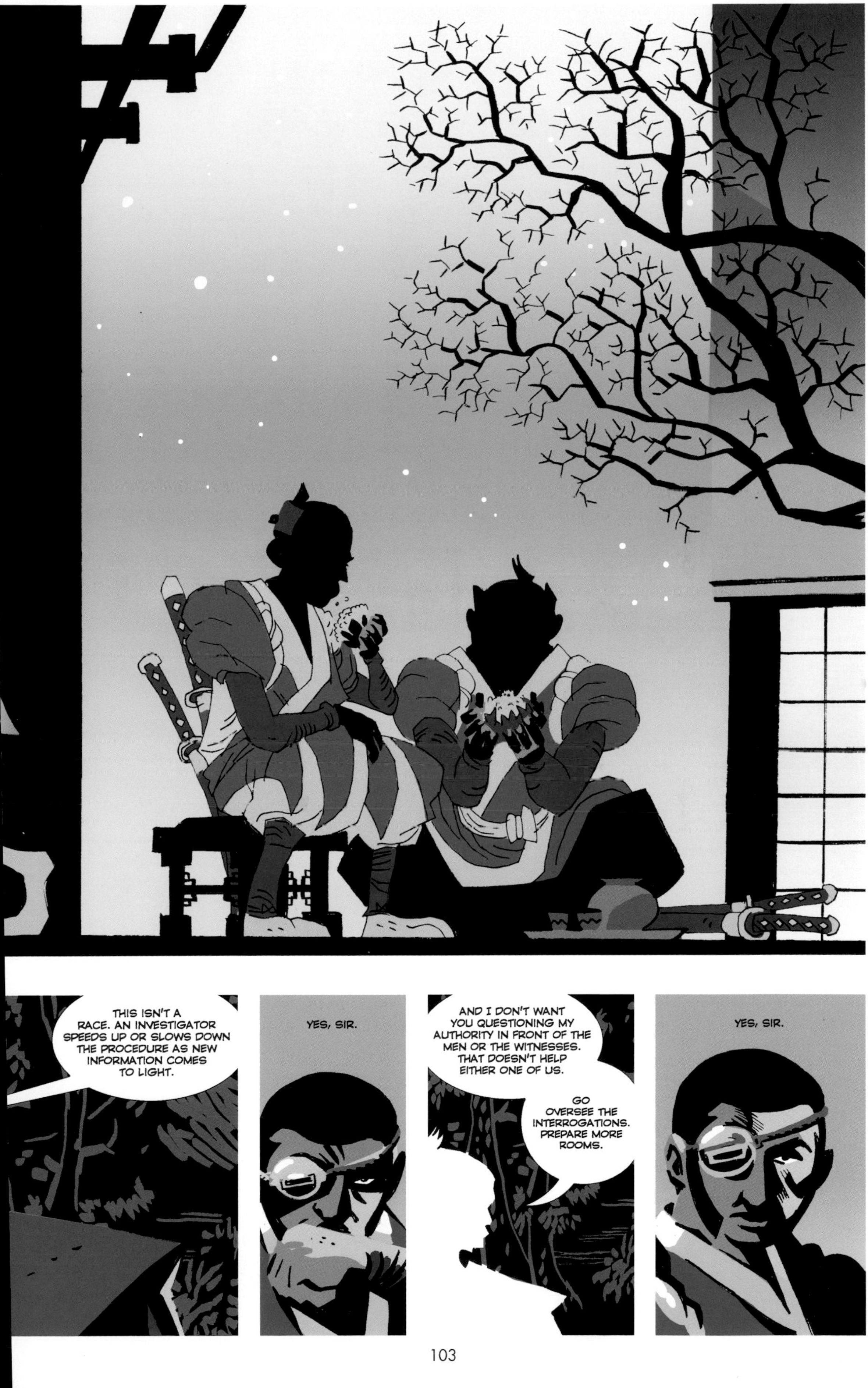
THIS ISN'T A RACE. AN INVESTIGATOR SPEEDS UP OR SLOWS DOWN THE PROCEDURE AS NEW INFORMATION COMES TO LIGHT.
YES, SIR.
AND I DON'T WANT YOU QUESTIONING MY AUTHORITY IN FRONT OF THE MEN OR THE WITNESSES. THAT DOESN'T HELP EITHER ONE OF US.
GO OVERSEE THE INTERROGATIONS. PREPARE MORE ROOMS.
YES, SIR.

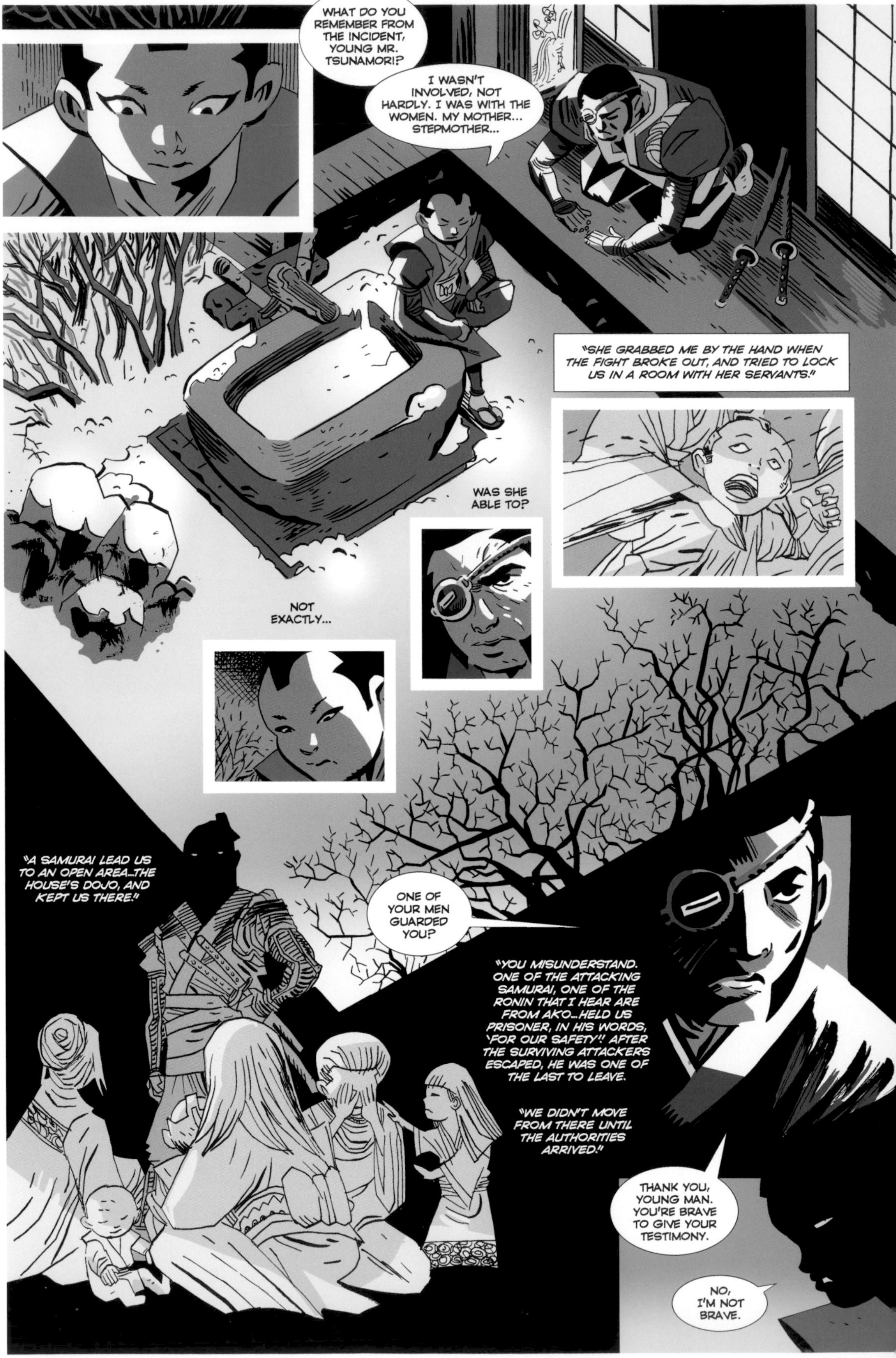
WHAT DO YOU REMEMBER FROM THE INCIDENT, YOUNG MR. TSUNAMORI?
I WASN'T HARDLY INVOLVED, NOT HARDLY. I WAS WITH THE WOMEN. MY MOTHER... STEPMOTHER...
"SHE GRABBED ME BY THE HAND WHEN THE FIGHT BROKE OUT, AND TRIED TO LOCK US IN A ROOM WITH HER SERVANTS."
WAS SHE ABLE TO?
NOT EXACTLY...
"A SAMURAI LEAD US TO AN OPEN AREA...THE HOUSE'S DOJO, AND KEPT US THERE."
ONE OF YOUR MEN GUARDED YOU?
"YOU MISUNDERSTAND. ONE OF THE ATTACKING SAMURAI, ONE OF THE RONIN THAT I HEAR ARE FROM AKO...HELD US PRISONER, IN HIS WORDS, 'FOR OUR SAFETY'! AFTER THE SURVIVING ATTACKERS ESCAPED, HE WAS ONE OF THE LAST TO LEAVE.
"WE DIDN'T MOVE FROM THERE UNTIL THE AUTHORITIES ARRIVED."
THANK YOU, YOUNG MAN. YOU'RE BRAVE TO GIVE YOUR TESTIMONY.
NO, I'M NOT BRAVE.

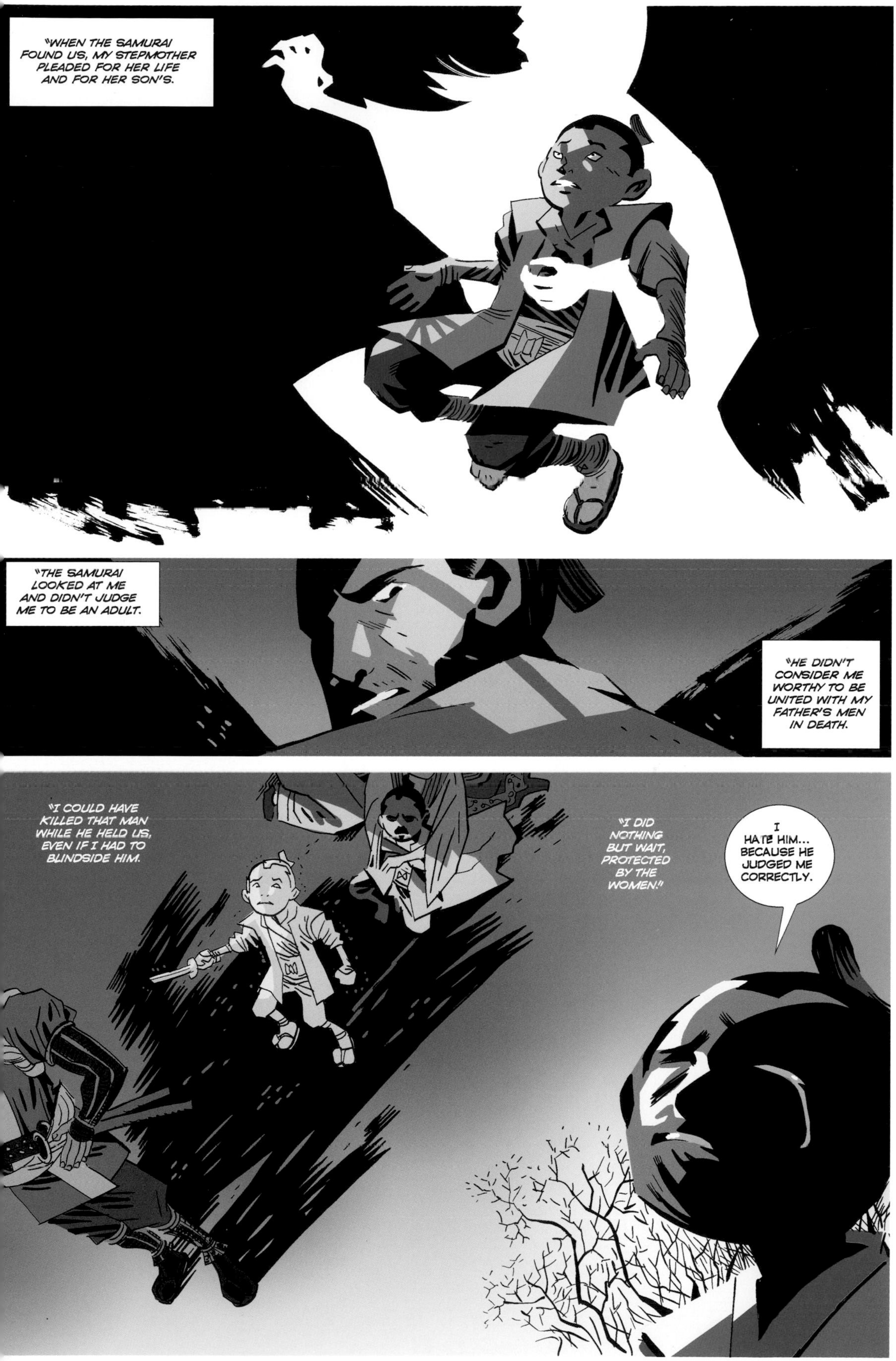
"WHEN THE SAMURAI FOUND US, MY STEPMOTHER PLEADED FOR HER LIFE AND FOR HER SON'S.
"THE SAMURAI LOOKED AT ME AND DIDN'T JUDGE ME TO BE AN ADULT.
"HE DIDN'T CONSIDER ME WORTHY TO BE UNITED WITH MY FATHER'S MEN IN DEATH.
"I COULD HAVE KILLED THAT MAN WHILE HE HELD US, EVEN IF I HAD TO BLINDSIDE HIM.
"I DID NOTHING BUT WAIT, PROTECTED BY THE WOMEN."
I HATE HIM... BECAUSE HE JUDGED ME CORRECTLY.

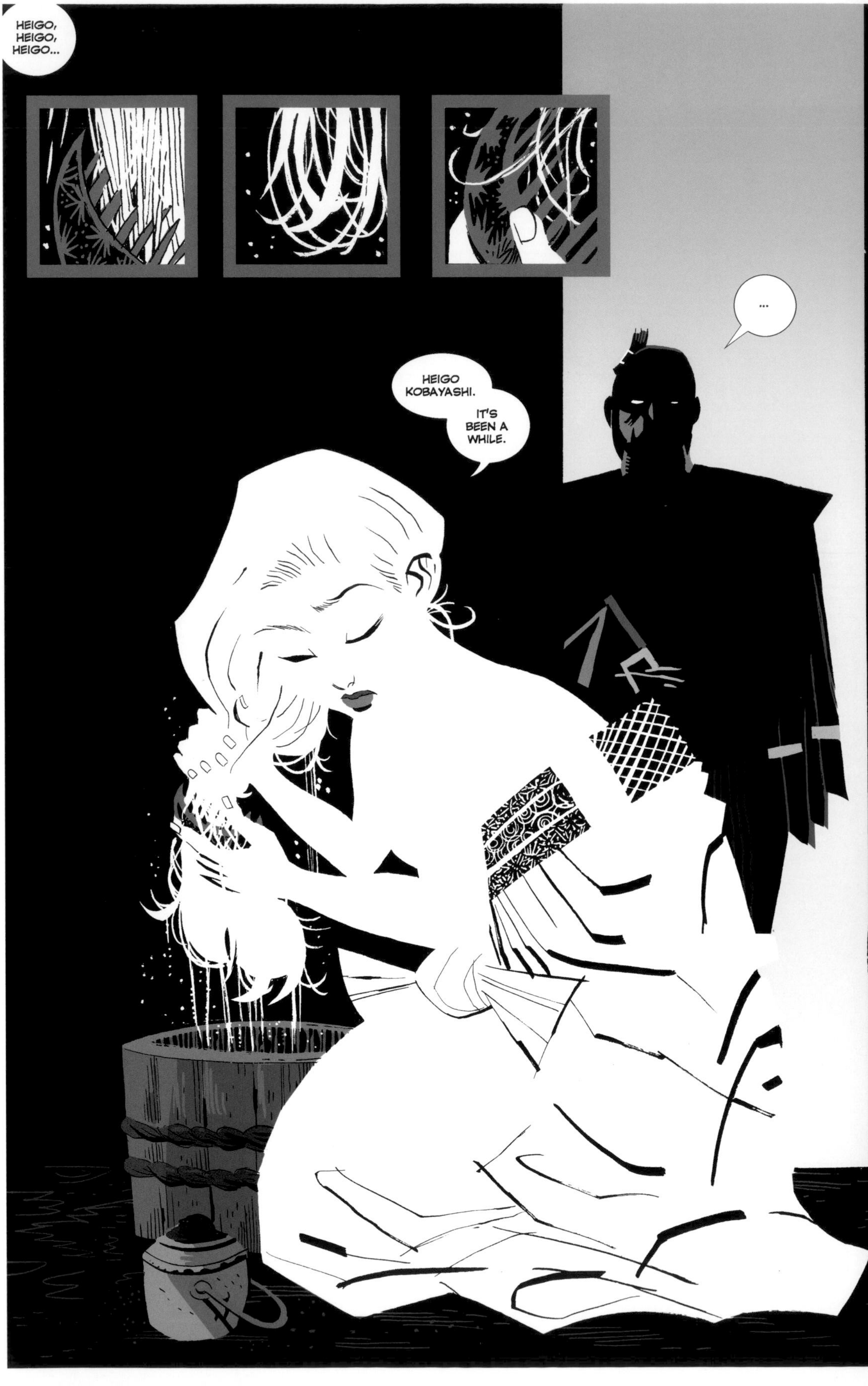
HEIGO, HEIGO, HEIGO...
...
HEIGO KOBAYASHI.
IT'S BEEN A WHILE.

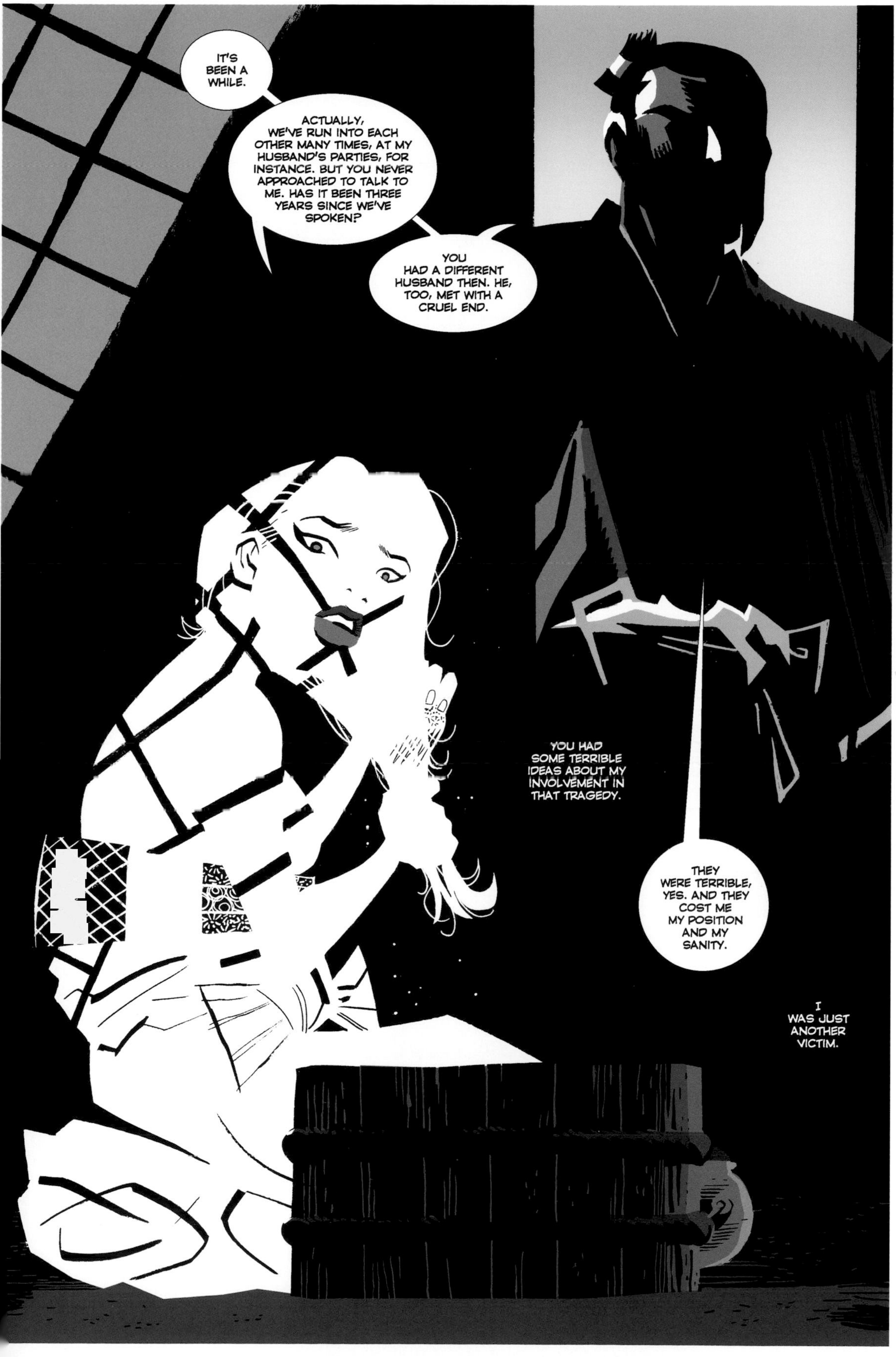
IT'S BEEN A WHILE.
ACTUALLY, WE'VE RUN INTO EACH OTHER MANY TIMES, AT MY HUSBAND'S PARTIES, FOR INSTANCE. BUT YOU NEVER APPROACHED TO TALK TO ME. HAS IT BEEN THREE YEARS SINCE WE'VE SPOKEN?
YOU HAD A DIFFERENT HUSBAND THEN. HE, TOO, MET WITH A CRUEL END.
YOU HAD SOME TERRIBLE IDEAS ABOUT MY INVOLVEMENT IN THAT TRAGEDY.
THEY WERE TERRIBLE, YES. AND THEY COST ME MY POSITION AND MY SANITY.
I WAS JUST ANOTHER VICTIM.

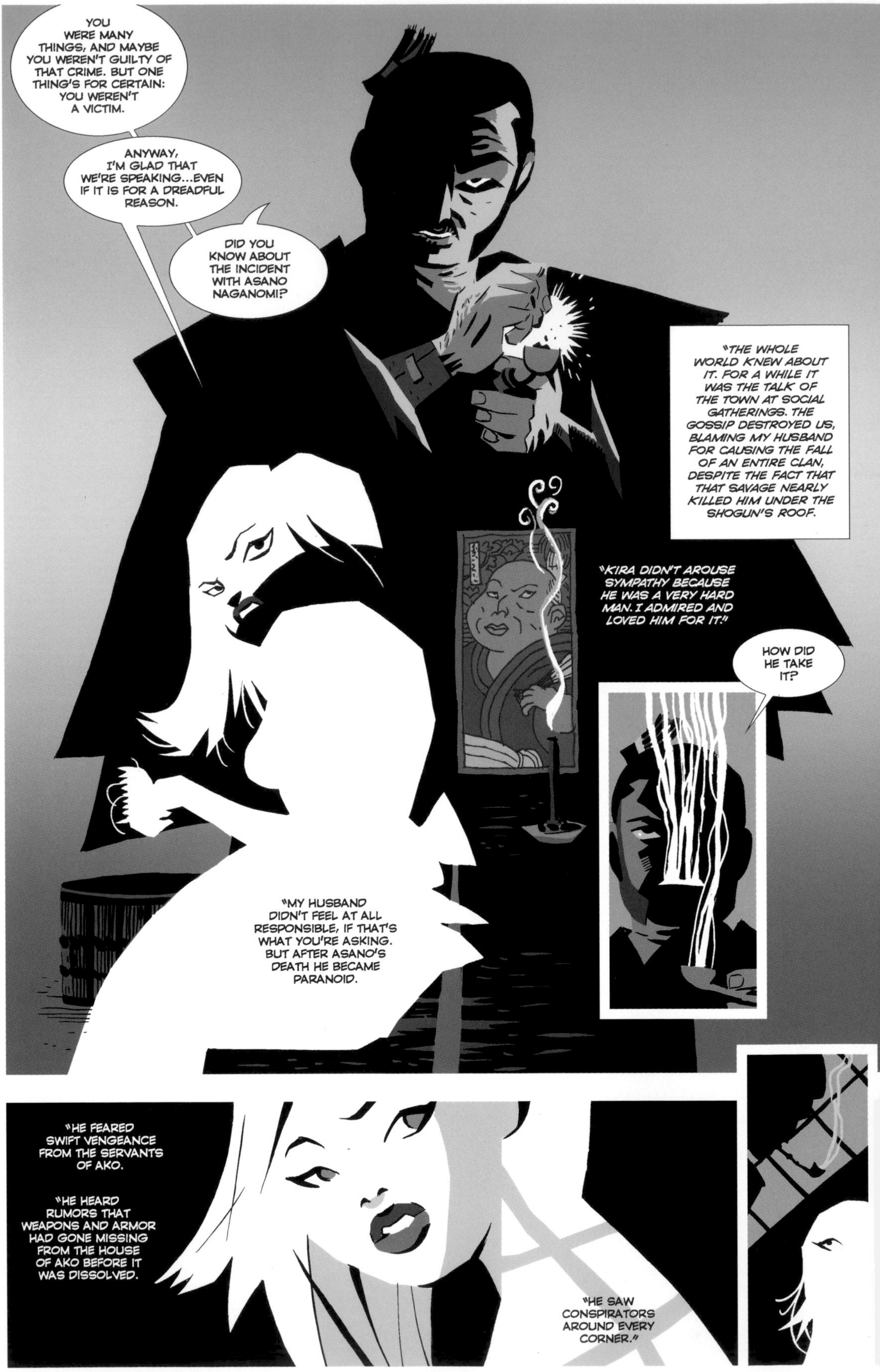

YOU WERE MANY THINGS, AND MAYBE YOU WEREN'T GUILTY OF THAT CRIME. BUT ONE THING'S FOR CERTAIN: YOU WEREN'T A VICTIM.
ANYWAY, I'M GLAD THAT WE'RE SPEAKING...EVEN IF IT IS FOR A DREADFUL REASON.
DID YOU KNOW ABOUT THE INCIDENT WITH ASANO NAGANOMI?
"THE WHOLE WORLD KNEW ABOUT IT. FOR A WHILE IT WAS THE TALK OF THE TOWN AT SOCIAL GATHERINGS. THE GOSSIP DESTROYED US, BLAMING MY HUSBAND FOR CAUSING THE FALL OF AN ENTIRE CLAN, DESPITE THE FACT THAT THAT SAVAGE NEARLY KILLED HIM UNDER THE SHOGUN'S ROOF.
"KIRA DIDN'T AROUSE SYMPATHY BECAUSE HE WAS A VERY HARD MAN. I ADMIRED AND LOVED HIM FOR IT."
HOW DID HE TAKE IT?
"MY HUSBAND DIDN'T FEEL AT ALL RESPONSIBLE, IF THAT'S WHAT YOU'RE ASKING. BUT AFTER ASANO'S DEATH HE BECAME PARANOID.
"HE FEARED SWIFT VENGEANCE FROM THE SERVANTS OF AKO.
"HE HEARD RUMORS THAT WEAPONS AND ARMOR HAD GONE MISSING FROM THE HOUSE OF AKO BEFORE IT WAS DISSOLVED.
"HE SAW CONSPIRATORS AROUND EVERY CORNER."

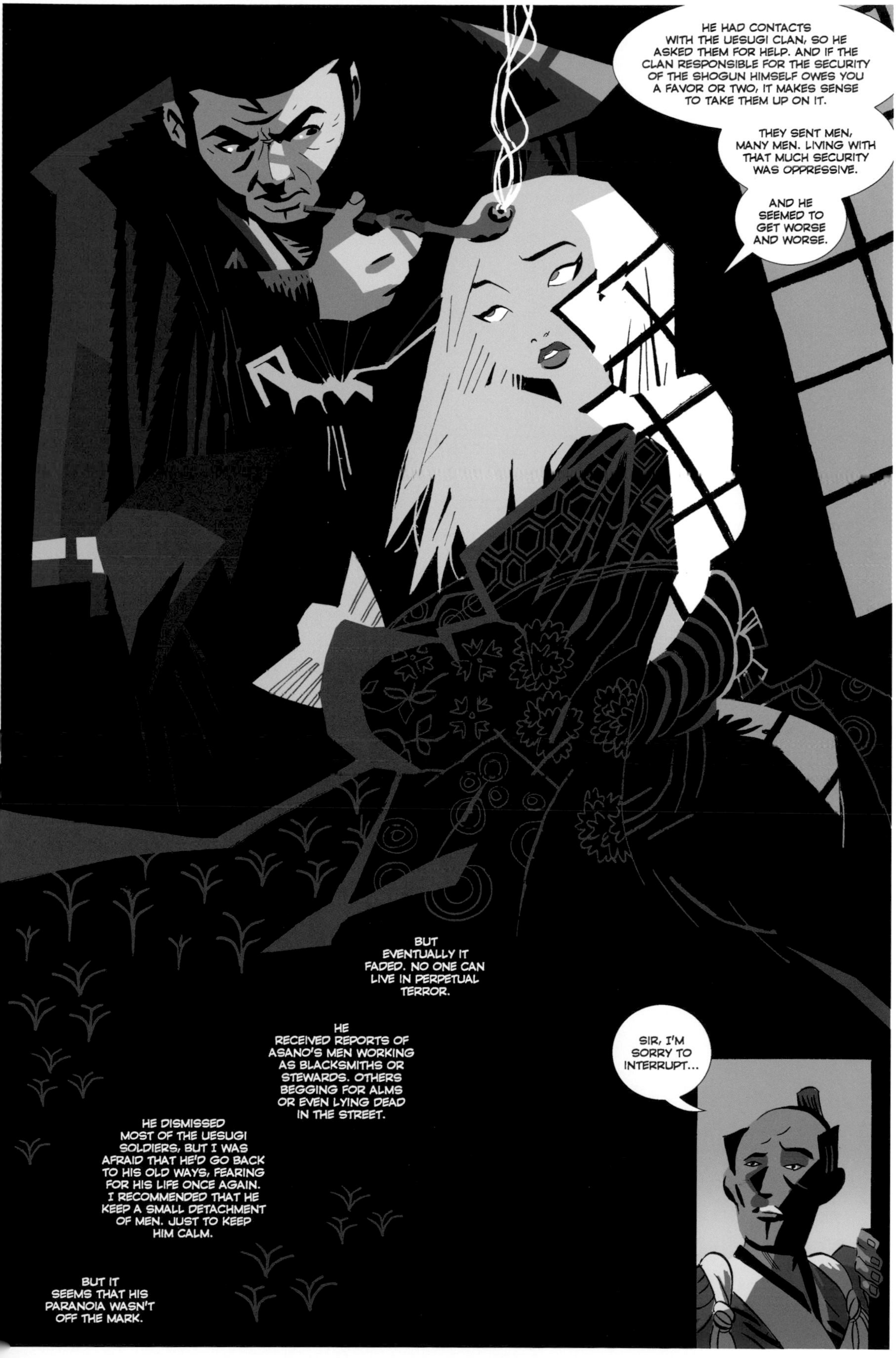

HE HAD CONTACTS WITH THE UESUGI CLAN, SO HE ASKED THEM FOR HELP. AND IF THE CLAN RESPONSIBLE FOR THE SECURITY OF THE SHOGUN HIMSELF OWES YOU A FAVOR OR TWO, IT MAKES SENSE TO TAKE THEM UP ON IT.
THEY SENT MEN, MANY MEN. LIVING WITH THAT MUCH SECURITY WAS OPPRESSIVE.
AND HE SEEMED TO GET WORSE AND WORSE.
BUT EVENTUALLY IT FADED. NO ONE CAN LIVE IN PERPETUAL TERROR.
HE RECEIVED REPORTS OF ASANO'S MEN WORKING AS BLACKSMITHS OR STEWARDS. OTHERS BEGGING FOR ALMS OR EVEN LYING DEAD IN THE STREET.
HE DISMISSED MOST OF THE UESUGI SOLDIERS, BUT I WAS AFRAID THAT HE'D GO BACK TO HIS OLD WAYS, FEARING FOR HIS LIFE ONCE AGAIN. I RECOMMENDED THAT HE KEEP A SMALL DETACHMENT OF MEN. JUST TO KEEP HIM CALM.
BUT IT SEEMS THAT HIS PARANOIA WASN'T OFF THE MARK.
SIR, I'M SORRY TO INTERRUPT...

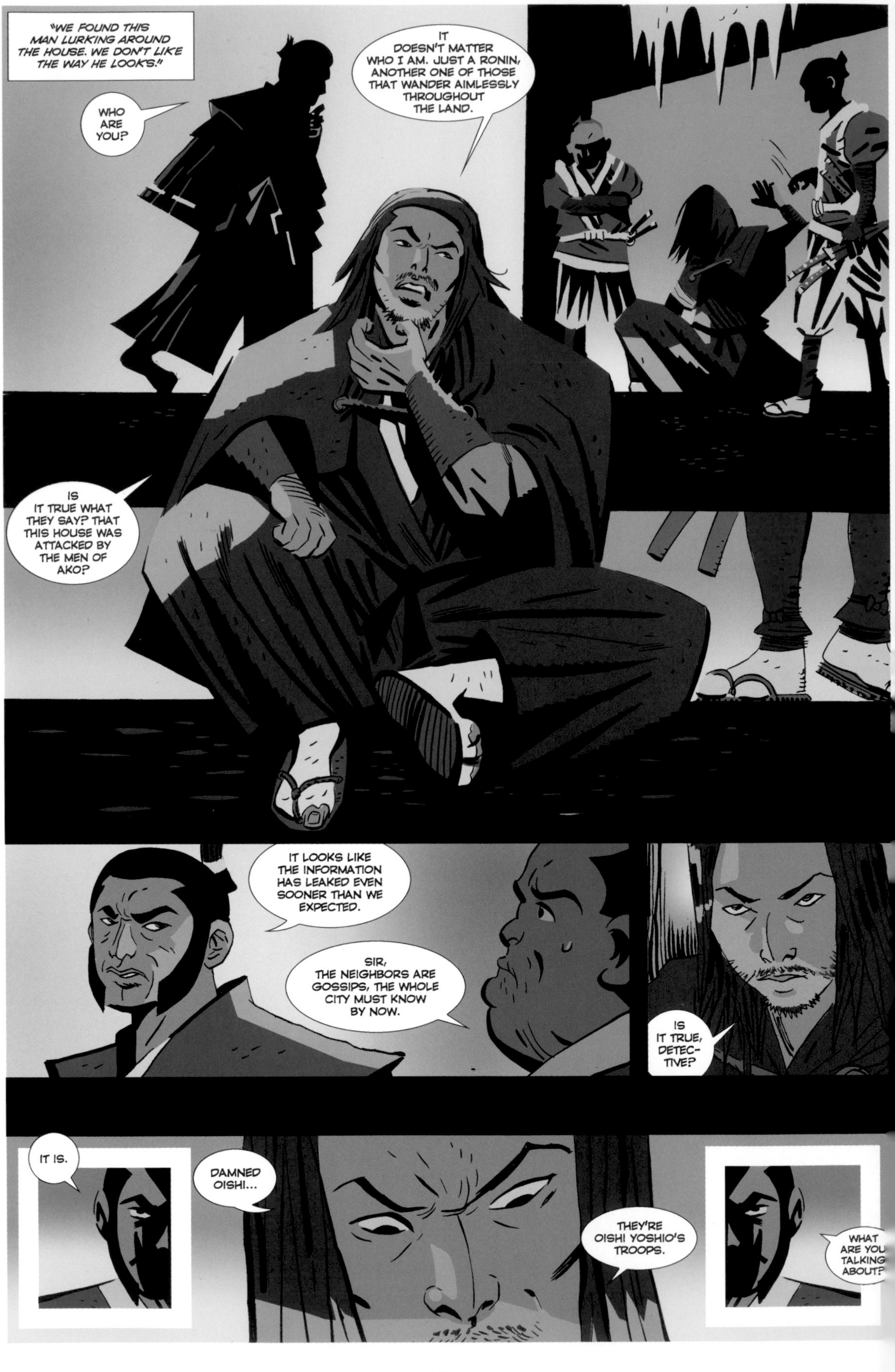
"WE FOUND THIS MAN LURKING AROUND THE HOUSE. WE DON'T LIKE THE WAY HE LOOKS."
WHO ARE YOU?
IT DOESN'T MATTER WHO I AM. JUST A RONIN, ANOTHER ONE OF THOSE THAT WANDER AIMLESSLY THROUGHOUT THE LAND.
IS IT TRUE WHAT THEY SAY? THAT THIS HOUSE WAS ATTACKED BY THE MEN OF AKO?
IT LOOKS LIKE THE INFORMATION HAS LEAKED EVEN SOONER THAN WE EXPECTED.
SIR, THE NEIGHBORS ARE GOSSIPS, THE WHOLE CITY MUST KNOW BY NOW.
IS IT TRUE, DETEC-TIVE?
IT IS.
DAMNED OISHI...
THEY'RE OISHI YOSHIO'S TROOPS.
WHAT ARE YOU TALKING ABOUT?

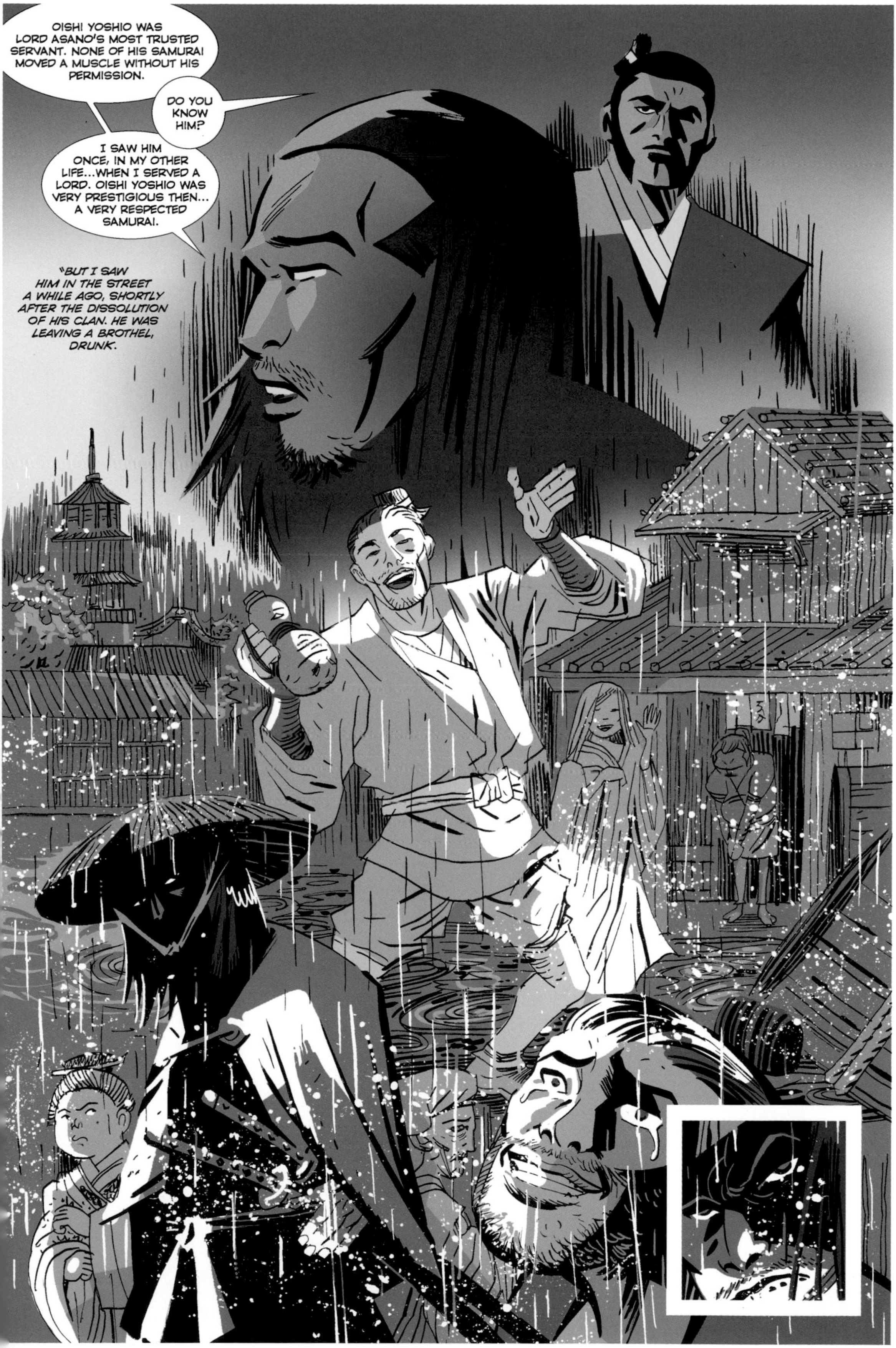
OISHI YOSHIO WAS LORD ASANO'S MOST TRUSTED SERVANT. NONE OF HIS SAMURAI MOVED A MUSCLE WITHOUT HIS PERMISSION.
DO YOU KNOW HIM?
I SAW HIM ONCE, IN MY OTHER LIFE...WHEN I SERVED A LORD. OISHI YOSHIO WAS VERY PRESTIGIOUS THEN... A VERY RESPECTED SAMURAI.
"BUT I SAW HIM IN THE STREET A WHILE AGO, SHORTLY AFTER THE DISSOLUTION OF HIS CLAN. HE WAS LEAVING A BROTHEL, DRUNK.

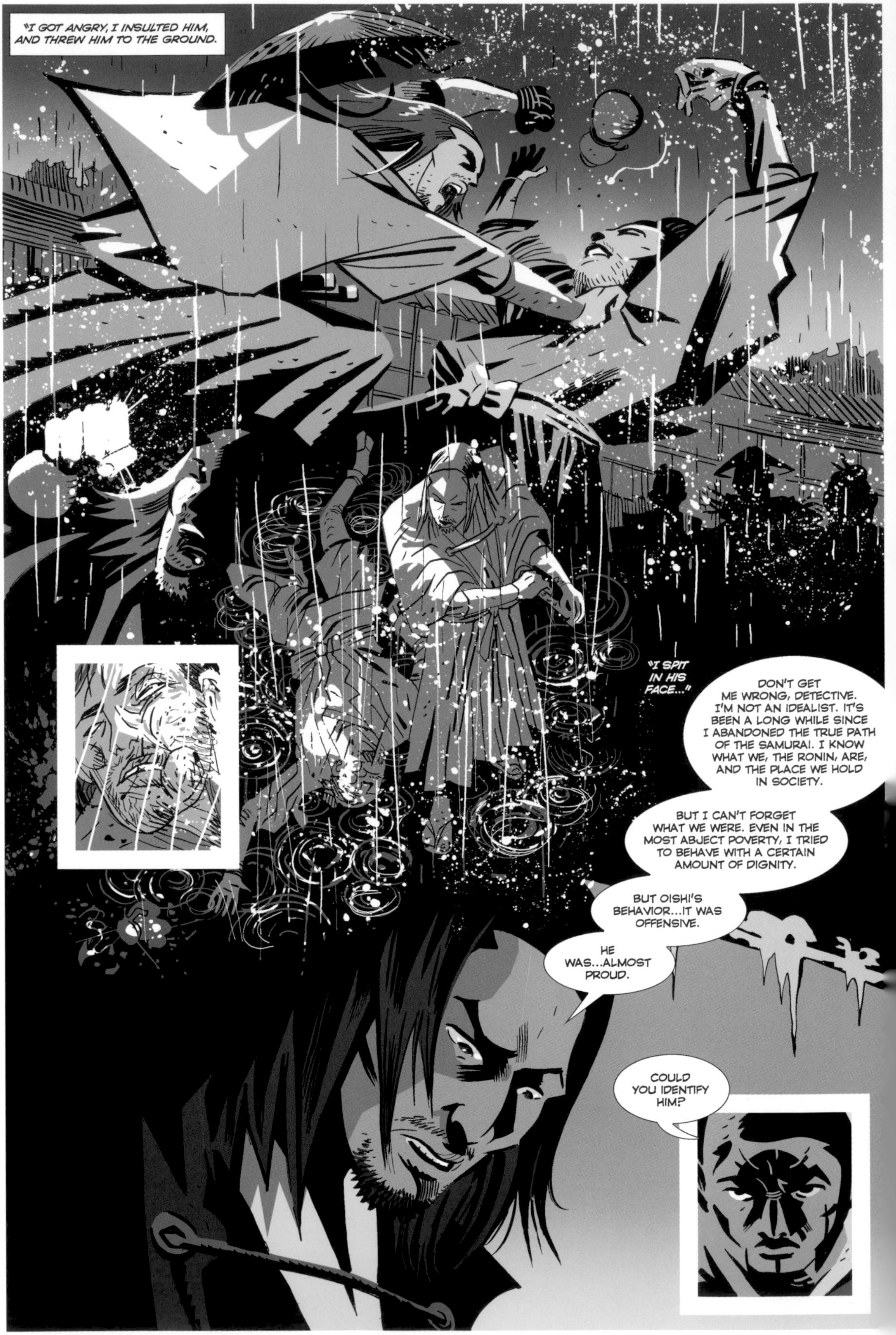
"I GOT ANGRY, I INSULTED HIM, AND THREW HIM TO THE GROUND.
"I SPIT IN HIS FACE..."
DON'T GET ME WRONG, DETECTIVE. I'M NOT AN IDEALIST. IT'S BEEN A LONG WHILE SINCE I ABANDONED THE TRUE PATH OF THE SAMURAI. I KNOW WHAT WE, THE RONIN, ARE, AND THE PLACE WE HOLD IN SOCIETY.
BUT I CAN'T FORGET WHAT WE WERE. EVEN IN THE MOST ABJECT POVERTY, I TRIED TO BEHAVE WITH A CERTAIN AMOUNT OF DIGNITY.
BUT OISHI'S BEHAVIOR...IT WAS OFFENSIVE.
HE WAS...ALMOST PROUD.
COULD YOU IDENTIFY HIM?

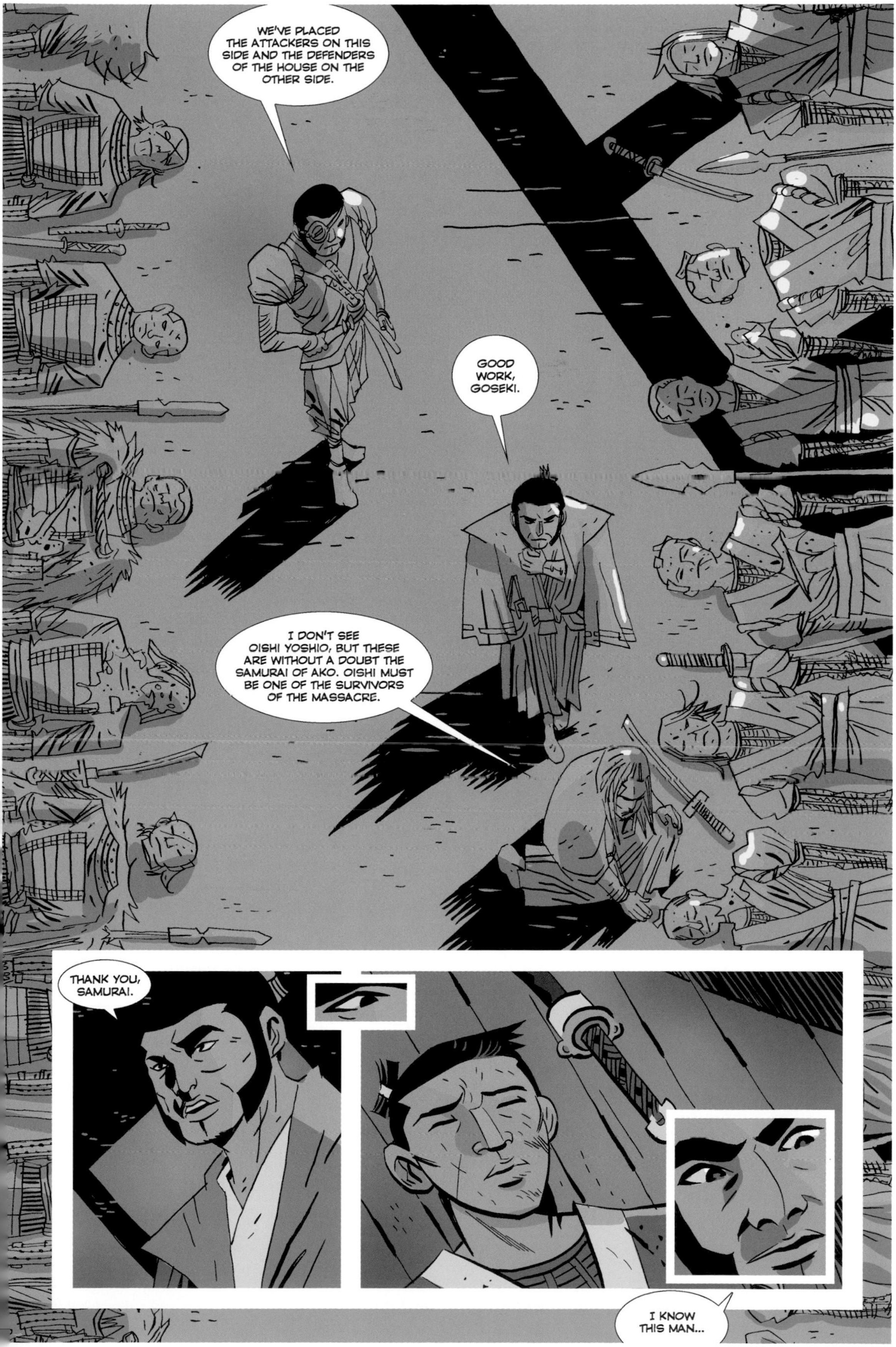
WE'VE PLACED THE ATTACKERS ON THIS SIDE AND THE DEFENDERS OF THE HOUSE ON THE OTHER SIDE.
GOOD WORK, GOSEKI.
I DON'T SEE OISHI YOSHIO, BUT THESE ARE WITHOUT A DOUBT THE SAMURAI OF AKO. OISHI MUST BE ONE OF THE SURVIVORS OF THE MASSACRE.
THANK YOU, SAMURAI.
I KNOW THIS MAN...

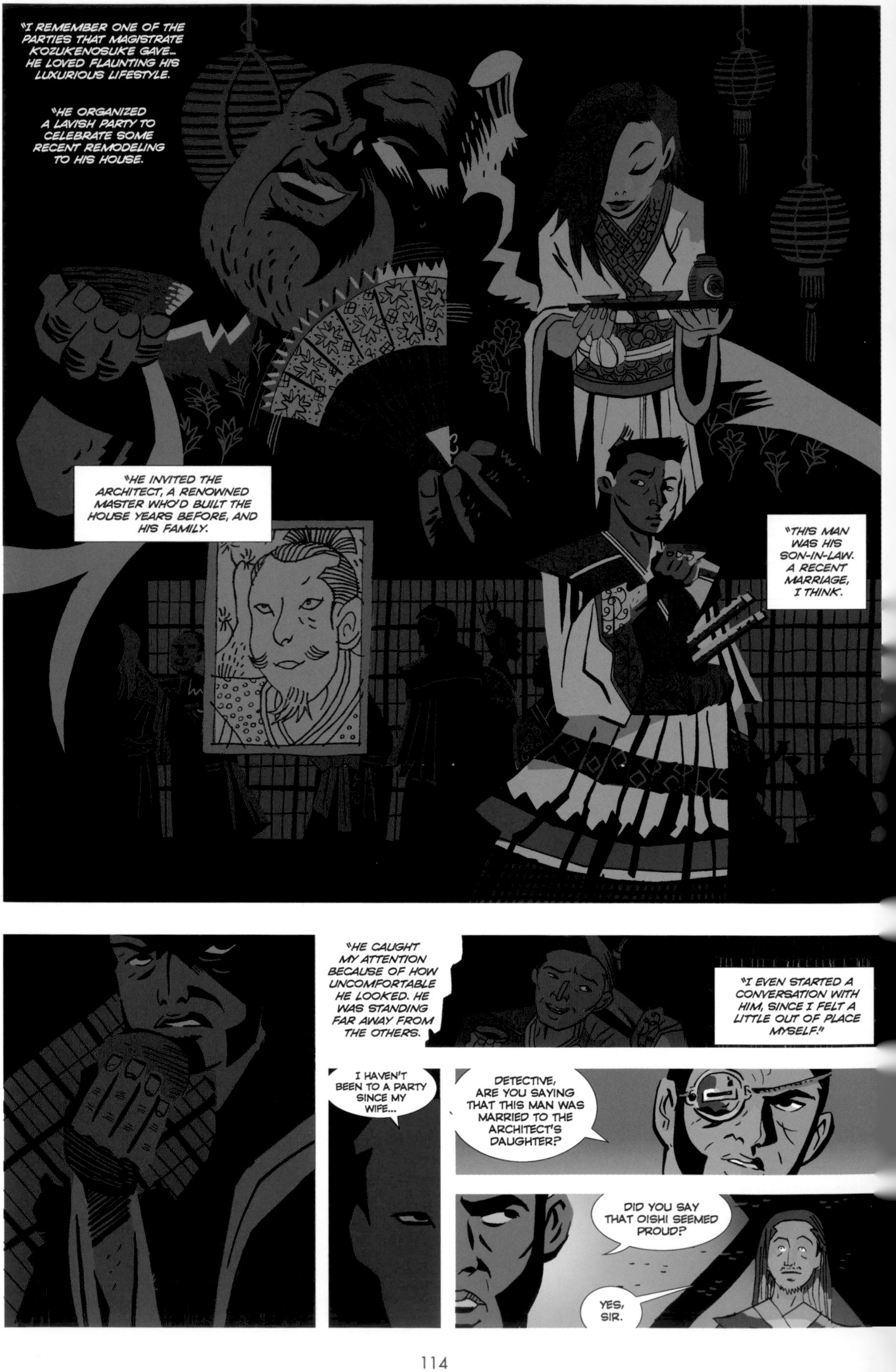
"I REMEMBER ONE OF THE PARTIES THAT MAGISTRATE KOZUKENOSUKE GAVE... HE LOVED FLAUNTING HIS LUXURIOUS LIFESTYLE.
"HE ORGANIZED A LAVISH PARTY TO CELEBRATE SOME RECENT REMODELING TO HIS HOUSE.
"HE INVITED THE ARCHITECT, A RENOWNED MASTER WHO'D BUILT THE HOUSE YEARS BEFORE, AND HIS FAMILY.
"THIS MAN WAS HIS SON-IN-LAW. A RECENT MARRIAGE, I THINK.
"HE CAUGHT MY ATTENTION BECAUSE OF HOW UNCOMFORTABLE HE LOOKED. HE WAS STANDING FAR AWAY FROM THE OTHERS.
"I EVEN STARTED A CONVERSATION WITH HIM, SINCE I FELT A LITTLE OUT OF PLACE MYSELF."
I HAVEN'T BEEN TO A PARTY SINCE MY WIFE...
DETECTIVE, ARE YOU SAYING THAT THIS MAN WAS MARRIED TO THE ARCHITECT'S DAUGHTER?
DID YOU SAY THAT OISHI SEEMED PROUD?
YES, SIR.

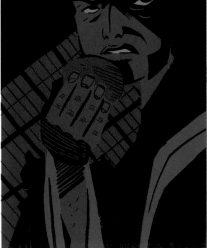

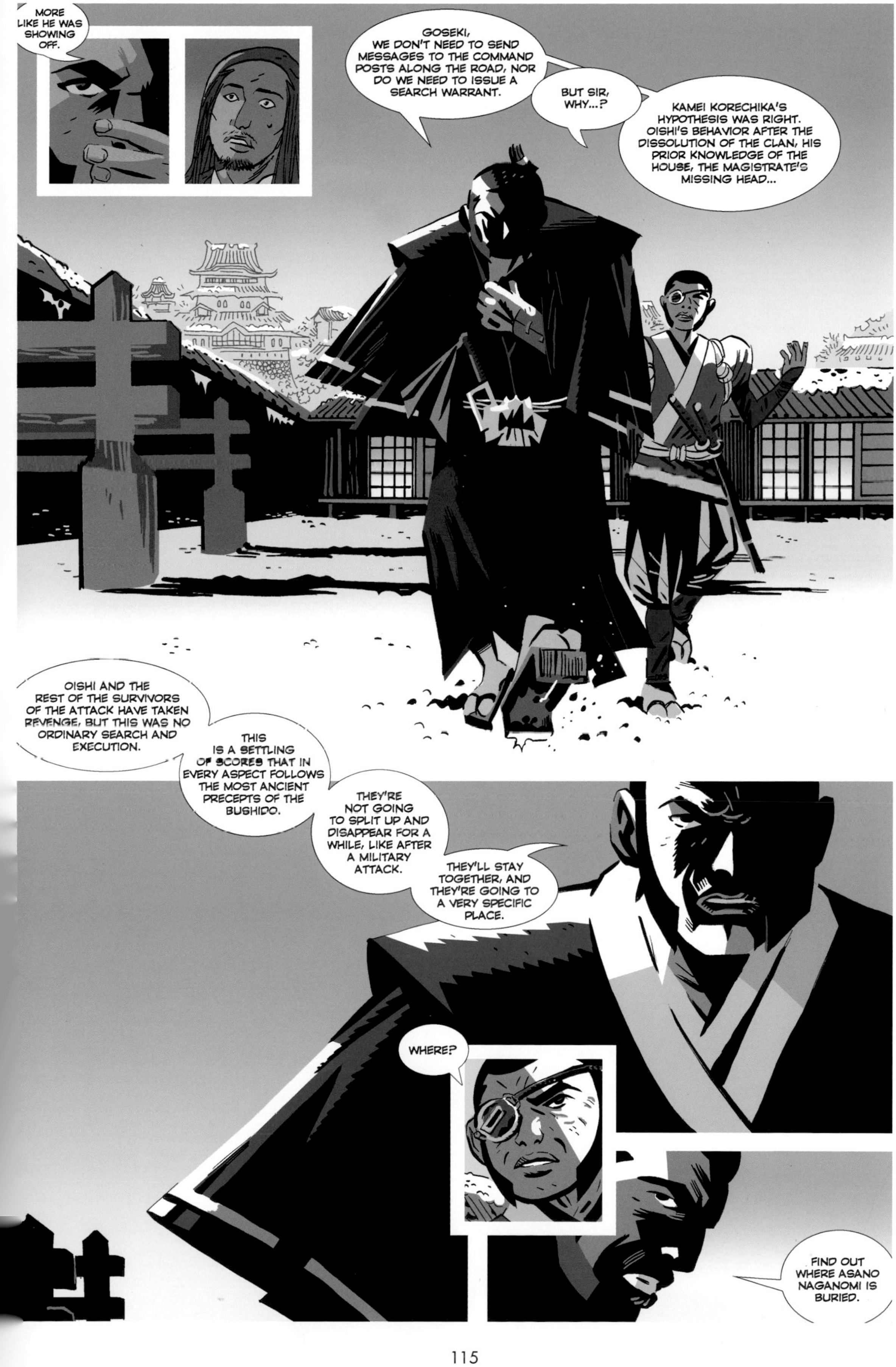
MORE LIKE HE WAS SHOWING OFF.
GOSEKI, WE DON'T NEED TO SEND MESSAGES TO THE COMMAND POSTS ALONG THE ROAD, NOR DO WE NEED TO ISSUE A SEARCH WARRANT.
BUT SIR, WHY...?
KAMEI KORECHIKA'S HYPOTHESIS WAS RIGHT. OISHI'S BEHAVIOR AFTER THE DISSOLUTION OF THE CLAN, HIS PRIOR KNOWLEDGE OF THE HOUSE, THE MAGISTRATE'S MISSING HEAD...
OISHI AND THE REST OF THE SURVIVORS OF THE ATTACK HAVE TAKEN REVENGE, BUT THIS WAS NO ORDINARY SEARCH AND EXECUTION.
THIS IS A SETTLING OF SCORES THAT IN EVERY ASPECT FOLLOWS THE MOST ANCIENT PRECEPTS OF THE BUSHIDO.
THEY'RE NOT GOING TO SPLIT UP AND DISAPPEAR FOR A WHILE, LIKE AFTER A MILITARY ATTACK.
THEY'LL STAY TOGETHER, AND THEY'RE GOING TO A VERY SPECIFIC PLACE.
WHERE?
FIND OUT WHERE ASANO NAGANOMI IS BURIED.

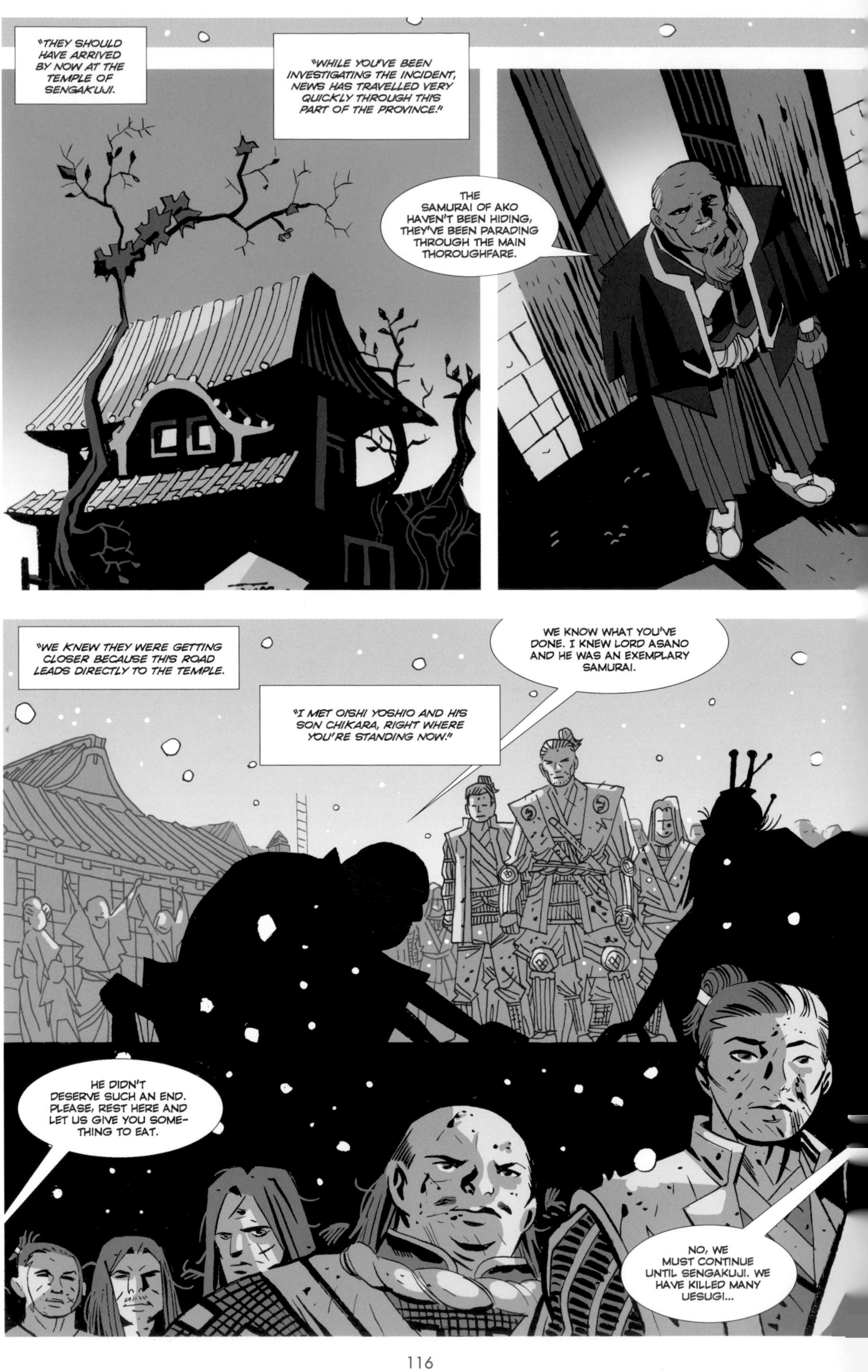

"THEY SHOULD HAVE ARRIVED BY NOW AT THE TEMPLE OF SENGAKUJI.
"WHILE YOU'VE BEEN INVESTIGATING THE INCIDENT, NEWS HAS TRAVELLED VERY QUICKLY THROUGH THIS PART OF THE PROVINCE."
THE SAMURAI OF AKO HAVEN'T BEEN HIDING, THEY'VE BEEN PARADING THROUGH THE MAIN THOROUGHFARE.
"WE KNEW THEY WERE GETTING CLOSER BECAUSE THIS ROAD LEADS DIRECTLY TO THE TEMPLE.
WE KNOW WHAT YOU'VE DONE. I KNEW LORD ASANO AND HE WAS AN EXEMPLARY SAMURAI.
"I MET OISHI YOSHIO AND HIS SON CHIKARA, RIGHT WHERE YOU'RE STANDING NOW."
HE DIDN'T DESERVE SUCH AN END. PLEASE, REST HERE AND LET US GIVE YOU SOME-THING TO EAT.
NO, WE MUST CONTINUE UNTIL SENGAKUJI. WE HAVE KILLED MANY UESUGI...

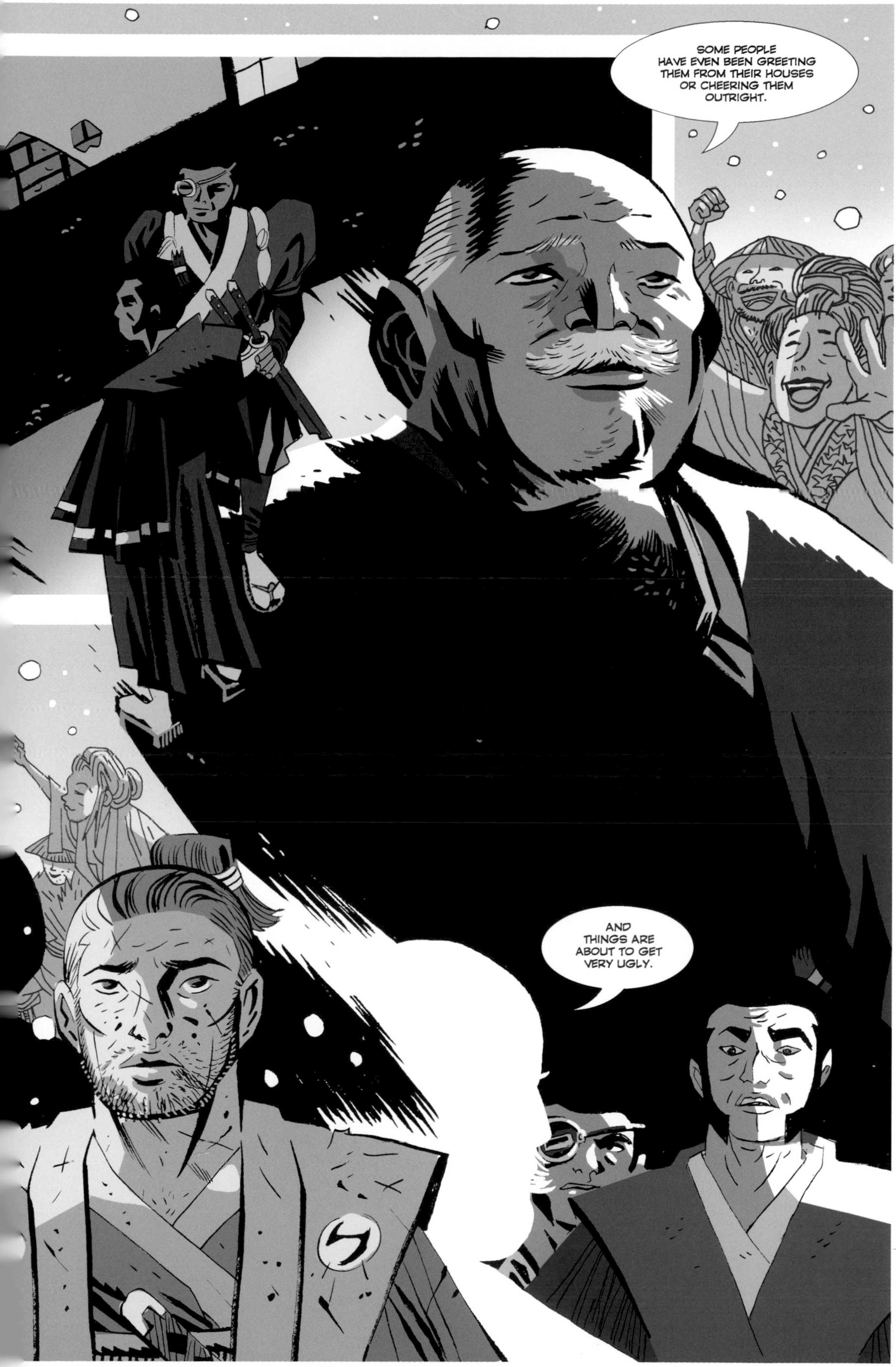
SOME PEOPLE HAVE EVEN BEEN GREETING THEM FROM THEIR HOUSES OR CHEERING THEM OUTRIGHT.
AND THINGS ARE ABOUT TO GET VERY UGLY.

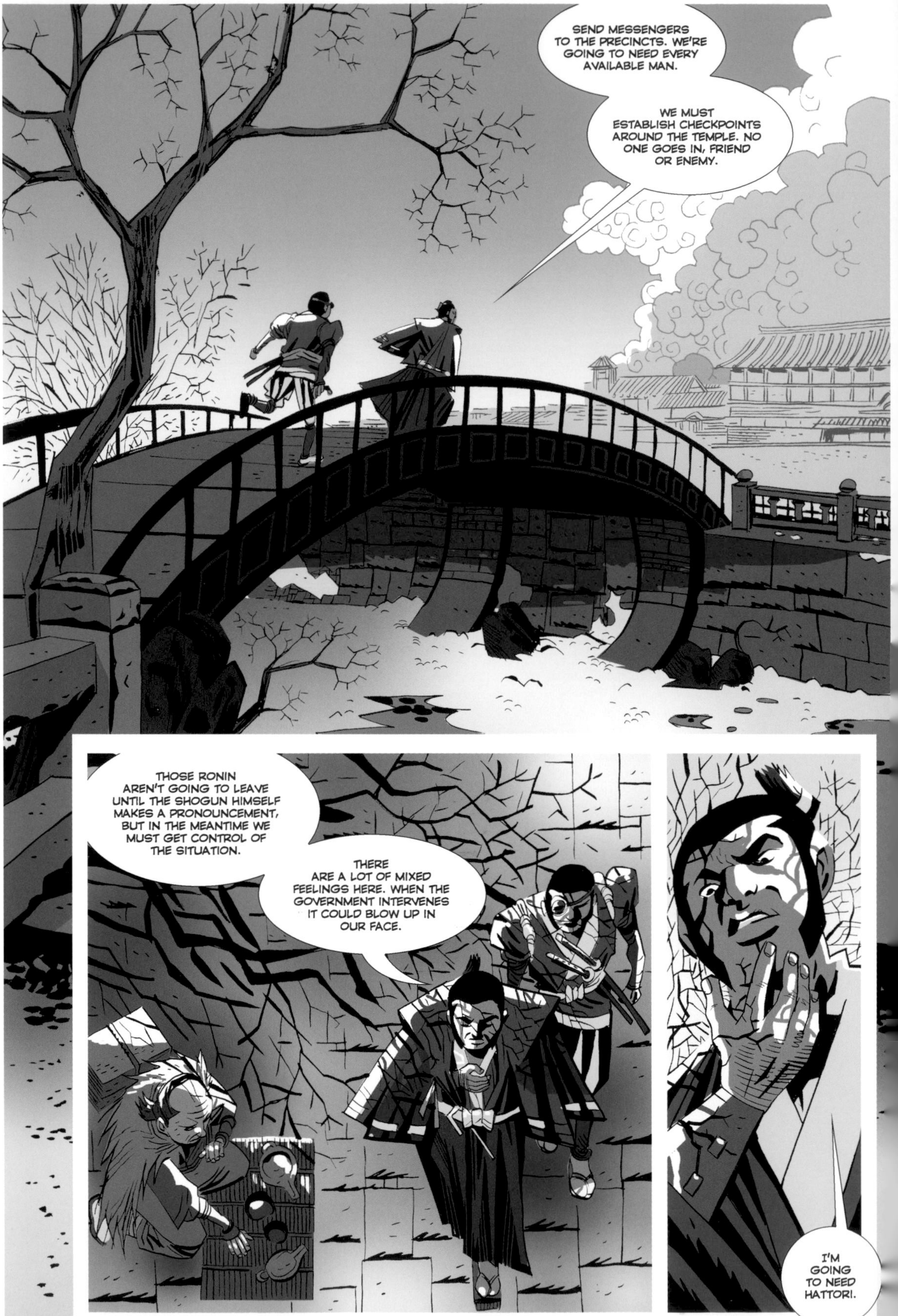
SEND MESSENGERS TO THE PRECINCTS. WE'RE GOING TO NEED EVERY AVAILABLE MAN.
WE MUST ESTABLISH CHECKPOINTS AROUND THE TEMPLE. NO ONE GOES IN, FRIEND OR ENEMY.
THOSE RONIN AREN'T GOING TO LEAVE UNTIL THE SHOGUN HIMSELF MAKES A PRONOUNCEMENT, BUT IN THE MEANTIME WE MUST GET CONTROL OF THE SITUATION.
THERE ARE A LOT OF MIXED FEELINGS HERE. WHEN THE GOVERNMENT INTERVENES IT COULD BLOW UP IN OUR FACE.
I'M GOING TO NEED HATTORI.

THE STORY OF FORTY-SEVEN RONIN WHO HAVE BARRICADED THEMSELVES IN THE SENGAKUJI TEMPLE HAS SWEPT THE NATION'S CONSCIENCE LIKE A GIANT TSUNAMI.

THE TOPIC FILLS HOURS AND HOURS AT SOCIAL GATHERINGS IN TAVERNS AND IN HOMES.

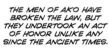

THE MEN OF AKO HAVE BROKEN THE LAW, BUT THEY UNDERTOOK AN ACT OF HONOR UNLIKE ANY SINCE THE ANCIENT TIMES.

THE RONIN REFUSED TO NEGOTIATE. THEY APPEALED THE VERDICT PROCLAIMED BY THE SHOGUN HIMSELF. POLITICIANS, SOLDIERS AND SCHOLARS PRESSURED THE BAKUFU TO TAKE ACTION.

BUT THE SHOGUN DIDN'T TAKE A STANCE.

IF HE WAS LENIENT WITH THE REBELS, IT WOULD SHOW WEAKNESS AND WOULD CREATE A DANGEROUS PRECEDENT IN A PERIOD OF GREAT SOCIAL STABILITY.

IF HE PUNISHED THE RONIN HARSHLY, HE WOULD BE ACTING AGAINST POPULAR AND MILITARY OPINION.

THE MEN OF KEBIISHI, COMMANDED BY HEIGO KOBAYASHI, MAINTAINED CONTROL OF THE TEMPLE AND ITS SURROUNDINGS.

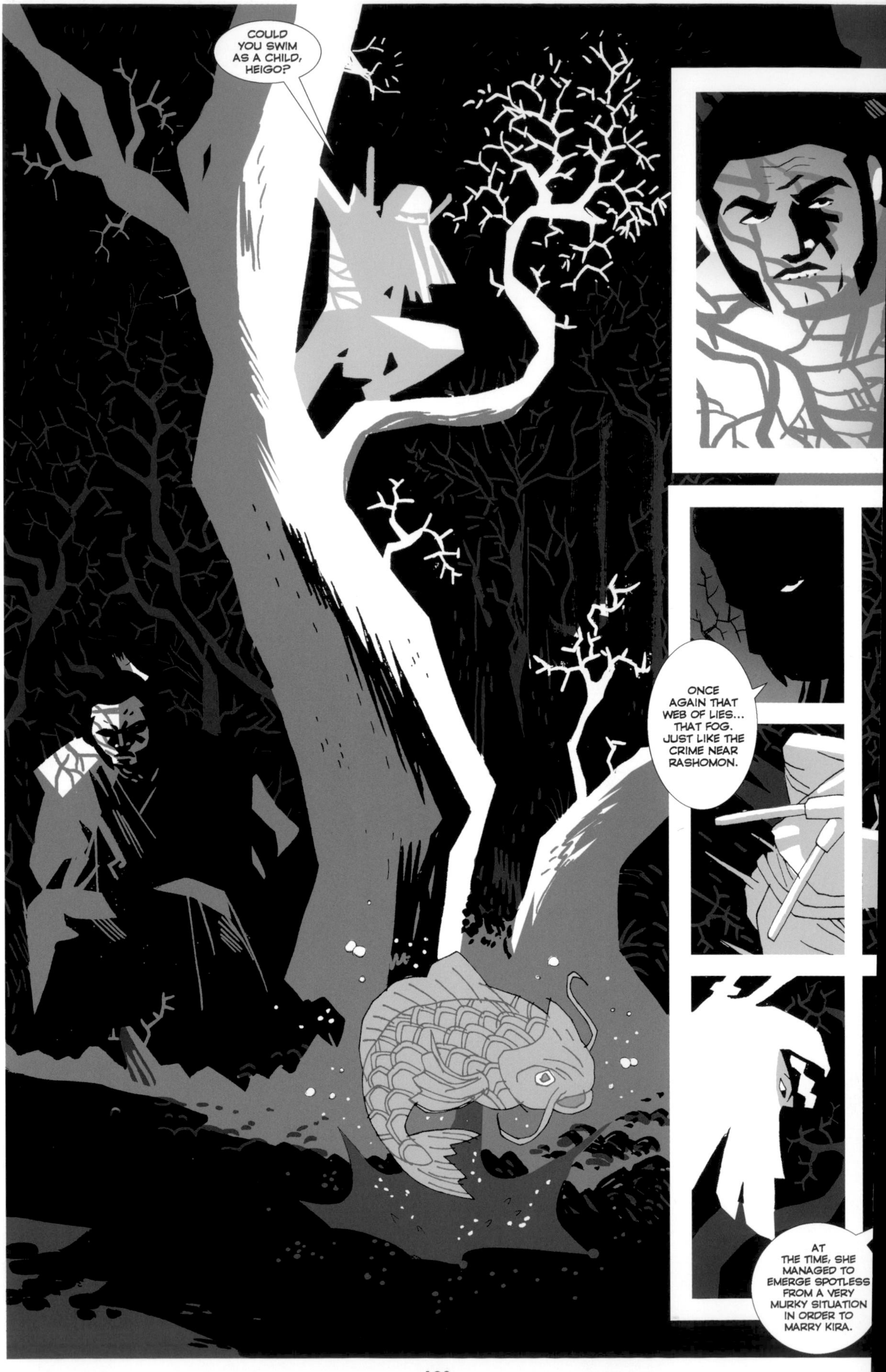
COULD YOU SWIM AS A CHILD, HEIGO?
ONCE AGAIN THAT WEB OF LIES... THAT FOG. JUST LIKE THE CRIME NEAR RASHOMON.
AT THE TIME, SHE MANAGED TO EMERGE SPOTLESS FROM A VERY MURKY SITUATION IN ORDER TO MARRY KIRA.

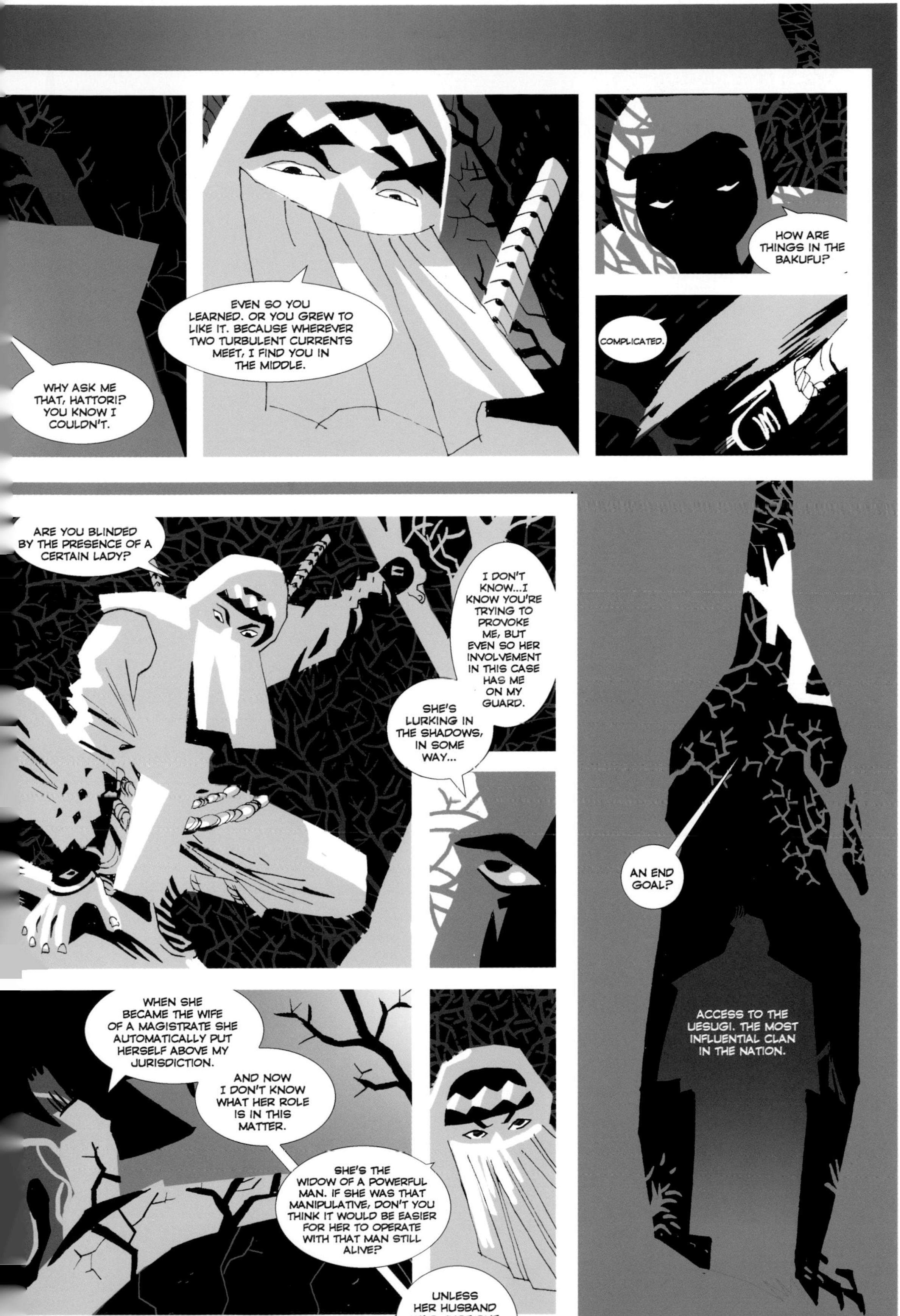
WHY ASK ME THAT, HATTORI? YOU KNOW I COULDN'T.
EVEN SO YOU LEARNED. OR YOU GREW TO LIKE IT. BECAUSE WHEREVER TWO TURBULENT CURRENTS MEET, I FIND YOU IN THE MIDDLE.
HOW ARE THINGS IN THE BAKUFU?
COMPLICATED.
ARE YOU BLINDED BY THE PRESENCE OF A CERTAIN LADY?
I DON'T KNOW...I KNOW YOU'RE TRYING TO PROVOKE ME, BUT EVEN SO HER INVOLVEMENT IN THIS CASE HAS ME ON MY GUARD.
SHE'S LURKING IN THE SHADOWS, IN SOME WAY...
WHEN SHE BECAME THE WIFE OF A MAGISTRATE SHE AUTOMATICALLY PUT HERSELF ABOVE MY JURISDICTION.
AND NOW I DON'T KNOW WHAT HER ROLE IS IN THIS MATTER.
SHE'S THE WIDOW OF A POWERFUL MAN. IF SHE WAS THAT MANIPULATIVE, DON'T YOU THINK IT WOULD BE EASIER FOR HER TO OPERATE WITH THAT MAN STILL ALIVE?
UNLESS HER HUSBAND WAS JUST ONE MORE STEP TOWARDS AN END GOAL.
AN END GOAL?
ACCESS TO THE UESUGI. THE MOST INFLUENTIAL CLAN IN THE NATION.

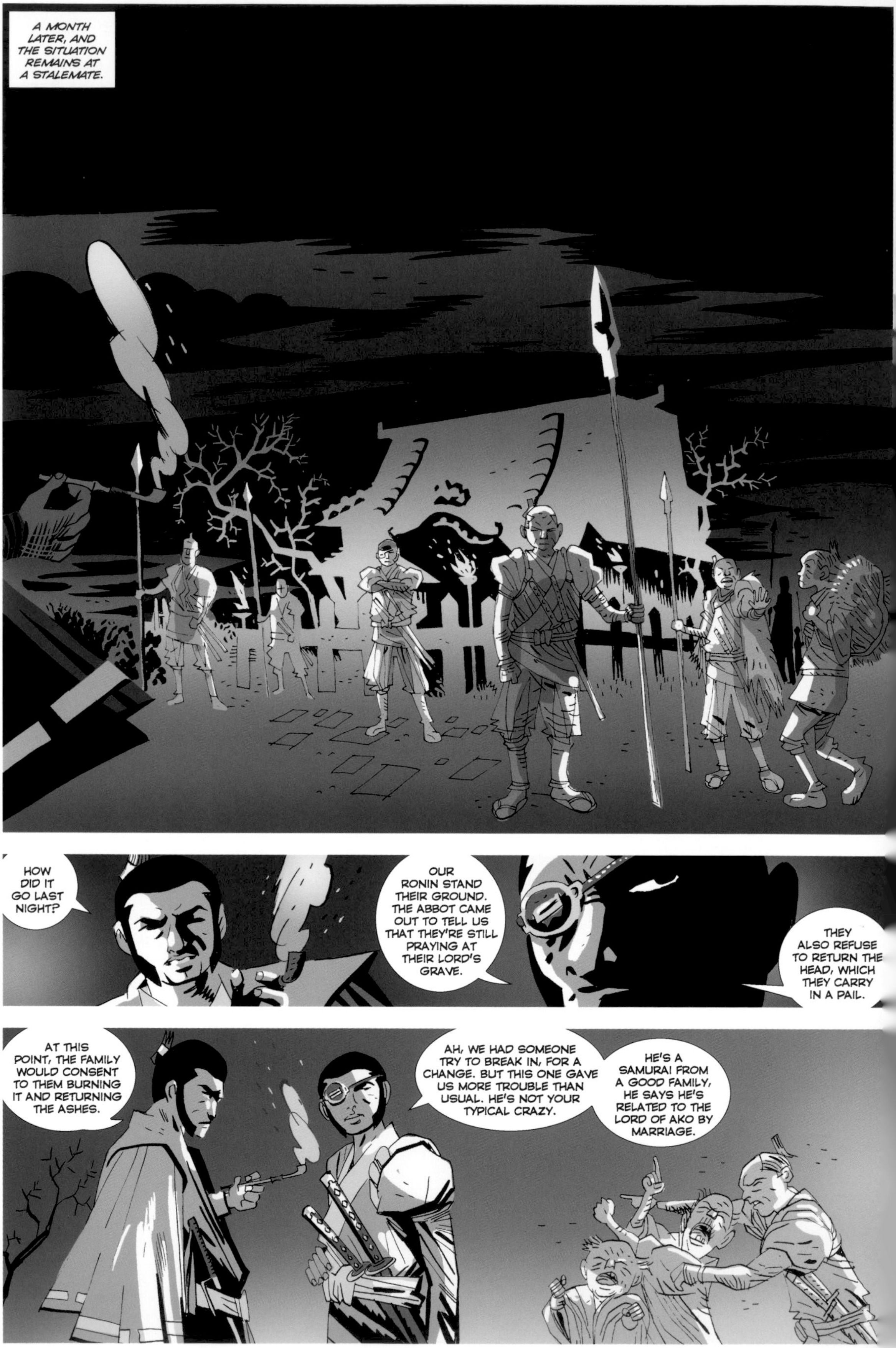
A MONTH LATER, AND THE SITUATION REMAINS AT A STALEMATE.
HOW DID IT GO LAST NIGHT?
OUR RONIN STAND THEIR GROUND. THE ABBOT CAME OUT TO TELL US THAT THEY'RE STILL PRAYING AT THEIR LORD'S GRAVE.
THEY ALSO REFUSE TO RETURN THE HEAD, WHICH THEY CARRY IN A PAIL.
AT THIS POINT, THE FAMILY WOULD CONSENT TO THEM BURNING IT AND RETURNING THE ASHES.
AH, WE HAD SOMEONE TRY TO BREAK IN, FOR A CHANGE. BUT THIS ONE GAVE US MORE TROUBLE THAN USUAL. HE'S NOT YOUR TYPICAL CRAZY.
HE'S A SAMURAI FROM A GOOD FAMILY, HE SAYS HE'S RELATED TO THE LORD OF AKO BY MARRIAGE.

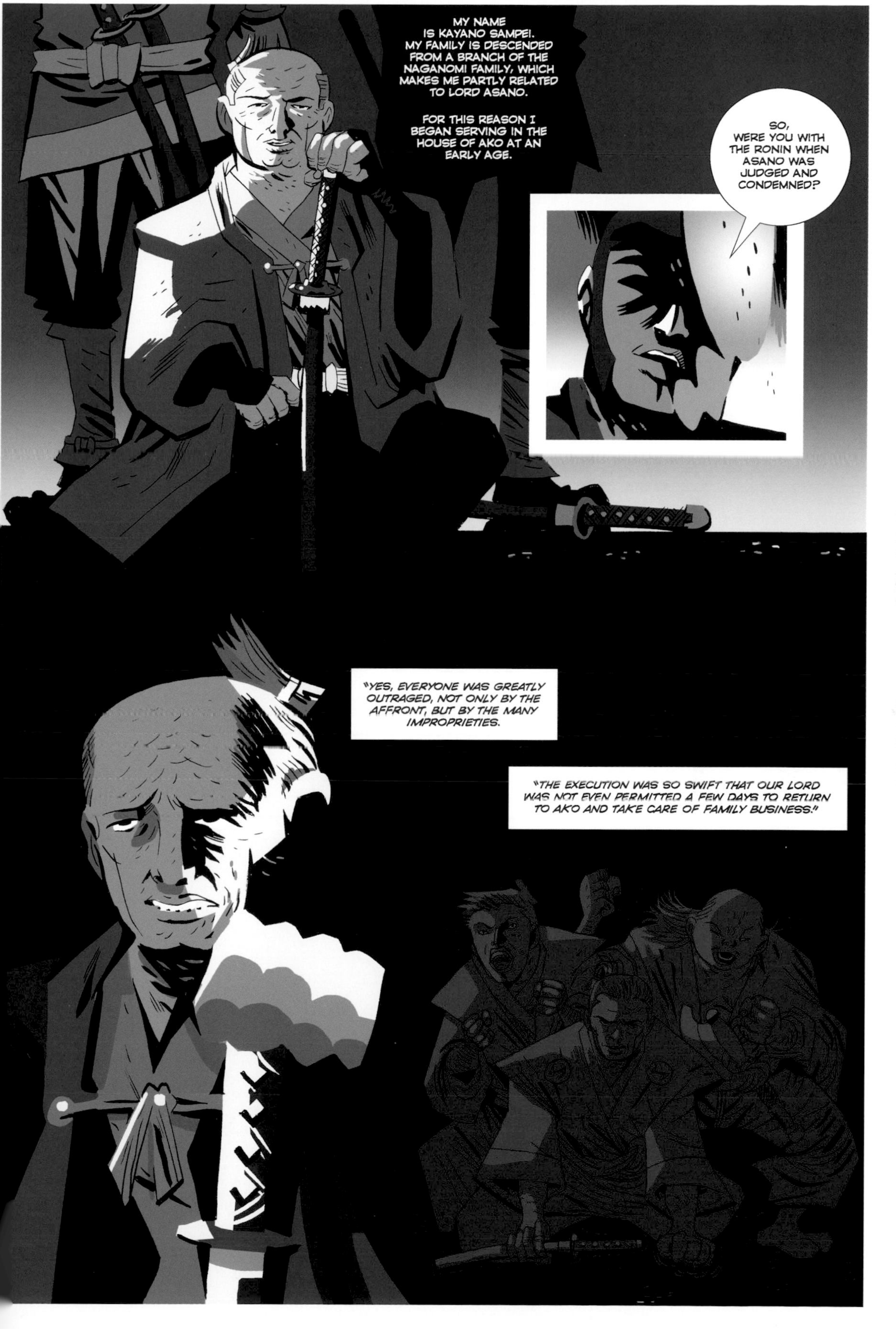
MY NAME IS KAYANO SAMPEI. MY FAMILY IS DESCENDED FROM A BRANCH OF THE NAGANOMI FAMILY, WHICH MAKES ME PARTLY RELATED TO LORD ASANO.
FOR THIS REASON I BEGAN SERVING IN THE HOUSE OF AKO AT AN EARLY AGE.
SO, WERE YOU WITH THE RONIN WHEN ASANO WAS JUDGED AND CONDEMNED?
"YES, EVERYONE WAS GREATLY OUTRAGED, NOT ONLY BY THE AFFRONT, BUT BY THE MANY IMPROPRIETIES.
"THE EXECUTION WAS SO SWIFT THAT OUR LORD WAS NOT EVEN PERMITTED A FEW DAYS TO RETURN TO AKO AND TAKE CARE OF FAMILY BUSINESS."

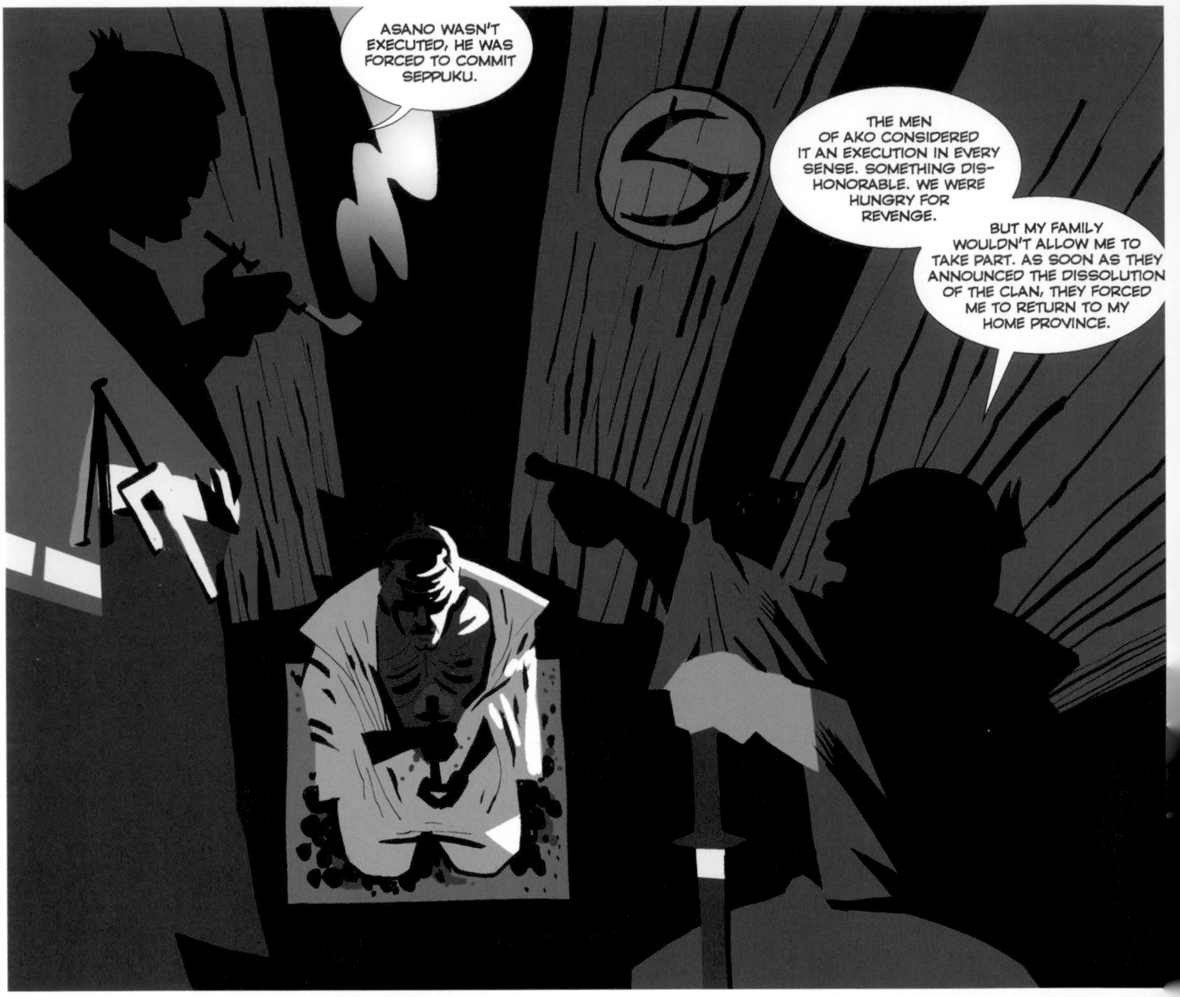
ASANO WASN'T EXECUTED, HE WAS FORCED TO COMMIT SEPPUKU.
THE MEN OF AKO CONSIDERED IT AN EXECUTION IN EVERY SENSE. SOMETHING DIS-HONORABLE. WE WERE HUNGRY FOR REVENGE.
BUT MY FAMILY WOULDN'T ALLOW ME TO TAKE PART. AS SOON AS THEY ANNOUNCED THE DISSOLUTION OF THE CLAN, THEY FORCED ME TO RETURN TO MY HOME PROVINCE.

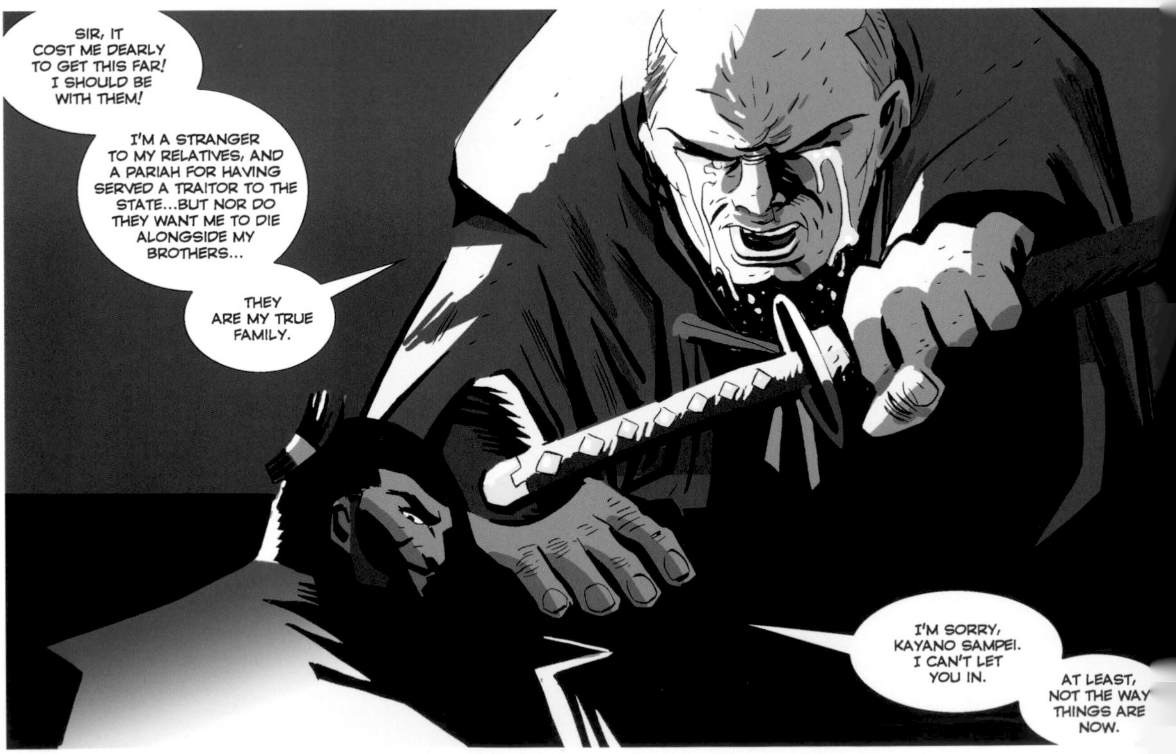
SIR, IT COST ME DEARLY TO GET THIS FAR! I SHOULD BE WITH THEM!
I'M A STRANGER TO MY RELATIVES, AND A PARIAH FOR HAVING SERVED A TRAITOR TO THE STATE...BUT NOR DO THEY WANT ME TO DIE ALONGSIDE MY BROTHERS...
THEY ARE MY TRUE FAMILY.
I'M SORRY, KAYANO SAMPEI. I CAN'T LET YOU IN.
AT LEAST, NOT THE WAY THINGS ARE NOW.

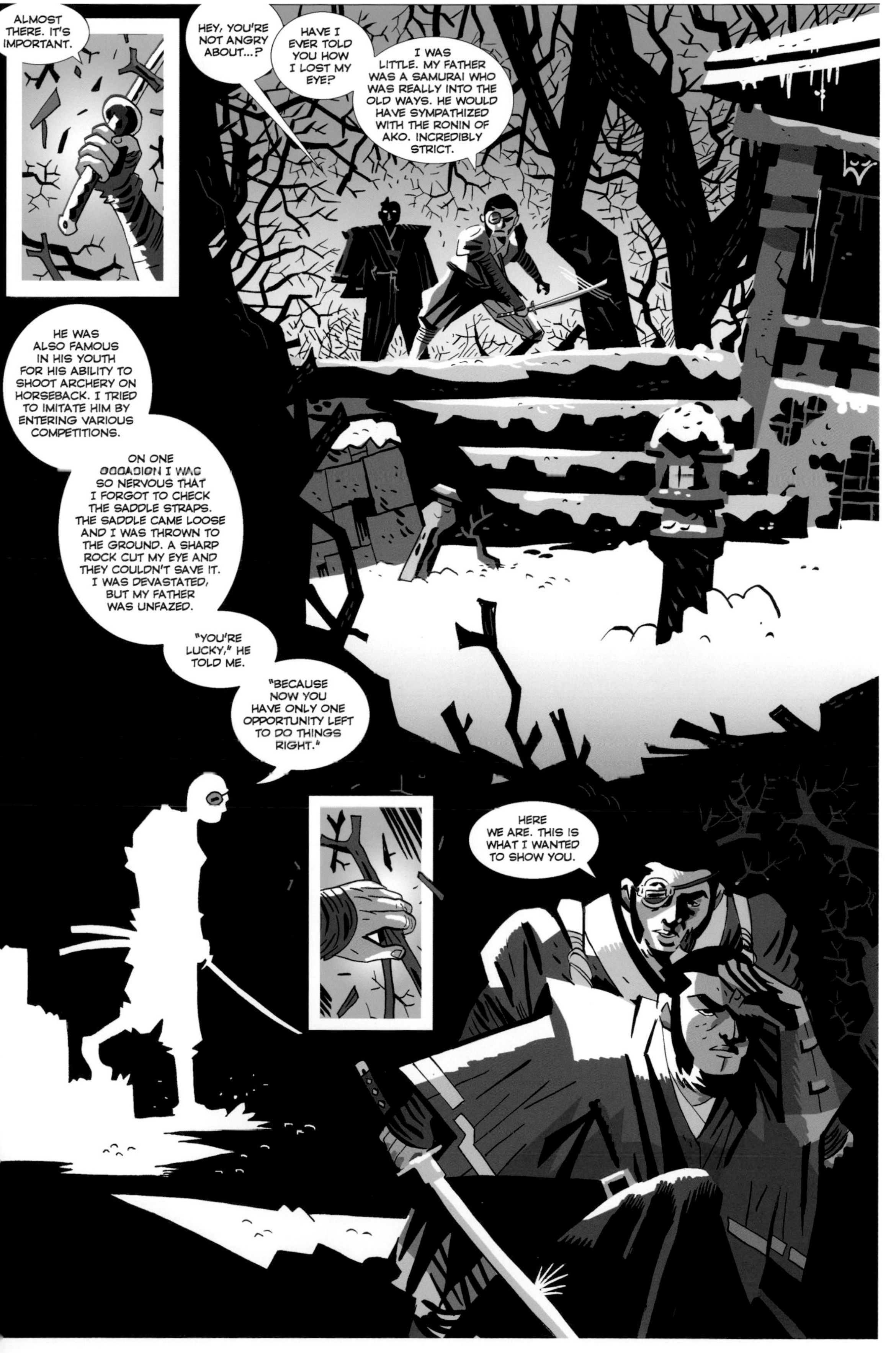
ALMOST THERE. IT'S IMPORTANT.
HEY, YOU'RE NOT ANGRY ABOUT...?
HAVE I EVER TOLD YOU HOW I LOST MY EYE?
I WAS LITTLE. MY FATHER WAS A SAMURAI WHO WAS REALLY INTO THE OLD WAYS. HE WOULD HAVE SYMPATHIZED WITH THE RONIN OF AKO. INCREDIBLY STRICT.
HE WAS ALSO FAMOUS IN HIS YOUTH FOR HIS ABILITY TO SHOOT ARCHERY ON HORSEBACK. I TRIED TO IMITATE HIM BY ENTERING VARIOUS COMPETITIONS.
ON ONE OCCASION I WAS SO NERVOUS THAT I FORGOT TO CHECK THE SADDLE STRAPS. THE SADDLE CAME LOOSE AND I WAS THROWN TO THE GROUND. A SHARP ROCK CUT MY EYE AND THEY COULDN'T SAVE IT. I WAS DEVASTATED, BUT MY FATHER WAS UNFAZED.
"YOU'RE LUCKY," HE TOLD ME.
"BECAUSE NOW YOU HAVE ONLY ONE OPPORTUNITY LEFT TO DO THINGS RIGHT."
HERE WE ARE. THIS IS WHAT I WANTED TO SHOW YOU.

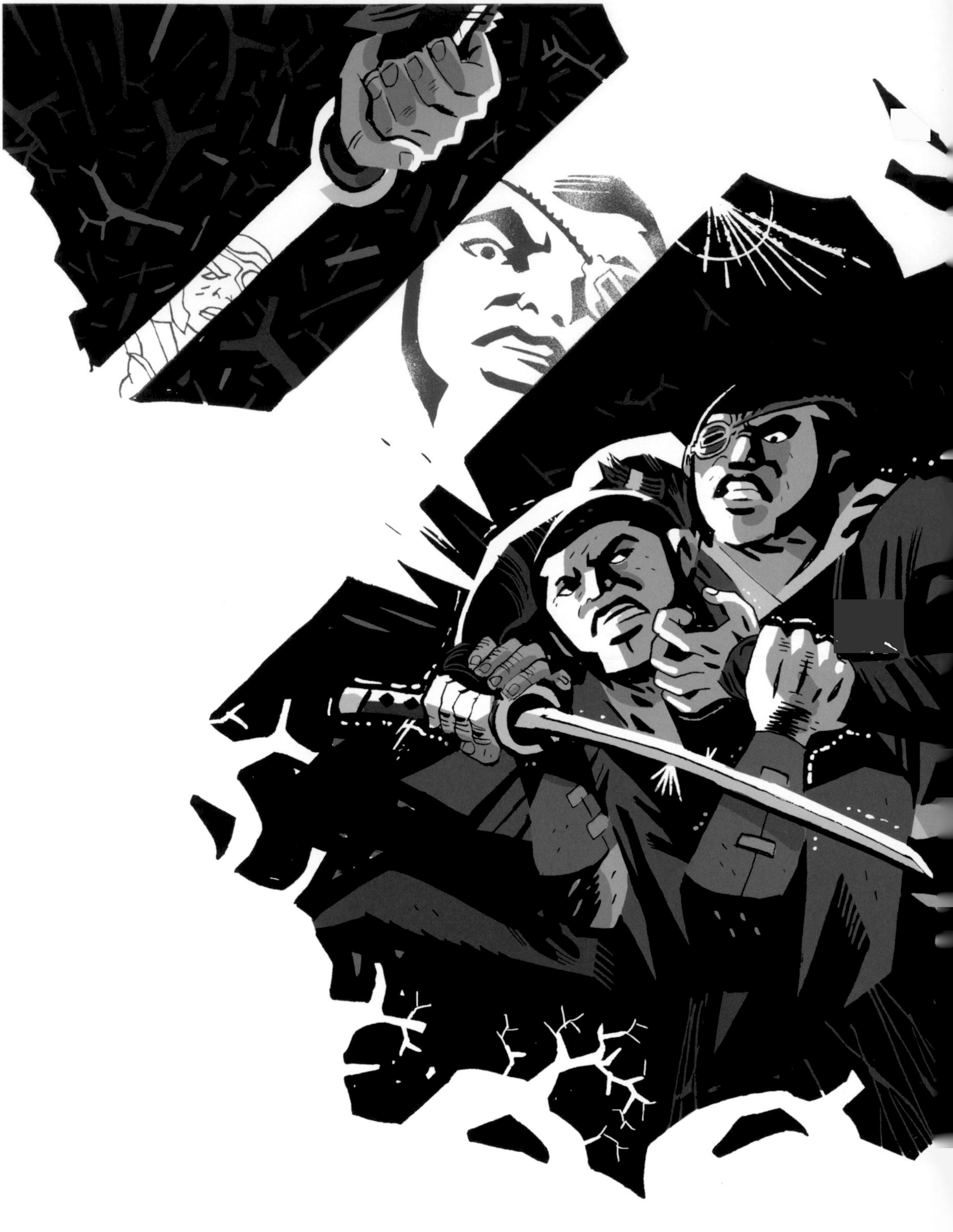

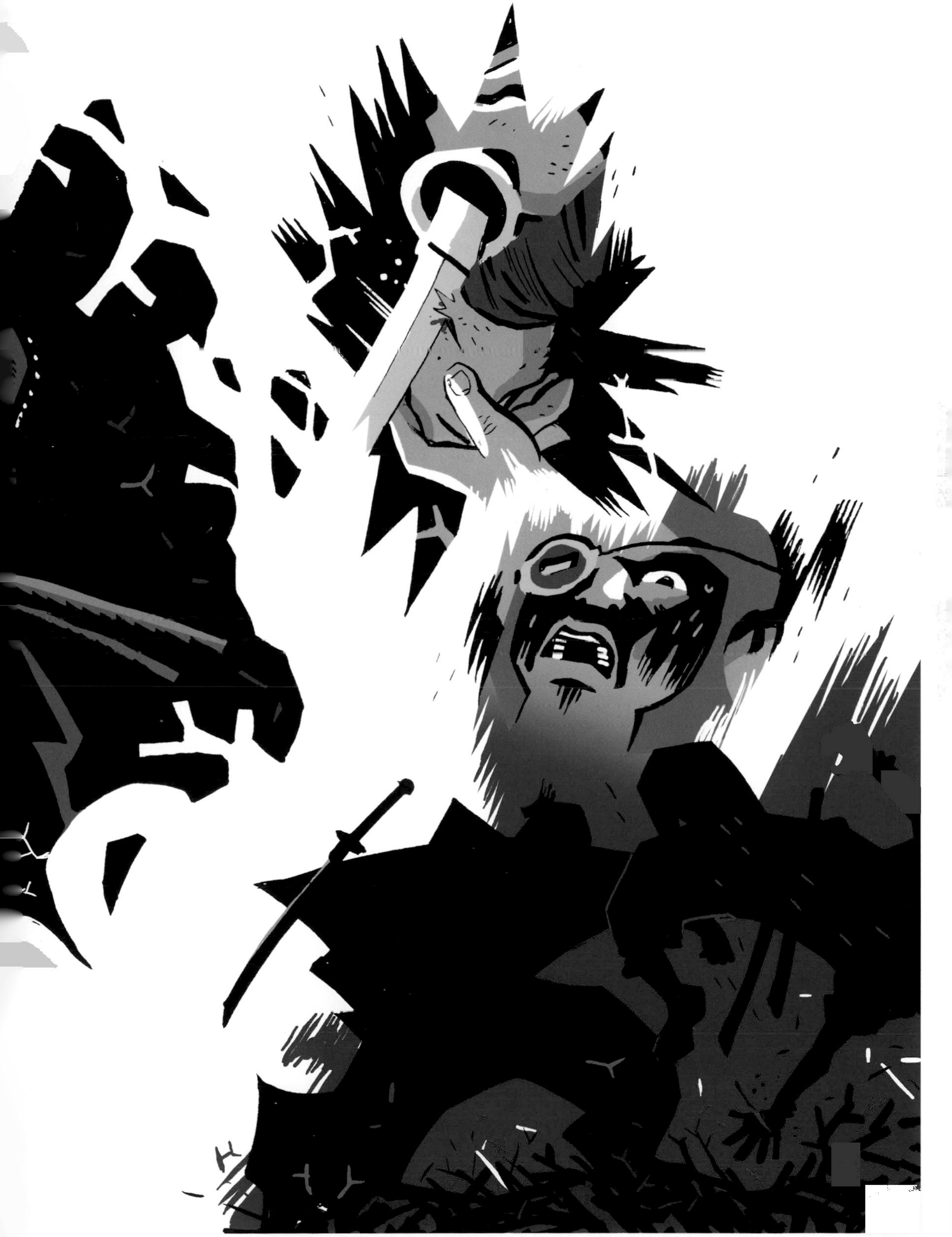

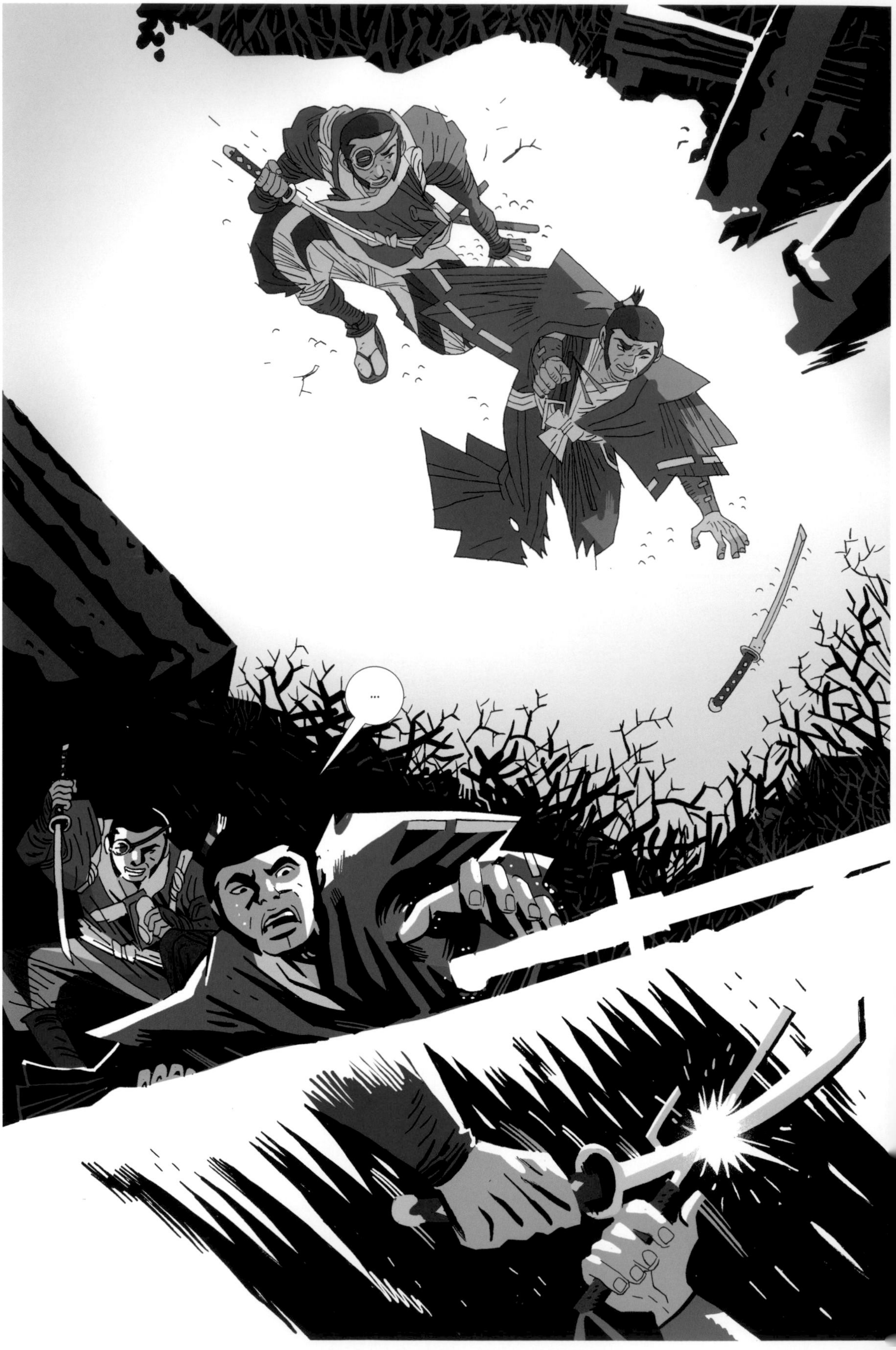
...

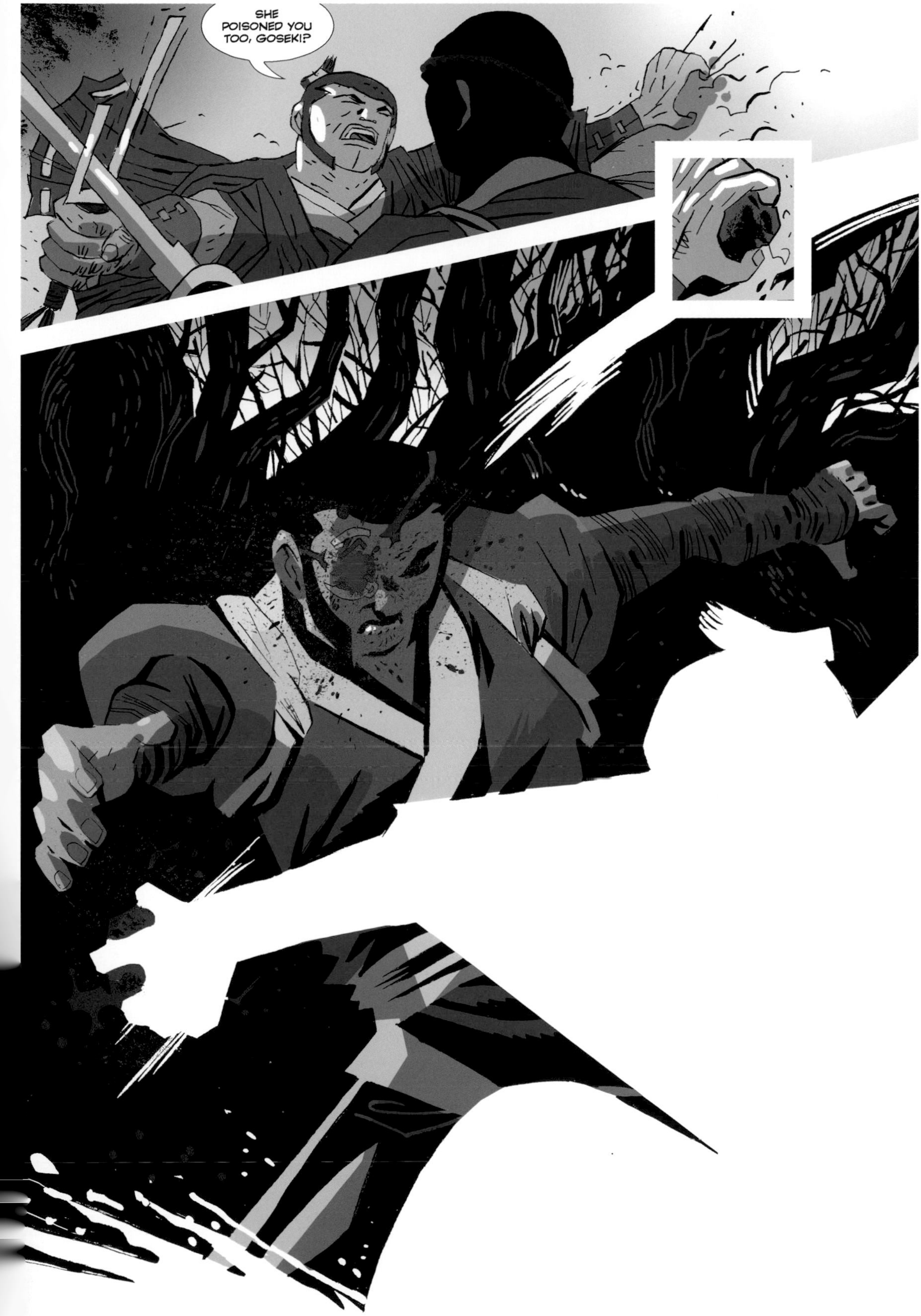
SHE POISONED YOU TOO, GOSEKI!?

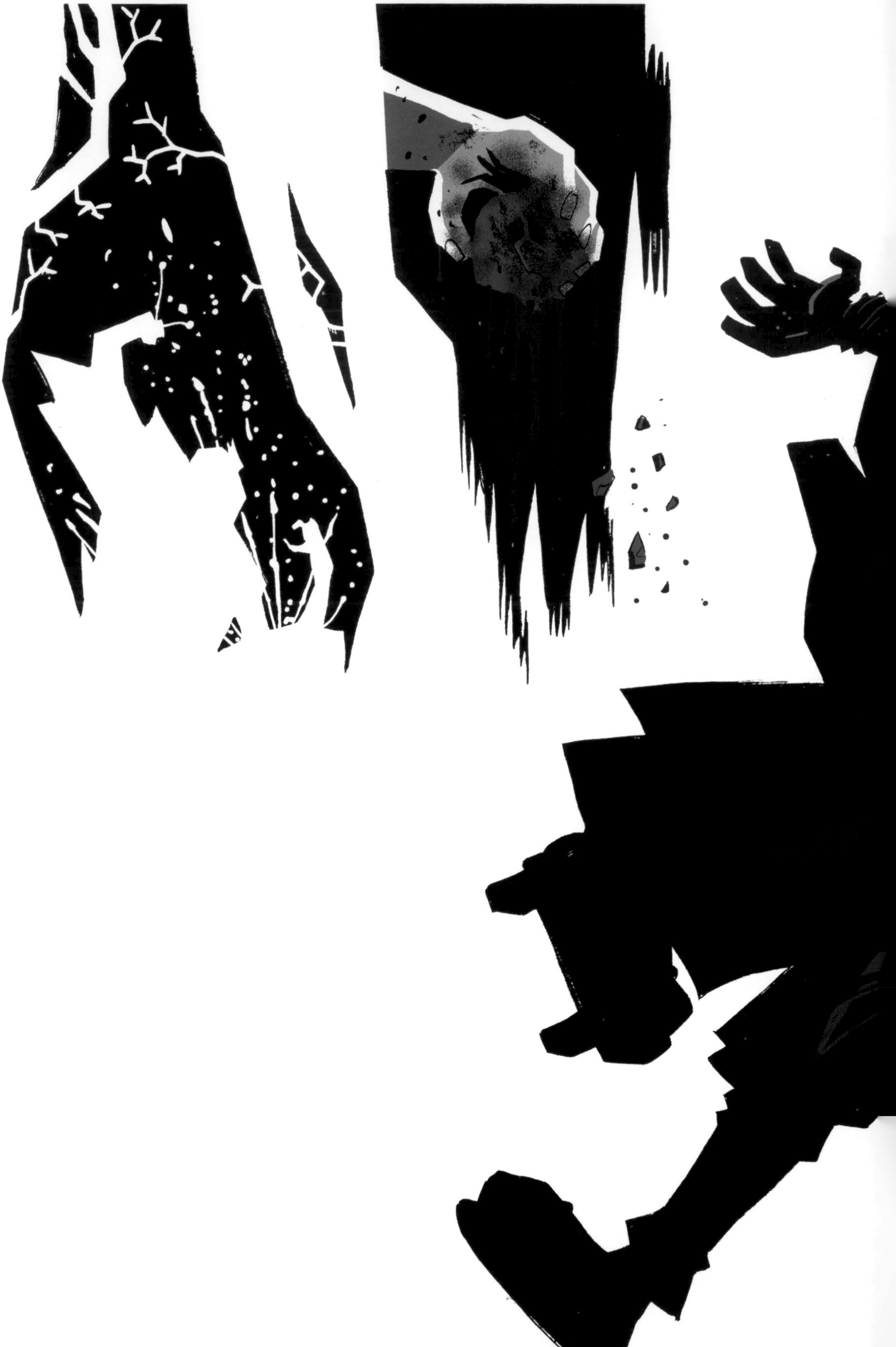

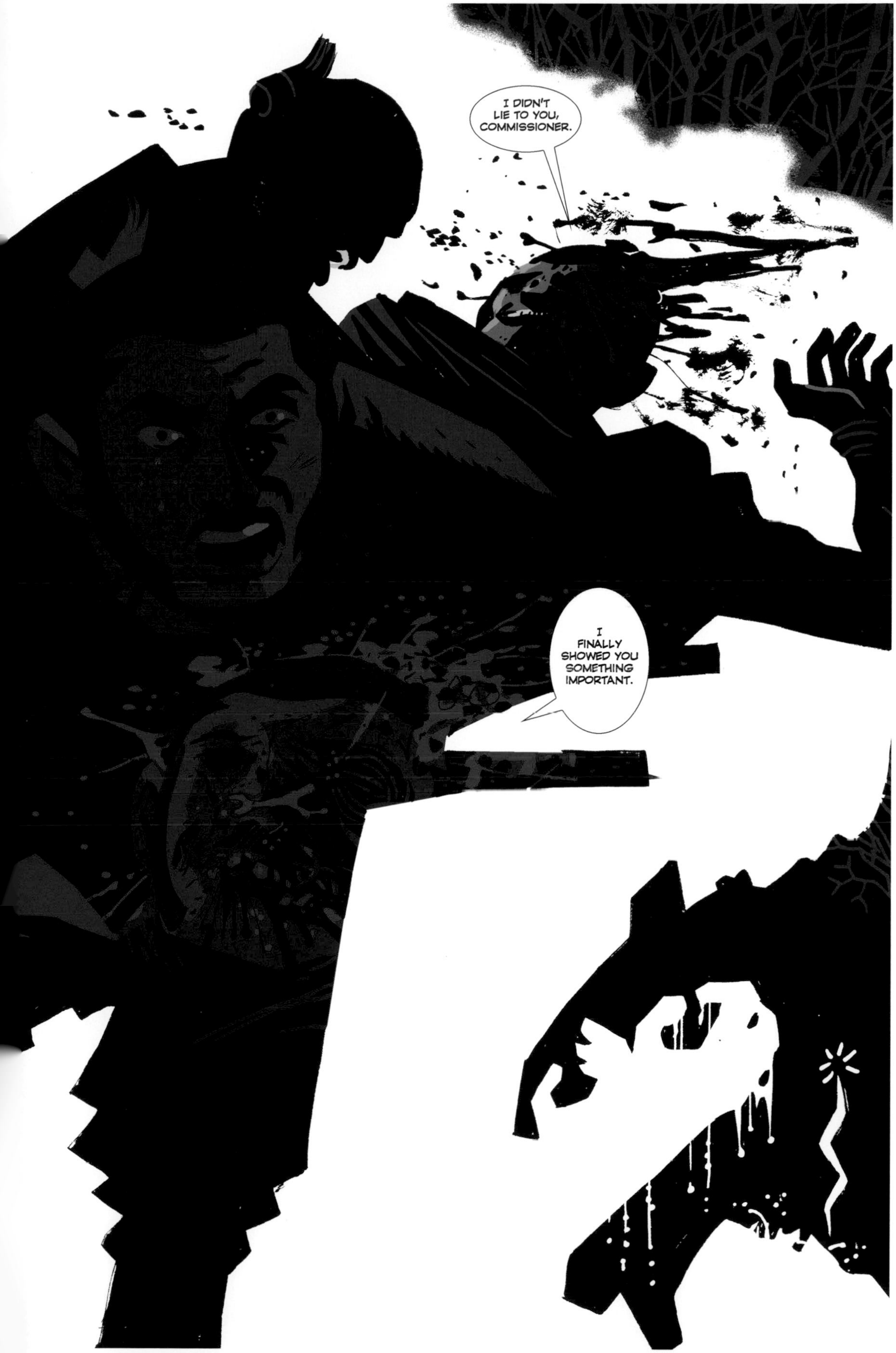
I DIDN'T LIE TO YOU, COMMISSIONER.
I FINALLY SHOWED YOU SOMETHING IMPORTANT.

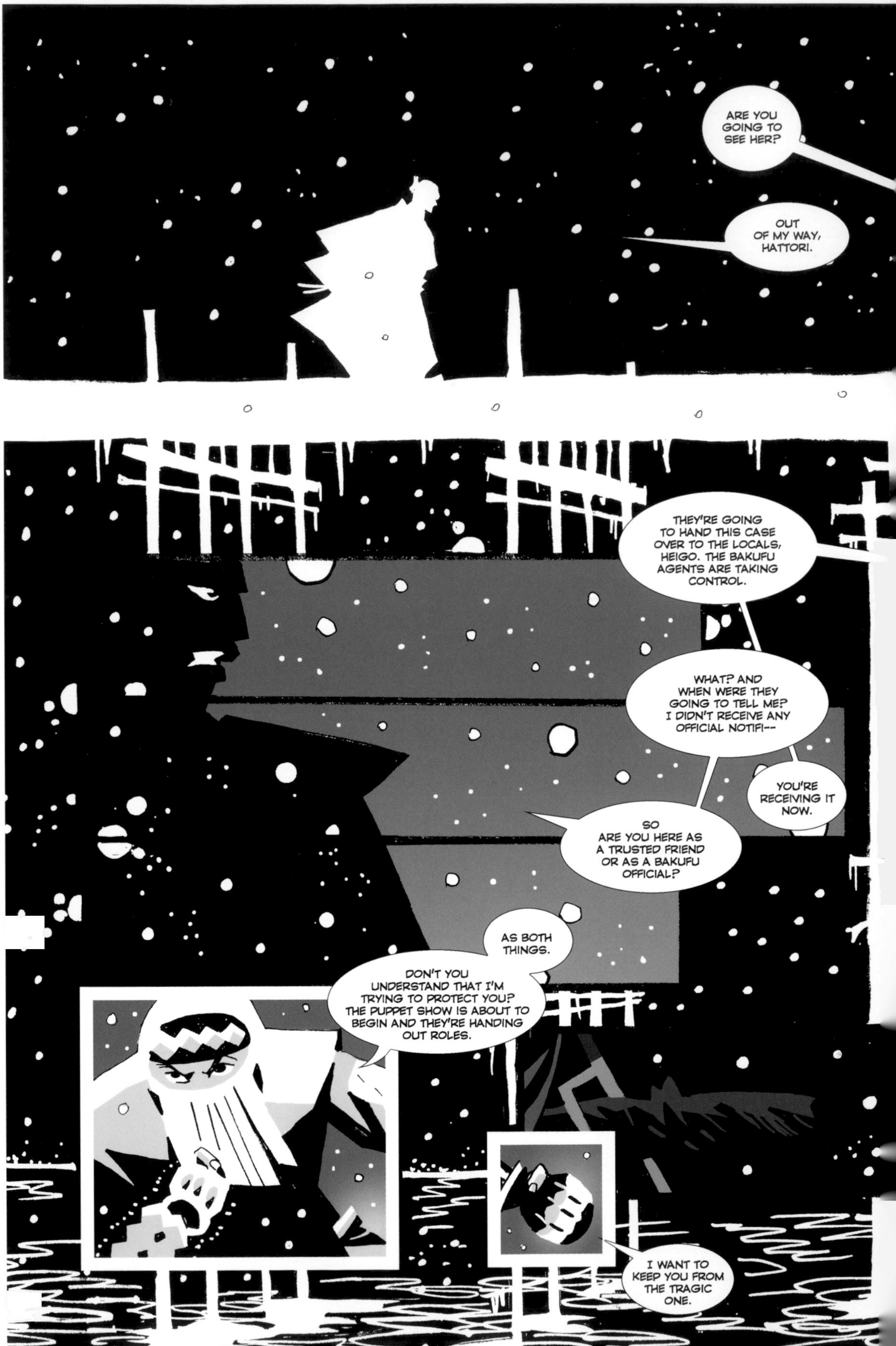
ARE YOU GOING TO SEE HER?
OUT OF MY WAY, HATTORI.
THEY'RE GOING TO HAND THIS CASE OVER TO THE LOCALS, HEIGO. THE BAKUFU AGENTS ARE TAKING CONTROL.
WHAT? AND WHEN WERE THEY GOING TO TELL ME? I DIDN'T RECEIVE ANY OFFICIAL NOTIFI--
YOU'RE RECEIVING IT NOW.
SO ARE YOU HERE AS A TRUSTED FRIEND OR AS A BAKUFU OFFICIAL?
AS BOTH THINGS.
DON'T YOU UNDERSTAND THAT I'M TRYING TO PROTECT YOU? THE PUPPET SHOW IS ABOUT TO BEGIN AND THEY'RE HANDING OUT ROLES.
I WANT TO KEEP YOU FROM THE TRAGIC ONE.

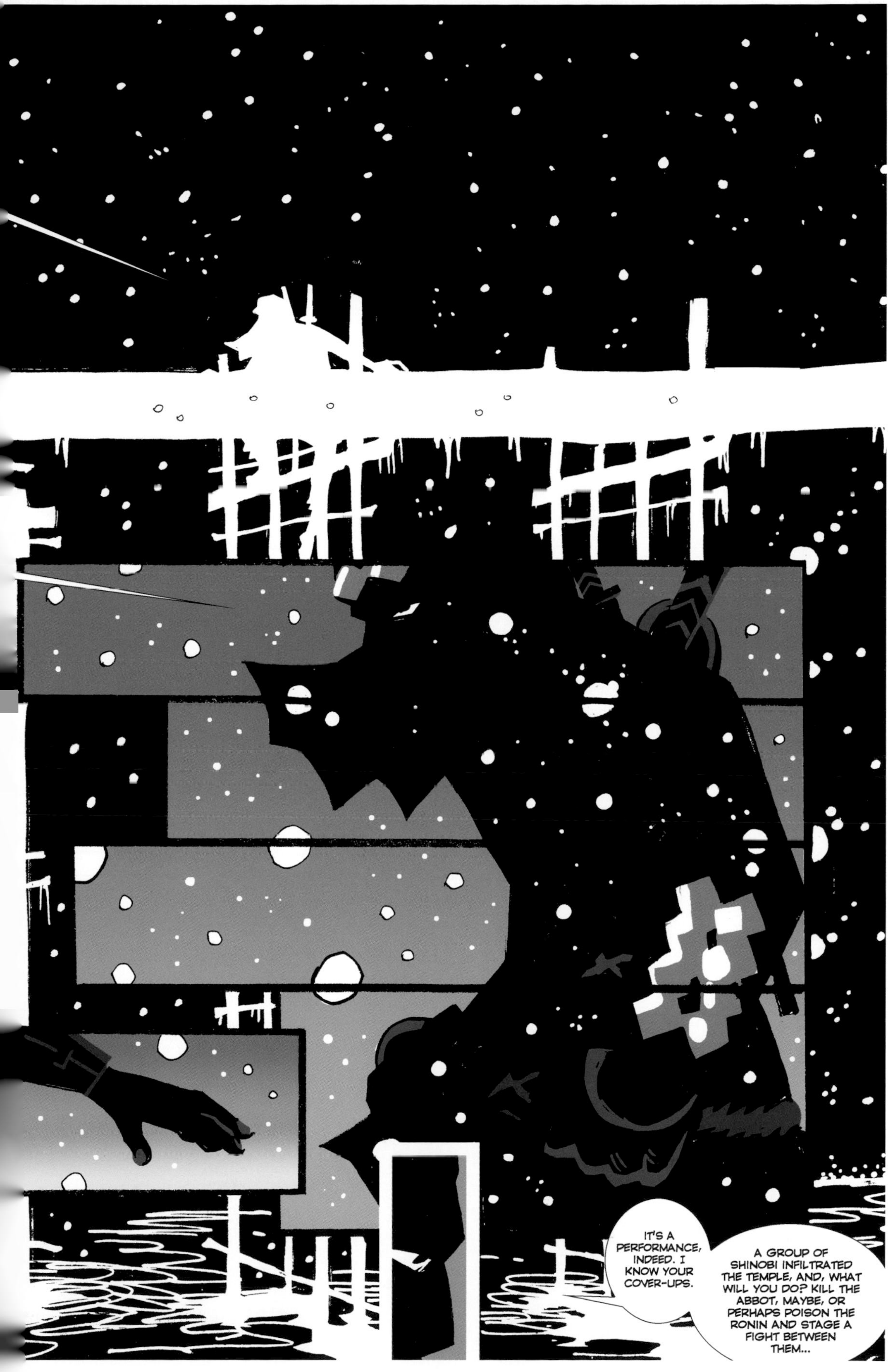
IT'S A PERFORMANCE, INDEED. I KNOW YOUR COVER-UPS.
A GROUP OF SHINOBI INFILTRATED THE TEMPLE, AND, WHAT WILL YOU DO? KILL THE ABBOT, MAYBE, OR PERHAPS POISON THE RONIN AND STAGE A FIGHT BETWEEN THEM...

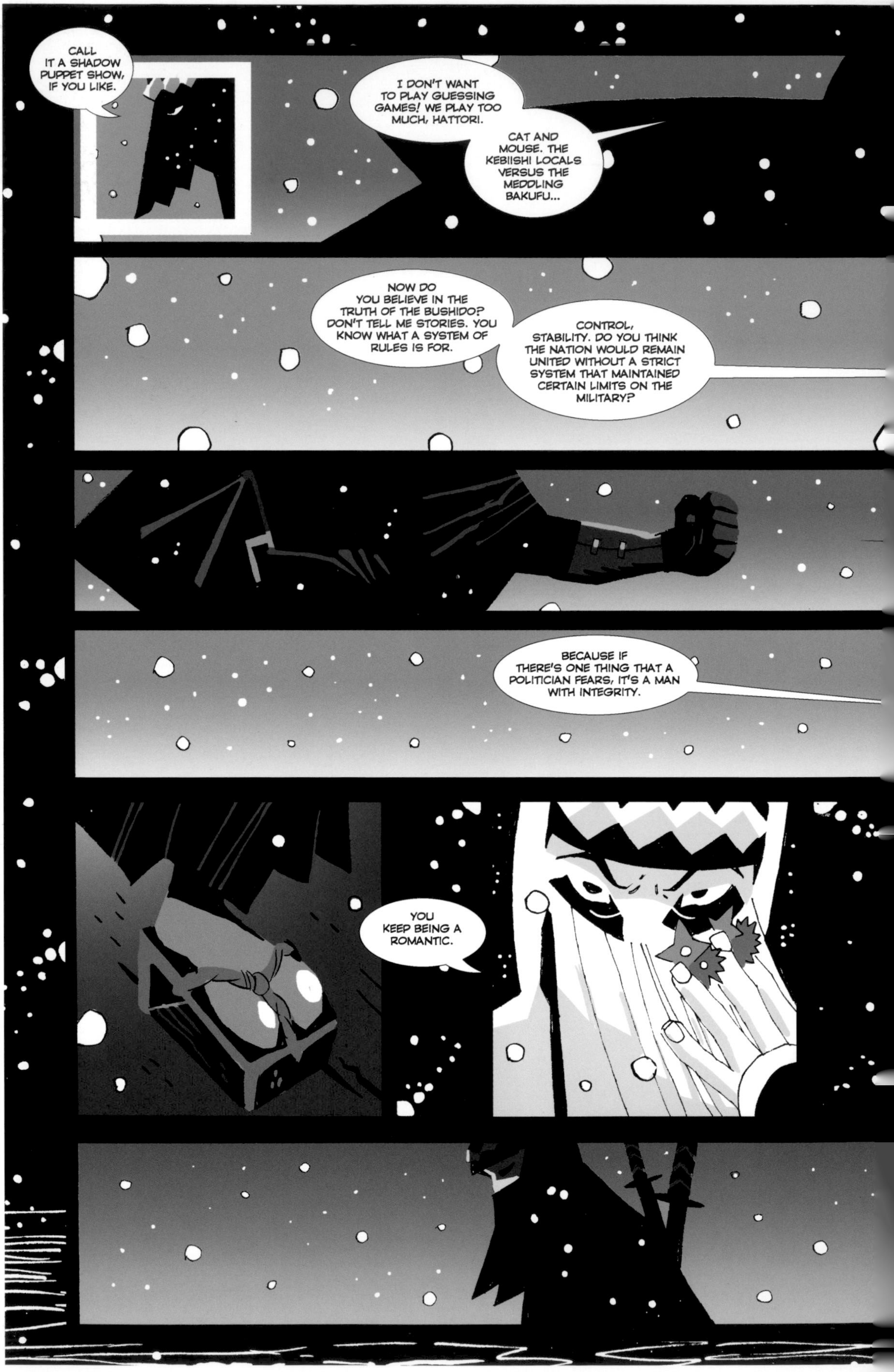
CALL IT A SHADOW PUPPET SHOW, IF YOU LIKE.
I DON'T WANT TO PLAY GUESSING GAMES! WE PLAY TOO MUCH, HATTORI.
CAT AND MOUSE. THE KEBIISHI LOCALS VERSUS THE MEDDLING BAKUFU...
NOW DO YOU BELIEVE IN THE TRUTH OF THE BUSHIDO? DON'T TELL ME STORIES. YOU KNOW WHAT A SYSTEM OF RULES IS FOR.
CONTROL, STABILITY. DO YOU THINK THE NATION WOULD REMAIN UNITED WITHOUT A STRICT SYSTEM THAT MAINTAINED CERTAIN LIMITS ON THE MILITARY?
BECAUSE IF THERE'S ONE THING THAT A POLITICIAN FEARS, IT'S A MAN WITH INTEGRITY.
YOU KEEP BEING A ROMANTIC.

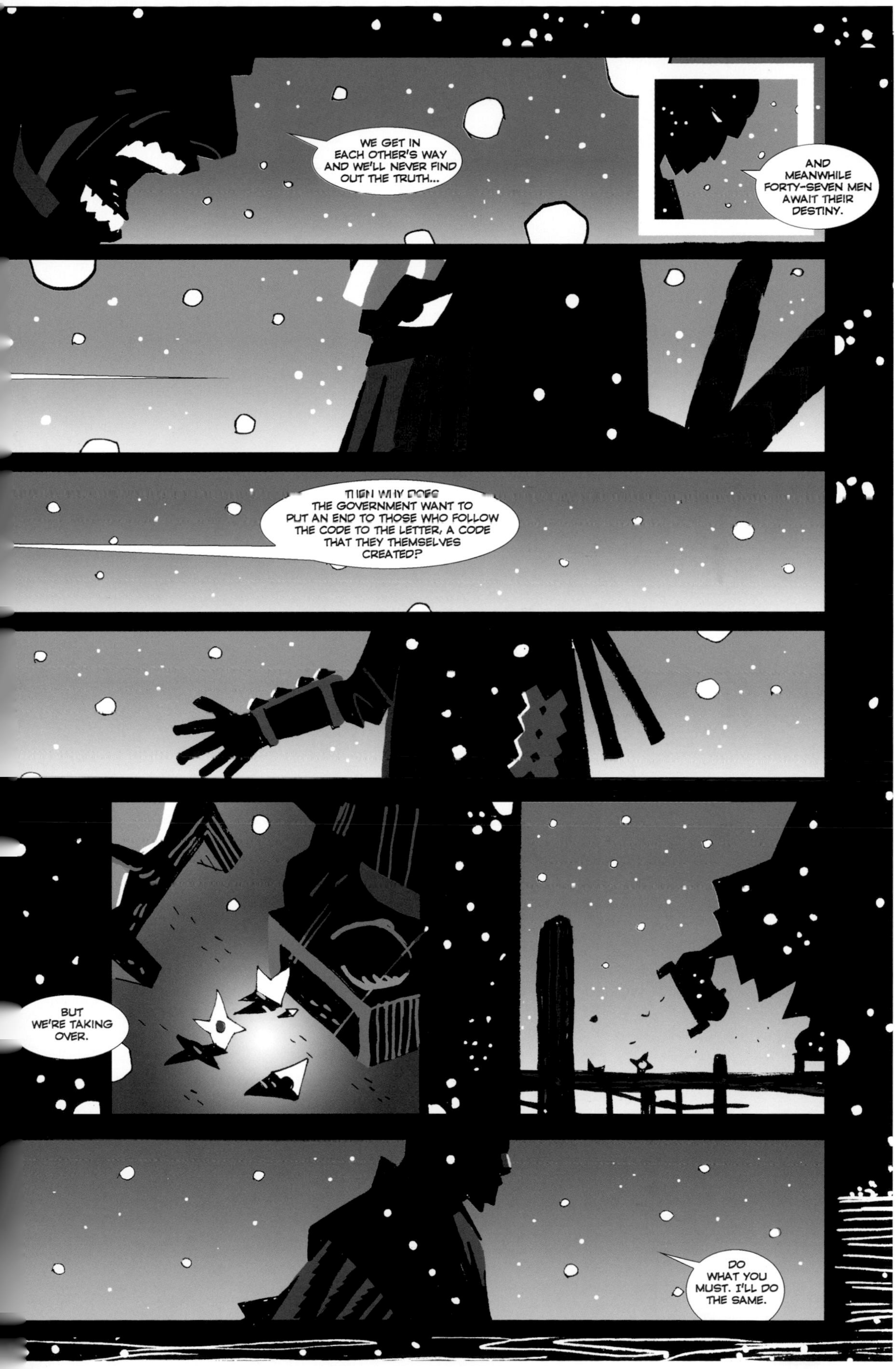
WE GET IN EACH OTHER'S WAY AND WE'LL NEVER FIND OUT THE TRUTH...
AND MEANWHILE FORTY-SEVEN MEN AWAIT THEIR DESTINY.
THEN WHY DOES THE GOVERNMENT WANT TO PUT AN END TO THOSE WHO FOLLOW THE CODE TO THE LETTER, A CODE THAT THEY THEMSELVES CREATED?
BUT WE'RE TAKING OVER.
DO WHAT YOU MUST. I'LL DO THE SAME.

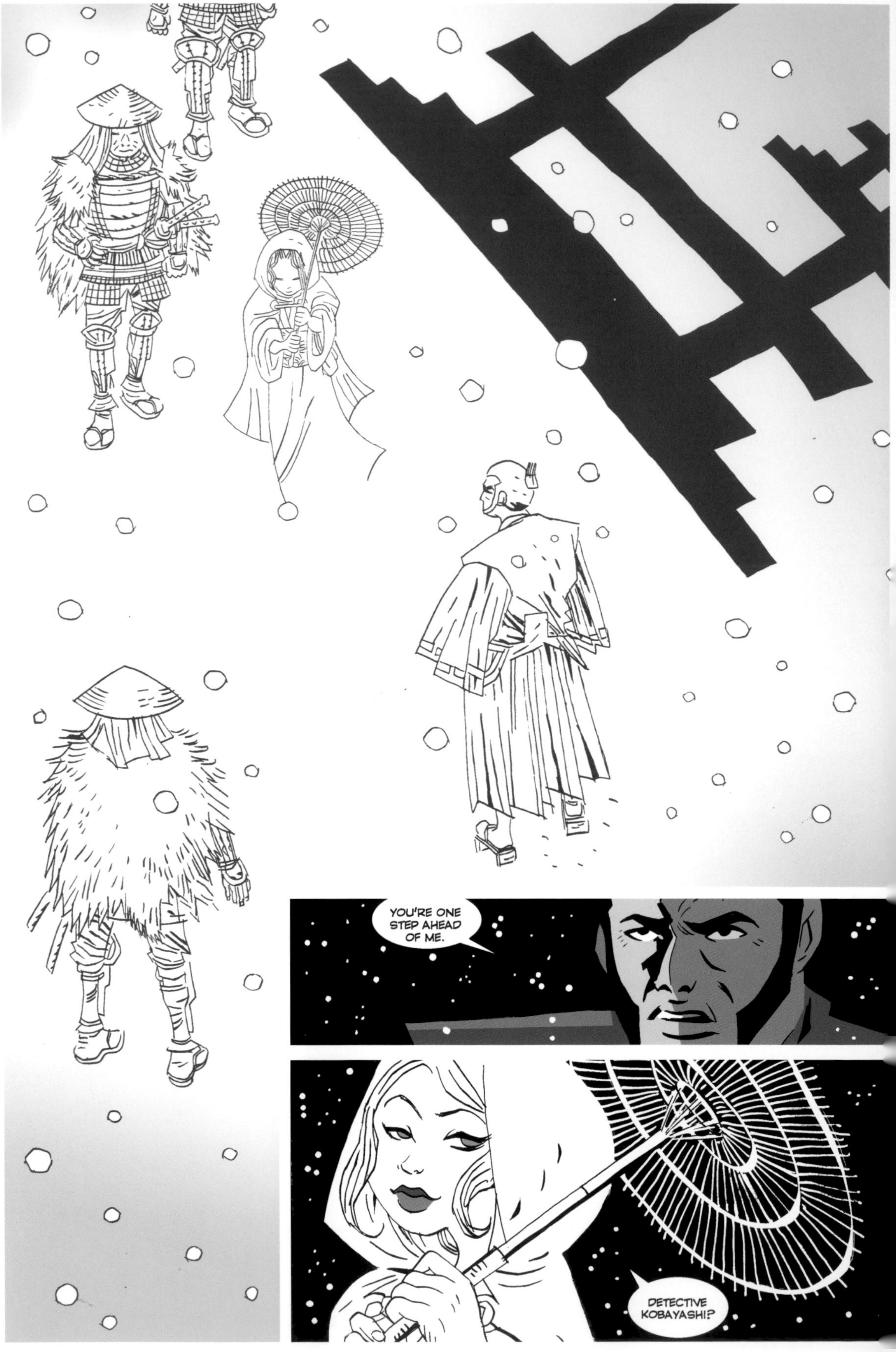
YOU'RE ONE STEP AHEAD OF ME.
DETECTIVE KOBAYASHI?

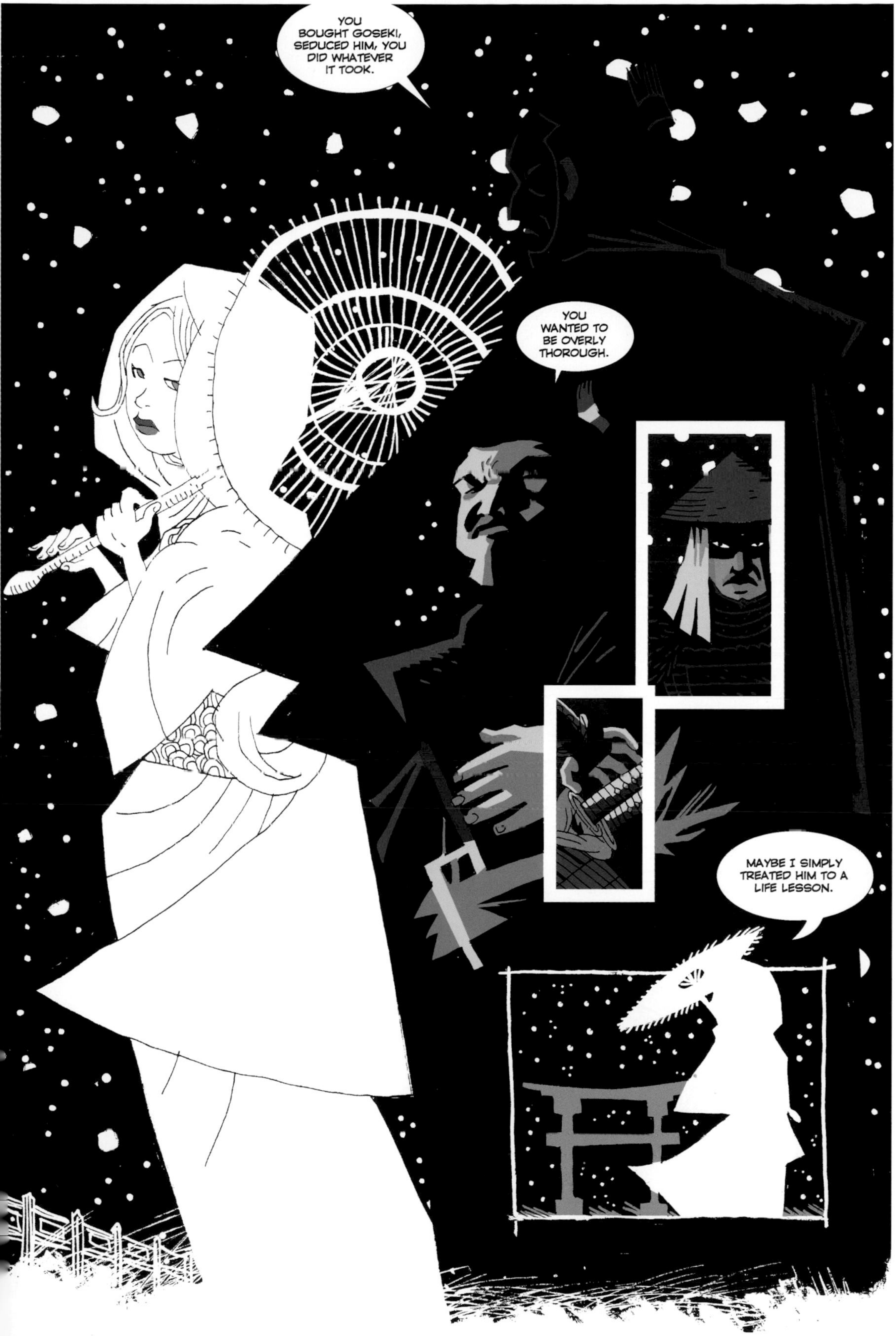
YOU BOUGHT GOSEKI, SEDUCED HIM, YOU DID WHATEVER IT TOOK.
YOU WANTED TO BE OVERLY THOROUGH.
MAYBE I SIMPLY TREATED HIM TO A LIFE LESSON.

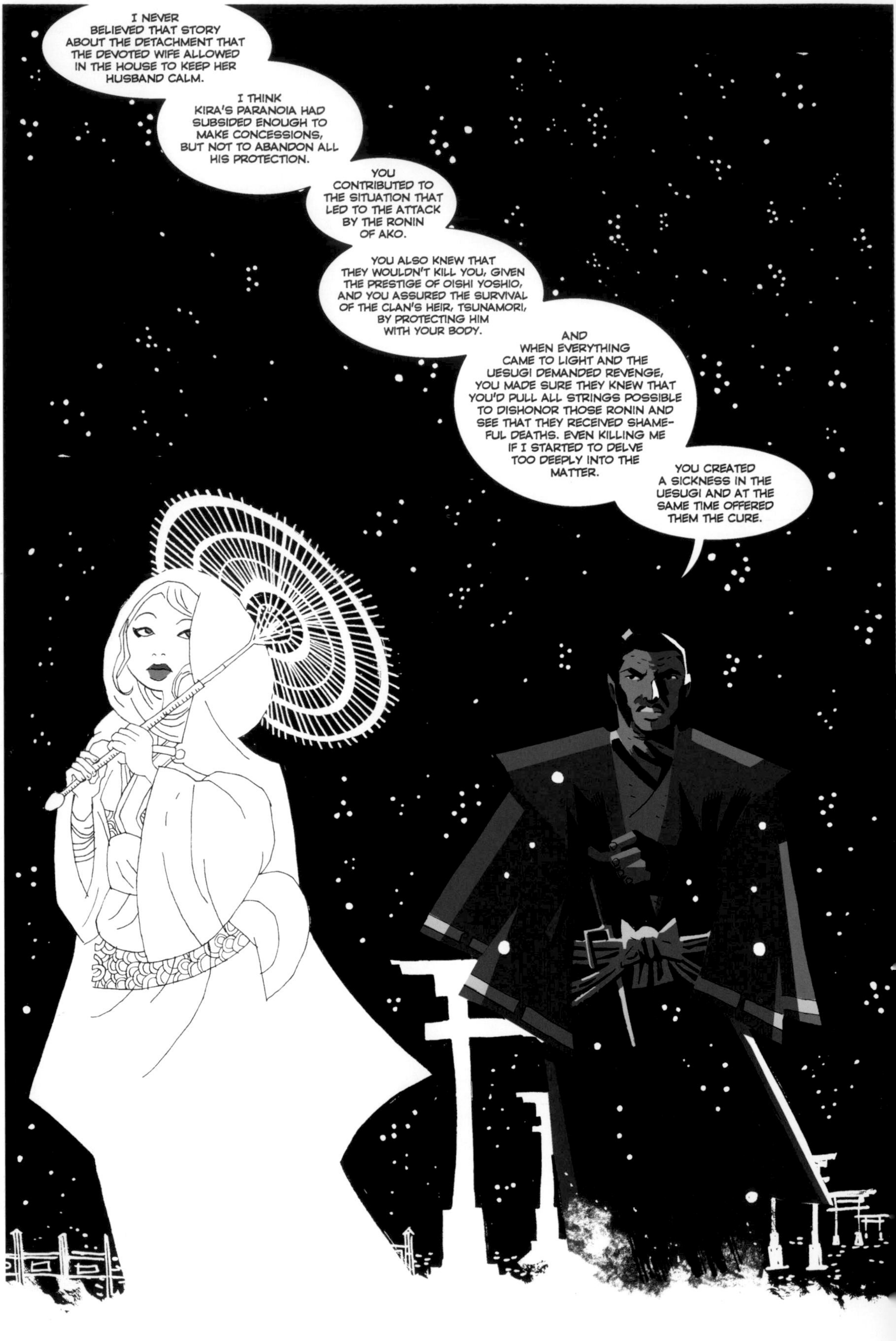
I NEVER BELIEVED THAT STORY ABOUT THE DETACHMENT THAT THE DEVOTED WIFE ALLOWED IN THE HOUSE TO KEEP HER HUSBAND CALM.
I THINK KIRA'S PARANOIA HAD SUBSIDED ENOUGH TO MAKE CONCESSIONS, BUT NOT TO ABANDON ALL HIS PROTECTION.
YOU CONTRIBUTED TO THE SITUATION THAT LED TO THE ATTACK BY THE RONIN OF AKO.
YOU ALSO KNEW THAT THEY WOULDN'T KILL YOU, GIVEN THE PRESTIGE OF OISHI YOSHIO, AND YOU ASSURED THE SURVIVAL OF THE CLAN'S HEIR, TSUNAMORI, BY PROTECTING HIM WITH YOUR BODY.
AND WHEN EVERYTHING CAME TO LIGHT AND THE UESUGI DEMANDED REVENGE, YOU MADE SURE THEY KNEW THAT YOU'D PULL ALL STRINGS POSSIBLE TO DISHONOR THOSE RONIN AND SEE THAT THEY RECEIVED SHAME-FUL DEATHS. EVEN KILLING ME IF I STARTED TO DELVE TOO DEEPLY INTO THE MATTER.
YOU CREATED A SICKNESS IN THE UESUGI AND AT THE SAME TIME OFFERED THEM THE CURE.

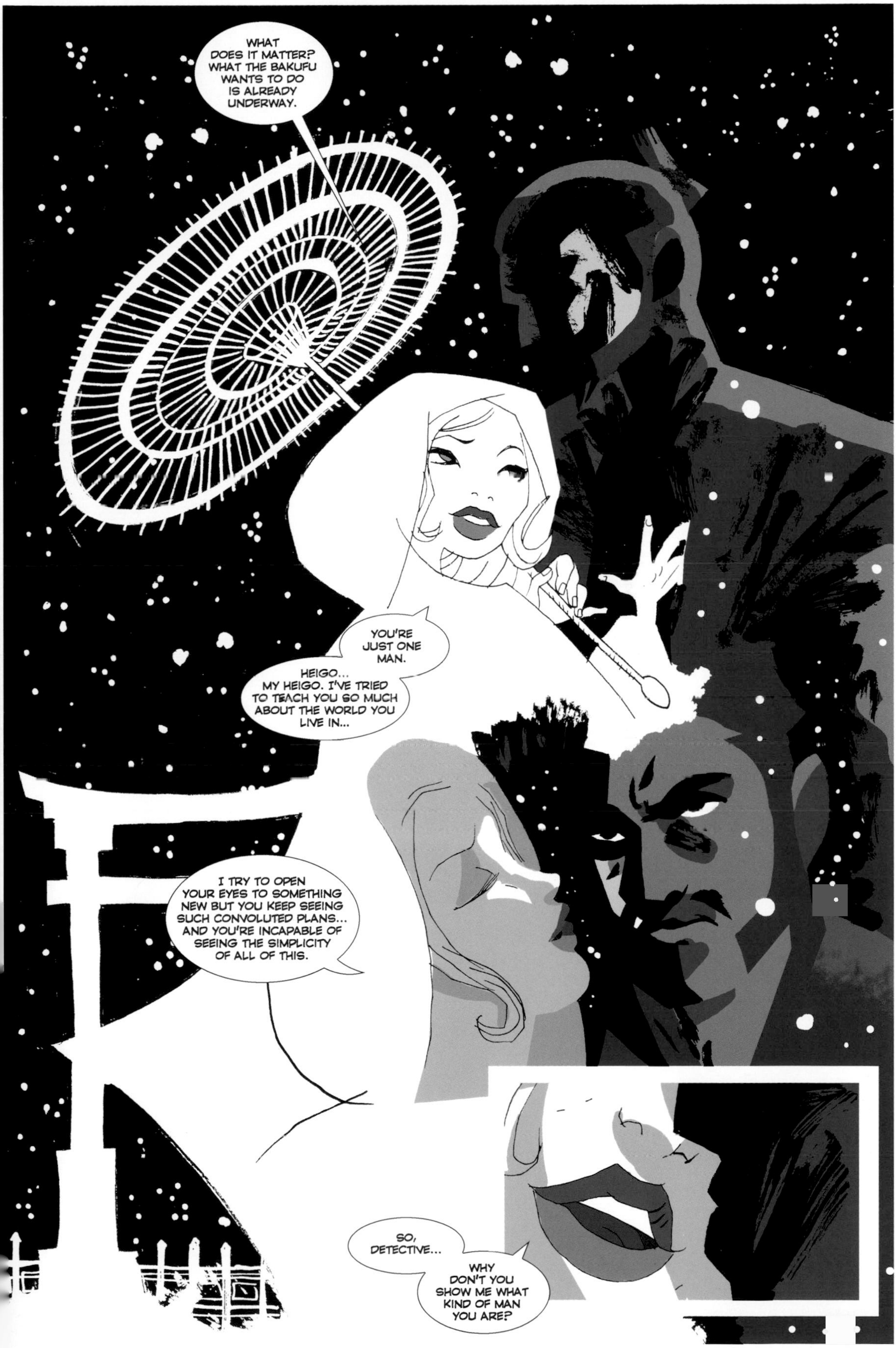
WHAT DOES IT MATTER? WHAT THE BAKUFU WANTS TO DO IS ALREADY UNDERWAY.
YOU'RE JUST ONE MAN.
HEIGO... MY HEIGO. I'VE TRIED TO TEACH YOU SO MUCH ABOUT THE WORLD YOU LIVE IN...
I TRY TO OPEN YOUR EYES TO SOMETHING NEW BUT YOU KEEP SEEING SUCH CONVOLUTED PLANS... AND YOU'RE INCAPABLE OF SEEING THE SIMPLICITY OF ALL OF THIS.
SO, DETECTIVE...
WHY DON'T YOU SHOW ME WHAT KIND OF MAN YOU ARE?

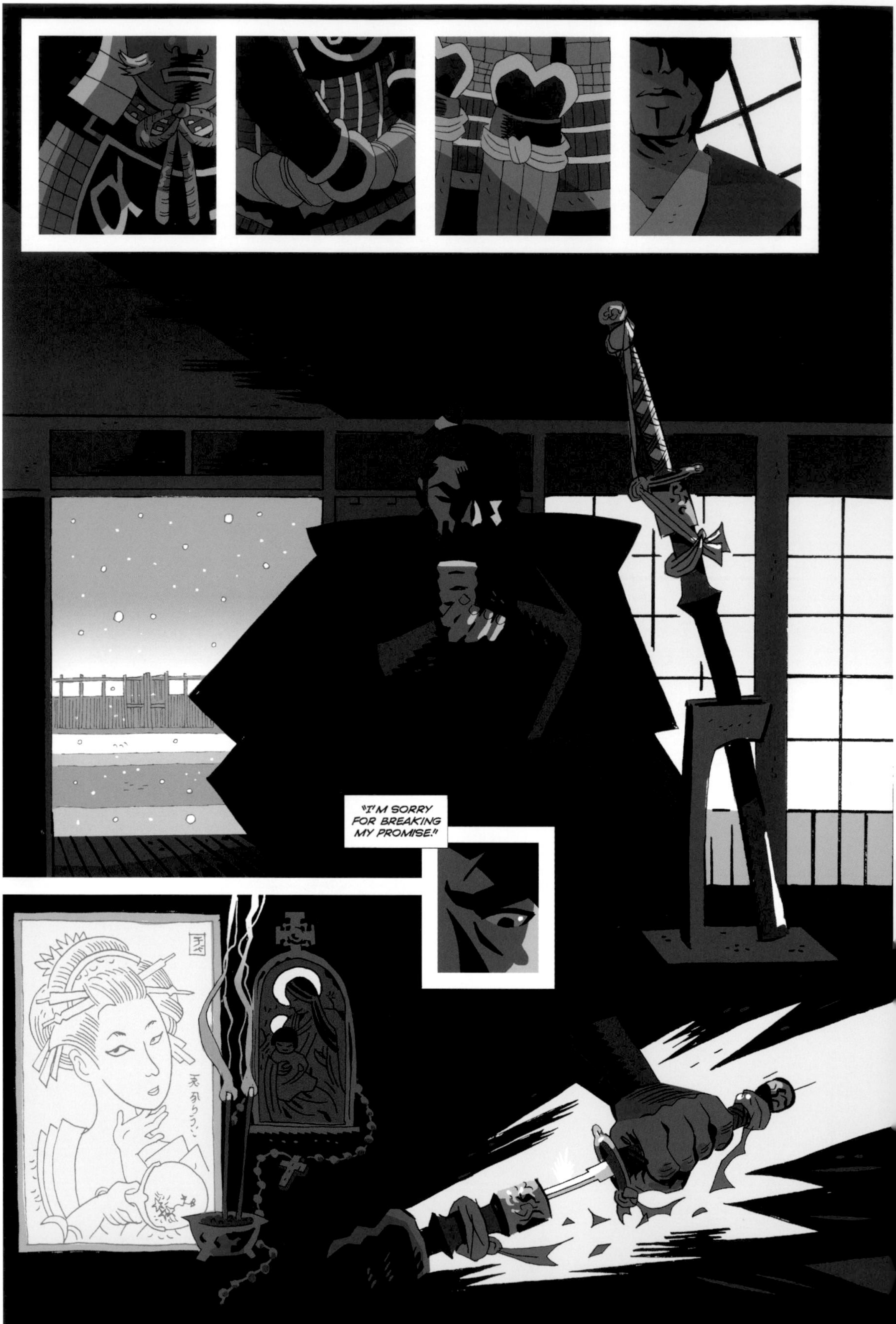
"I'M SORRY
FOR BREAKING
MY PROMISE."

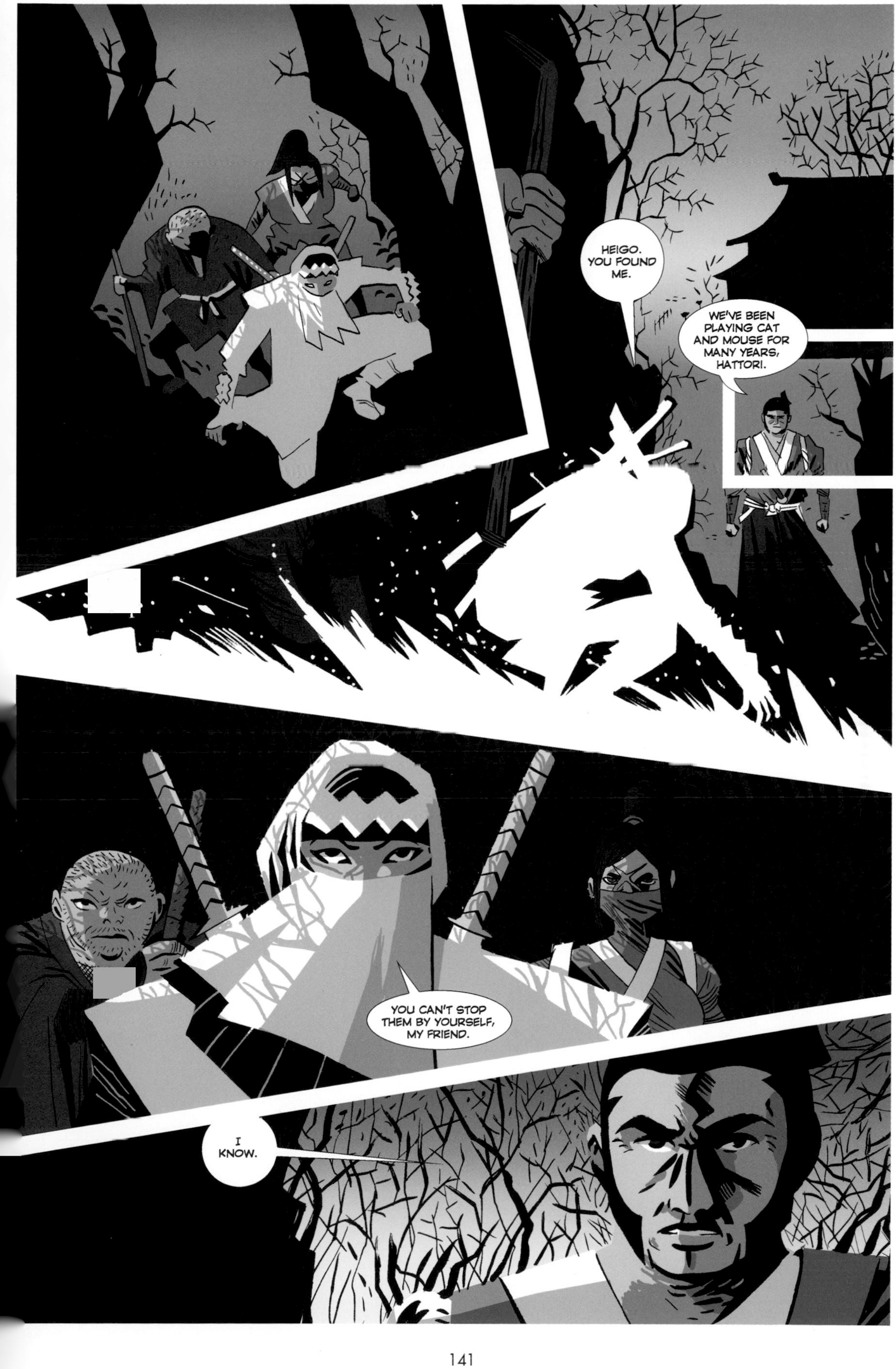
HEIGO. YOU FOUND ME.
WE'VE BEEN PLAYING CAT AND MOUSE FOR MANY YEARS, HATTORI.
YOU CAN'T STOP THEM BY YOURSELF, MY FRIEND.
I KNOW.

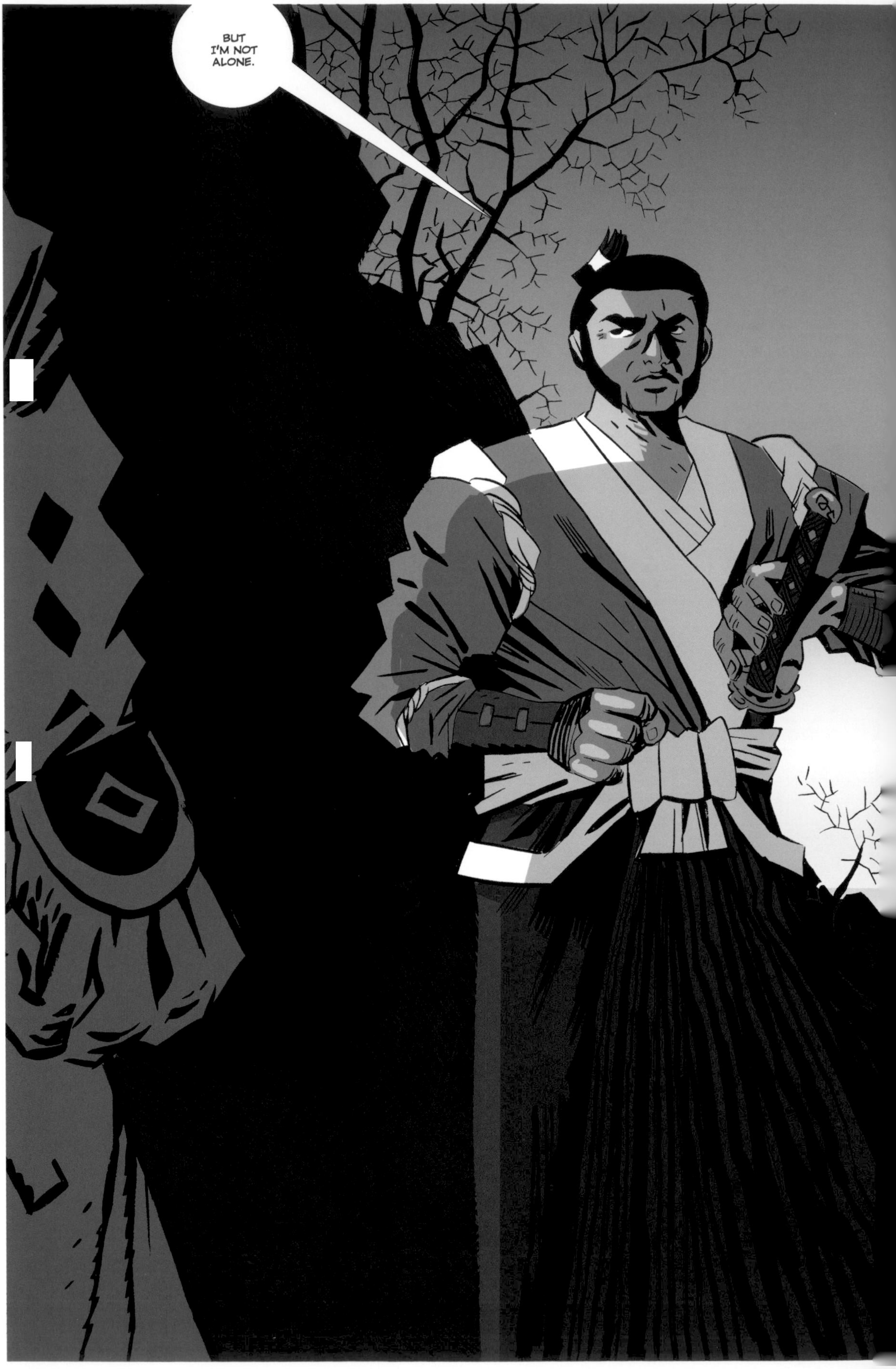
BUT I'M NOT ALONE.

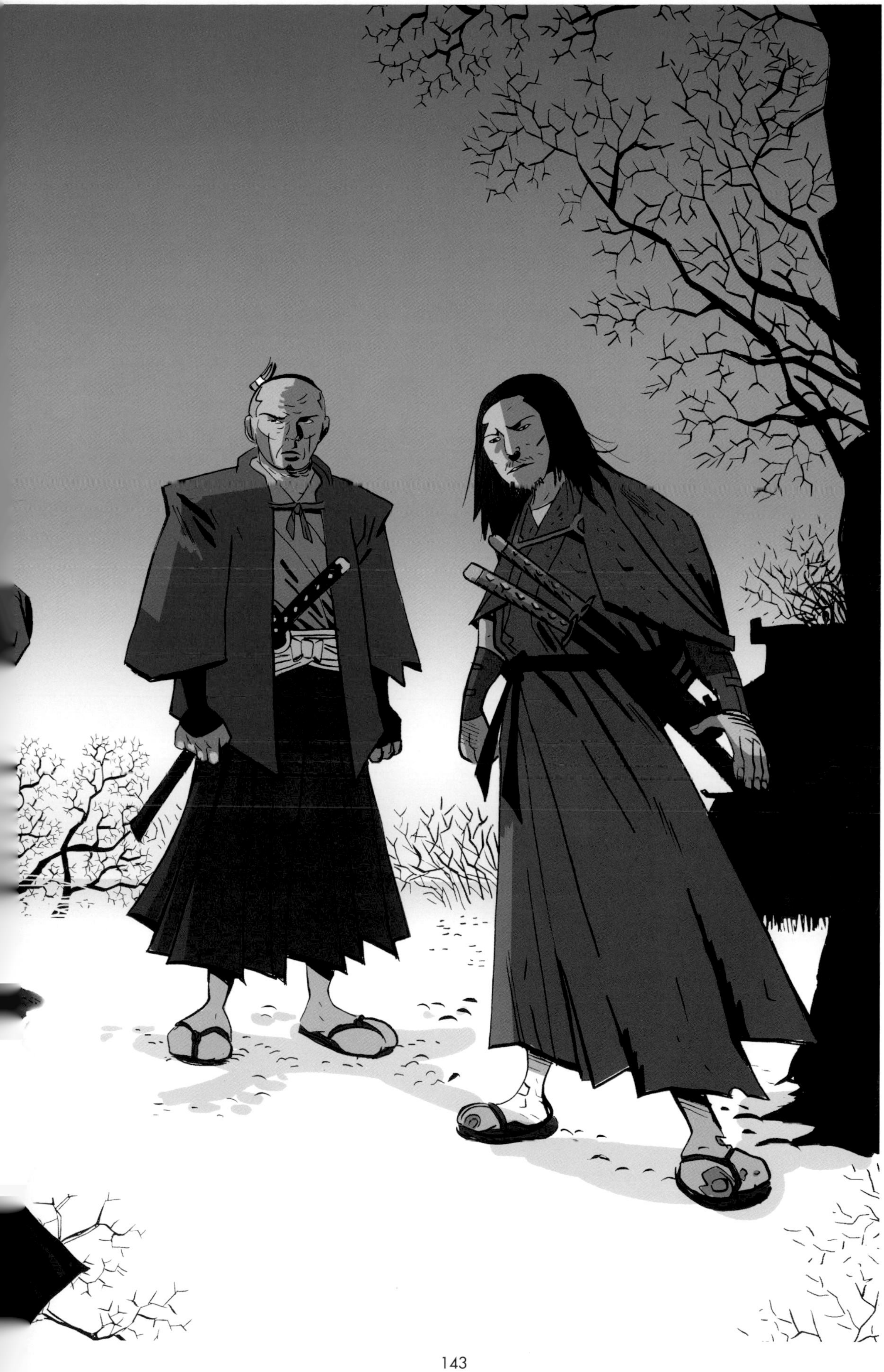

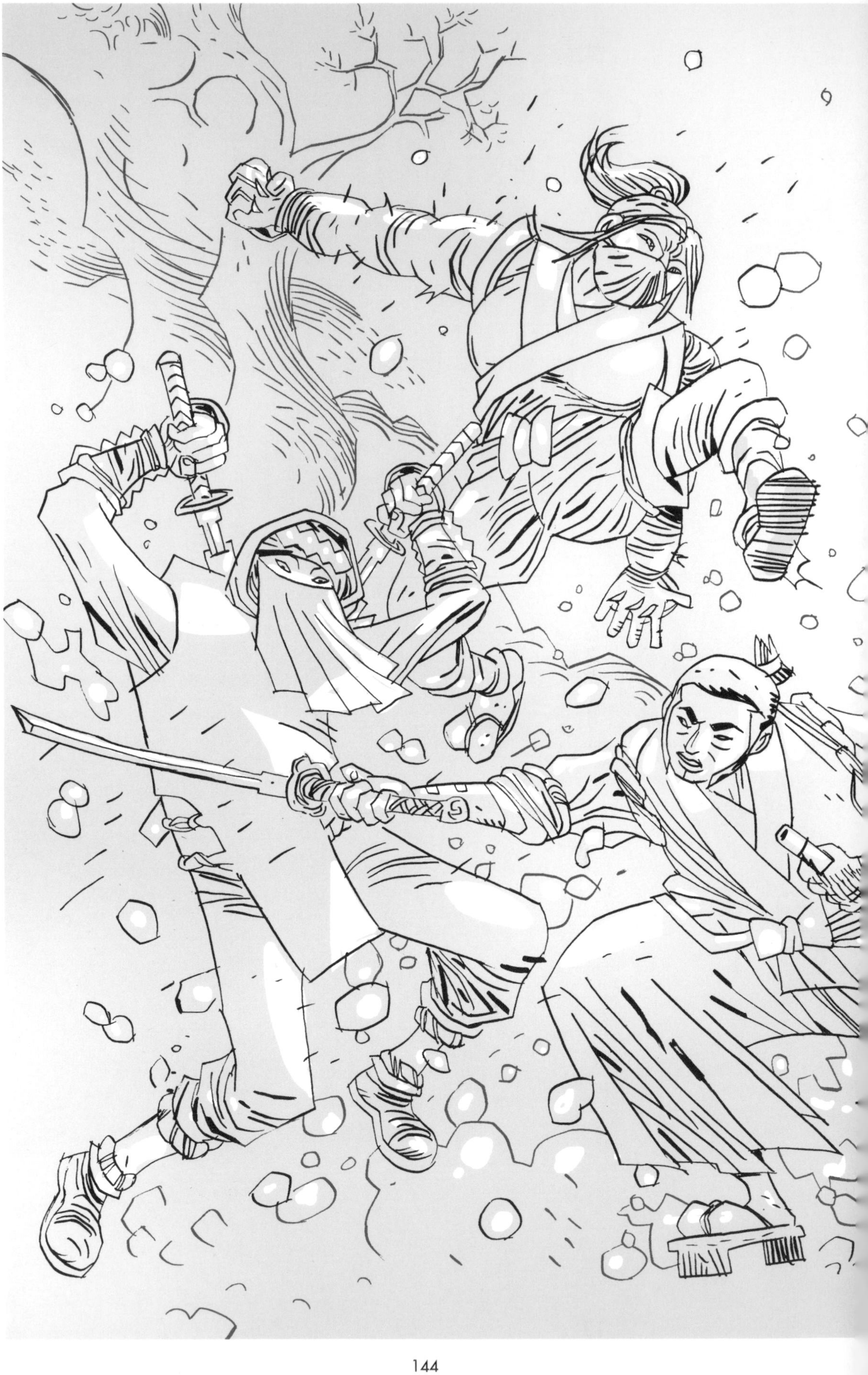

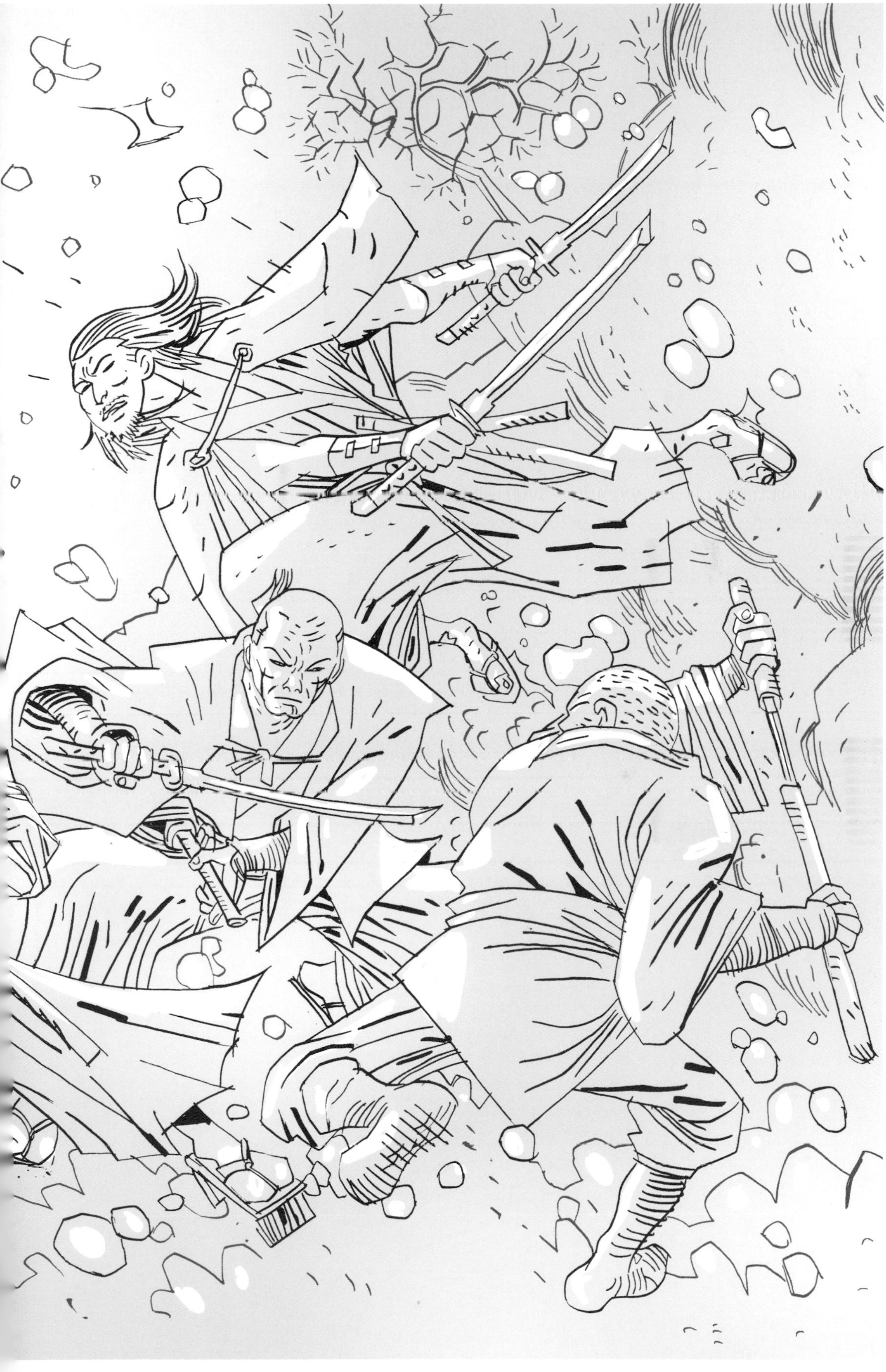

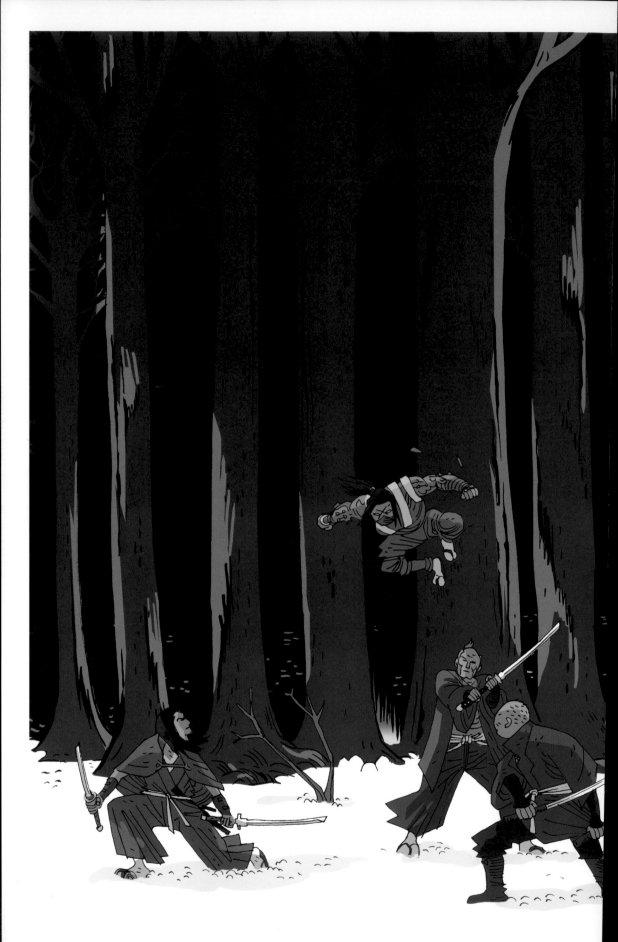

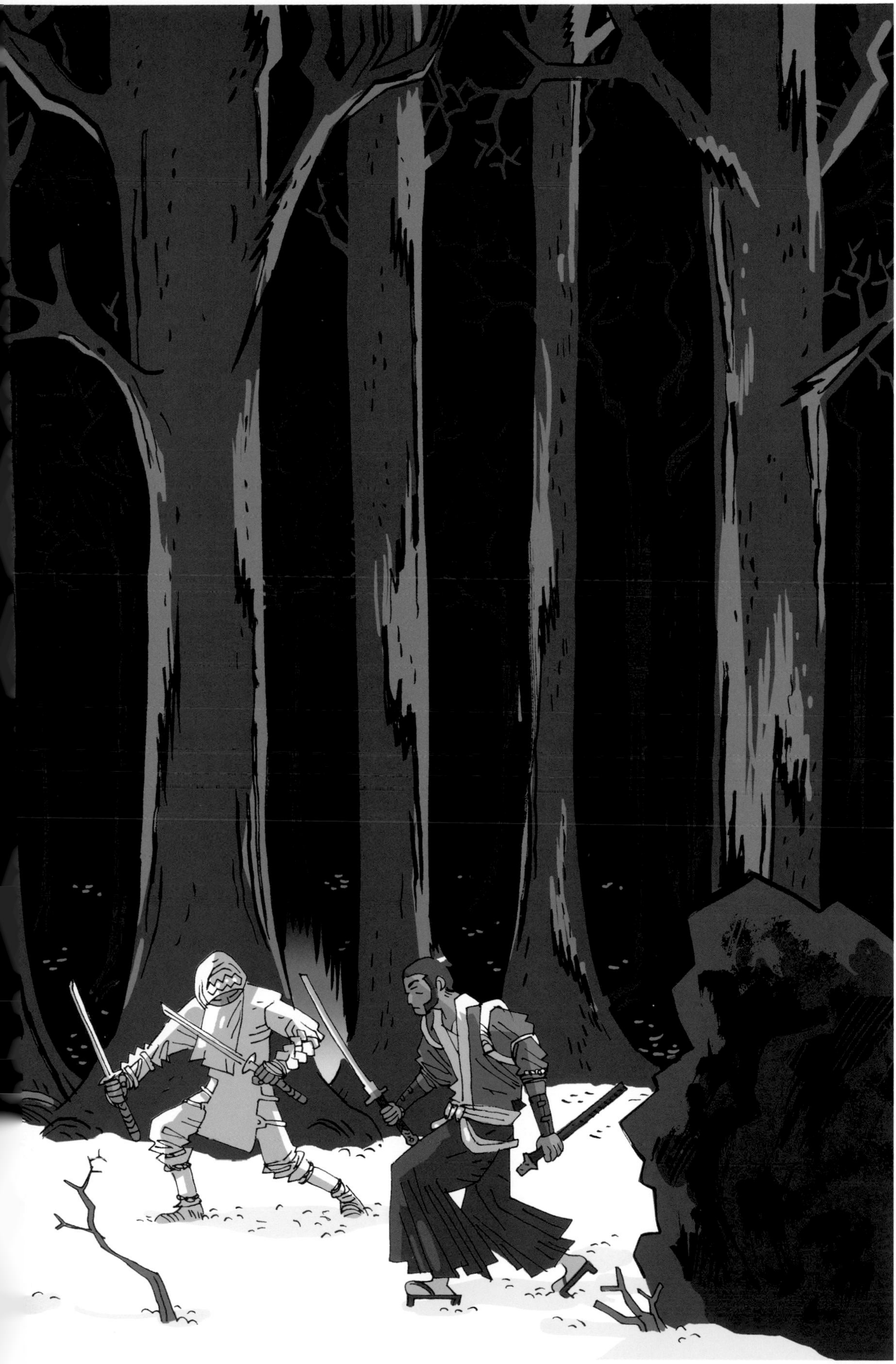

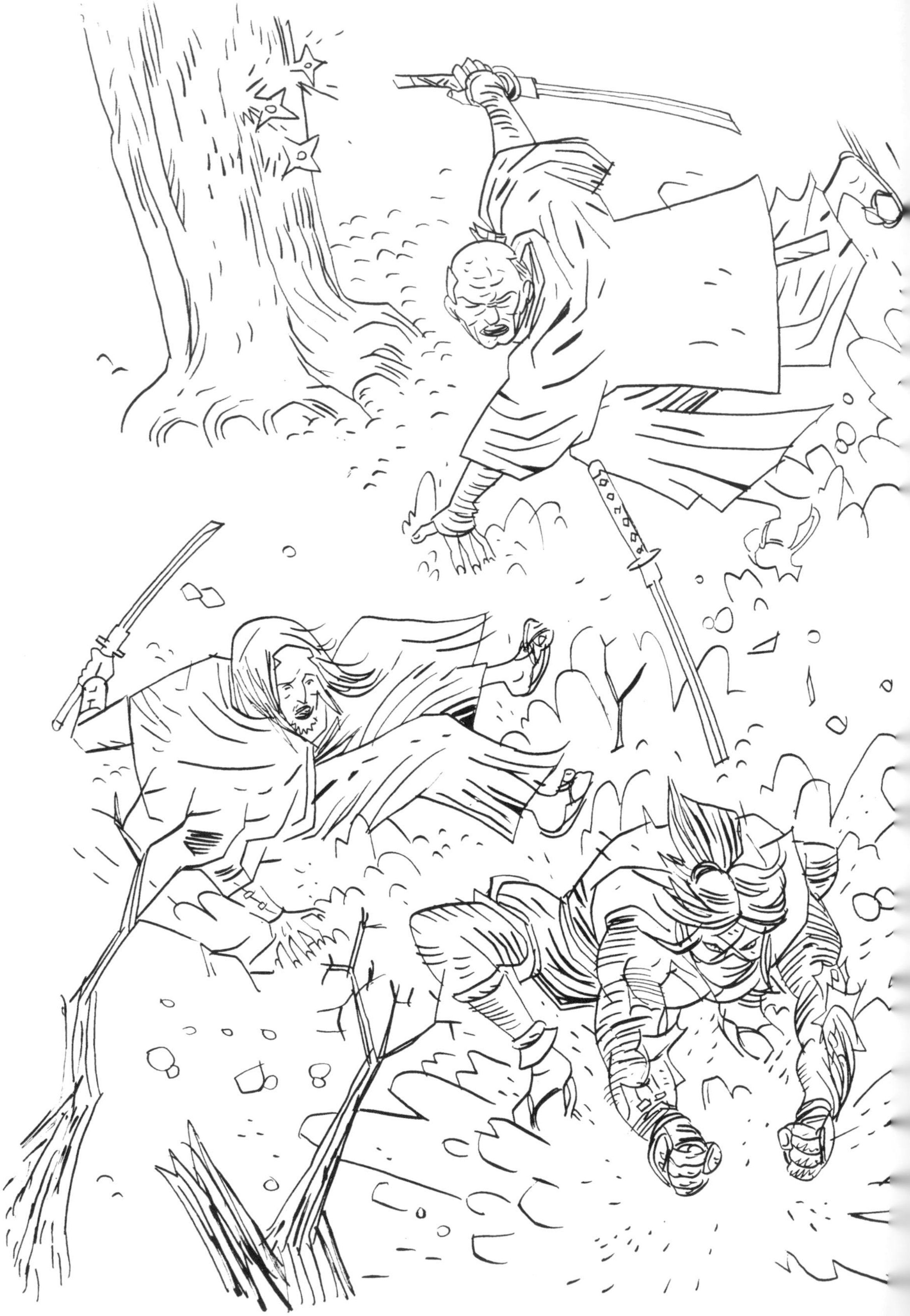

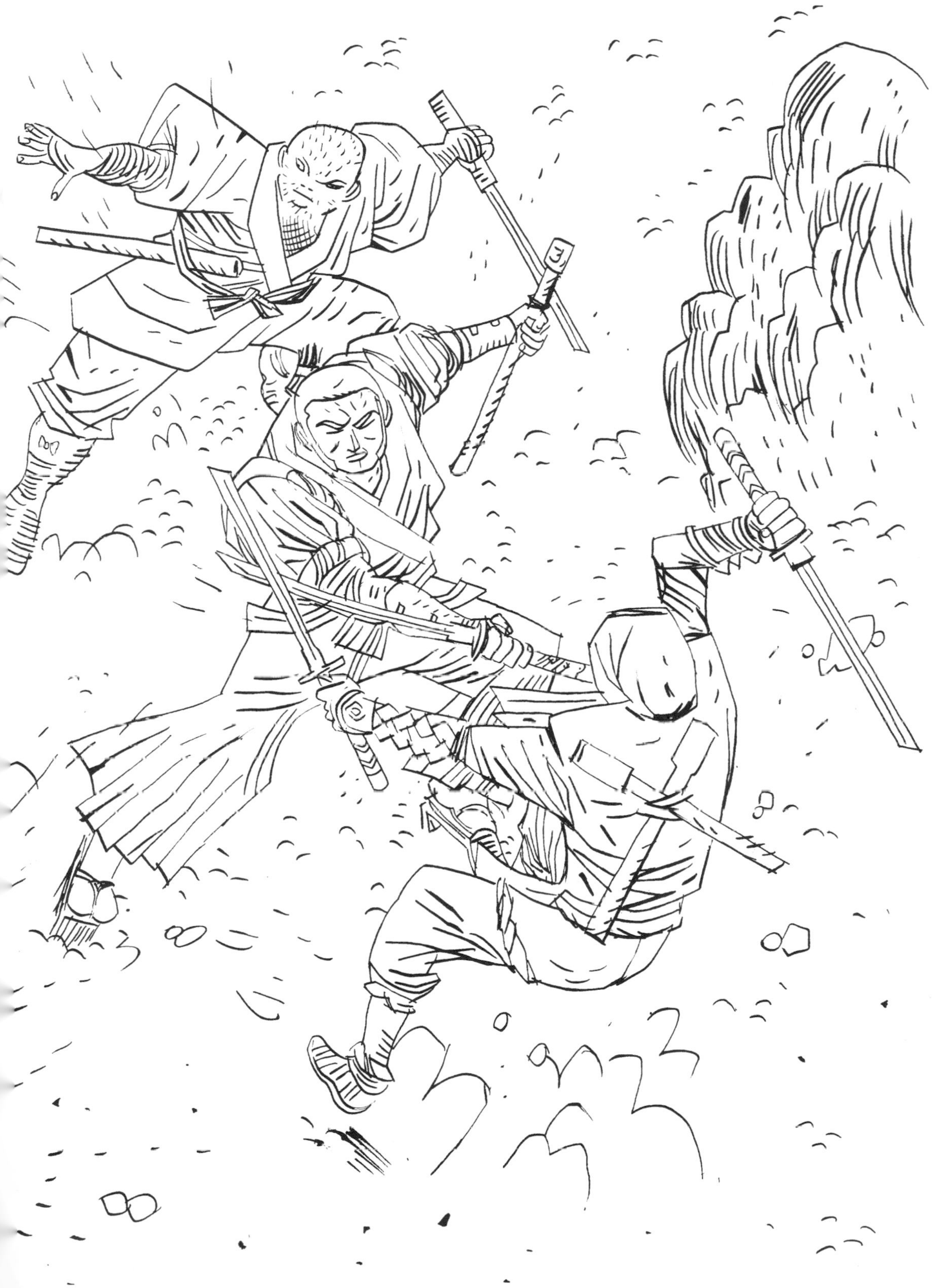

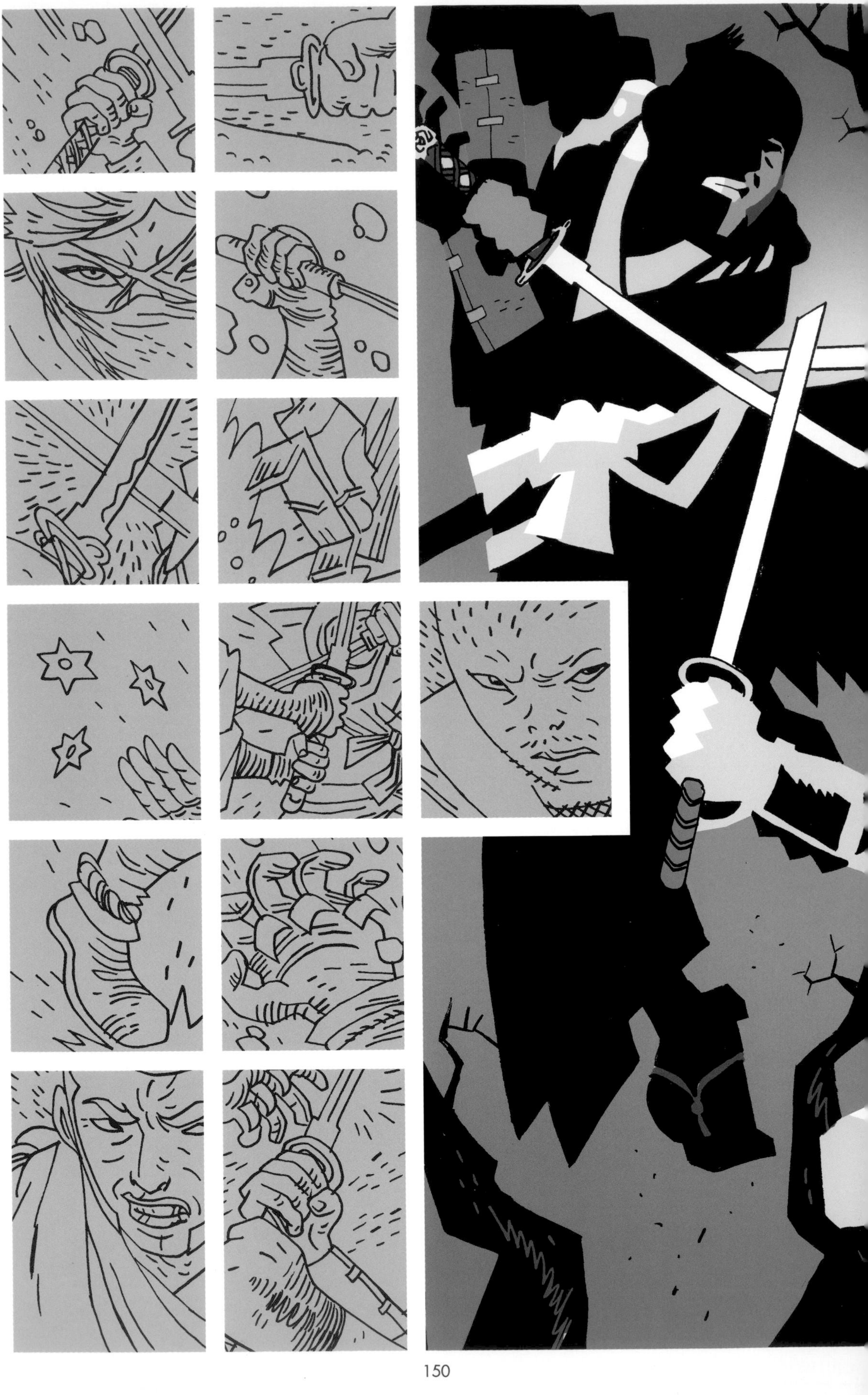

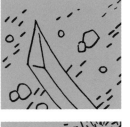

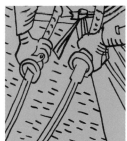

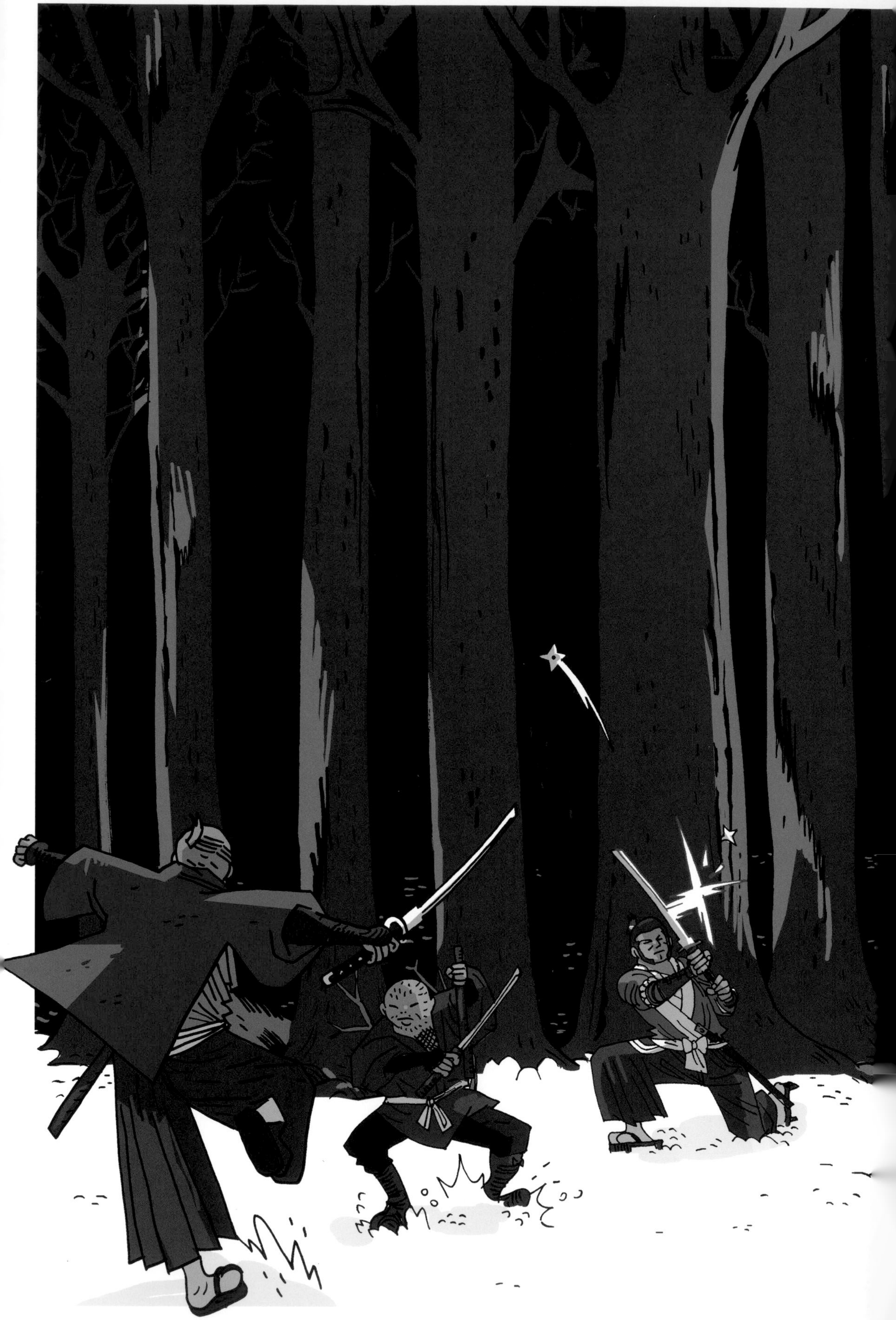

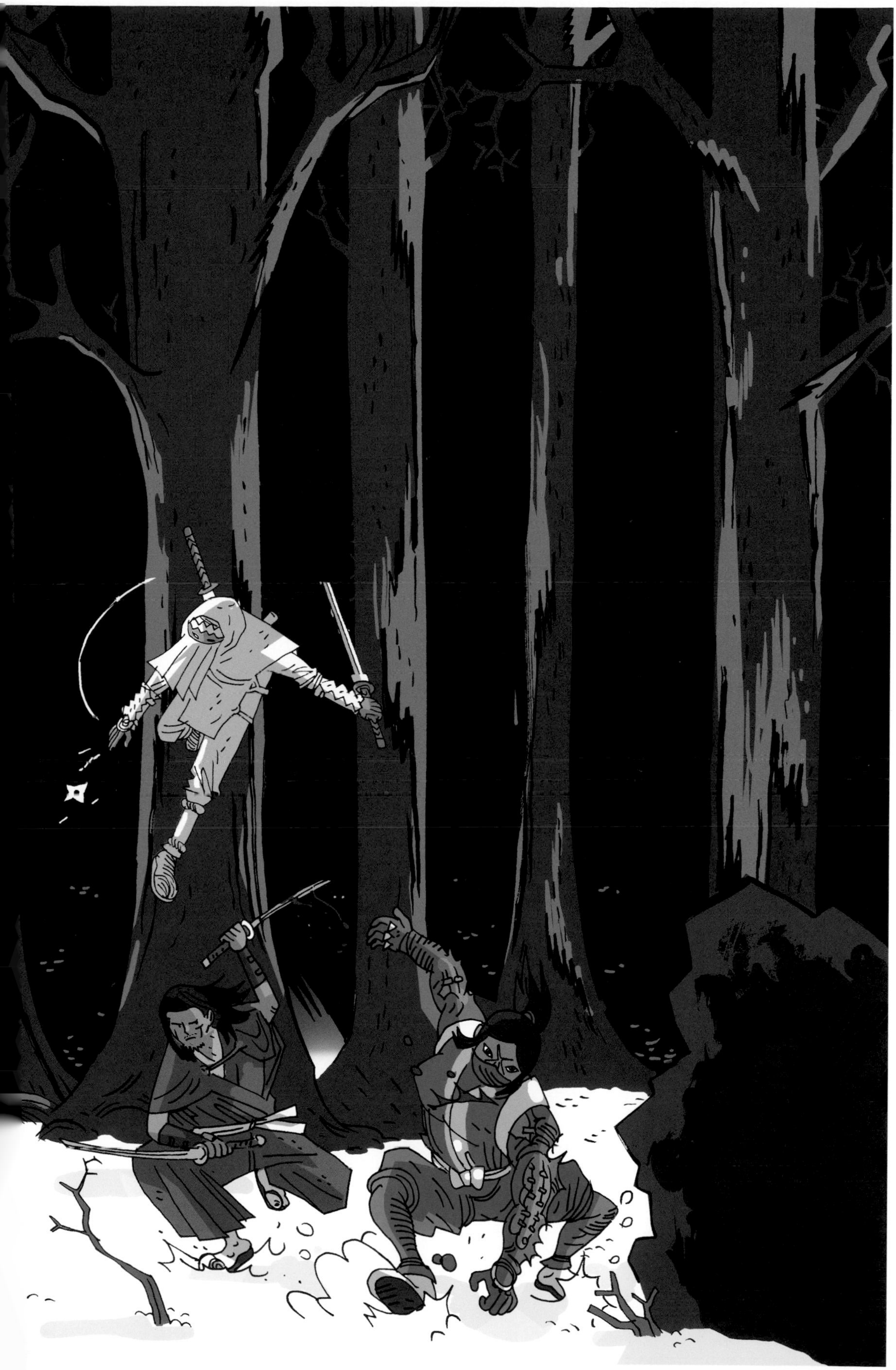

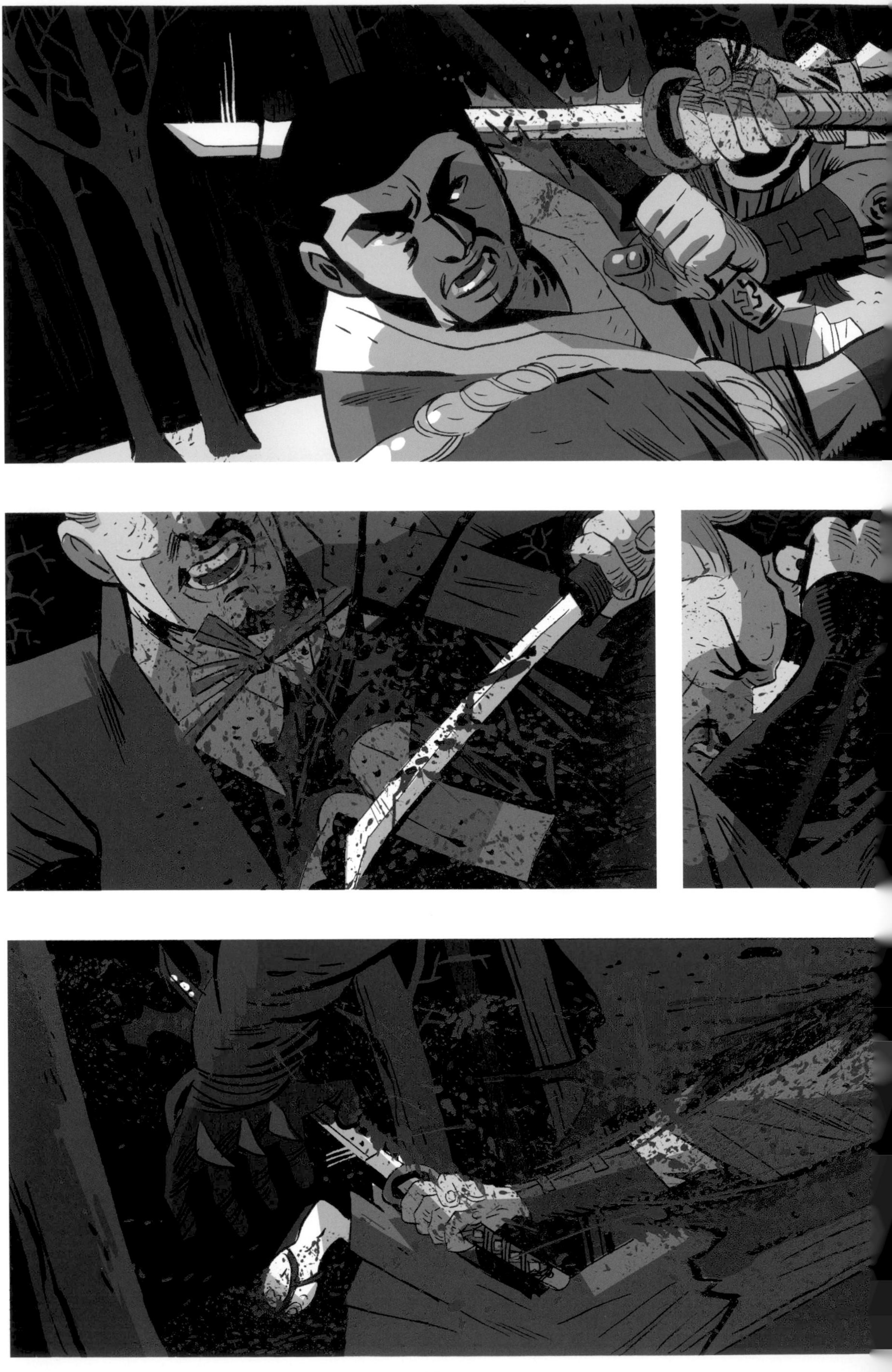

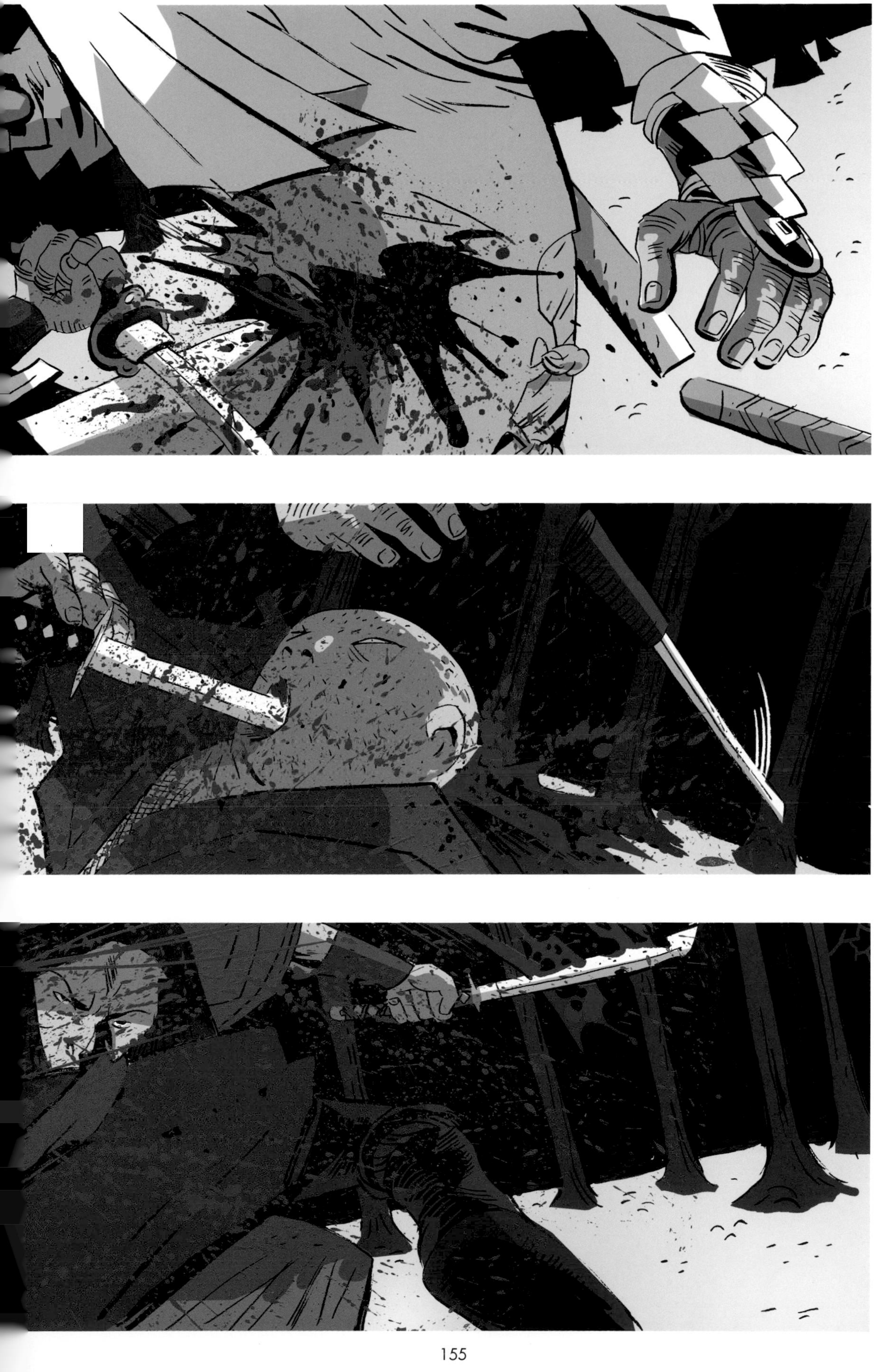

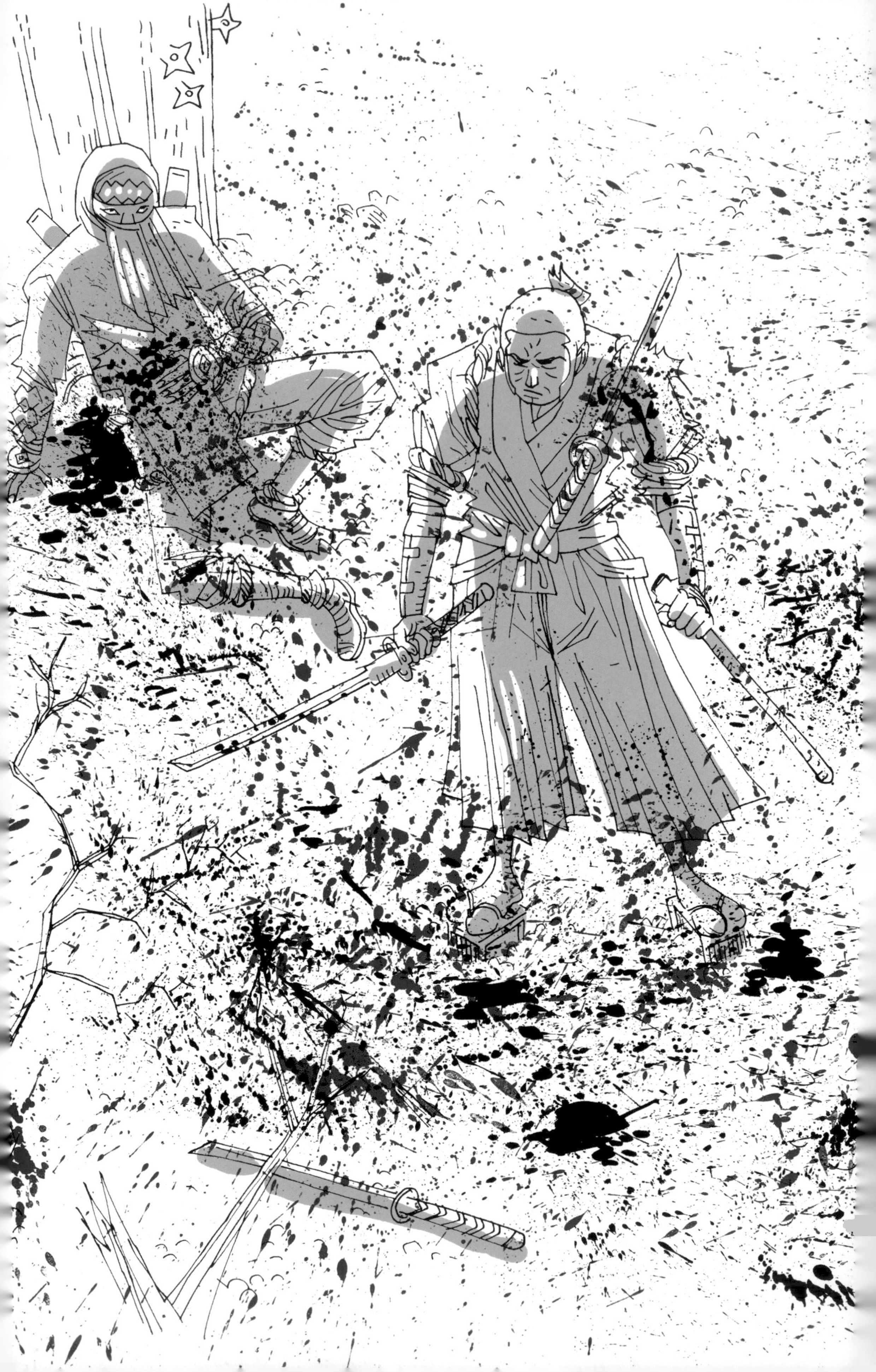

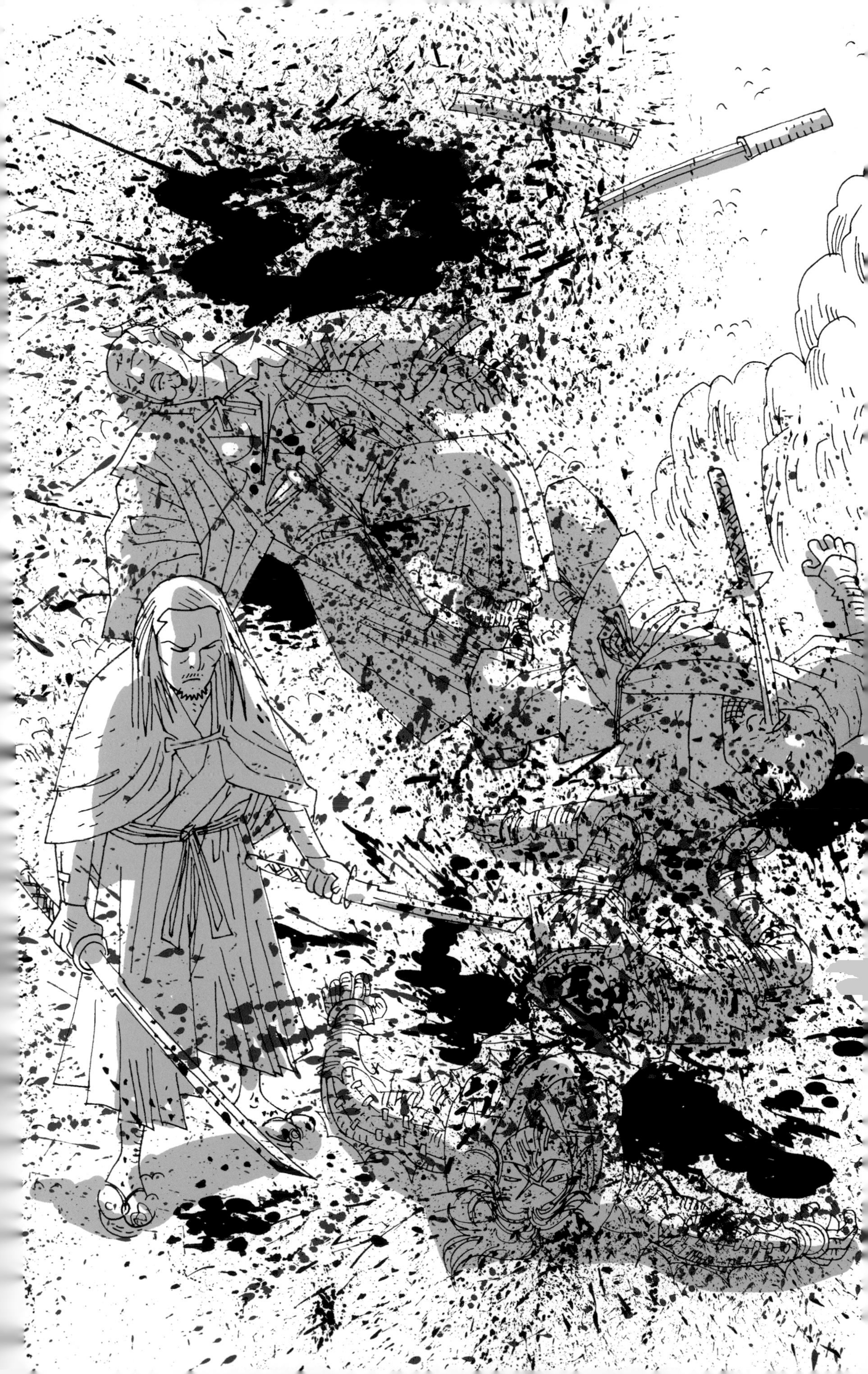

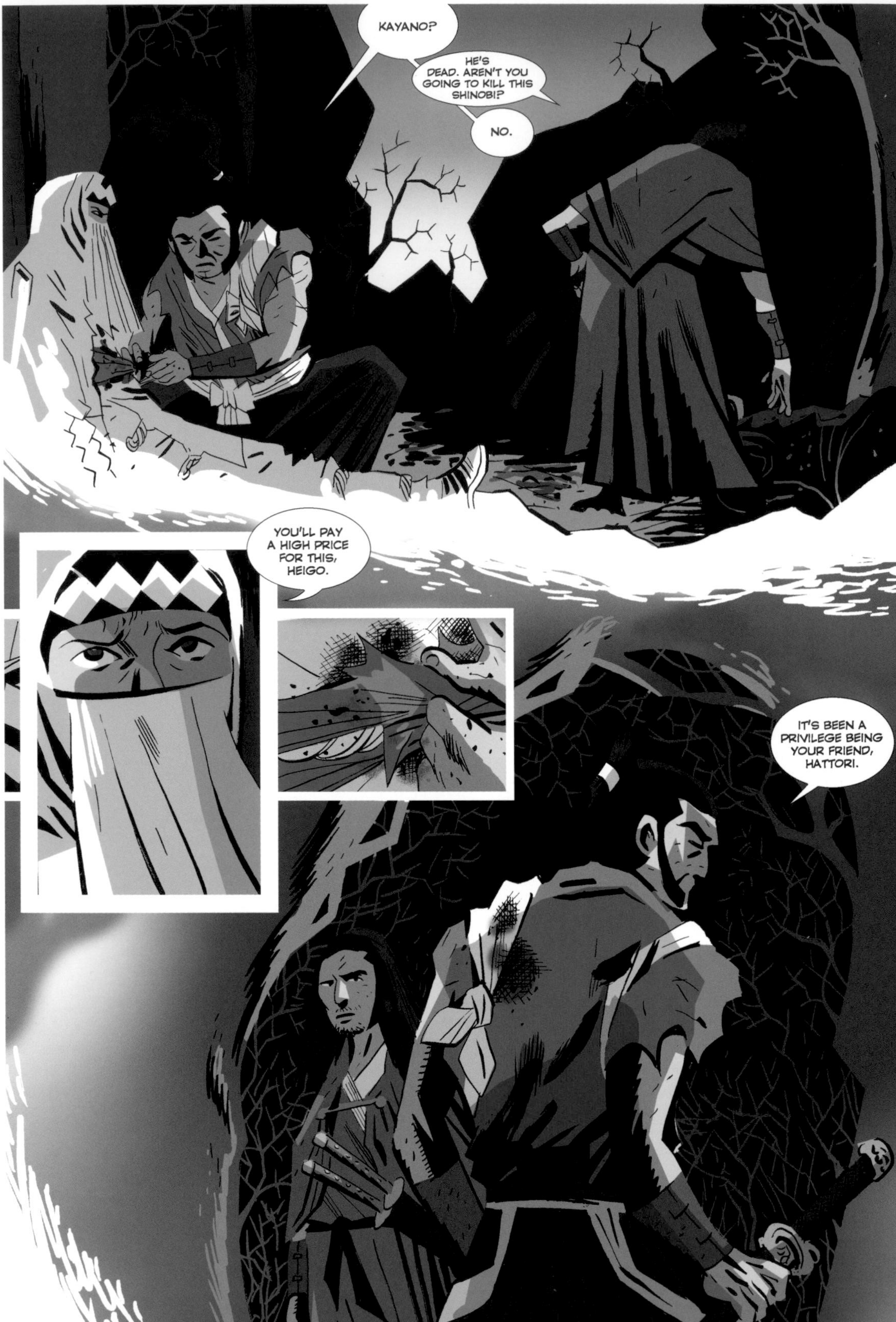
KAYANO?
HE'S DEAD. AREN'T YOU GOING TO KILL THIS SHINOBI?
NO.
YOU'LL PAY A HIGH PRICE FOR THIS, HEIGO.
IT'S BEEN A PRIVILEGE BEING YOUR FRIEND, HATTORI.

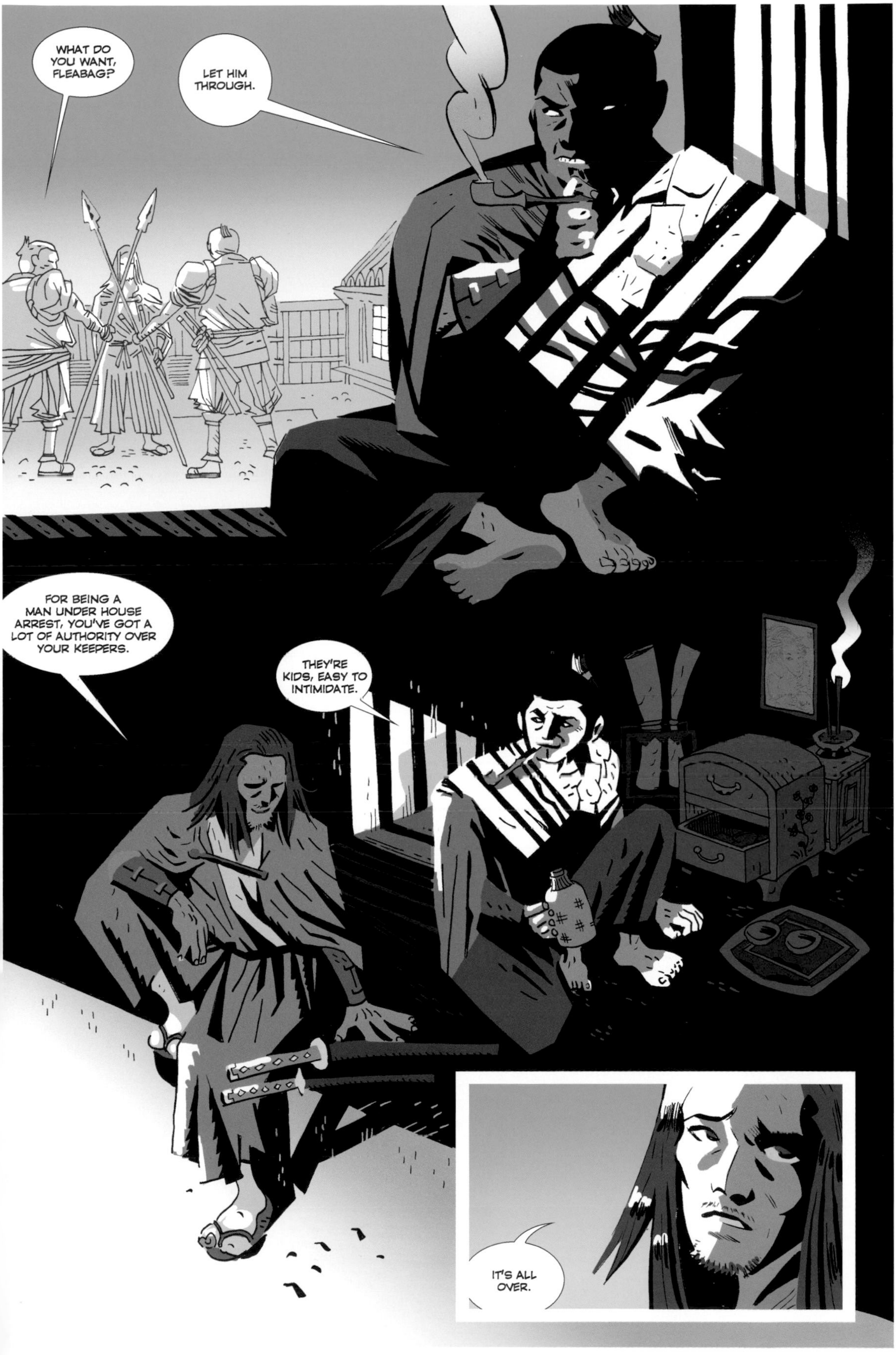
WHAT DO YOU WANT, FLEABAG?
LET HIM THROUGH.
FOR BEING A MAN UNDER HOUSE ARREST, YOU'VE GOT A LOT OF AUTHORITY OVER YOUR KEEPERS.
THEY'RE KIDS, EASY TO INTIMIDATE.
IT'S ALL OVER.

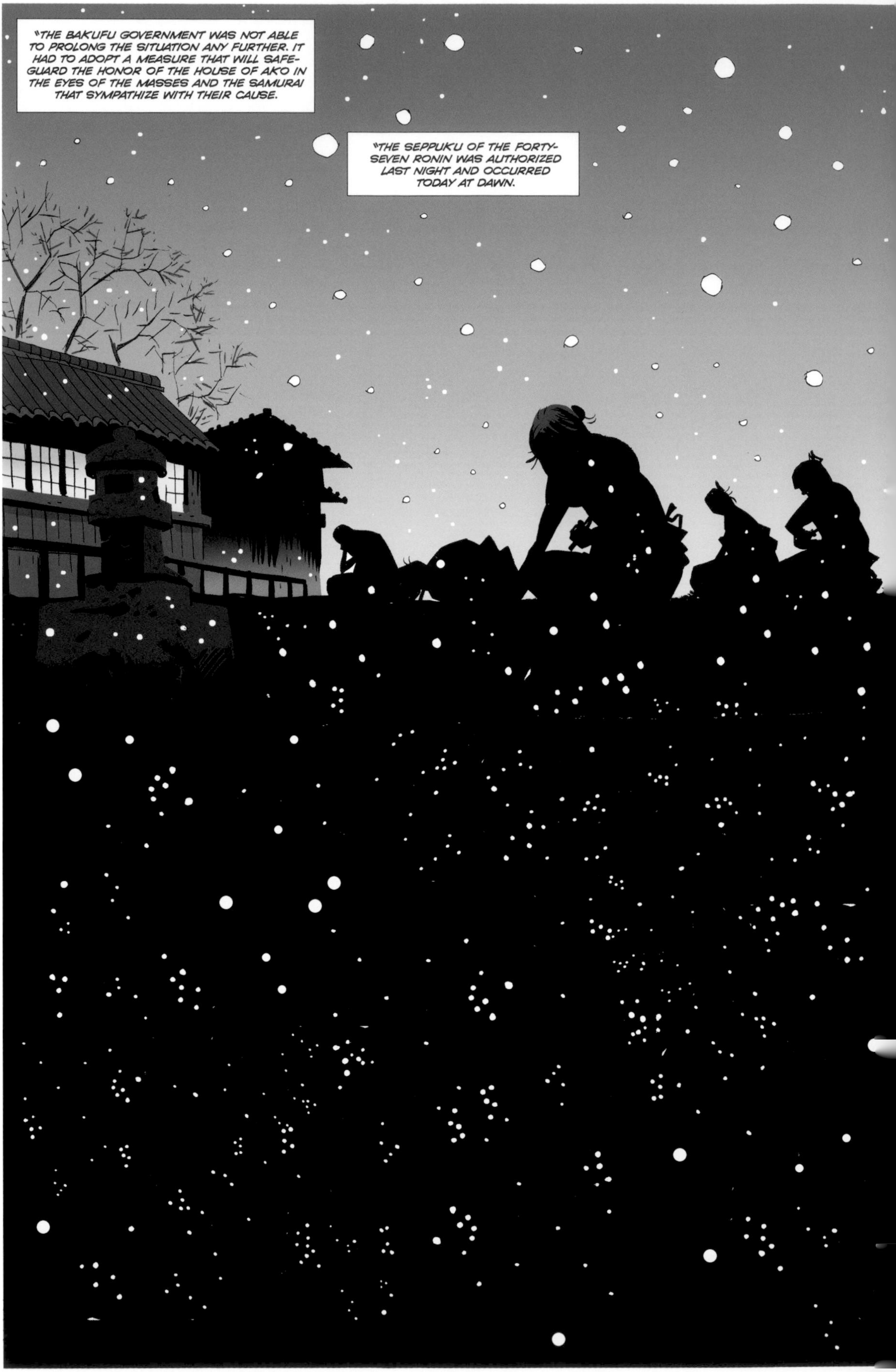
"THE BAKUFU GOVERNMENT WAS NOT ABLE TO PROLONG THE SITUATION ANY FURTHER. IT HAD TO ADOPT A MEASURE THAT WILL SAFEGUARD THE HONOR OF THE HOUSE OF AKO IN THE EYES OF THE MASSES AND THE SAMURAI THAT SYMPATHIZE WITH THEIR CAUSE.
"THE SEPPUKU OF THE FORTY-SEVEN RONIN WAS AUTHORIZED LAST NIGHT AND OCCURRED TODAY AT DAWN.

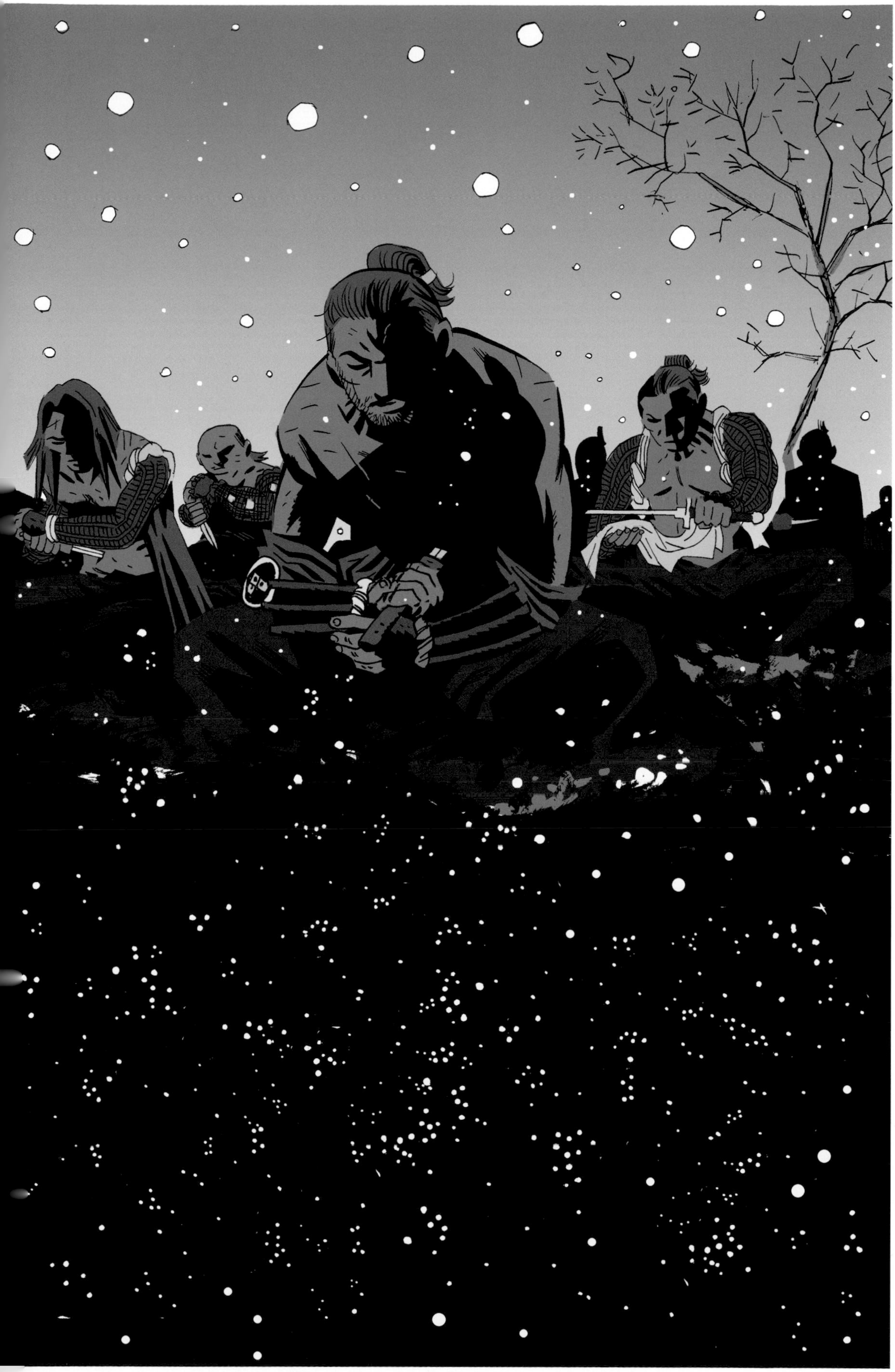

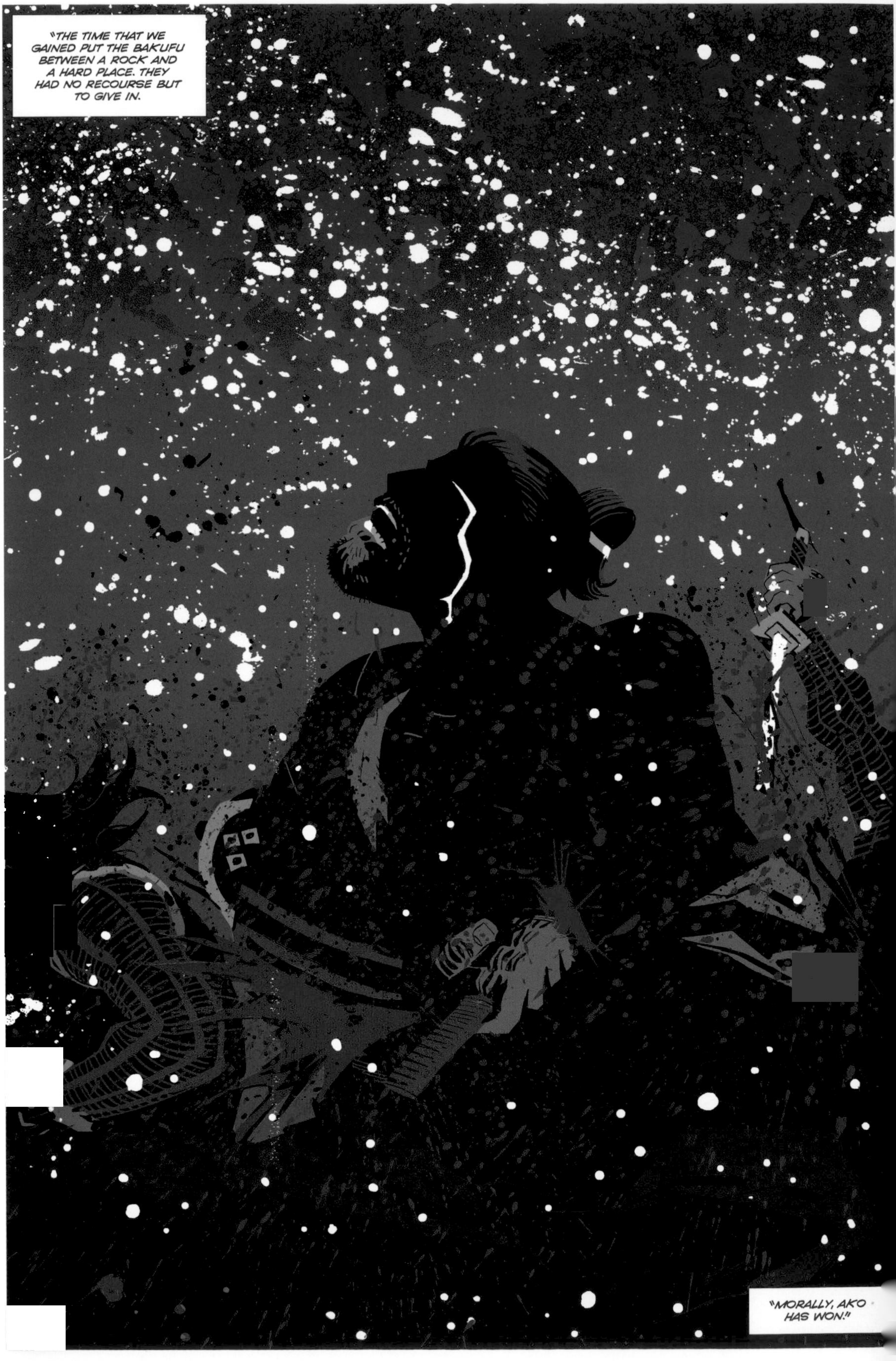
"THE TIME THAT WE GAINED PUT THE BAKUFU BETWEEN A ROCK AND A HARD PLACE. THEY HAD NO RECOURSE BUT TO GIVE IN.
"MORALLY, AKO HAS WON."

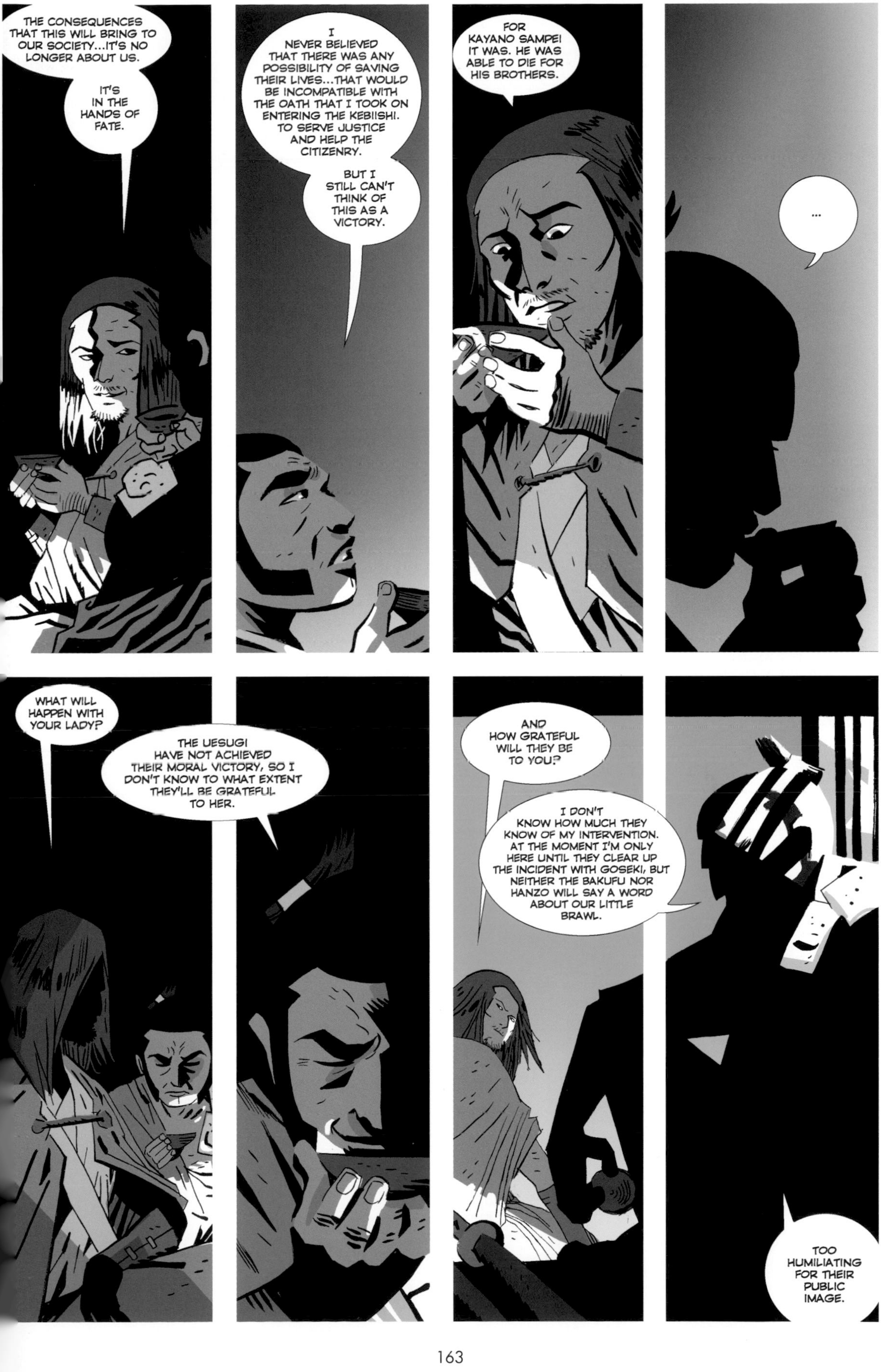
THE CONSEQUENCES THAT THIS WILL BRING TO OUR SOCIETY...IT'S NO LONGER ABOUT US.
IT'S IN THE HANDS OF FATE.
I NEVER BELIEVED THAT THERE WAS ANY POSSIBILITY OF SAVING THEIR LIVES...THAT WOULD BE INCOMPATIBLE WITH THE OATH THAT I TOOK ON ENTERING THE KEBIISHI. TO SERVE JUSTICE AND HELP THE CITIZENRY.
BUT I STILL CAN'T THINK OF THIS AS A VICTORY.
FOR KAYANO SAMPEI IT WAS. HE WAS ABLE TO DIE FOR HIS BROTHERS.
...
WHAT WILL HAPPEN WITH YOUR LADY?
THE UESUGI HAVE NOT ACHIEVED THEIR MORAL VICTORY, SO I DON'T KNOW TO WHAT EXTENT THEY'LL BE GRATEFUL TO HER.
AND HOW GRATEFUL WILL THEY BE TO YOU?
I DON'T KNOW HOW MUCH THEY KNOW OF MY INTERVENTION. AT THE MOMENT I'M ONLY HERE UNTIL THEY CLEAR UP THE INCIDENT WITH GOSEKI, BUT NEITHER THE BAKUFU NOR HANZO WILL SAY A WORD ABOUT OUR LITTLE BRAWL.
TOO HUMILIATING FOR THEIR PUBLIC IMAGE.

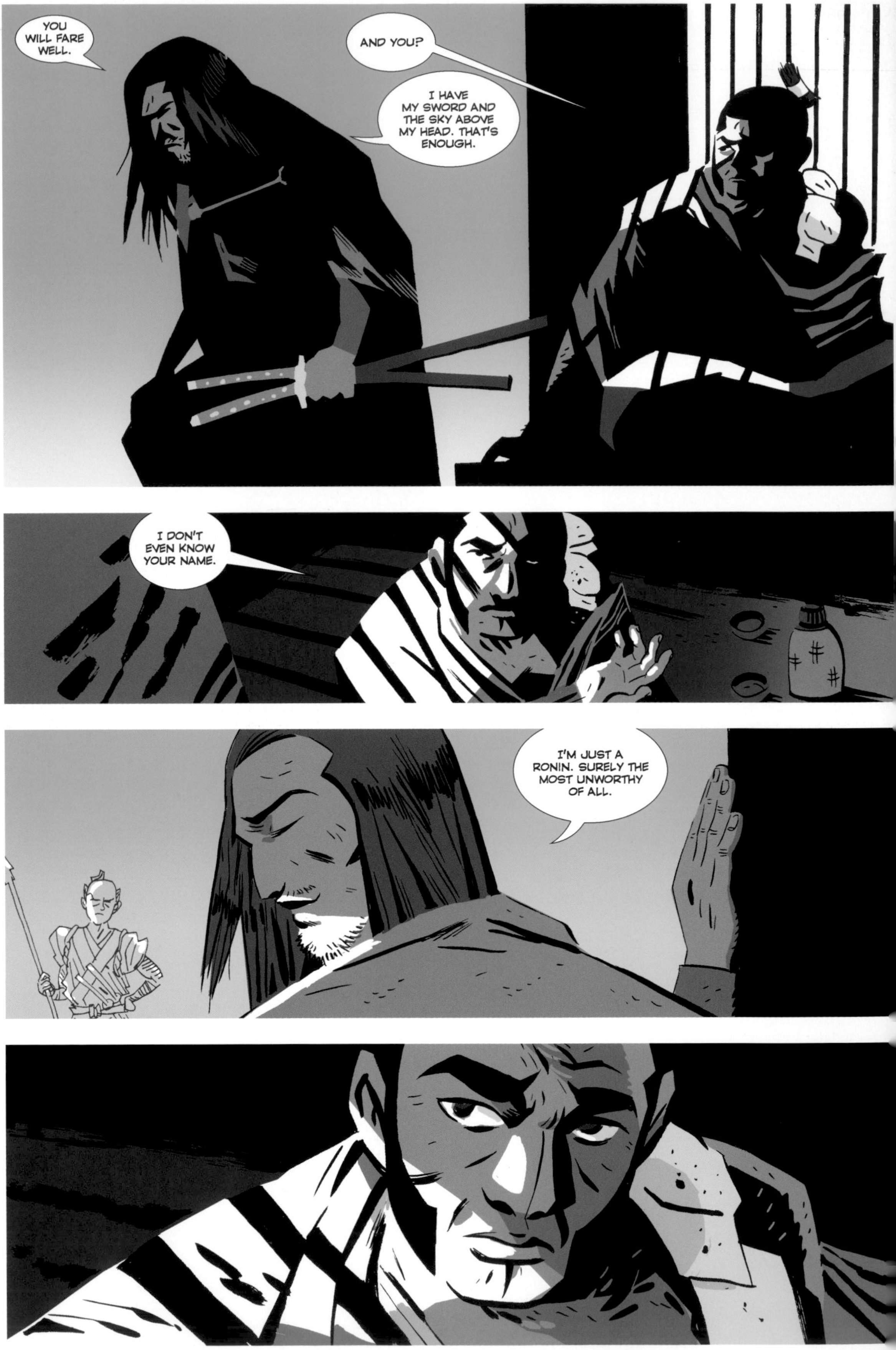
YOU WILL FARE WELL.
AND YOU?
I HAVE MY SWORD AND THE SKY ABOVE MY HEAD. THAT'S ENOUGH.
I DON'T EVEN KNOW YOUR NAME.
I'M JUST A RONIN. SURELY THE MOST UNWORTHY OF ALL.

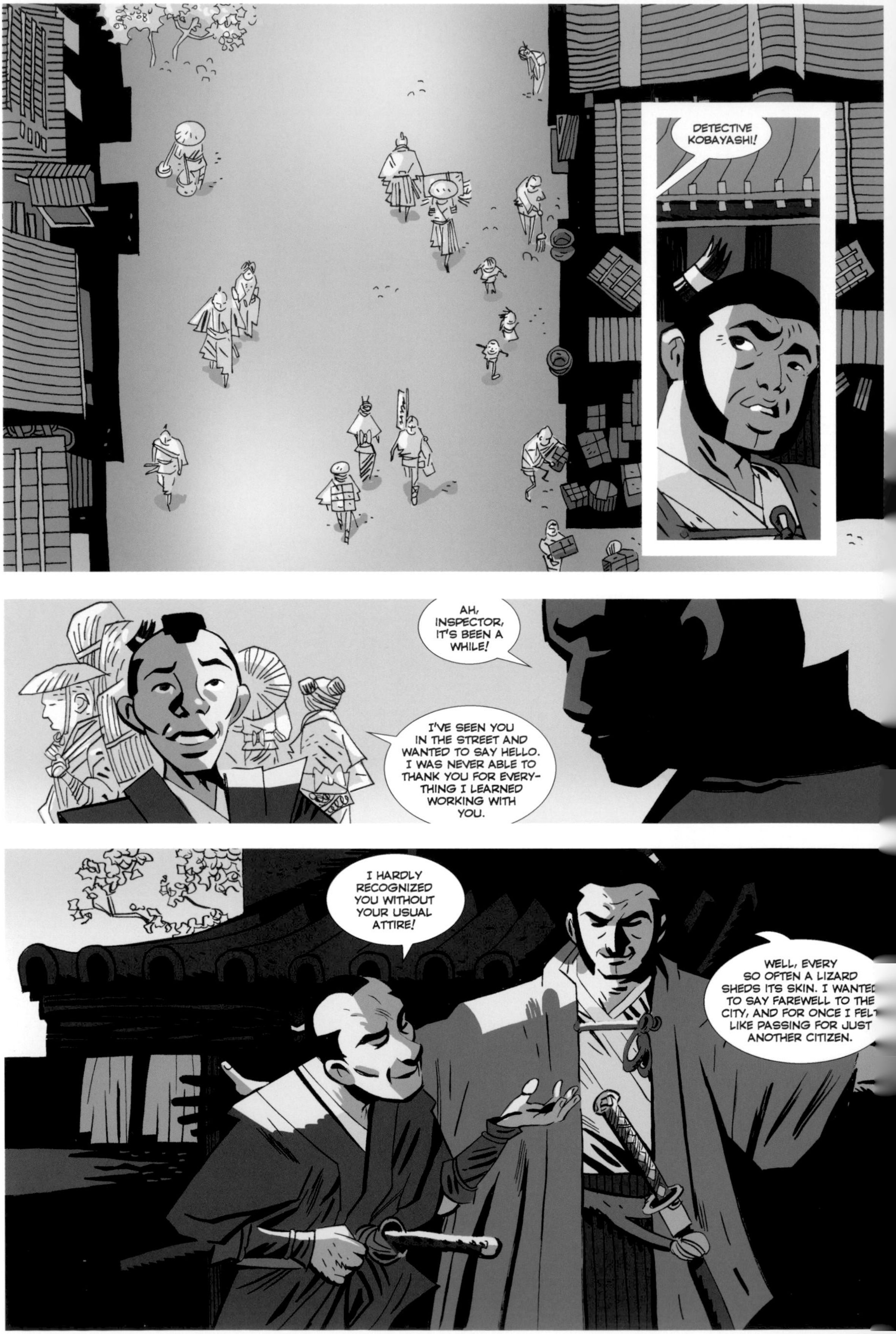
DETECTIVE KOBAYASHI!
AH, INSPECTOR, IT'S BEEN A WHILE!
I'VE SEEN YOU IN THE STREET AND WANTED TO SAY HELLO. I WAS NEVER ABLE TO THANK YOU FOR EVERY-THING I LEARNED WORKING WITH YOU.
I HARDLY RECOGNIZED YOU WITHOUT YOUR USUAL ATTIRE!
WELL, EVERY SO OFTEN A LIZARD SHEDS ITS SKIN. I WANTED TO SAY FAREWELL TO THE CITY, AND FOR ONCE I FELT LIKE PASSING FOR JUST ANOTHER CITIZEN.

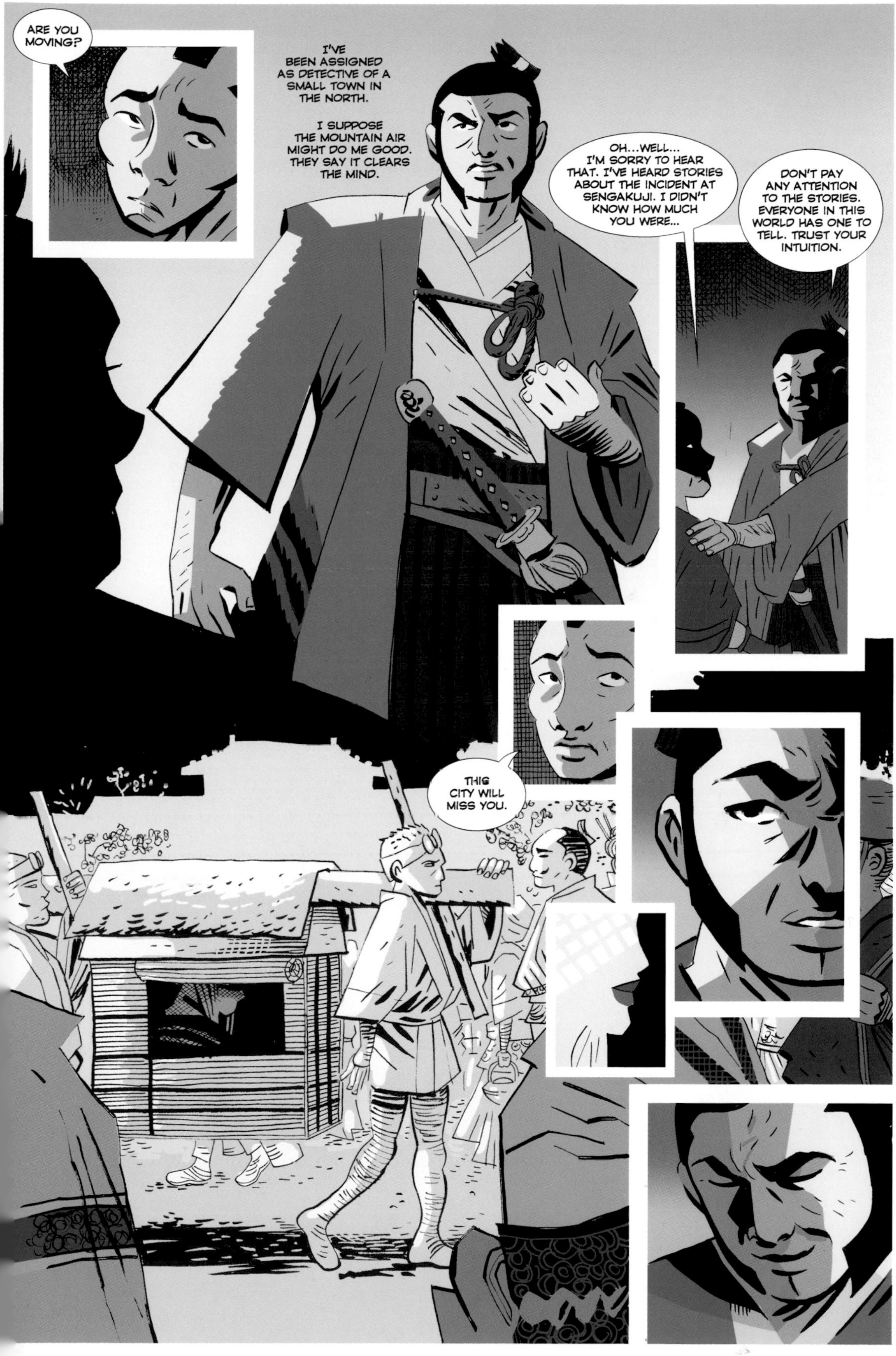
ARE YOU MOVING?
I'VE BEEN ASSIGNED AS DETECTIVE OF A SMALL TOWN IN THE NORTH.
I SUPPOSE THE MOUNTAIN AIR MIGHT DO ME GOOD. THEY SAY IT CLEARS THE MIND.
OH...WELL... I'M SORRY TO HEAR THAT. I'VE HEARD STORIES ABOUT THE INCIDENT AT SENGAKUJI. I DIDN'T KNOW HOW MUCH YOU WERE...
DON'T PAY ANY ATTENTION TO THE STORIES. EVERYONE IN THIS WORLD HAS ONE TO TELL. TRUST YOUR INTUITION.
THIS CITY WILL MISS YOU.

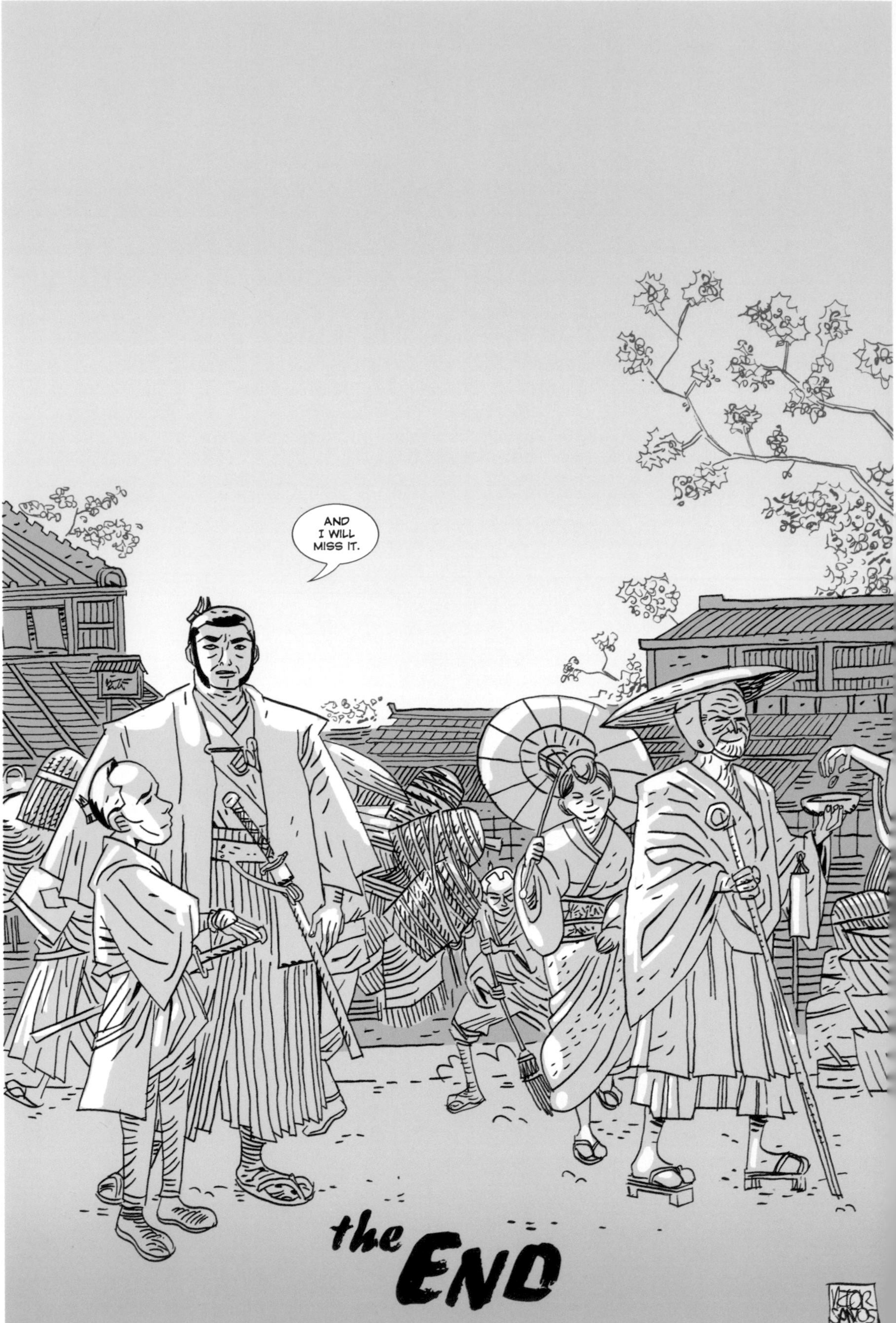
AND I WILL MISS IT.
the END
VICTOR SANTOS

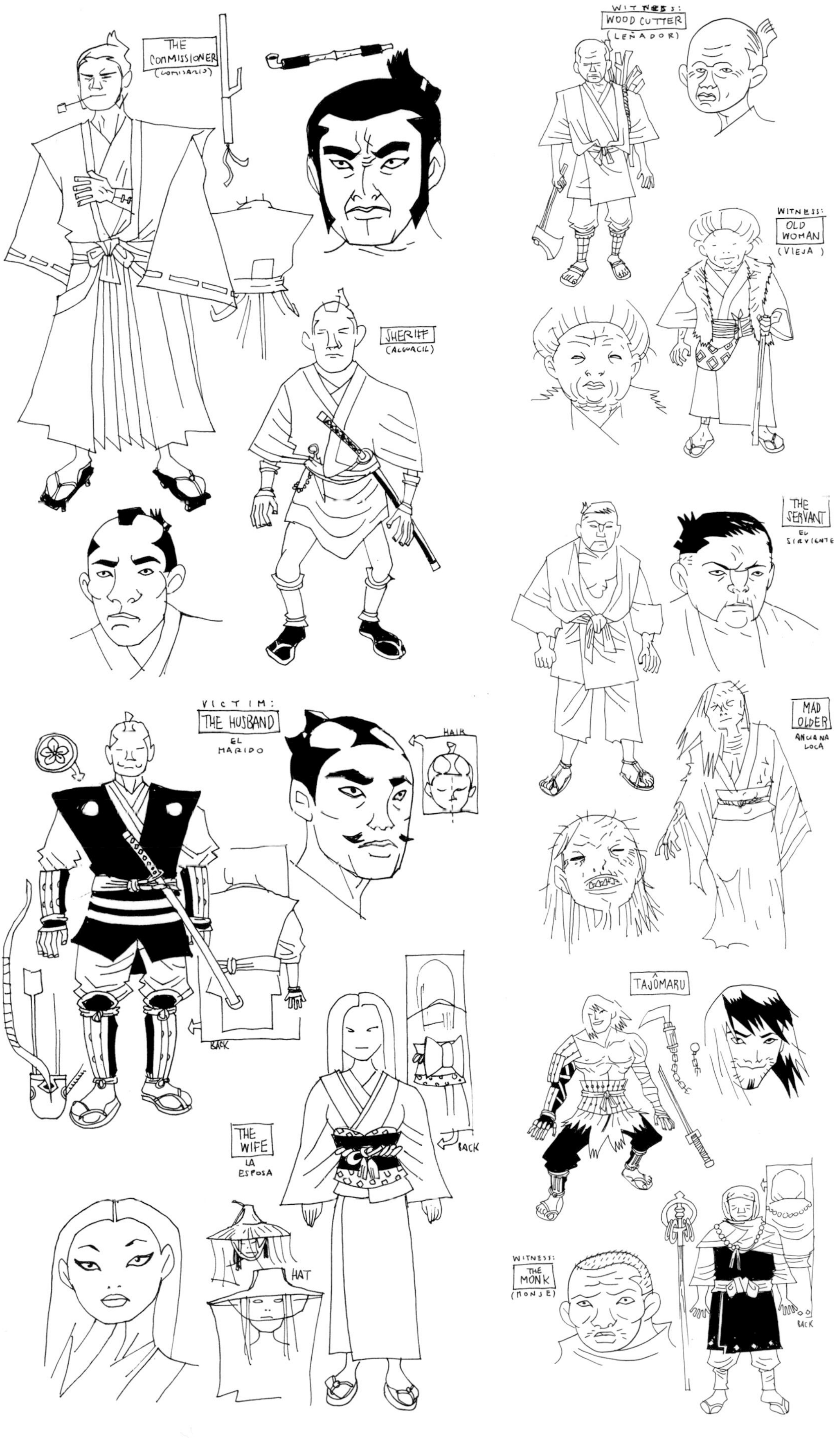
THE COMMISSIONER
(COMISARIO)
SHERIFF
(ALGUACIL)
VICTIM:
THE HUSBAND
EL MARIDO
HAIR
BACK
THE WIFE
LA ESPOSA
HAT
BACK
WITNESS:
WOOD CUTTER
(LEÑADOR)
WITNESS:
OLD WOMAN
(VIEJA)
THE SERVANT
EL SIRVIENTE
MAD OLDER
ANCIANA LOCA
TAJÔMARU
WITNESS:
THE MONK
(MONJE)
BACK

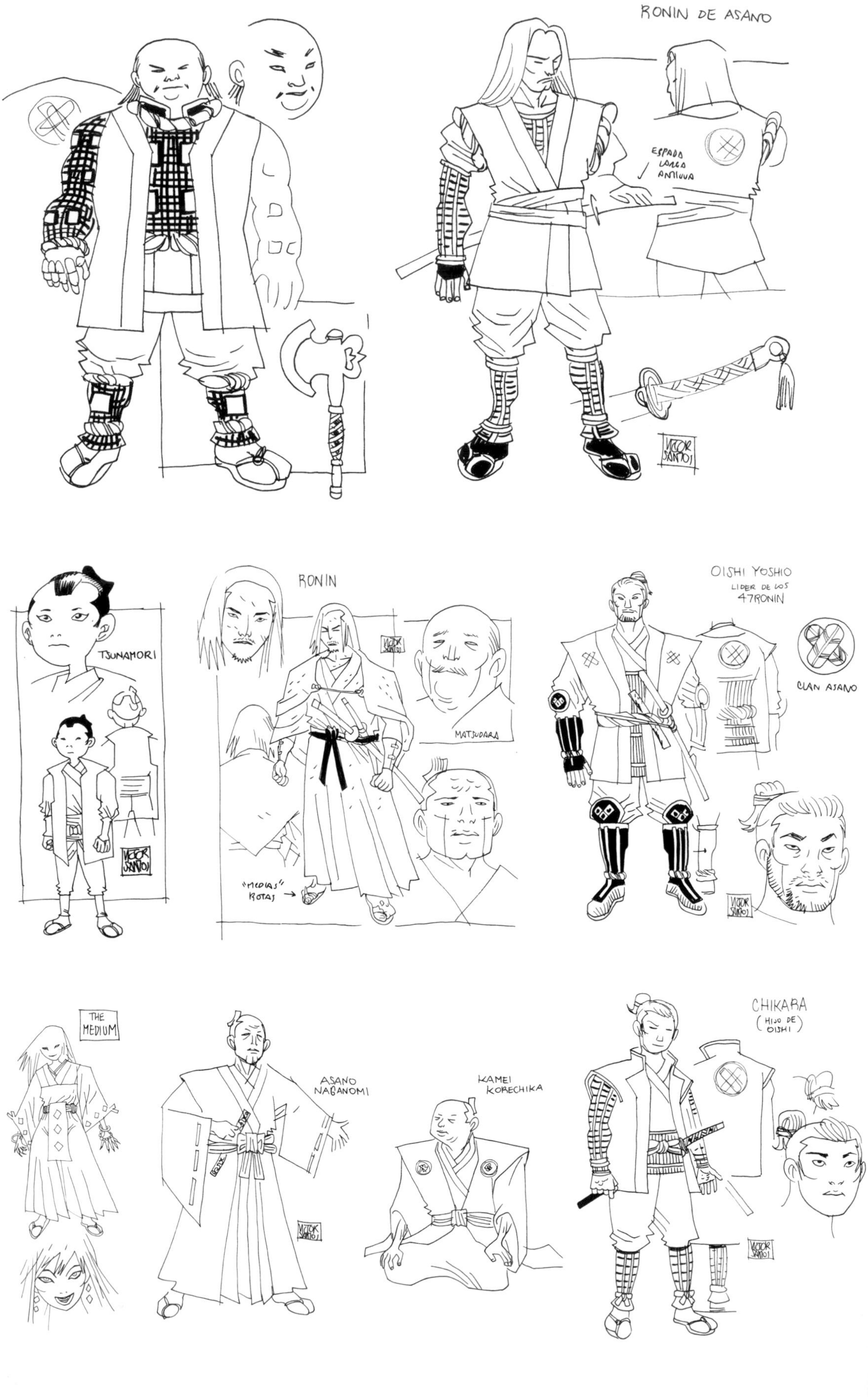

RONIN DE ASANO
ESPADA LARGA ANTIGUA
TSUNAMORI
RONIN
MATSUDARA
"MEDIAS" BOTAS
OISHI YOSHIO
LIDER DE LOS 47RONIN
CLAN ASANO
THE MEDIUM
ASANO NAGANOMI
KAMEI KORECHIKA
CHIKARA
(HIJO DE OISHI)

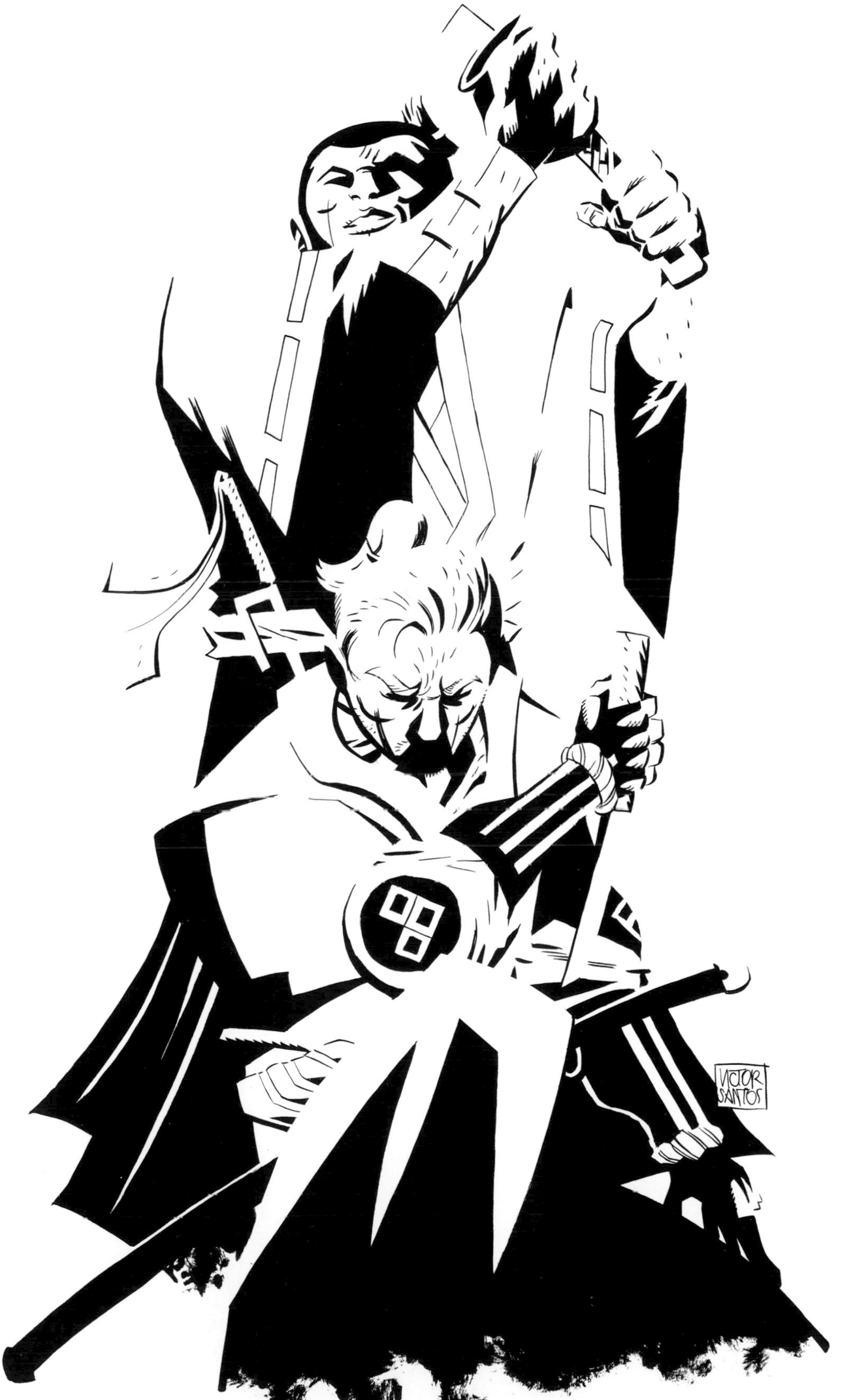
VICTOR SANTOS

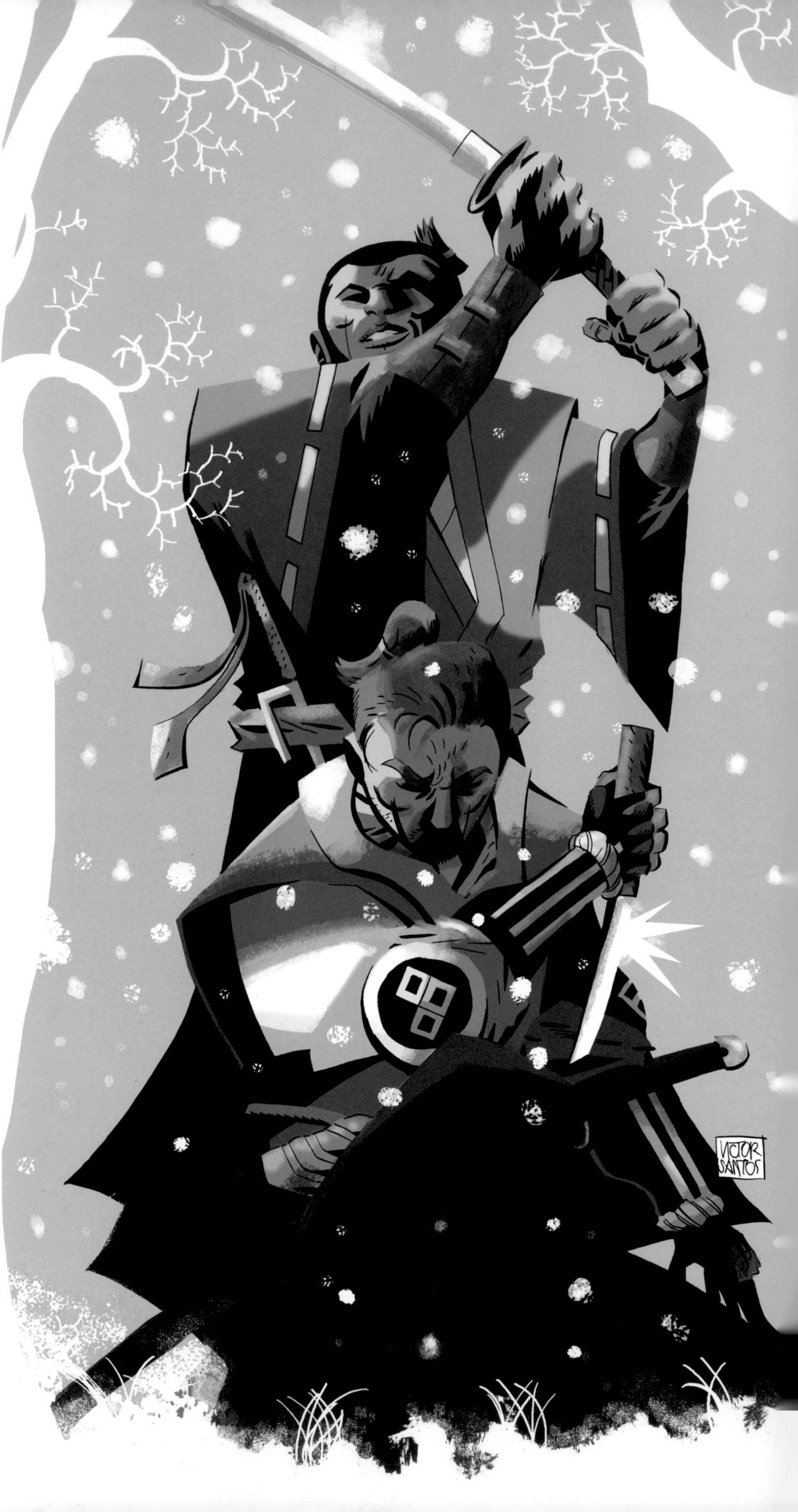
VICTOR SANTOS

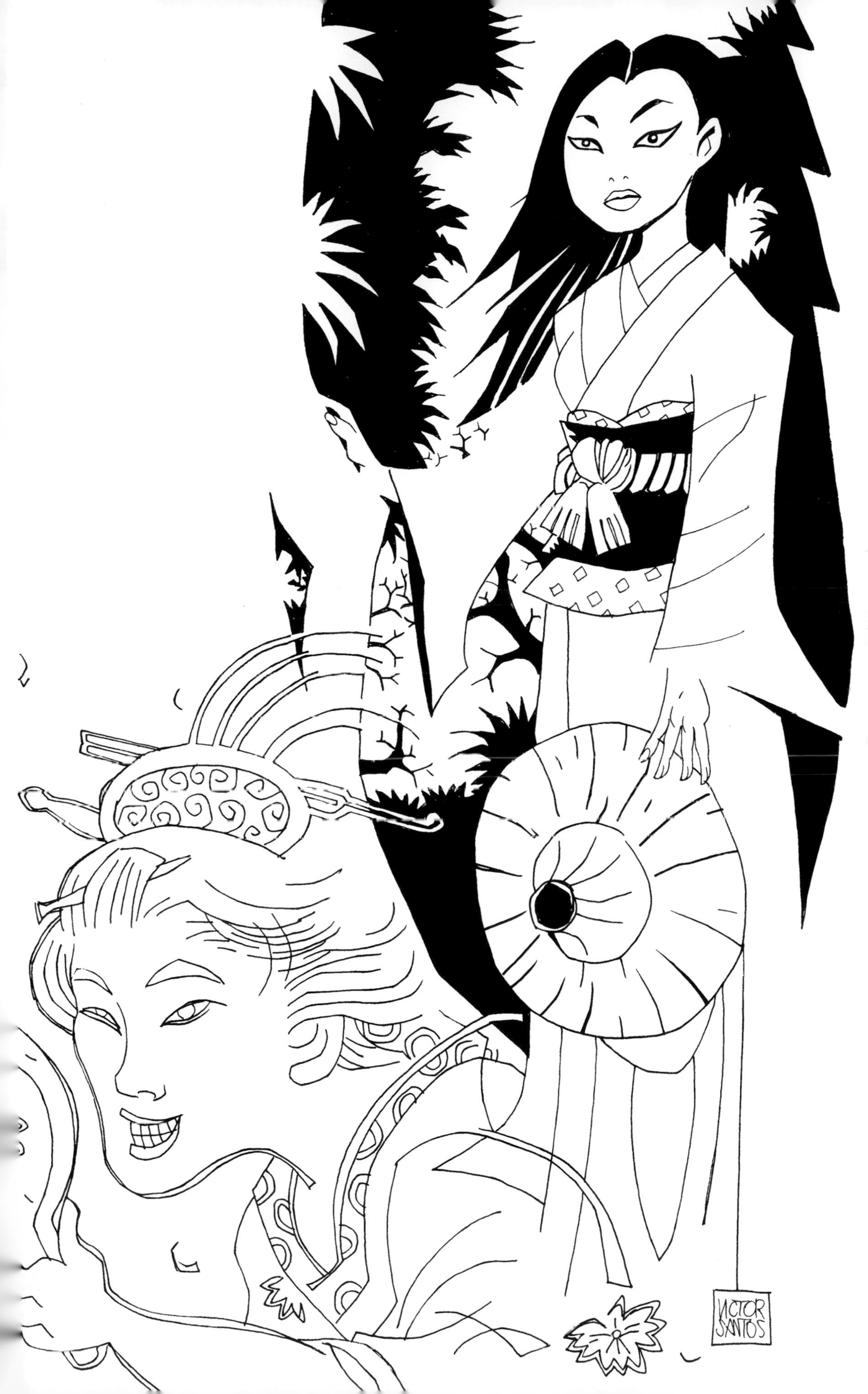
VICTOR
SANTOS

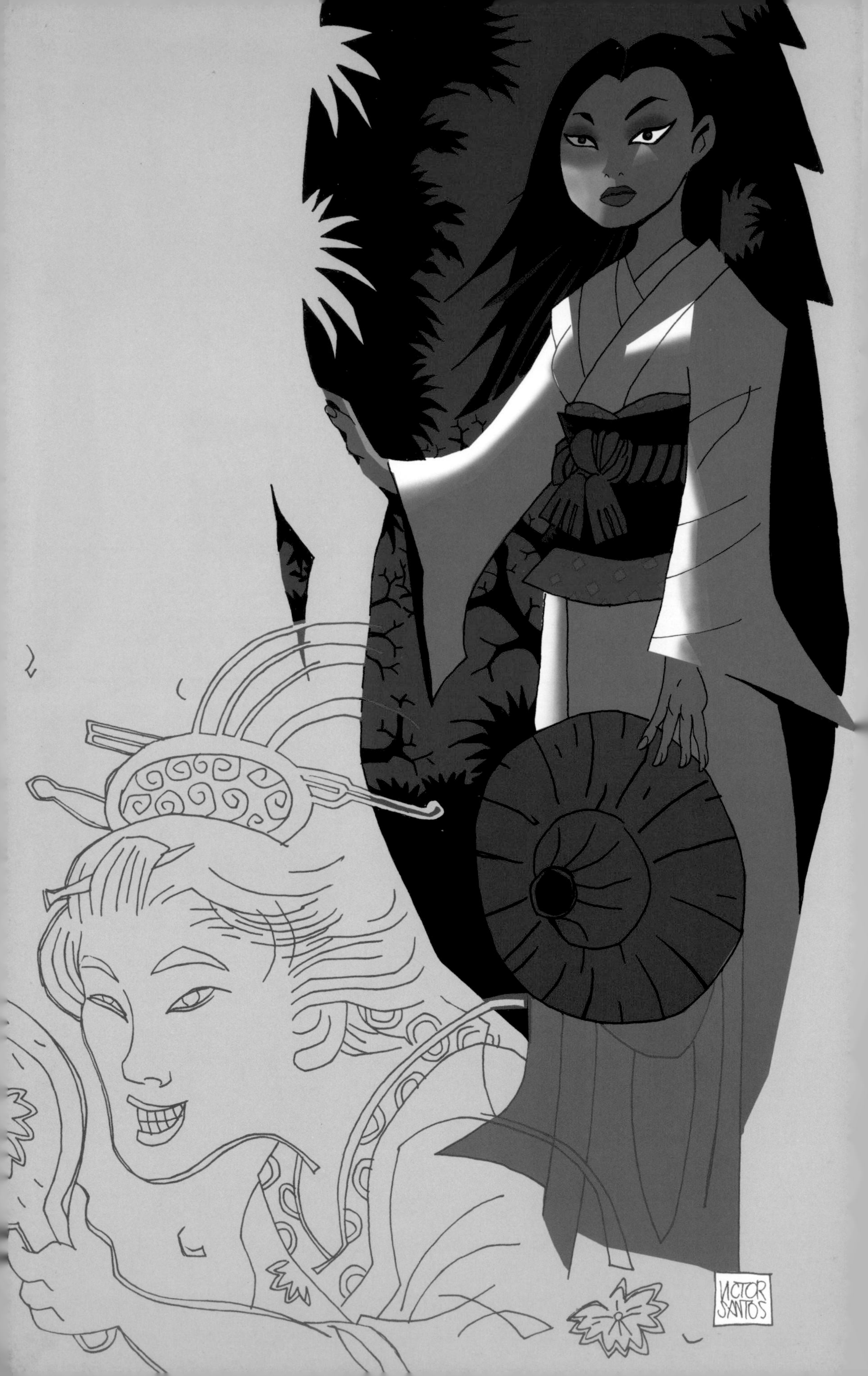
VICTOR SANTOS

MORE EUROPEAN INTRIGUE FROM
DARK HORSE BOOKS

BLACKSAD

BLACKSAD
Juan Díaz Canales and Juanjo Guarnido

The *Blacksad* books first took Europe by storm in 2000 and sold over 200,000 copies in France alone. Now Dark Horse Comics presents the beautifully painted stories of private investigator John Blacksad, up to his feline ears in mystery, digging into the backstories behind murders, child abductions, and nuclear secrets.

Volume 1
978-1-59582-393-9 | $29.99
Volume 2: A Silent Hell
978-1-59582-931-3 | $19.99

VAMPIRE BOY
CARLOS TRILLO
EDUARDO RISSO

VAMPIRE BOY
Carlos Trillo and Eduardo Risso

Left nameless by his father and sentenced to eternal life by a trick of fate and fortune, the protagonist of Carlos Trillo and Eduardo Risso's *Vampire Boy* has spent fifty centuries in a body that never ages, locked in an eternal struggle with a rival as immortal as he. Acclaimed writer Carlos Trillo teams with legendary artist Eduardo Risso (100 Bullets) to produce a poignantly engrossing twist on the classic vampire mythos, now presented in English for the first time!

978-1-59582-562-9 | $24.99

MORE THAN 56 MILLION COPIES SOLD WORLDWIDE!
THE
DYLAN DOG
CASE FILES

THE DYLAN DOG CASE FILES
Tiziano Sclavi and others

Unavailable in English for almost a decade, one of the most popular comics in the world—selling more than a million copies every month throughout Europe—returns! An ex-cop who now battles against evil as a "nightmare investigator," Dylan Dog is unlike any private eye you've ever met. If creatures from beyond the unknown are after you, and if you can hire him, he just might save your life.

978-1-59582-206-2 | $24.99

ENTER A WORLD OF MAGIC AND FANTASY!
DRAGONERO
Luca Enoch • Stefano Vietti • Giuseppe Matteoni

DRAGONERO
Luca Enoch, Stefano Vietti, and Giuseppe Matteoni

Beyond the civilized lands of Erondàr, the Stone Towers are crumbling. The great monoliths are falling one after another under the wild thrusts of an evil force. The Ancient Prohibition that binds the Abominables inside their dark world is soon to be broken. Alben the Wizard will send for Myrva, a young follower of the powerful Technocrats; he will choose Ecuba, the fighting nun, to protect him; and he will call back Ian Aranill, a former Empire officer—followed by Gmor the Orc, his loyal friend—to use his scouting experience. Together they will face the Painers, the evil beings who still live in the barren Dragonlands. Can Ian prevail against the last, horrible threat they will be facing?

978-1-59582-291-8 | $19.99

AVAILABLE AT YOUR LOCAL COMICS SHOP OR BOOKSTORE! • **To find a comics shop in your area, call 1-888-266-4226.**
For more information or to order direct visit DarkHorse.com or call 1-800-862-0052 Mon.–Fri. 9 AM to 5 PM Pacific Time. Prices and availability subject to change without notice.

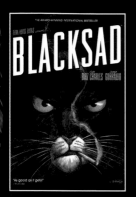

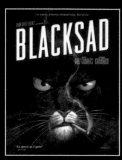

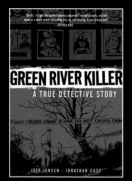

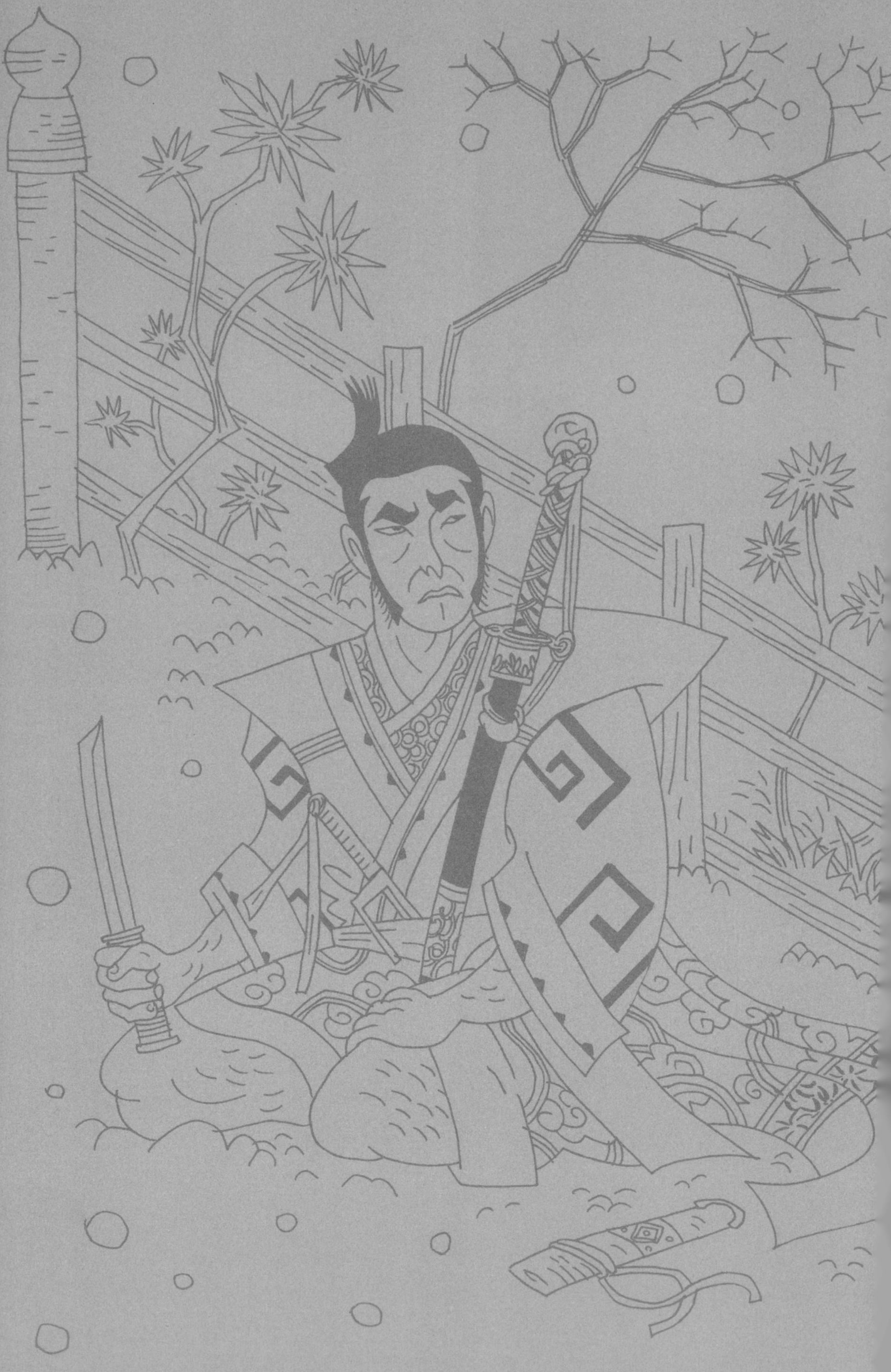